CIGA ... ALUES

1984 ... e and

...rade Cards

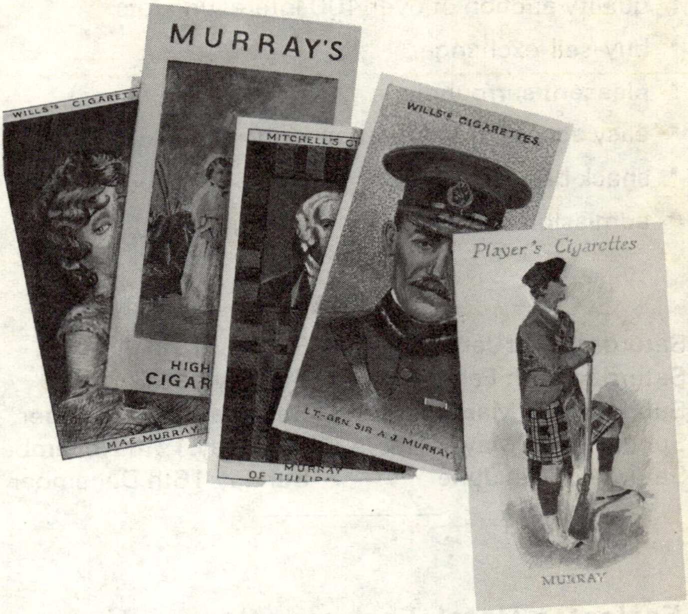

Compiled and published by

MURRAY CARDS (INTERNATIONAL) LIMITED

51 Watford Way, Hendon Central, London NW4 3JH
Tel: (01) 202-5688

Opening hours – 10am-5pm Monday-Friday

Watford Way is the A41 road into London, and is one mile from the end of the M1 Motorway. It can be reached via Hendon Central Underground Station (Northern Line), which is 100 yards away, and is also served by a number of bus routes and Green Line.

 ISBN 0 946942 00 5

Introduction

We are proud to present a completely new and enlarged Catalogue, after five successful editions of our last version. There are several important new features in this volume. British and overseas tobacco firms have now been separated. The British section includes *all* series that have been traced by the compilers up to 31st August 1983, and several sets are shown which have never been recorded previously. The overseas, and in particular the trade sections have also been enlarged. Guides to values, if not actual selling prices, have been allotted to all tobacco issues. And the introduction of colour illustrations will enable collectors to appreciate the full beauty of many of the series.

During the last ten years our Catalogues have come to be acknowledged by the majority of collectors and dealers as the definitive work on cigarette cards and their values. However it must be remembered that this book is basically a list of the selling prices of cards which we hold in stock. Unlike some of our competitors we do not price an item unless we actually had some in stock at the time of compilation. Our prices are therefore totally realistic, and are finely tuned each year to react to changes in both supply and demand.

Demand does increase each year, and prices thus show in some cases a steady, and in other instances a spectacular increase. We have no doubt that this situation will continue to apply as more people turn to cigarette card collecting as a source of education, nostalgia and pleasure. Fortunately there are many new sets of cards issued each year, with commodities as diverse as bubble gum, periodicals, cereals and tea. In particular we are pleased to welcome the appearance of regular issues with several brands of cigars – perhaps their success will eventually lead to the introduction of genuine cigarette cards once again!

Our exclusive "Nostalgia" plastic albums have become increasingly more popular in the past year. A number of modifications have been made recently to improve both the quality and the versatility of this most modern method of displaying cards, and have helped to retain its place in the forefront of the market. We are indeed so confident in the attractiveness of these albums that we have introduced one more important feature this year. *With all pre-1940 sets purchased from us we will give the appropriate Nostalgia album pages absolutely free.* We are certain that once you have sampled them you will want to insert all your cards into our superlative albums (see page 16).

HOW TO USE THE CATALOGUE

The Catalogue is in three parts.

Part I contains all known issues by British-based tobacco companies. Thus all cards by the firm W.D. & H.O. Wills, which was located in Bristol, are shown, even though they may have been issued in a Wills brand abroad. Issues from the Channel Islands and the Republic of Ireland are included in this part. Excluded are most post cards and larger non-insert items.

Part II contains tobacco issues by most of the major manufacturers in the English-speaking world, and a selection of other series, including all the sets readily available to collectors.

Part III comprises series issued with commodities other than tobacco (commonly known as "trade cards"). Although mainly British issues, there are a number of overseas sets included. Each issuer's name is followed by the commodity with which the cards were issued; where the set was not given away free, but produced in order to be sold, the issuer is described as "commercial".

Parts I and III commence with an index of brand names, and the issuer's name under which that item appears. Series are listed in alphabetical order of series title under the issuing firm, regardless of country of origin. Where the issuer was not normally located in the United Kingdom the country of origin is given. In the case of certain larger issuers series have been listed in logical groups so that they may be more readily found.

For each set the following information is given:–

(1) **Size information.** Cards are assumed to be standard size unless otherwise stated. Sizes used correspond to the page sizes used for our plastic albums (see separate notice) i.e. when a letter is used it may be assumed that at least one dimension is greater than the size shown by the previous letter. Abbreviations used are:–

K	smaller than standard.	51 x 41 mm.
B	bigger than standard.	80 x 46 mm.
M	medium size.	80 x 52 mm.
L	large size.	80 x 71 mm.
T	Typhoo/Doncella size.	110 x 54 mm.
X	extra large size.	80 x 110 mm.
P	postcard size.	165 x 105 mm.
G	cabinet size.	223 x 165 mm.
E	too large for albums.	
D	dual (more than one) size.	
S	stereoscopic series.	
F	photographic production.	

(2) **Number of cards in set.** When there are several rare numbers in a set the quantity normally available is shown. Thus 35/37 means that the series consists of 37 cards, but that only 35 are usually obtainable.

(3) **Series title.** Where the set has no name then the title accepted by common usage is given. Sect. = sectional series. Silk = silk, satin or canvas. P/C = playing card.

(4) **Year of issue.** This is approximate only, and should in no way be considered to be binding. Particularly in the case of overseas and pre-1900 issues the date should be treated as merely an indication of the era in which the set was produced.

(5) **Price of odd cards.** Because of high labour costs and overheads it is not an economic proposition to offer odd cards from many post-1945 series. Where shown the price is that of normal cards in the set. End numbers (e.g. numbers 1 and 50 from a set of 50 cards) are DOUBLE the price shown. Known scarce subjects from a series, and also thematic subjects from general series (e.g. cricketers from general interest series) would be more expensive than the price shown here. In

response to many requests we have this year adopted a coding system to indicate the comparative scarcity of all tobacco cards that we do not actually price, since we have none in stock. A letter appears in the odds column as follows:–

A Value under £25.00 per card.
B Value £25-50 per card.
C Value £50-100 per card.
D Value £100 or more per card.

The wide range of valuations is accounted for by the fact that the discovery of just a few cards from a scarcer series can greatly affect the price.

(6) **Price of complete sets.** Prices shown are for sets in clean, undamaged condition. Where mint sets are required (and available) there will be a premium of 50% extra for sets 1920-1940, and 100% for pre 1920 sets. Where no set price is quoted we had no complete sets in stock at the time of compilation; however, when available these will be sold at prices based on the odds figure. *With each pre 1940 set the appropriate Nostalgia album pages are presented FREE!*

UNLISTED SERIES

Because our stocks are constantly changing we always have in stock a large number of series which are unlisted. In particular we can presently offer an excellent selection of German sets, loose or in their special albums. If you require a specific item please send us a stamped addressed envelope for an immediate quotation.

ALIKE SERIES

There are many instances where affiliated companies, or indeed completely independent groups issued identical series, where the pictures are the same, and only the issuer's name is altered. Examples are Fish & Bait issued by Churchman, I.T.C. (Canada) and Wills; British Cavalry Uniforms of the Nineteenth Century issued by Badshah, Brown, Empson, Rington and Willcocks & Willcocks; or even Interesting Animals by Hignett or Church & Dwight. In many instances alphabetical code names have been generally adopted to group similar series of the more prolific subjects, e.g. Actresses FROGA, Boer War Generals CLAM, where the letters of the adopted name indicate some of the leading issuers.

TERMS OF BUSINESS

All previous lists are cancelled.

Cash with order. Any unsatisfactory items may be returned for credit or refund within seven days of receipt.

Condition. All prices are based on cards in clean, undamaged condition. Where available mint sets 1920-1940 will be at a premium of 50% above the normal price, and mint sets pre 1920 and all mint odd cards will be an extra 100%.

Minimum Order. We are unable to accept orders totalling less than £1.00.

Postage. Inland second class post is included in all prices quoted. Overseas letter post is sent free by surface mail; parcels and (if requested) air mail are charged at cost.

Overseas payments in currencies other than sterling are acceptable, but allow £1.30 for bank conversion charges.

Value Added Tax where applicable is included in all prices shown.

When ordering cards please quote the issuer's name, the name of the set, the date of issue, and the price. This will enable us to identify the precise series.

Odd Lists must be submitted on a separate sheet of paper with the name and address clearly shown; this will be returned with the cards for checking. Remember that end cards are double the normal price. Please write all the numbers required, i.e. NOT "17-20" but 17, 18, 19, 20. If the cards are required to complete an unnumbered set, and you do not know the missing titles, we can supply them provided that you list all the cards that you HAVE in alphabetical order.

Alternatives. Although this catalogue is based upon current stocks, these are bound to fluctuate. Therefore, whenever possible please give alternatives.

Credit Notes. When items are out of stock a credit note is normally sent. This may be utilised or encashed at any time, but MUST be returned when so doing.

Unlisted series. We are always pleased to quote for series unlisted, or unpriced.

Purchasing. We are always pleased to purchase or exchange collectors' unwanted cards. Please write with full details before sending cards.

Enquiries. We are always pleased to offer our advice on all collectors' queries. Please enclose a stamped addressed envelope with all enquiries.

Callers. Our shop is open from 10.00 a.m. to 5.00 p.m. each Monday to Friday, and collectors are always welcome to select from our complete range of cards and accessories. Watford Way is at Hendon Central (Underground, Northern Line), and is served by a number of buses, including Green Line.

No Hidden Extras. Remember that all prices shown include postage, packing, insurance and (where applicable) V.A.T. And that with every pre 1940 set we include Nostalgia pages *absolutely free!*

CARTOPHILIC SOCIETY REFERENCE BOOKS

A number of the earlier Reference Books have been unavailable for some years. However we are now pleased to be able to offer the following paper backed reprints at exceptionally low cost.

No. 1 Faulkner.
No. 2 Hill.
No. 4 Gallaher.
No. 5 Abdulla, Adkin & Anstie.
No. 6 Ardath.
No. 7 Directory of British Cigarette Card Issuers (16 cards illustrated).
No. 8 Glossary of Cartophilic Terms (27 cards illustrated).
No. 9 Lambert & Butler (25 cards illustrated).
No. 10 Churchman (29 cards illustrated).
No. 12 Taddy (30 cards illustrated).
No. 13 Phillips (225 cards illustrated).
No. 17 Player (26 cards illustrated).

ONLY £1.50 Per Booklet!

The following reprints have been combined in hard covers. The information contained cannot be found elsewhere, and each book represents excellent value. Each contains lists of unnumbered series, illustrations of untitled cards, and background information to most sets.

The Cigarette Card Issues of Wills. Originally 5 parts, now in one volume. 200 pages, 559 cards illustrated. **PRICE £5.00**

The Ogden Reference Book (including Guinea Golds). 244 pages, 536 cards illustrated. **PRICE £10.00**

The Tobacco War and B.A.T. Book, 336 pages, 2,959 cards illustrated! **PRICE £10.00**

A MUST FOR ALL COLLECTORS THE WORLD TOBACCO ISSUES INDEX

Published by the Cartophilic Society of G.B. Ltd., this work is now in four volumes, which between them list every card issued by tobacco manufacturers that was known at the end of 1980.

Part I. World Index and Handbook reprinted as one volume. 701 pages, 1977 cards illustrated. This is the basic reference work for all serious collectors, including details of nearly every British cigarette card. First published in 1956. **PRICE £10.00**

Part II. 452 pages, with 3,600 cards illustrated. This volume covers additions to Part I, which are mainly overseas cards. In particular it includes most of the information from the American Book of Checklists. **PRICE £10.00**

Part III. 504 pages, 666 cards illustrated. Published in 1978, this latest work updates the information in Parts I and II, and also repeats the lists (amended) which were previously in the Churchman, Lambert & Butler, Taddy, Phillips and Australasian Booklets. Also featured are American non-insert cards, blankets and pins. **PRICE £10.00**

Part IV. 688 pages. Lists of U.S. Baseball, photographic, Maltese etc. as well as additions to three previous parts. **PRICE £20.00**

OTHER LITERATURE

GENERAL WORKS

Collecting Cigarette Cards by Dorothy Bagnall. 112 pages, illustrated. The best book on the hobby currently in print. **£3.50**

Cigarette Cards and Novelties by Frank Doggett. 96 pages, 1291 cards illustrated in colour. Paper back reprint. **£5.00**

Pipe Dreams by Mike Dempsey. 96 pages, many fine illustrations, mainly in full colour. Comprises advertising by Imperial Tobacco Co. **£8.00**

Antiques and Their Values – Cigarette Cards by Tessa Bennett. 126 pages, approx. 1000 cards illustrated, nearly all different series. **£3.00**

An Album of Cigarette Cards published by David & Charles. 4 books, each with a general introduction, a section on a particular theme, album pages with backs of cards printed, and plain backed card reproductions.

(1) Birds.
(2) Flowers.
(3) History & General Knowledge.
(4) Travel & Transport. **Each £3.50**

REFERENCE BOOKS

Handbook Part I. Published by L.C.C.C. Lists and illustrations of pre-1918 unnumbered and alike series (tobacco only). Essential reference. **£5.00**

Handbook Part II. Published by L.C.C.C. Lists of post-1918 series and all silks, with additions to Part I. **£5.00**

Smith Cigarette Cards. 36 pages with illustrations. Lists all known series, including back varieties. **£2.00**

British Trade Index, Part I. Series up to 1940. 216 pages, many illustrations. **£7.00**

British Trade Index, Part II. 232 pages. Additions to Part I and also Issues 1945-1968. **£7.00**

Typhoo Tea Cards. 36 pages with illustrations. Lists of back varieties. **£1.50**

A. & B.C. Gum Cards. 40 pages with illustrations. Many lists. **£2.75**

CRICKET BOOKS

Cricket Cigarette Cards. An initial listing by Derek Deadman. 80 pages. All subjects detailed. **£3.50**

Cricket Trade Cards. An initial listing by Derek Deadman. 135 pages. Companion to book above. **£5.50**

Classic Cricket Cards. Reproductions of 154 cards in colour – Wills 1896 onwards. Designed to be cut out. **£2.50**

More Classic Cricket Cards. 160 cards, different from above. **£2.50**

FOREIGN CARDS

Australian & New Zealand Index. Published by Cartophilic Society. Over 300 pages – 600 cards illustrated. Lists all tobacco and trade cards. Published 1983. **£10.50**

Liebig Catalogue in English. See page 180 for full details. **£2.50**

Fada Liebig Catalogue. 300 pages, listing all titles from 1863 different sets. Index in three languages (not English), text in Italian. **£5.00**

Sanguinetti Liebig Catalogue. 1982 Edition. 347 pages, listing all titles from 1871 sets and menus, Italian text. Illustrations of 700 sets. **£8.50**

German Album Catalogue, Part I. 1872-1945. 260 pages. German text. **£7.50**

German Album Catalogue, Part II. 1946-1980. 149 pages. German text. **£7.50**

Card Collectors Price Guide. U.S. Series, mainly Gum. Many illustrations. **£4.00**

Sport Americana Price Guide to the Non-Sports Cards. Tobacco and Gum. Lists of all subjects. Illustrations of every series. A remarkable work. 316 pages. **£8.00**

OTHER LITERATURE—cont.

MISCELLANEOUS

I.P.M. Postcard Catalogue, 1984 Edition. **£3.50**

Picton's Postcard Catalogue, 1984 Edition. **£5.00**

Sweet Cigarette Packets, by Michael Johnston. 36 pages, 127 packets illustrated. Published 1983. **£2.50**

•••

INDEX OF BRANDS (Tobacco)

HONEST LONG CUT—See Duke or American Tobacco Co. (Part 2)
HUSTLER LITTLE CIGARS—See American Tobacco Co. (Part 2)

ISLANDER, FAGS, SPECIALS, CUBS—See Bucktrout (Part 1)

JACK ROSE LITTLE CIGARS—See American Tobacco Co. (Part 2)
JERSEY LILY CIGARETTES—See Bradford (Part 1)
JUST MEMBER CIGARETTES—See Pattreiouex (Part 1)

KENSITAS CIGARETTES—See J. Wix (Part 1)

LENOX CIGARETTES—See American Tobacco Co. (Part 2)
LE ROY CIGARS—See Miller (Part 2)
LEVANT FAVOURITES—See B. Morris (Part 1)
LIFEBOAT CIGARETTES—See United Tobacco Co. (Part 2)
LIFE RAY CIGARETTES—See Ray (Part 1)
LITTLE RHODY CUT PLUG—See Geo. F. Young (Part 2)
LOTUS CIGARETTES—See United Tobacco Co. (Part 2)
LUCANA CIGARETTES—See Sandorides (Part 1)
LUCKY STRIKE CIGARETTES—See American Tobacco Co. (Part 2)
LUXURY CIGARETTES—See American Tobacco Co. (Part 2)

MAGPIE CIGARETTES—See Schuh (Part 2)
MANIKIN CIGARS—See Freeman (Part 1)
MATTOSSIANS IMPORTED EGYPTIAN CIGARETTES—See Henly & Watkins (Part 1)
MAX CIGARETTES—See A. & M. Wix (Part 1)
MAYBLOSSOM CIGARETTES—See Lambert & Butler (Part 1)
MECCA CIGARETTES—See American Tobacco Co. (Part 2)
MILLBANK CIGARETTES—See Imperial Tobacco Co. (Canada) (Part 2)
MILLS CIGARETTES—See Amalgamated Tobacco Corporation (Part 1)
MILO CIGARETTES—See Sniders & Abrahams (Part 2)
MINERS EXTRA SMOKING TOBACCO—See American Tobacco Co. (Part 2)
MOGUL CIGARETTES—See American Tobacco Co. (Part 2)
MURAD CIGARETTES—See American Tobacco Co. (Part 2)

NEBO CIGARETTES—See American Tobacco Co. (Part 2)

OK CIGARETTES—See African Tobacco Mfrs. (Part 2)
OBAK CIGARETTES—See American Tobacco Co. (Part 2)
OFFICERS MESS CIGARETTES—See African Tobacco Mfrs. (Part 2)
OLD GOLD CIGARETTES—See American Tobacco Co. (Part 2)
OLD JUDGE CIGARETTES—See Goodwin (Part 2)
ONE OF THE FINEST—See Buchner (Part 2)
ORACLE CIGARETTES—See Tetley (Part 1)
OUR LITTLE BEAUTIES—See Allen & Ginter (Part 2)
OXFORD CIGARETTES—See American Tobacco Co. (Part 2)

PAN HANDLE SCRAP—See American Tobacco Co. (Part 2)
PETER PAN CIGARETTES—See Sniders & Abrahams (Part 2)
PICADILLY LITTLE CIGARS—See American Tobacco Co. (Part 2)
PICK-ME-UP CIGARETTES—See Drapkin & Millhoff (Part 1)
PIEDMONT CIGARETTES—See American Tobacco Co. (Part 2)
PINHEAD CIGARETTES—See British American Tobacco Co. (Part 2)
PINNACE—See G. Phillips (Part 1)
PIONEER CIGARETTES—See Richmond Cavendish (Part 1)
PIRATE CIGARETTES—See Wills (Part 1)
POLO MILD CIGARETTES—See Murray (Part 1)
PURITAN LITTLE CIGARS—See American Tobacco Co. (Part 2)
PURPLE MOUNTAIN CIGARETTES—See Wills (Part 1)

R.S.—See R. Sinclair (Part 1)
RECRUIT LITTLE CIGARS—See American Tobacco Co. (Part 2)

RED CROSS—See Lorillard or American Tobacco Co. (Part 2)
REINA REGENTA CIGARS—See B. Morris (Part 1)
RICHMOND GEM CIGARETTES—See Allen & Ginter (Part 2)
RICHMOND STRAIGHT CUT CIGARETTES—See American Tobacco Co. (Part 2)
ROSELAND CIGARETTES—See Glass (Part 1)
ROYAL BENGALS LITTLE CIGARS—See American Tobacco Co. (Part 2)

ST. DUNSTANS CIGARETTES—See Carreras (Part 1)
ST. LEGER LITTLE CIGARS—See American Tobacco Co. (Part 2)
SCOTS CIGARETTES—See African Tobacco Mfrs. (Part 2)
SCRAP IRON SCRAP—See American Tobacco Co. (Part 2)
SENATOR CIGARETTES—See Scerri (Part 2)
SENIOR SERVICE CIGARETTES—See Pattreiouex (Part 1)
SENSATION CUT PLUG—See Lorillard (Part 2)
SHANTUNG CIGARETTES—See British American Tobacco Co. (Part 2)
SILKO CIGARETTES—See American Tobacco Co. (Part 2)
SMILE AWAY TOBACCO—See Carreras (Part 1)
SOVEREIGN CIGARETTES—See American Tobacco Co. (Part 2)
SPANISH PUFFS—See Mandelbaum (Part 2)
SPINET CIGARETTES—See Hill (Part 1)
SPOTLIGHT TOBACCOS—See Hill (Part 1)
SPRINGBOK CIGARETTES—See United Tobacco Co. (Part 2)
STAG TOBACCO—See American Tobacco Co. (Part 2)
STANDARD CIGARETTES—See Carreras (Part 1) or Sniders & Abrahams (Part 2)
STATE EXPRESS CIGARETTES—See Ardath (Part 1)
SUB ROSA CIGARROS—See American Tobacco Co. (Part 2)
SUMMIT—See International Tobacco Co. (Part 1)
SUNRIPE CIGARETTES—See Hill (Part 1)
SUNSPOT CIGARETTES—See Theman (Part 1)
SWEET CAPORAL—See Kinney or American Tobacco Co. (Part 2)
SWEET LAVENDER—See Kimball (Part 2)

TATLEY CIGARETTES—See Walkers (Part 1)
TEAL CIGARETTES—See British American Tobacco Co. (Part 2)
THREE BELLS CIGARETTES—See Bell (Part 1)
THREE CASTLES CIGARETTES—See Wills (Part 1)
TIGER CIGARETTES—See British American Tobacco Co. (Part 1)
TIPSY LOO CIGARETTES—See H. C. Lloyd (Part 1)
TOKIO CIGARETTES—See American Tobacco Co. (Part 2)
TRAWLER CIGARETTES—See Pattreiouex (Part 1)
TRUMPS LONG CUT—See Moore & Calvi (Part 2)
TURF CIGARETTES—See Carreras (Part 1)
TURKEY RED CIGARETTES—See American Tobacco Co. (Part 2)
TURKISH TROPHY CIGARETTES—See American Tobacco Co. (Part 2)
TWELFTH NIGHT CIGARETTES—See American Tobacco Co. (Part 2)

U.S. MARINE—See American Tobacco Co. (Part 2)
UZIT CIGARETTES—See American Tobacco Co. (Part 2)

VANITY FAIR CIGARETTES—See Kimball (Part 2)
VICE REGAL CIGARETTES—See Wills (Part 1)
VIRGINIA BRIGHTS CIGARETTES—See Allen & Ginter (Part 2)

WINGS CIGARETTES—See Brown & Williamson (Part 2)

ZIRA CIGARETTES—See American Tobacco Co. (Part 2)

Part 1

BRITISH TOBACCO MANUFACTURERS

(Including Channel Islands, Eire, and Overseas Issues by British-based firms)

ABDULLA & CO.

Qty		Date	Odds	Sets
50	Beauties of Today	1938	£1.50	—
25	British Butterflies	1935	24p	£6.00
F52	Cinema Stars, Set 1	1932	£2.00	—
30	Cinema Stars, Set 2	1932	£2.50	—
30	Cinema Stars, Set 3	1933	£2.00	—
32	Cinema Stars, Set 4	1933	60p	£19.00
32	Cinema Stars, Set 5	1934	60p	£19.00
30	Cinema Stars, Set 6	1934	£1.50	—
25	Feathered Friends	1935	24p	£6.00
50	Film Favourites	1934	£1.50	—
50	Film Stars	1934	A	—
P24	Film Stars (Series of Cards)	1934	A	—
P24	Film Stars (Series of 24 Cards)	1934	A	—
P24	Film Stars, 2nd (25-48)	1934	A	—
18	Message Cards	1936	£2.00	—
K18	Message Cards	1936	£3.00	—
L1	Princess Mary Gift Card	1914	—	£7.50
25	Old Favourites	1936	12p	£3.00
40	Screen Stars	1939	30p	£12.00
50	Stage and Cinema Beauties	1935	£2.00	—
30	Stars of The Stage & Screen	1934	£2.50	—
German Issues				
M150	Autobilder Serie I	1931	35p	—
M150	Autobilder Serie II	1932	35p	—
M160	Im Auto Mit Abdulla Durch Die Welt	1930	35p	£56.00
B110	Landerwappen–Sammlung	1932	30p	£33.00
B110	Landerwappen–Sammlung Serie II	1932	30p	£33.00
B150	Landerwappen–Sammlung Serie III	1932	30p	£45.00
B200	Nationale Und Internationale Sport–Rekorde	1931	40p	—
B50	Soldatenbilder Europaischer Armeen Der Gegenwart	1928	£1.00	—
X80	Wappenkarten	1928	40p	£32.00

ADCOCK & SON

11/12	Ancient Norwich	1928	70p	£7.50

ADKIN & SONS

25	Actresses–French	1898	C	—
12	A Living Picture	1901	£2.50	£30.00
12	A Royal Favourite	1900	£5.00	—
15	Beauties "PAC"	1898	C	—
50	Butterflies & Moths	1924	50p	£25.00
12	Character Sketches	1902	£2.50	£30.00
25	Notabilities	1915	£1.60	£40.00
12	Pretty Girl Series (Actresses)	1897	£17.50	—
12	Pretty Girl Series "RASH"	1900	£8.00	—
50	Soldiers of The Queen	1899	£2.00	—
59	Soldiers of The Queen (Series of 60)	1900	£2.00	—
31	Soldiers of The Queen & Portraits	1901	£3.00	£90.00
30	Sporting Cups & Trophies	1914	£6.00	—
25	War Trophies	1917	£2.50	£62.50
50	Wild Animals of the World	1923	35p	£17.50

AIKMAN'S

Qty		Date	Odds	Sets
30	Army Pictures, Cartoons, etc.	1916	B	—

H. J. AINSWORTH

30	Army Pictures, Cartoons, etc.	1916	B	—

ALBERGE & BROMET

25	Boer War & General Interest	1900	B	—
40	Naval & Military Phrases	1904	B	—
30	Proverbs	1903	B	—

PHILLIP ALLMAN & CO. LTD.

50	Coronation Series	1953	15p	£7.50
12	Pin Up Girls, 1st Series (numbered)	1953	25p	£3.00
12	Pin Up Girls, 1st Series (unnumbered)	1953	25p	£3.00
L12	Pin Up Girls, 1st Series	1953	£1.00	—
12	Pin Up Girls, 2nd Series	1953	£1.00	—
L12	Pin Up Girls, 2nd Series	1953	£1.00	—

AMALGAMATED TOBACCO CORPORATION LTD. (Mills)

25	Aircraft of the World	1958	—	50p
25	A Nature Series	1958	—	50p
25	Animals of the Countryside	1958	—	75p
25	Aquarium Fish	1961	—	75p
25	Army Badges—Past & Present	1961	—	£1.25
25	British Coins & Costumes	1958	—	75p
25	British Locomotives	1961	—	£1.50
25	British Uniforms of the 19th Century	1957	—	£2.00
25	Butterflies & Moths	1957	—	50p
25	Cacti	1961	—	60p
25	Castles of Britain	1961	—	£4.00
25	Coins of The World	1961	—	75p
25	Communications	1961	—	£5.00
25	Dogs	1958	—	£1.00
25	Evolution of The Royal Navy	1957	—	£1.50
M25	Famous British Ships, 1st	1952	—	50p
M25	Famous British Ships, 2nd	1952	—	50p
25	Football Clubs and Badges	1961	—	£10.00
25	Freshwater Fish	1958	—	50p
25	Guerriers a Travers Les Ages (French Text)	1961	—	£5.00
25	Histoire de l'Aviation, Premiere Serie (French)	1961	—	60p
25	Histoire de l'Aviation, Seconde Serie (French)	1962	—	50p
25	Historical Buildings	1959	—	£3.50
M25/50	History of Aviation	1952	—	£1.00
M50	History of Aviation	1952	—	£20.00
25	Holiday Resorts	1957	—	50p
25	Interesting Hobbies	1959	—	£2.00
25	Into Space	1959	—	75p
25	Kings of England	1954	50p	£12.50
25	Les Autos Modernes (French Text)	1961	—	£2.50
25	Medals of The World	1959	—	£1.25
25	Merchant Ships of The World	1961	—	£1.00
25	Merveilles Modernes (French Text)	1961	—	£5.00
25	Miniature Cars and Scooters	1958	—	£7.50
25	Naval Battles	1959	—	75p

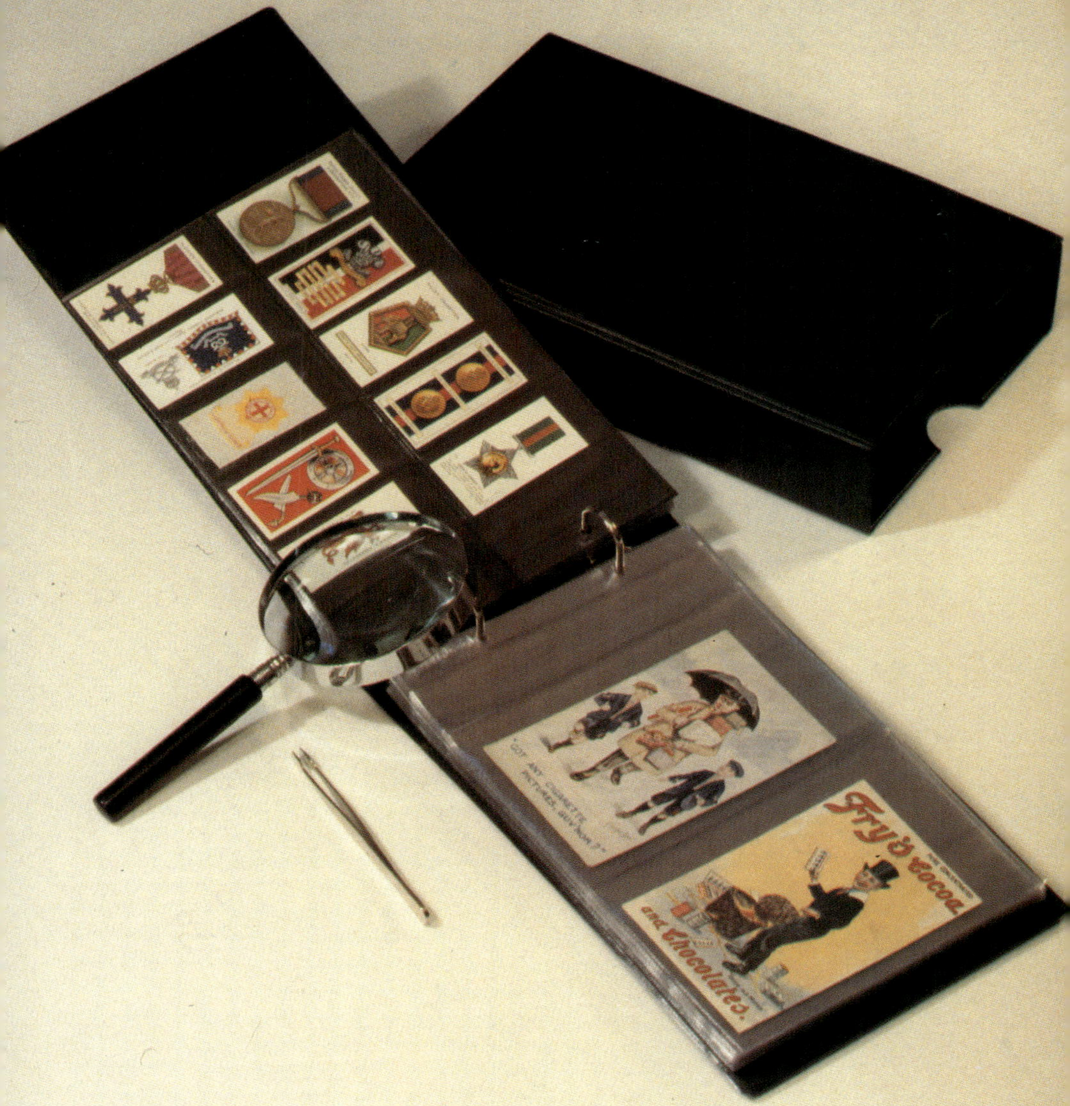

NOSTALGIA ALBUMS

Preserve the best of the past in the best of the present. See opposite page for details.

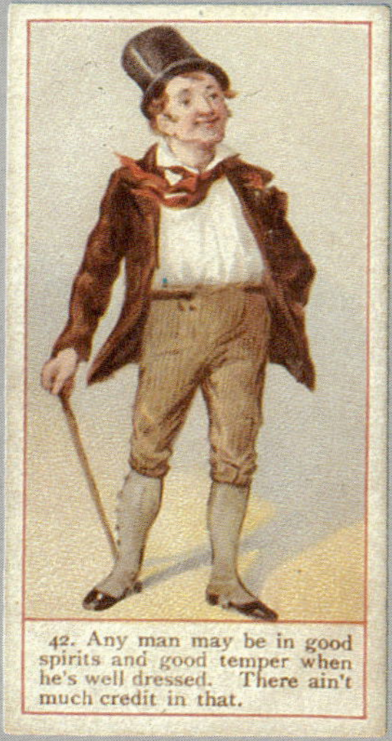

Dickens Gallery. Cope

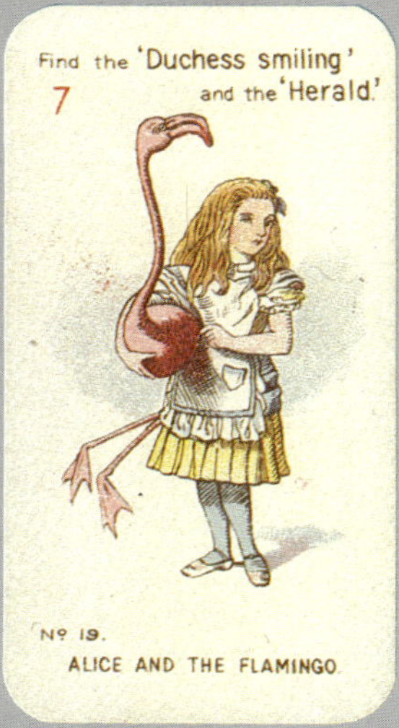

Alice in Wonderland.
Carreras

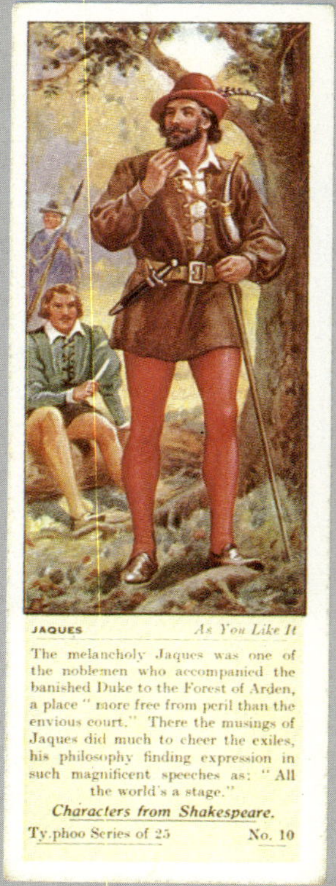

Characters from Shakespeare.
Typhoo

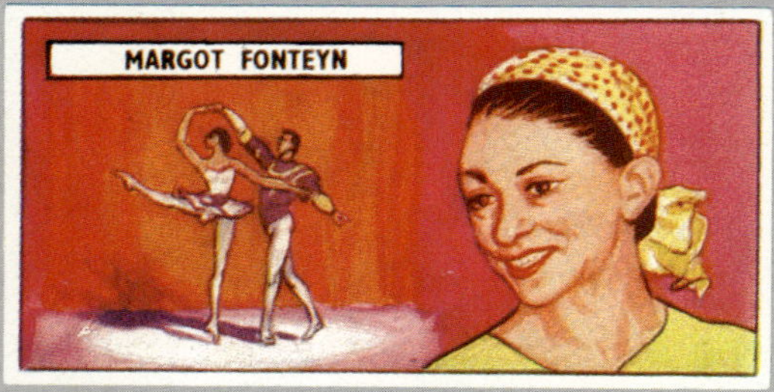

Famous People. Lyons

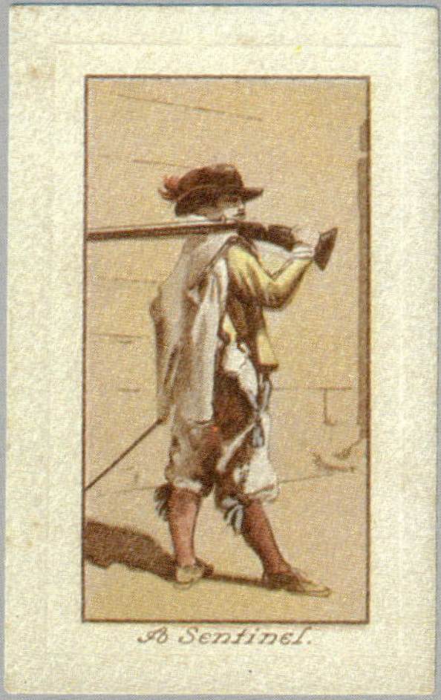

Art Treasures. Millhoff

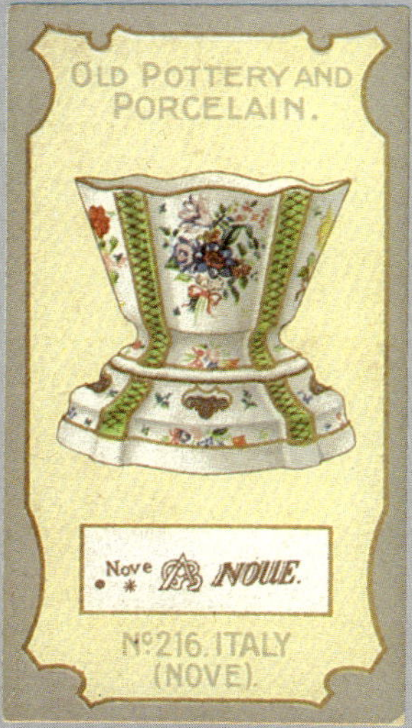

Old Pottery & Porcelain. Lea

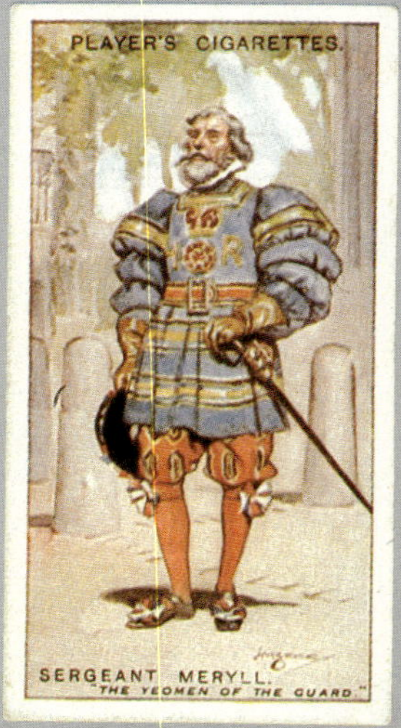

Gilbert & Sullivan.
Player

AMALGAMATED TOBACCO CORP. LTD. (Mills)—cont.

Qty		Date	Odds	Sets
25	Ports of The World	1959	—	50p
25	Propelled Weapons	1953	—	60p
25	Ships of The Royal Navy	1961	—	£3.00
25	Sports and Games	1958	—	£4.00
25	The Wild West	1960	—	£3.00
25	Tropical Birds	1958	A	—
25	Weapons of Defence	1961	—	£1.50
25	Wild Animals	1958	—	50p
25	World Locomotives	1959	—	£2.00

THE ANGLO-AMERICAN CIG. MAKING CO. LTD.

20	Russo Japanese War Series	1902	C	—

ANGLO CIGARETTE MFG. CO. LTD.

36	Tariff Reform Series	1909	£10.00	—

ANONYMOUS ISSUES

Printed Backs

41	V.C. Heroes	1916	£2.50	£100.00

Plain Backs

25	Actors & Actresses "FROGA"—C	1900	£4.00	—
?25	Actresses "ANGLO"	1896	B	—
?20	Actresses "ANGOOD"	1898	£5.00	—
20	Actresses "BLARM"	1900	£3.00	£60.00
?50	Actresses "DAVAN"	1902	A	—
26	Actresses "FROGA" A (Brown)	1900	£4.00	£100.00
26	Actresses "FROGA" A (Coloured)	1900	£5.00	—
?25	Actresses "HAGG"	1900	£4.00	—
15	Actresses "RUTAN"	1900	£7.50	—
24	Beauties "BOCCA"	1900	£6.00	—
50	Beauties "CHOAB" (Brown)	1902	£5.00	—
50	Beauties "CHOAB" (Coloured)	1902	£3.50	—
50	Beauties "FECKSA"	1903	£4.00	—
20	Beauties "FENA"	1899	A	—
25	Beauties "GRACC"	1898	£5.00	£125.00
26	Beauties "HOL"	1900	£5.00	—
25	Boer War & General Interest	1901	£10.00	—
20	Boer War Cartoons	1900	£7.50	—
7	Boer War Celebrities "RUTTER"	1901	£6.00	—
20	Boer War Generals "CLAM"	1901	£6.00	—
12	Boer War Generals "FLAC"	1901	£7.50	—
25	Boxer Rebellion—Sketches	1904	£4.00	—
M108	British Naval Crests	1916	£1.50	—
16	British Royal Family	1902	£4.00	—
50	Colonial Troops	1902	£3.00	—
M108	Crest & Badges of the British Army	1916	£1.50	—
20	Cricketers Series	1902	B	—
50	Dogs (as Taddy)	1900	A	—
30	Flags & Flags with Soldiers (Flag Draped)	1902	£2.50	£75.00
15	Flags & Flags with Soldiers (Flag Undraped)	1902	£3.00	—
24	Flags Arms & Types of Nations	1904	£3.00	—
30	Flags of Nations (As Cope)	1903	£3.00	—
40	Home & Colonial Regiments	1900	£3.50	—
2	King Edward & Queen Alexandra	1902	£10.00	£20.00

ANONYMOUS ISSUES—cont.

Qty		Date	Odds	Sets
40	Naval & Military Phrases	1904	£2.50	—
F30	Photographs (Animal Studies)	1935	50p	£15.00
?50	Pretty Girl Series "BAGG"	1898	£7.50	—
12	Pretty Girl Series "RASH"	1899	£5.00	—
30	Proverbs	1901	£3.00	—
19	Russo Japanese Series	1902	A	—
20	Russo Japanese War Series	1902	A	—
25	Star Girls	1900	£4.00	£100.00
20	The European War Series	1915	£2.00	£40.00
25	Types of British & Colonial Troops	1900	A	—
25	Types of British Soldiers	1914	£2.00	£50.00

E. & W. ANSTIE

25	Aesop's Fables	1934	50p	£12.50
16	British Empire Series	1904	£5.00	£80.00
10	Clifton Suspension Bridge (Sect.)	1938	25p	£2.50
B40	Flags (Silk)	1915	60p	—
X9	Flags (Silk)	1915	£2.00	—
40	Nature Notes	1939	£3.00	—
50	People of Africa	1926	£1.50	£75.00
50	People of Asia	1926	£1.50	£75.00
50	People of Europe	1925	£1.20	£60.00
40	Places of Interest	1939	13p	£5.25
8	Puzzle Series	1900	B	—
25	Racing Series (1-25)	1922	75p	£19.00
25	Racing Series (26-50)	1922	£1.00	£25.00
60/82	Regimental Badges (Silk)	1915	40p	£24.00
M5	Royal Mail Series	1900	C	—
X5	Royal Standard & Portraits (Silk)	1915	£2.00	—
50	Scout Series	1923	£1.25	£62.50
10	Stonehenge (Sect.)	1936	25p	£2.50
10	The Victory (Sect.)	1936	40p	—
50	The World's Wonders	1924	75p	£37.50
20	Wells Cathedral (Sect.)	1935	35p	£7.00
40	Wessex	1938	35p	£14.00
20	Wiltshire Downs (Sect.)	1935	35p	£7.00
10	Windsor Castle (Sect.)	1937	25p	£2.50

HENRY ARCHER & CO.

26	Actresses "FROGA"	1900	B	—
50	Beauties "CHOAB" (Brown)	1900	£7.50	—
25	Beauties "CHOAB" (Coloured)	1900	B	—
20	Prince of Wales Series	1912	£10.00	—

ARDATH TOBACCO CO. LTD.

50	Animals at The Zoo	1924	60p	—
F54	Beautiful English Women	1930	£1.00	—
25	Big Game Hunting	1930	£1.20	£30.00
L30	Boucher Series	1915	£1.25	£37.50
50	Britain's Defenders	1936	16p	£8.00
50	British Born Film Stars	1934	30p	£15.00
M50	British Born Film Stars	1934	50p	—
X1	Calendar 1942	1941	—	40p
X1	Calendar 1942-3	1942	—	50p

Qty		Date	Odds	Sets
X1	Calendar 1943	1942	—	50p
X1	Calendar 1943-4	1943	—	40p
X1	Calendar 1944	1943	—	50p
F36	Camera Studies	1939	50p	£18.00
LF45	Camera Studies	1939	40p	£18.00
X25	Champion Dogs	1934	16p	£4.00
X100	Contract Bridge Contest Hands	1930	A	—
50	Cricket, Tennis & Golf Celebrities (brown back—NZ)	1935	50p	£25.00
50	Cricket, Tennis & Golf Celebrities (grey back)	1935	20p	£10.00
X25	Dog Studies (State Express etc.)	1938	40p	£10.00
X25	Dog Studies (New Zealand)	1938	A	—
25	Eastern Proverbs	1932	50p	£12.50
48	Empire Flying Boat (Sect.)	1938	30p	£15.00
50	Empire Personalities	1937	25p	£12.50
50	Famous Film Stars	1934	20p	£10.00
50	Famous Footballers	1934	16p	£8.00
25	Famous Scots	1935	24p	£6.00
X25	Fighting & Civil Aircraft	1936	60p	£15.00
50	Figures of Speech	1936	16p	£4.00
50	Film, Stage and Radio Stars	1935	25p	£12.50
X25	Film, Stage & Radio Stars (Different)	1935	20p	£5.00
M50	Flags 4th Series (Silk)	1914	A	—
M50	Flags 5th Series (Silk)	1914	A	—
D50	Flags 6th Series (Silk)	1914	B	—
L40	Franz Hals Series	1916	A	—
X50	From Screen and Stage	1936	25p	£12.50
L30	Gainsborough Series	1915	£1.25	£37.50
L30	Girls of all Nations	1916	£5.00	—
50	Great War Series	1916	£2.50	—
50	Great War Series "B"	1916	£2.50	—
50	Great War Series "C"	1916	£2.50	—
25	Hand Shadows	1930	A	—
X25	Historic Grand Slams	1936	A	—
L50	Hollandsche Oude Meesters	1916	A	—
X48	How to Recognise The Service Ranks	1940	£1.50	—
X2	Industrial Posters	1942	—	60p
X150	Information Slips	1940	£1.00	—
L24	It All Depends On Me	1940	30p	£7.50
50	Life in The Services (adhesive)	1938	15p	£7.50
50	Life in The Services (non-adhesive NZ)	1938	40p	£20.00
96	Modern School Atlas	1936	60p	£60.00
50	National Fitness (adhesive)	1938	12p	£6.00
50	National Fitness (non-adhesive NZ)	1938	40p	£20.00
50	New Zealand Views	1928	£1.50	—
L1	On The Kitchen Front	1942	—	60p
50	Our Empire	1937	60p	£30.00
LF110	Photocards "A" (Lancs. Football Teams)	1936	24p	£25.00
LF110	Photocards "B" (N.E. Football Teams)	1936	30p	£33.00
LF110	Photocards "C" (Yorks. Football Teams)	1936	30p	£33.00
LF165	Photocards "D" (Scots Footballs Teams)	1936	25p	£42.00
LF110	Photocards "E" (Midlands Football Teams)	1936	30p	£33.00
LF110	Photocards "F" (Southern Football Teams)	1936	16p	£17.50
LF99	Photocards "Z" (Sport & General Interest)	1936	12p	£4.00

Qty		*Date*	*Odds*	*Sets*
LF11	Photocards "Supplementary"	1936	75p	£8.00
LF22	Photocards Group "A" (Sports)	1937	12p	£2.50
LF21/22	Photocards Group "B" (Coronation, Sports) ...	1937	16p	£3.50
LF21/22	Photocards Group "C" (Lancs. Personalities) ...	1937	40p	£8.00
LF22	Photocards Group "D" (Irish Personalities) ...	1937	40p	£9.00
LF22	Photocards Group "E" (Films, Sports)	1938	25p	£5.50
LF22	Photocards Group "F" (Films, Sports)	1938	60p	£13.00
LF11	Photocards Group "G" (Cricketers)	1938	£8.00	—
LF66	Photocards Group "GS" (Various)	1938	60p	£40.00
LF22	Photocards Group "H" (Films, Sport)	1938	40p	£9.00
LF22	Photocards Group "I" (Films, Various)	1938	75p	£16.50
LF22	Photocards Group "J" (Films, Various)	1939	16p	£3.50
LF22	Photocards Group "K" (Various)	1939	40p	£9.00
LF44	Photocards Group "L" (Various)	1939	20p	£9.00
F45	Photocards Group "M" (Films, Various)	1939	24p	£11.00
LF45	Photocards Group "M" (Films, Various)	1939	24p	£11.00
F45	Photocards Group "N" (Films)	1939	24p	£11.00
LF45	Photocards Group "N" (Films)	1939	24p	£11.00
LF66	Photocards Views of the World	1938	24p	£15.00
25	Proverbs (1-25)	1936	12p	£3.00
25	Proverbs (26-50)	1936	60p	£15.00
L30	Raphael Series	1916	£1.25	£37.50
LF45	Real Photographs Group "O" (Films)	1939	30p	£13.50
F45	Real Photos 1st Series	1939	40p	£20.00
XF18	Real Photos 1st Series (Views)	1937	£1.00	—
F54	Real Photos 2nd Series	1939	40p	£20.00
XF18	Real Photos 2nd Series	1937	£1.00	—
XF18	Real Photos 3rd Series (Views)	1937	£1.00	—
XF18	Real Photos 4th Series	1938	£1.00	—
XF18	Real Photos 5th Series (Views)	1938	£1.00	—
XF18	Real Photos 6th Series	1938	£1.00	—
LF44	Real Photos Series 1—GP1	1939	30p	£13.00
LF44	Real Photos Series 2—GP2	1939	12p	£3.00
LF44	Real Photos Series 3—GP3	1939	£1.25	—
LF44	Real Photos Series 3—CV3 (Views)	1939	30p	£13.00
LF44	Real Photos Series 4—CV4 (Views)	1939	12p	£3.50
XF36	Real Photos Series 7	1938	50p	£18.00
XF54	Real Photos Series 8	1938	30p	£16.00
LF54	Real Photos Series 9	1938	25p	£13.50
XF54	Real Photos Series 9	1938	25p	£13.50
LF54	Real Photos Series 10	1939	25p	£13.50
XF54	Real Photos Series 10	1939	30p	£16.00
LF54	Real Photos Series 11	1939	25p	£13.50
XF54	Real Photos Series 11	1939	50p	£27.00
LF54	Real Photos Series 12	1939	25p	£13.50
LF54	Real Photos Series 13	1939	25p	£13.50
LF36	Real Photographs of Famous Landmarks ...	1939	£1.00	—
XF36	Real Photographs of Famous Landmarks ...	1939	60p	£20.00
LF36	Real Photographs of Modern Aircraft	1939	£1.25	—
XF36	Real Photographs of Modern Aircraft	1939	75p	£27.00
L30	Rembrandt Series	1916	£1.50	£45.00
X30	Rembrandt Series	1916	£2.00	£60.00
L30	Rubens Series	1916	£1.25	£37.50
100	Scenes From Big Films	1935	40p	—

ARDATH TOBACCO CO. LTD.—cont.

Qty		Date	Odds	Sets
M100	Scenes From Big Films	1935	50p	—
50	Silver Jubilee	1935	16p	£8.00
50	Speed Land Sea & Air (State Express)	1935	30p	£15.00
50	Speed Land Sea & Air ("Ardath"—N.Z.)	1935	60p	£30.00
X25	Speed Land Sea & Air (Different)	1938	30p	£7.50
50	Sports Champions (title in 1 line)	1935	16p	£8.00
50	Sports Champions (title in 2 lines—N.Z.)	1935	60p	£30.00
6	Sportsmen (Double Ace)	1953	£1.50	—
50	Stamps Rare & Interesting	1939	50p	£25.00
50	Swimming Diving and Life-Saving	1937	50p	£25.00
50	Tennis	1938	50p	£25.00
9	The Office of Chief Whip	1955	£1.50	—
48	Trooping the Colour (Sect.)	1939	60p	£30.00
X?	Types of British Manhood	1935	A	—
L30	Velasquez Series	1916	£1.50	£45.00
X30	Velasquez Series	1916	£2.50	—
50	Who is this? (Film Stars)	1936	15p	£7.50
X?	Wonderful Handcraft	1935	A	—
X24/25	World Views	1937	12p	£2.50
50	Your Birthday Tells Your Fortune	1937	13p	£6.50

ASSOCIATED TOBACCO MANUFACTURERS

25	Cinema Stars	1926	A	—

ATKINSON

30	Army Pictures, Cartoons, etc.	1916	B	—

AVISS BROS. LTD.

40	Naval & Military Phrases	1904	B	—

J. A. BAILEY

40	Naval & Military Phrases	1904	C	—

A. BAKER & CO. LTD.

25	Actresses, 3 Sizes	1901	£7.50	—
L25	Actresses, 3 Sizes (different)	1901	£15.00	—
P?25	Actresses, 3 Sizes	1901	C	—
20	Actresses, "BLARM"	1900	£10.00	—
10	Actresses, "HAGG"	1900	£10.00	—
41	Baker's Tobacconists Shops	1901	B	—
25	Beauties of All Nations (Albert Baker)	1898	£6.00	—
25	Beauties of All Nations (A. Baker)	1899	£4.00	£100.00
16	British Royal Family	1902	£15.00	—
20	Cricketers Series	1902	C	—
25	Star Girls	1898	C	—

BAYLEY AND HOLDSWORTH

26	Flag Signalling Code Series	1912	£50.00	—

THOMAS BEAR & SONS LTD.

50	Aeroplanes	1924	£1.25	—
50	Cinema Artistes, Set 2	1936	A	—
50	Cinema Artistes, Set 4	1937	A	—
50	Cinema Stars "BAMT"	1928	75p	—
50	Do You Know?	1923	60p	£30.00

THOMAS BEAR & SONS LTD.—cont.

Qty		Date	Odds	Sets
270	Javanese Series (Blue)	1925	50p	£135.00
100	Javanese Series (Yellow)	1925	A	—
50	Stage and Film Stars	1926	£1.00	—

E. C. BEESTON

30	Army Pictures, Cartoons, etc.	1916	B	—

BELFAST SHIPS STORES

?10	Dickens Characters Burlesqued	1900	D	—

J. & F. BELL LTD.

10	Actresses "HAGG"	1900	£25.00	—
25	Beauties (Tobacco Leaf Back)	1898	£35.00	—
25	Colonial Series	1901	£16.00	—
30	Footballers	1902	£8.00	—
60	Rigsvaabner	1925	A	—
25	Scottish Clan Series	1903	£4.00	£100.00
60	Women of All Nations	1925	A	—

R. BELLWOOD

18	Motor Cycle Series	1913	B	—

RICHARD BENSON LTD.

L24	Old Bristol Series	1925	£1.25	£30.00
X24	Old Bristol Series (Reprint)	1946	80p	£20.00

BENSON & HEDGES LTD.

1	Advertisement Card, Original Shop	1973	—	60p
3	Advertisement Cards, Silk Cut	1974	40p	£1.20
48	Ancient & Modern Fire-Fighting Equipment	1947	£1.00	£48.00
L10	B.E.A. Aircraft	1958	£1.00	—

FELIX S. BERLYN

25	The Burline Mixture (Golfers Blend) Series	1910	C	—

BERRY'S

20	London Views	1904	C	—

BEWLAY & CO.

5	Comic Advertisement Cards	1909	C	—
12	War Series (Portraits)	1915	£6.00	£72.00
25	War Series (Scenes)	1915	£3.00	—

W. O. BIGG & CO.

37	Flags of All Nations	1904	£3.50	—
50	Life on Board a Man Of War	1905	£5.00	—

JAS BIGGS & SON

26	Actresses "FROGA A"	1900	£15.00	—
26	Actresses "FROGA B"	1900	B	—
24	Beauties "BOCCA"	1900	B	—
25	Beauties "CHOAB"	1902	B	—
30	Colonial Trops	1901	£12.50	—
30	Flags & Flags With Soldiers	1903	£12.50	—
25	Star Girls	1900	C	—

J. S. BILLINGHAM

Qty		Date	Odds	Sets
30	Army Pictures, Cartoons, etc.	1916	B	—

R. BINNS

?15	Halifax Town Footballers	1924	C	—

BLANKS CIGARETTES

50	Keystrokes in Break-building	1910	C	—

BOCNAL TOBACCO CO.

25	Luminous Silhouettes of Beauty & Charm ...	1938	50p	£12.50
25	Proverbs Up To Date	1938	50p	£12.50

ALPHONSE BODE & SON

30	Proverbs	1903	C	—

ALEXANDER BOGULSAVSKY LTD.

X12	Big Events on the Turf	1924	£3.00	—
25	Conan Doyle Characters (black back)	1923	£1.20	£30.00
25	Conan Doyle Characters (green back)	1923	£1.20	£30.00
25	Mythological Gods and Goddesses	1924	30p	£7.50
25	Sports Records (1-25)	1925	24p	£6.00
25	Sports Records, 2nd Series (26-50)	1925	16p	£4.00
25	Winners on the Turf	1925	40p	£10.00
L25	Winners on the Turf	1925	50p	£12.50

R. & E. BOYD LTD.

B25	Places of Interest	1938	A	—
L25	Wild Birds at Home	1938	A	—

WM. BRADFORD

50	Beauties "CHOAB"	1902	£12.50	—
?25	Beauties, Jersey Lily	1900	C	—
20	Boer War Cartoons	1901	B	—

THOS. BRANKSTON & CO. LTD.

30	Colonial Troops	1901	£12.50	—

BRIGHAM & CO.

L16	Down The Thames From Henley to Windsor ...	1912	B	—
16	Reading Football Players	1912	B	—
X3	Tobacco Growing in Hampshire, England ...	1912	£3.50	£10.50

BRITANNIA ANONYMOUS SOCIETY

?20	Beauties & Couples	1914	B	—

BRITISH & COLONIAL TOBACCO CO.

25	Armies of the World	1900	C	—

BRITISH FASCISTS CIGARETTES

?3	Recruiting Cards	1935	B	—

J. M. BROWN

30	Army Pictures, Cartoons, etc.	1916	B	—

JOHN BRUMFIT

50	The Public Schools Ties Series	1925	£1.25	£62.50

BUCKTROUT & CO. LTD. (Channel Isles)

Qty		*Date*	*Odds*	*Sets*
M416	Around the World/Places of Interest	1924	25p	£100.00
24	Birds of England	1924	£1.00	£24.00
50	Cinema Stars, 1st	1926	60p	£30.00
50	Cinema Stars, 2nd	1927	£1.00	£50.00
M50	Football Teams	1928	75p	£37.50
L22	Football Teams of the Bailiwick	1927	25p	£5.50
123	Guernsey Footballers	1923	£1.00	£120.00
20	Inventors Series	1924	25p	£5.00
25	Marvels of the Universe Series	1919	£1.00	£25.00
M53	Playing Cards	1930	40p	£20.00
25	Sports & Pastimes	1926	£1.20	£30.00

G. A. BULLOGH

30	Army Pictures, Cartoons, etc.	1916	B	—

BURSTEIN ISAACS & CO. LTD.

50	Famous Prize Fighters	1923	£1.00	£50.00
F28	London View Series	1922	£1.20	—

BYRT WOOD & CO.

25	Pretty Girl Series "BAGG"	1900	£40.00	—

CABANA CIGAR CO.

B1	Little Manturios Advertisement Card	1904	C	—

PERCY E. CADLE & CO.

20	Actresses "BLARM"	1900	£10.00	—
26	Actresses "FROGA" (Chocolate)	1900	£15.00	—
26	Actresses "FROGA" (Coloured)	1900	£20.00	—
?25	Boer War & Boxer Rebellion Sketches	1901	£25.00	—
10	Boer War Generals	1901	B	—
20	Footballers	1904	£7.50	—

CARRERAS LTD.

F24	Actresses and Their Pets	1926	£1.75	£42.00
50	A Kodak at the Zoo, A Series	1924	15p	£7.50
50	A Kodak at the Zoo, 2nd Series	1925	15p	£7.50
48	Alice in Wonderland (round corners)	1930	12p	£6.00
48	Alice in Wonderland (square corners)	1930	50p	£25.00
L48	Alice in Wonderland	1930	15p	£7.50
X1	Alice in Wonderland (Instructions)	1930	A	—
50	Amusing Tricks & How To Do Them	1937	16p	£8.00
22	Battle of Waterloo	1934	60p	—
L15	Battle of Waterloo	1934	£1.50	—
B1	Battle of Waterloo (Instructions)	1934	—	£2.50
50	Believe It Or Not	1934	12p	£6.00
50	Birds of the Countryside	1939	12p	£6.00
200	Black Cat Library	1913	£6.00	—
50	Britain's Defences	1938	15p	£7.50
25	British Costumes	1927	50p	£12.50
L25	British Costumes	1927	50p	£12.50
F27	British Prime Ministers	1928	50p	£13.50
1	Calendar	1934	A	—

Qty		Date	Odds	Sets
50	Celebrities of British History	1935	12p	£3.00
25	Christie Comedy Girls	1928	£1.00	£25.00
30	Cricketers	1934	75p	£22.50
50	Cricketers (A Series of 50)	1934	60p	£30.00
F50	Dogs & Friend	1936	12p	£3.50
50	Do You Know?	1939	12p	£2.50
50	Famous Airmen & Airwomen	1936	30p	£15.00
25	Famous Escapes	1926	40p	£10.00
L25	Famous Escapes	1926	30p	£7.50
P10	Famous Escapes	1926	60p	£6.00
96	Famous Film Stars	1935	25p	£25.00
48	Famous Footballers	1935	12p	£6.00
25	Famous Men	1927	60p	£15.00
LF24	Famous Naval Men	1929	50p	£12.50
X6	Famous Posters (St. Dunstans)	1923	£12.00	—
LF12	Famous Soldiers	1928	£2.00	£24.00
F27	Famous Women	1929	60p	£16.00
25	Figures of Fiction	1924	60p	£15.00
F54	Film & Stage Beauties	1939	12p	£4.00
LF54	Film and Stage Beauties	1939	12p	£6.00
LF36	Film and Stage Beauties	1939	15p	£7.50
XF36	Film and Stage Beauties	1939	25p	—
50	Film Favourites	1938	25p	£12.50
F54	Film Stars, A Series	1937	15p	£7.50
LF54	Film Stars (as 2nd Series)	1938	25p	£13.50
XF36	Film Stars (Different)	1936	£1.25	£45.00
F54	Film Stars, 2nd Series	1938	12p	£4.00
XF36	Film Stars, 2nd Series (Different)	1936	60p	£21.50
XF36	Film Stars, 3rd Series	1937	60p	£21.50
XF36	Film Stars, 4th Series	1938	75p	£27.00
50	Film Stars (By Desmond)	1936	12p	£6.00
72	Film Stars (Oval)	1934	25p	£18.00
F72	Film Stars (Oval) "Real Photos"	1934	35p	—
60	Flags of All Nations (Unissued)	—	—	£32.00
K6	Flags & Arms (Circular)	1915	35p	—
K6	Flags of the Allies (Shaped)	1915	A	—
50	Flowers	1936	12p	£4.00
75	Footballers	1934	13p	£10.00
36	Fortune Telling (Card Inset)	1926	20p	£7.50
36	Fortune Telling (Head Inset)	1926	12p	£3.50
L36	Fortune Telling (Card Inset)	1926	12p	£5.00
L36	Fortune Telling (Head Inset)	1926	20p	£7.50
X1	Fortune Telling (Instructions)	1926	—	£2.00
F54	Glamour Girls of Stage and Films	1939	12p	£3.00
LF54	Glamour Girls of Stage and Films	1939	12p	£4.00
LF36	Glamour Girls of Stage and Films	1939	12p	£4.00
XF36	Glamour Girls of Stage and Films	1939	15p	£5.00
50	Gran-Pop	1934	12p	£5.00
L50	Gran-Pop	1934	12p	£2.00
M16	Guards Series (Sectional)	1970	40p	£6.00
M8	Guards Series (Full Length)	1970	40p	£3.25
M4	Guards Series (Mugs)	1971	50p	£2.00
48	Happy Family	1925	12p	£6.00
L48	Happy Family	1925	12p	£3.00

CARRERAS LTD.—cont.

Qty		Date	Odds	Sets
25	Highwaymen	1924	80p	£20.00
50	History of Army Uniforms	1937	50p	£25.00
50	History of Naval Uniforms	1937	25p	£12.50
25	Horses and Hounds	1926	50p	£12.50
L20	Horses and Hounds	1926	30p	£6.00
P10	Horses and Hounds	1926	60p	£6.00
50	Kings & Queens of England	1935	35p	£17.50
L50	Kings & Queens of England	1935	60p	£30.00
L?84	Lace Motifs	1915	£2.00	—
F27	Malayan Industries	1929	12p	£2.50
F24	Malayan Scenes	1928	60p	£15.00
LF24	Malayan Scenes	1928	12p	£3.00
K53	Miniature Playing Cards	1934	12p	£3.50
50	Notable M.P.s	1929	12p	£6.00
L50	Notable M.P.s	1929	12p	£4.00
F25	Notable Ships Past & Present	1929	50p	£12.50
24	Old Staffordshire Figures	1926	35p	£8.50
L24	Old Staffordshire Figures (Different)	1926	60p	£15.00
P12	Old Staffordshire Figures	1926	£1.25	£15.00
24	Orchids	1925	12p	£3.00
L24	Orchids	1925	12p	£3.00
P24	Orchids	1925	£1.00	—
50	Our Navy	1937	25p	£12.50
50	Palmistry	1933	12p	£4.00
F27	Paramount Stars	1929	20p	£5.50
25	Picture Puzzle Series	1923	50p	£12.50
52	Playing Cards	1926	75p	£40.00
52	Playing Cards & Dominoes (Numbered)	1929	12p	£5.00
52	Playing Cards & Dominoes (Unnumbered)	1929	15p	£7.50
L26	Playing Cards & Dominoes (Numbered)	1929	15p	£4.00
L26	Playing Cards & Dominoes (Unnumbered)	1929	22p	£6.00
48	Popular Footballers	1936	12p	£4.00
72	Popular Personalities (Oval)	1935	15p	£11.00
25	Races Historic & Modern	1927	30p	£15.00
L25	Races Historic & Modern	1927	30p	£15.00
P12	Races Historic & Modern	1927	£1.00	£12.00
140	Raemaekers War Cartoons (Black Cat)	1916	50p	£70.00
140	Raemaekers War Cartoons (Carreras)	1916	£1.50	—
25	Regalia Series	1925	12p	£3.00
L20	Regalia Series	1925	25p	£5.00
P10	Regalia Series	1925	50p	£5.00
L50	Round the World Scenic Models	1925	20p	£10.00
50	School Emblems	1929	20p	£10.00
L40	School Emblems	1929	25p	£10.00
P20	School Emblems	1929	50p	£10.00
L216	Sportsman's Guide—Fly Fishing (Canada)	1950	50p	—
48	Tapestry Reproductions of Famous Paintings (Sect.)	1938	25p	£12.50
52	The Greyhound Racing Game	1926	12p	£3.50
L52	The Greyhound Racing Game	1926	12p	£2.50
X1	The Greyhound Racing Game (Instructions)	1926	A	—
B5	The Handy English-French Dictionary	1915	£6.00	—
50	The Nose Game	1927	12p	£6.50
L50	The Nose Game	1927	12p	£3.50

Qty		Date	Odds	Sets
X1	The Nose Game (Instructions)	1927	A	—
50	The Science of Boxing (Black Cat)	1914	60p	£30.00
50	The Science of Boxing (Carreras)	1914	£1.50	£75.00
50	Tools and How To Use Them	1935	20p	£10.00
80	Types of London	1919	65p	£52.00
F27	Views of London	1929	12p	£2.50
F27	Views of the World	1927	35p	£9.00
25	Wild Flower Art Series	1923	30p	£7.50
50	Women on War Work	1916	£3.00	£150.00

TURF SLIDES

50	British Aircraft	1953	12p	£4.00
50	British Fish	1954	12p	£2.50
50	British Railway Locomotives	1952	16p	£8.00
50	Celebrities of British History	1951	20p	£10.00
50	Famous British Fliers	1956	30p	£15.00
50	Famous Cricketers	1950	£1.00	£50.00
50	Famous Dog Breeds	1952	15p	£7.50
50	Famous Film Stars	1949	12p	£8.00
50	Famous Footballers	1951	25p	£12.50
50	Film Favourites	1948	35p	£17.50
50	Film Stars	1947	25p	£12.50
50	Footballers	1948	30p	£15.00
50	Olympics 1948	1948	40p	£20.00
50	Radio Celebrities	1950	20p	£10.00
50	Sports	1949	20p	£10.00
50	Zoo Animals	1954	12p	£2.50

"BLACK CAT" MODERN ISSUES

50	British Birds	1976	6p	£1.50
50	Flowers All The Year Round	1977	12p	£6.00
50	Kings & Queens of England	1977	12p	£6.00
50	Military Uniforms	1976	6p	£1.50
50	Palmistry	1979	40p	—
50	Sport Fish	1978	6p	£1.50
50	Vintage Cars (with "Filter")	1976	10p	£5.00
50	Vintage Cars (without "Filter")	1976	6p	£1.50

AUSTRALIAN ISSUES

72	Film Stars Series (Smile Away)	1933	75p	—
72	Film Stars Series (Standard)	1933	60p	£45.00
72	Football Series	1933	60p	£42.50
24	Personality Series	1933	60p	£15.00
72	Personality Series, Film Stars	1933	60p	£42.50
72	Personality Series, Footballers	1933	60p	£45.00

CARRERAS & MARCIANUS

1	Photo Miniatures Folder	1909	—	£35.00
100	War Series	1915	B	—

CARRICK

12	Military Terms	1900	£25.00	—

P. J. CARROLL & CO.

Qty		*Date*	*Odds*	*Sets*
25	Birds	1939	12p	£3.00
25	British Naval Series	1915	£10.00	—
25	Derby Winners	1914	B	—
24	Jig Saw Puzzles	1935	£5.00	—
20	Louth—All Ireland Champions	1912	£5.00	—
25	Ship Series	1934	£2.50	—

THE CASKET TOBACCO & CIGARETTE CO. LTD.

?	Cricket Fixture Cards	1905	D	—
1	Cyclists Lighting Up Table	1909	D	—
?	Football Fixture Cards	1909	C	—
?	Road Maps	1909	D	—

S. CAVANDER & CO.

?25	Beauties "PLUMS"	1898	C	—

CAVANDERS LTD.

25	Ancient Chinese	1926	24p	£6.00
25	Ancient Egypt	1928	24p	£6.00
L25	Ancient Egypt (Different)	1928	16p	£4.00
F36	Animal Studies	1936	12p	£3.00
F50	Beauty Spots of Great Britain	1927	12p	£6.00
MF50	Beauty Spots of Great Britain	1927	12p	£6.00
F54	Camera Studies	1926	12p	£3.50
MF56	Camera Studies	1926	12p	£4.00
30	Cinema Stars	1934	20p	£6.00
MS50	Coloured Stereoscopic	1931	16p	£8.00
25	Feathered Friends	1926	80p	£20.00
25	Foreign Birds	1926	40p	£10.00
MS50	Glorious Britain	1930	20p	£10.00
25	Little Friends	1924	30p	£7.50
FS72	Peeps into Many Lands, A Series	1927	12p	£7.50
MFS72	Peeps into Many Lands, A Series	1927	12p	£7.50
XFS36	Peeps into Many Lands, A Series	1927	£1.00	£36.00
FS72	Peeps into Many Lands 2nd Series	1928	12p	£6.00
MFS72	Peeps into Many Lands 2nd Series	1928	12p	£7.50
FS48	Peeps into Many Lands 3rd Series	1929	12p	£5.00
MFS48	Peeps into Many Lands 3rd Series	1929	12p	£5.00
MFS48	Peeps into Many Lands 3rd (Reprinted)	1929	15p	£7.50
FS48	Peeps into Prehistoric Times 4th Series	1930	16p	£8.00
MFS48	Peeps into Prehistoric Times 4th Series	1930	16p	£8.00
F33	Photographs	1935	60p	£20.00
L48	Regimental Standards	1923	£4.00	—
25	Reproductions of Celebrated Oil Paintings	1925	50p	£12.50
F108	River Valleys	1926	20p	£20.00
MF108	River Valleys	1926	25p	£25.00
25	School Badges (Dark Blue Back)	1928	16p	£4.00
25	School Badges (Light Blue Back)	1928	16p	£4.00
MF30	The Colonial Series	1925	20p	£6.00
F54	The Homeland Series (Black Back)	1924	15p	£10.00
F50	The Homeland Series (Blue Back)	1924	25p	£12.50
MF50	The Homeland Series (Coloured)	1924	12p	£6.00
MF56	The Homeland Series (Uncoloured)	1924	15p	£8.50
M25	The Nation's Treasures	1925	16p	£4.00
MF30	Wordsworth's Country	1926	25p	£7.50

R. S. CHALLIS & CO. LTD.

Qty		Date	Odds	Sets
50	Comic Animals	1936	15p	£7.50
?30	Flickits (Fresher Cigarettes)	1936	A	—
36	Wild Birds at Home	1935	12p	£3.50
36	Wild Birds at Home (Baldric deleted)	1935	40p	£15.00

CHAPMAN

Qty		Date	Odds	Sets
30	Army Pictures, Cartoons, etc.	1916	B	—

CHARLESWORTH & AUSTIN

Qty		Date	Odds	Sets
50	Beauties "BOCCA"	1900	£8.00	—
16	British Royal Family	1902	£15.00	—
30	Colonial Troops	1901	£12.50	—
20	Cricketers Series	1902	C	—
30	Flags & Flags with Soldiers	1903	£12.50	—

CHESTERFIELD CIGARETTES

Qty		Date	Odds	Sets
M6	Chesterfield Cocktails	1980	20p	£1.25

A. CHEW & CO.

Qty		Date	Odds	Sets
30	Army Pictures, Cartoons, etc.	1916	B	—

CHING & CO. (Channel Isles)

Qty		Date	Odds	Sets
L24	Around & About in Jersey 1st Series	1963	12p	£2.00
L24	Around & About in Jersey 2nd Series	1964	30p	£7.50
25	Do You Know?	1962	—	50p
B48	Flowers	1962	40p	£20.00
L24	Jersey Past & Present 1st Series	1960	—	60p
L24	Jersey Past & Present 2nd Series	1962	—	£2.00
L24	Jersey Past & Present 3rd Series	1963	—	75p
25	Ships and their Workings	1961	—	60p
50	Veteran and Vintage Cars	1960	12p	£6.00

W. A. & A. C. CHURCHMAN

Qty		Date	Odds	Sets
?25	Actresses, Unicoloured	1897	£25.00	—
26	Actresses, "FROGA A"	1900	£15.00	—
26	Actresses, "FROGA B"	1900	£20.00	—
M48	Air Raid Precautions	1938	12p	£3.50
25	Army Badges of Rank	1916	£3.00	£75.00
50	Association Footballers, A Series	1938	12p	£3.50
50	Association Footballers, 2nd Series	1939	12p	£6.00
50	A Tour Round The World	1911	£2.50	—
12	Beauties "CERF"	1899	£20.00	—
25	Beauties "CHOAB"	1900	C	—
M?25	Beauties "CHOAB" (Circular)	1900	D	—
25	Beauties "FECKSA"	1903	B	—
25	Beauties "GRACC"	1898	£30.00	—
50	Birds & Eggs	1906	£2.50	£125.00
20	Boer War Cartoons	1901	C	—
41	Boer War Celebrities & Actresses	1901	£6.00	—
20	Boer War Generals "CLAM"	1901	£15.00	—
25	Boxing	1922	£1.20	£30.00
50	Boxing Personalities	1938	16p	£8.00
50	Boy Scouts A Series	1916	£2.00	£100.00
50	Boy Scouts 2nd Series	1916	£2.00	£100.00

W. A. & A. C. CHURCHMAN—cont.

Qty		Date	Odds	Sets
50	Boy Scouts 3rd Series (Blue Back)	1916	£4.00	—
50	Boy Scouts 3rd Series (Brown Back)	1916	£2.00	£100.00
25	British Film Stars	1934	50p	£12.50
54/55	Can You Beat Bogey at St. Andrews?	1934	50p	£27.00
54/55	Can You Beat Bogey (Red Overprint)	1934	50p	£27.00
25	Cathedrals & Churches	1924	80p	£20.00
X12	Cathedrals & Churches	1924	£3.00	£36.00
50	Celebrated Gateways	1925	80p	£40.00
M1	Christmas Greeting Card	1938	—	50p
25	Civic Insignia and Plate	1926	60p	£15.00
50	Contract Bridge	1935	12p	£6.00
50	Cricketers	1936	80p	£40.00
25	Curious Dwellings	1926	60p	£15.00
L12	Curious Dwellings	1926	£1.25	£15.00
25	Curious Signs	1925	60p	£15.00
38	Dogs and Fowls	1908	£3.00	£100.00
25	Eastern Proverbs A Series	1931	14p	£3.50
L12	Eastern Proverbs A Series	1931	£1.25	£15.00
25	Eastern Proverbs 2nd Series	1932	24p	£6.00
L12	Eastern Proverbs 2nd Series	1932	50p	£6.00
L12	Eastern Proverbs 3rd Series	1933	25p	£3.00
L12	Eastern Proverbs 4th Series	1934	15p	£2.00
50	East Suffolk Churches (Black)	1912	80p	£40.00
50	East Suffolk Churches (Sepia)	1917	80p	£40.00
50	Empire Railways	1931	80p	£40.00
25	Famous Cricket Colours	1928	£1.20	£30.00
50	Famous Golfers	1927	75p	£37.50
L12	Famous Golfers 1st Series	1927	£2.00	£25.00
L12	Famous Golfers 2nd Series	1928	£2.00	—
25	Famous Railway Trains	1929	80p	£20.00
L12	Famous Railway Trains 1st Series	1929	£1.50	£18.00
L12	Famous Railway Trains 2nd Series	1929	£1.50	£18.00
50	Fish & Bait	1914	£2.00	£100.00
50	Fishes of the World	1924	£1.20	—
50	Flags & Funnels of Leading Steamship Lines ...	1912	£2.50	£125.00
50	Football Club Colours	1909	£3.00	—
50	Footballers (Brown)	1914	£7.50	—
50	Footballers (Coloured)	1914	£3.00	—
52	Frisky	1925	20p	£10.00
1	Frisky (Instructions)	1925	—	£1.00
50	History & Development of the British Empire ...	1934	35p	£17.50
M48	Holidays in Britain (Views & Maps)	1937	12p	£4.00
M48	Holidays in Britain (Views Only)	1938	12p	£4.50
40	Home & Colonial Regiments	1902	£15.00	—
40	Howlers	1937	12p	£3.00
L16	Howlers	1937	18p	£3.00
50	Interesting Buildings	1905	£2.50	£125.00
25	Interesting Door Knockers	1928	60p	£15.00
25	Interesting Experiments	1929	40p	£10.00
50	In Town To-Night	1938	12p	£3.50
L12	Italian Art Exhibition, 1930 1st Series	1930	60p	£7.50
L12	Italian Art Exhibition, 1930 2nd Series	1931	60p	£7.50
50	Kings of Speed	1939	12p	£4.00
50	Landmarks in Railway Progress	1931	80p	£40.00

Qty		Date	Odds	Sets
L12	Landmarks in Railway Progress 1st Series	1932	£1.00	£12.00
L12	Landmarks in Railway Progress 2nd Series	1932	£1.00	£12.00
50	Lawn Tennis	1928	30p	£15.00
L12	Lawn Tennis	1928	£1.00	—
50	Legends of Britain	1936	30p	£15.00
L12	Legends of Britain	1936	60p	£7.50
25	Life in a Liner	1930	20p	£5.00
L12	Life in a Liner	1930	£1.00	£12.00
50	Medals	1910	£3.00	£150.00
50	Men of the Moment in Sport	1928	80p	£40.00
L12	Men of the Moment in Sport 1st Series	1928	£1.25	—
L12	Men of the Moment in Sport 2nd Series	1928	£1.25	—
M48	Modern Wonders	1938	15p	£7.50
25	Musical Instruments	1924	£1.00	£25.00
25	Nature's Architects	1930	24p	£6.00
L12	Nature's Architects	1930	£1.00	£12.00
D55	Olympic Winners Through the Years	1956	60p	—
50	Phil May Sketches (Gold Flake)	1912	£2.50	£125.00
50	Phil May Sketches (no brand)	1912	£4.00	£200.00
25	Pipes of the World	1927	£1.00	£25.00
50	Prominent Golfers	1931	75p	£37.50
L12	Prominent Golfers	1931	£2.00	—
50	Racing Greyhounds	1934	30p	£15.00
25	Railway Working A Series	1926	£1.00	£25.00
L12	Railway Working A Series	1926	£2.50	—
25	Railway Working 2nd Series	1927	50p	£12.50
L13	Railway Working 2nd Series	1926	£2.50	—
L12	Railway Working 3rd Series	1927	£2.50	—
50	Regimental Colours & Cap Badges	1912	£2.00	£100.00
50	Rivers & Broads	1921	£2.50	—
50	Rivers & Broads of Norfolk & Suffolk	1922	£1.50	£75.00
50	Rugby Internationals	1935	25p	£12.50
50	Sectional Cycling Map	1913	£2.00	£100.00
50	Silhouettes of Warships	1915	£3.00	£150.00
50	Sporting Celebrities	1931	60p	£30.00
25	Sporting Trophies	1927	50p	£12.50
L12	Sporting Trophies	1927	£1.50	£18.00
25	Sports & Games in Many Lands	1929	30p	£7.50
25	The Houses of Parliament & Their Story	1931	50p	£12.50
25	The Inns of Court	1922	60p	£15.00
50	The King's Coronation	1937	12p	£3.00
L15	The King's Coronation	1937	30p	£4.50
M48	The Navy at Work	1937	12p	£3.00
50	The Queen Mary	1936	35p	£17.50
L16	The Queen Mary	1936	40p	£6.50
M48	The RAF at Work	1937	15p	£7.50
50	The Story of London	1934	40p	£20.00
L12	The Story of London	1934	£1.00	£12.00
50	The Story of Navigation	1937	12p	£3.50
L12	The Story of Navigation	1937	50p	£6.00
D40	The World of Sport	1961	60p	—
36	3 Jovial Golfers in Search of the Perfect Course	1934	40p	£15.00
72	3 Jovial Golfers (Irish Issue)	1934	£1.50	—
50	Treasure Trove	1937	12p	£3.00

W. A. & A. C. CHURCHMAN—cont.

Qty		Date	Odds	Sets
L12	Treasure Trove	1937	25p	£3.00
25	Types of British & Colonial Troops	1899	£25.00	—
25	Warriors of All Nations	1929	60p	£15.00
L12	Warriors of All Nations A Series	1929	75p	£9.00
L12	Warriors of All Nations 2nd Series	1931	£1.00	£12.00
50	Well Known Ties A Series	1934	20p	£10.00
L12	Well Known Ties A Series	1934	50p	£6.00
50	Well Known Ties 2nd Series	1935	12p	£5.00
L12	Well Known Ties 2nd Series	1935	50p	£6.00
25	Wembley Exhibition	1924	80p	£20.00
50	West Suffolk Churches	1919	£1.00	£50.00
50	Wild Animals of the World	1907	£3.00	£150.00
M48	Wings Over The Empire	1939	12p	£3.00
50	Wonderful Railway Travel	1937	15p	£7.50
L12	Wonderful Railway Travel	1937	40p	£5.00
50	World Wonders Old and New (Unissued) ...	—	—	£10.00
Overseas Issues (No. I.T.C. Clause)				
M48	Air Raid Precautions	1938	50p	—
M48	Holidays in Britain (Views & Maps)	1937	50p	—
M48	Holidays in Britain (Views only)	1938	50p	—
M48	Modern Wonders	1938	50p	—
M48	The Navy at Work	1937	50p	—
M48	The R.A.F. at Work	1937	50p	—
M48	Wings over the Empire	1939	50p	—

CIGARETTE COMPANY (Channel Isles)

72	Jersey Footballers	1910	£2.00	—

WM. CLARKE & SON

25	Army Life	1915	£3.50	—
16	Boer War Celebrities	1901	£12.50	£200.00
50	Butterflies & Moths	1912	£2.50	£125.00
30	Cricketer Series	1901	£40.00	—
66	Football Series	1902	£4.00	—
25	Marine Series	1907	£4.00	£100.00
50	Royal Mail	1914	£2.50	—
50	Sporting Terms	1900	£10.00	—
20	Tobacco Leaf Girls	1898	£200.00	—
25	Well Known Sayings	1900	£6.00	£150.00

J. H. CLURE & SON

30	Army Pictures, Cartoons, etc.	1916	B	—
50	War Portraits	1916	B	—

J. LOMAX COCKAYNE

50	War Portraits	1916	B	—

COHEN WEENEN & CO.

F40	Actresses, Footballers & Jockeys	1901	£12.50	—
26	Actresses "FROGA"	1900	B	—
24	Beauties "BOCCA"	1899	B	—
25	Beauties "GRACC"	1899	B	—
65	Celebrities (Black & White) ("250" back) ...	1900	£2.00	—

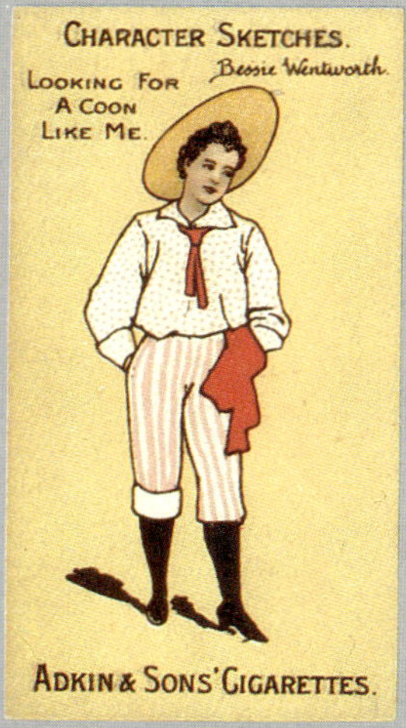

Character Sketches. Adkin

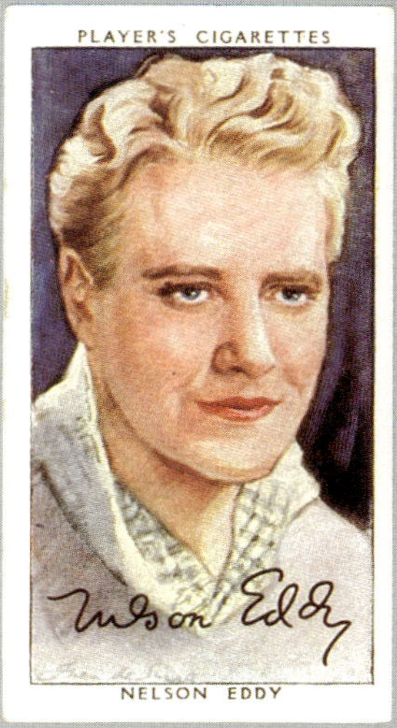

Film Stars. 3rd. Player

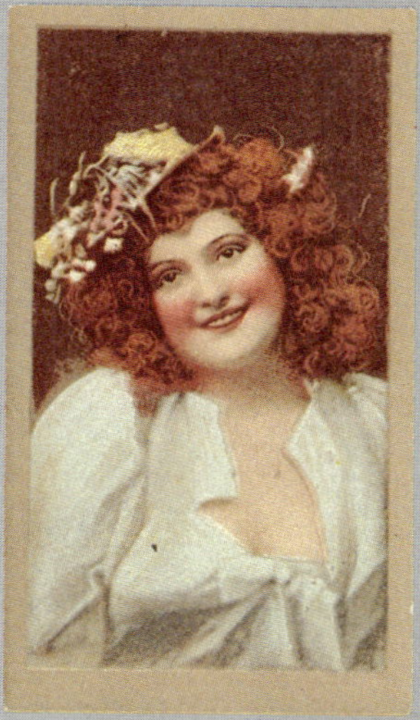

Beauties. American Tobacco Co.

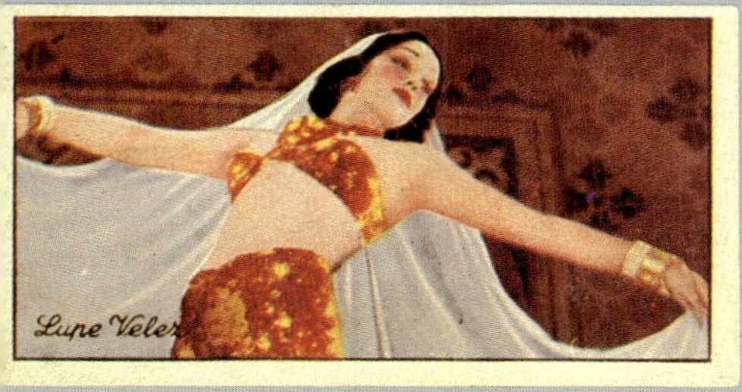

Famous Film Stars. Carreras

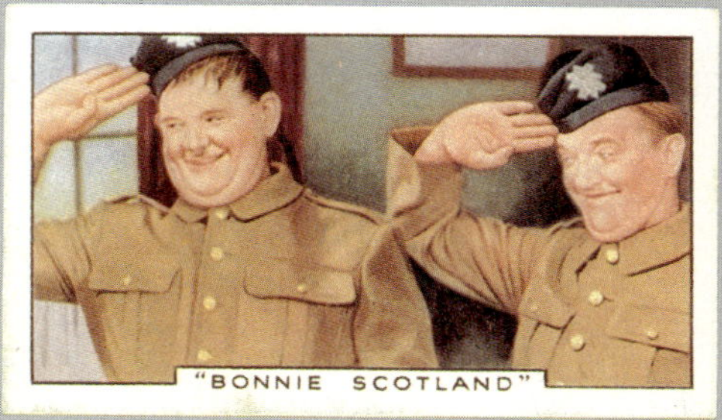

Film Episodes. Gallaher

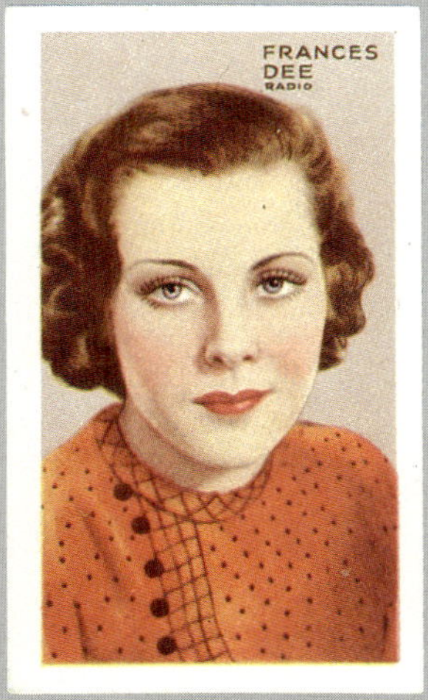

Stars of Screen & Stage. Gallaher

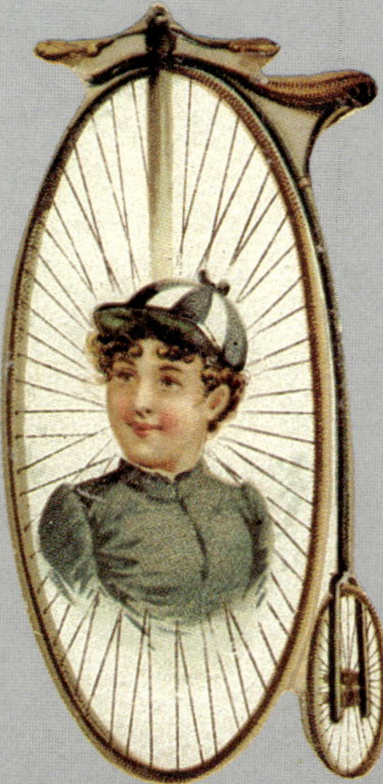

Novelties. Kinney

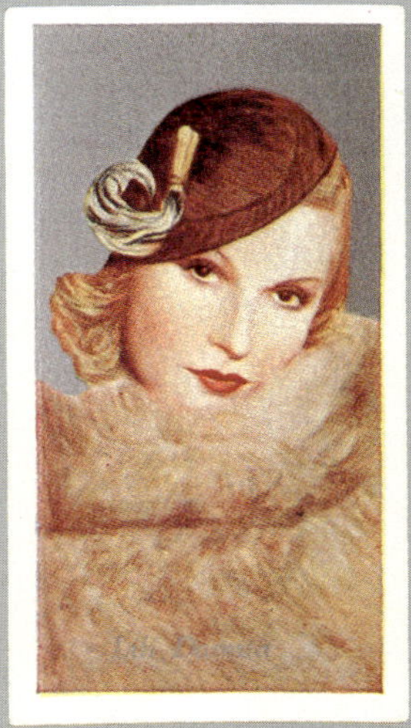

Film Favourites. Phillips or Abdulla

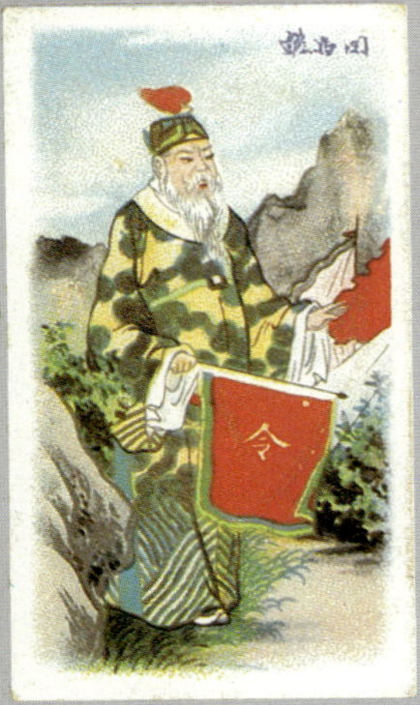

China's Ancient Warriors.
Wills (Pirate)

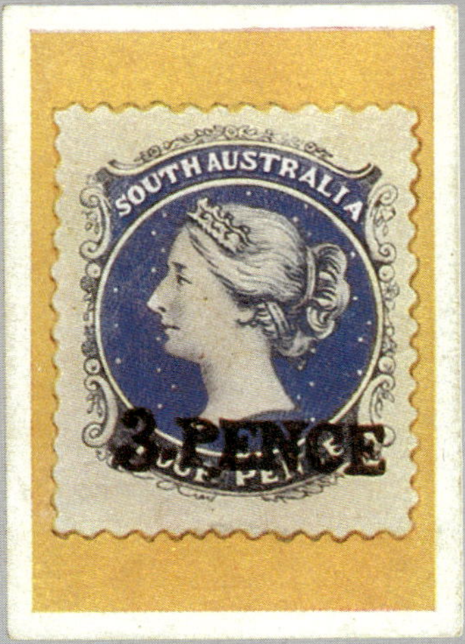

Postage Stamps—Rarest Varieties.
African Tob. Mfrs.

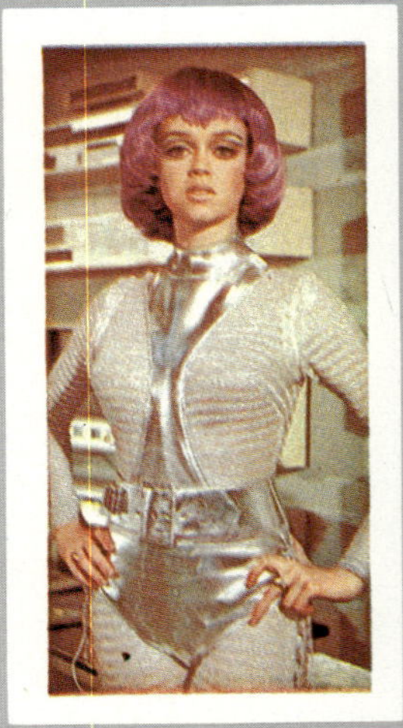

U.F.O. Barratt

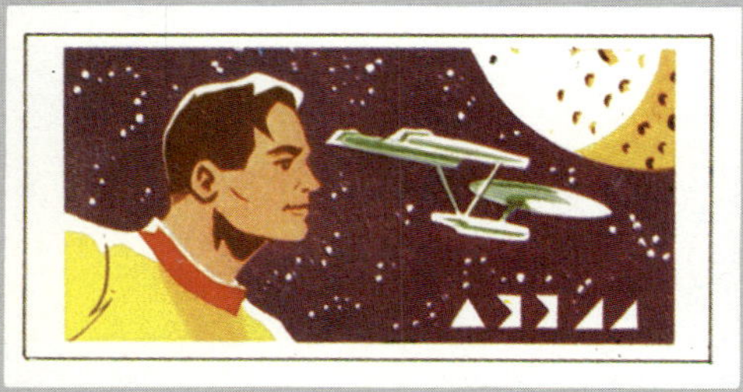

Star Trek. Primrose

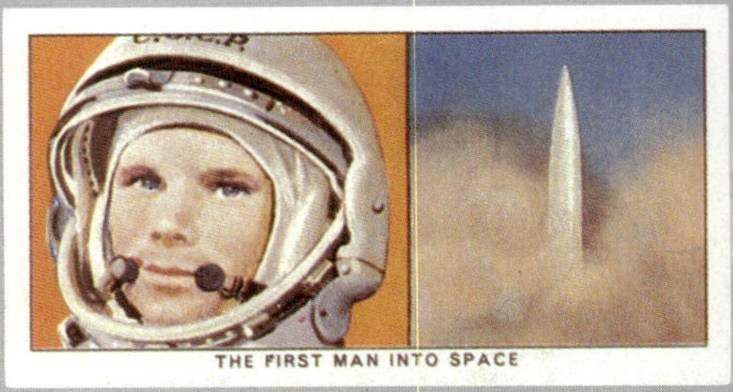

Famous Firsts. Kellogg

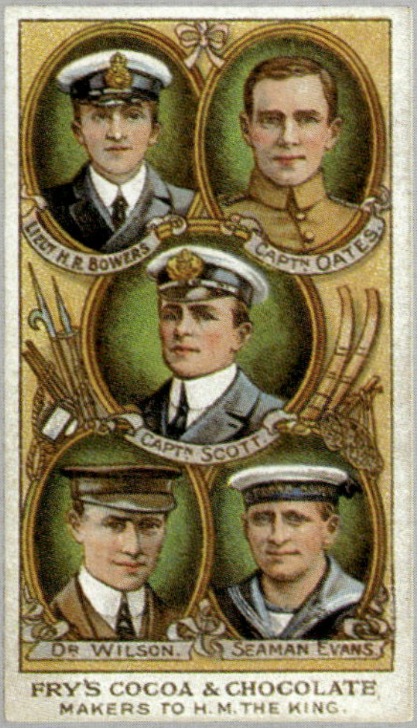

With Captain Scott to the South Pole.
Fry

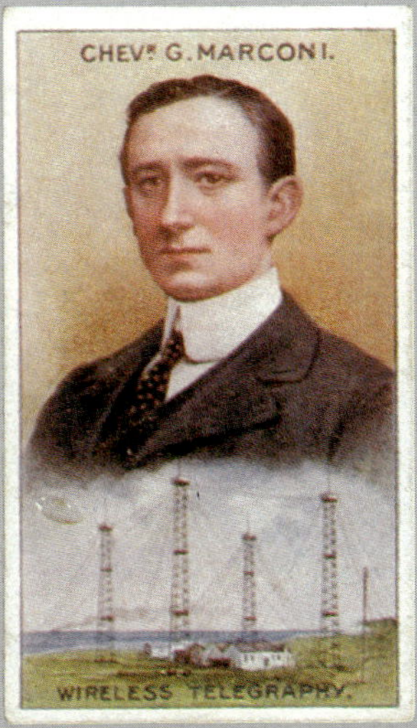

Inventors. Bucktrout, Hill, Teofani
or Whitford

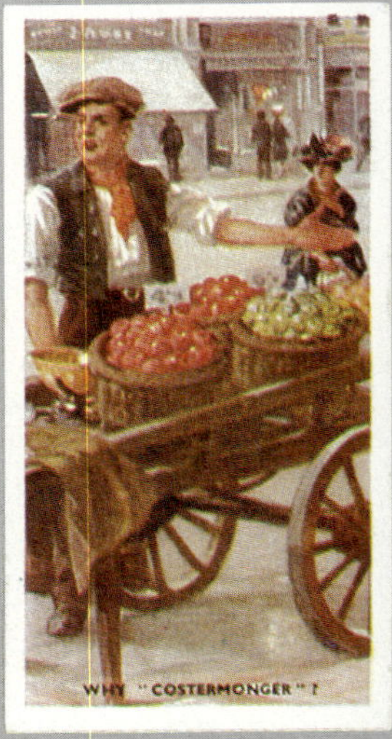

Do You Know. Carreras

COHEN WEENEN & CO.—cont.

Qty		Date	Odds	Sets
25	Celebrities (Black & White) ("500" back) ...	1900	£4.00	—
45	Celebrities, Coloured ("100" back)	1901	£2.00	£90.00
121	Celebrities, Coloured ("250" back)	1901	£2.00	—
30	Celebrities, Gainsborough ("400" Back) ...	1902	£5.00	£150.00
B39	Celebrities, Gainsborough ("250" back) ...	1902	£20.00	—
BF?150	Celebrities, Gainsborough	1901	£3.00	—
MF?150	Celebrities, Gainsborough (Metal Framed) ...	1901	£10.00	—
25	Cricketers	1926	£2.50	—
20	Cricketers, Footballers & Jockeys	1900	£10.00	£200.00
25	Famous Boxers (black back)	1912	£5.00	—
25	Famous Boxers (green back)	1912	£3.00	£100.00
40	Fiscal Phrases	1902	£6.00	£240.00
60	Football Captains	1908	£3.00	£180.00
100	Heroes of Sport	1898	£20.00	—
40	Home & Colonial Regiments ("100" back) ...	1901	£5.00	£200.00
40	Home & Colonial Regiments ("250" back) ...	1901	£6.00	£240.00
20	Interesting Buildings & Views	1902	£5.00	£100.00
K53	Miniature Playing Cards (Bandmaster)	1910	£2.00	—
20	Nations (Non Descriptive)	1902	£6.00	£120.00
20	Nations (Descriptive)	1923	£1.25	£25.00
40	Naval & Military Phrases (Blue Back)	1904	£15.00	—
40	Naval & Military Phrases (Red Back)	1906	£7.50	—
50	Owners, Jockeys, Footballers, Cricketers Series 2	1906	£2.50	£125.00
20	Owners, Jockeys, Footballers, Cricketers Series 3	1907	£3.50	£70.00
30	Proverbs	1903	£8.00	—
20	Russo Japanese War Series	1902	£7.50	£150.00
25	Silhouettes of Celebrities	1903	£6.00	£150.00
50	Star Artistes	1907	£4.00	£200.00
L16	Victoria Cross Heroes (Silk)	1915	£15.00	—
50	Victoria Cross Heroes (51-100)	1916	£4.00	£200.00
50	War Series	1916	£4.00	£200.00
30	Wonders of the World (Green Back)	1908	£3.00	£90.00
30	Wonders of the World (Grey Back)	1923	70p	£21.00

T. H. COLLINS

25	Homes of England	1924	£2.00	—
25	Sports & Pastimes	1923	£1.50	—

F. COLTON JR.

30	Army Pictures, Cartoons, etc.	1916	B	—
50	War Portraits	1916	B	—

T. W. CONQUEST

30	Army Pictures, Cartoons, etc.	1916	B	—

CONTINENTAL CIGARETTE FACTORY

25	Charming Portraits (Firm's name)	1920	£2.00	—
25	Charming Portraits (Club mixture)	1920	£2.50	—
25	Charming Portraits (Plain back)	1920	£2.00	—

COOPER & CO.

25	Boer War Celebrities "STEW"	1901	C	—

CO-OPERATIVE WHOLESALE SOCIETY (C.W.S.)

Qty		Date	Odds	Sets
5	Advertisement Cards	1915	D	—
24	African Types	1936	12p	£3.00
M50	Beauty Spots of Britain	1936	12p	£4.00
50	Boy Scout Badges	1939	15p	£7.50
25	Boy Scout Series	1912	£6.00	—
48	British and Foreign Birds	1938	12p	£6.00
50	British Sports Series	1904	£12.50	—
25	Cooking Recipes	1923	£1.00	£25.00
28	Co-operative Buildings & Works	1909	£7.00	£200.00
24	English Roses	1924	£1.60	£40.00
50	Famous Bridges	1937	25p	£12.50
48	Famous Buildings	1935	12p	£6.00
25	How To Do It	1924	80p	£20.00
48	Musical Instruments	1934	£1.00	£50.00
25	Parrot Series	1910	£12.00	£300.00
48	Poultry	1927	£1.00	£50.00
48	Railway Engines	1936	£1.50	£72.00
24	Sailing Craft	1935	50p	£12.00
18	War Series	1914	£8.00	—
48	Wayside Flowers (Brown Back)	1923	80p	£40.00
48	Wayside Flowers (Grey Back) (different)	1928	12p	£6.00
48	Wayside Woodland Trees	1924	£1.00	£50.00
24	Western Stars	1957	—	60p

COPE BROS. & CO. LTD.

Qty		Date	Odds	Sets
KF?50	Actors & Actresses	1900	£12.50	—
20	Actresses "BLARM"	1902	£12.50	—
6	Actresses "COPEIS"	1898	C	—
26	Actresses "FROGA"	1900	C	—
F50	Actresses & Beauties	1900	£6.00	£300.00
52	Beauties, P/C Inset	1899	£20.00	—
15	Beauties "PAC"	1898	£30.00	—
50	Boats of the World	1912	£3.00	£150.00
25	Boxers (1-25)	1915	£1.60	£40.00
25	Boxers (26-50)	1915	£2.00	£50.00
25	Boxers (51-75)	1915	£2.00	£50.00
25	Boxers (76-100)	1915	£6.00	£150.00
25	Boxers (101-125)	1915	£2.50	£62.50
1	Boxers (New World Champion)	1915	—	£7.50
25	Boxing Lessons	1935	30p	£7.50
35	Boy Scouts & Girl Guides	1910	£4.00	£140.00
X25	Bridge Problems	1924	A	—
25	British Admirals	1915	£6.00	£150.00
50	British Warriors	1912	£3.00	£150.00
25	Castles	1939	12p	£2.50
25	Cathedrals	1939	30p	£7.50
50	Characters From Scott	1905	£3.00	£150.00
115	Chinese Series	1903	£5.00	—
50	Copes Golfers	1904	£10.00	—
L25	Dickens Character Series	1939	12p	£2.50
50	Dickens Gallery	1910	£2.50	£125.00
50	Dogs of the World	1912	£2.50	£125.00
25	Eminent British Regiments Officers Uniforms	1908	£6.00	£150.00
24	Flags, Arms & Types of All Nations	1904	£4.00	£100.00

COPE BROS & CO. LTD.—cont.

Qty		Date	Odds	Sets
30	Flags of Nations	1903	£6.00	—
B50	General Knowledge	1925	£1.25	—
B32	Golf Strokes	1923	£2.00	—
60	Happy Families	1937	40p	£24.00
B50	Household Hints	1925	60p	£30.00
X20	Kenilworth Phrases	1910	C	—
25	Lawn Tennis Strokes	1924	60p	£15.00
5	Lawn Tennis Strokes (26-30)	1925	£2.00	—
L50	Modern Dancing	1926	£5.00	—
50	Music Hall Artistes ("Series of 50")	1913	£10.00	—
50	Music Hall Artistes (no number in series) ...	1913	£3.00	£150.00
472	Noted Footballers (Clips Cigarettes)	1910	£2.00	—
195	Noted Footballers (Solace Cigarettes)	1910	£2.50	—
24	Occupations for Women	1897	£40.00	—
X12	Photo Albums for the Million (Buff)	1902	£10.00	—
X12	Photo Albums for the Million (Green)	1902	£10.00	£120.00
25	Pigeons	1926	80p	£20.00
52	Playing Cards	1900	£7.50	—
30	Scandinavian Actors & Actresses	1910	A	—
50	Shakespeare Gallery	1906	£3.00	£150.00
25	Song Birds	1926	£1.00	£25.00
25	Sports & Pastimes	1925	80p	£20.00
L25	The Game of Poker	1936	12p	£2.00
25	The World's Police	1937	£1.00	£25.00
L25	Toy Models—The Country Fair	1925	12p	£2.50
25	Uniforms of Soldiers & Sailors (circular medal)	1898	£15.00	—
25	Uniforms of Soldiers & Sailors (square medal)	1898	£12.50	—
50	V.C. & D.S.O. Naval & Flying Heroes (Unnumbered)	1916	£2.50	£125.00
25	V.C. & D.S.O. Naval & Flying Heroes (Numbered 51-75)	1916	£3.50	—
20	War Pictures	1915	£6.00	£120.00
50	War Series	1915	£7.50	—
25	Wild Animals & Birds	1907	£7.50	—

E. CORONEL

25	Types of British & Colonial Troops	1900	£30	—

DAVID CORRE & CO.

1	Advertisement Card	1903	D	—
40	Naval & Military Phrases	1904	£35	—

JOHN COTTON LTD.

L50	Bridge Hands	1934	£2.00	—
50	Golf Strokes A/B	1936	£1.20	£60.00
50	Golf Strokes C/D	1937	£1.50	—
50	Golf Strokes E/F	1938	£2.00	—
50	Golf Strokes G/H	1939	A	—
50	Golf Strokes I/J	1939	A	—

A. & J. COUDENS LTD.

F60	British Beauty Spots	1923	60p	£36.00
F60	Holiday Resorts in East Anglia	1924	50p	£30.00
25	Sports Alphabet	1924	£1.50	—

THE CRAIGMILLAR CREAMERY CO.

Qty		Date	Odds	Sets
M?	Scottish Views	1901	D	–

W. R. DANIEL

30	Colonial Troops	1902	£40.00	—
25	National Flags & Flowers—Girls	1901	C	—

W. T. DAVIES & SONS

?50	Actresses	1902	B	—
30	Aristocrats of the Turf A Series (1-30)	1924	£1.00	£30.00
12	Aristocrats of the Turf A Series (31-42)	1924	£6.00	—
36	Aristocrats of the Turf 2nd Series	1924	£1.00	£36.00
25	Army Life	1915	£6.00	—
12	Beauties	1903	£15.00	—
25	Boxing	1924	80p	£20.00
50	Flags & Funnels of Leading Steamship Lines	1913	£2.50	—
?10	Newport Football Club	1904	C	—
?5	Royal Welsh Fusiliers	1904	C	—

S. H. DAWES

30	Army Pictures, Cartoons, etc.	1916	B	—

J. W. DEWHURST

30	Army Pictures, Cartoons, etc.	1916	B	—

R. I. DEXTER

30	Borough Arms	1900	40p	£12.00

DIANELLOS & VERGOPOULOS

XF?	Views of Cyprus	1926	A	—

GEORGE DOBIE & SON LTD.

M25	Bridge Problems	1933	A	—
M32	Four Square Books (1-32)	1959	50p	—
M32	Four Square Books (33-64)	1960	12p	£4.00
M32	Four Square Books (65-96)	1960	15p	£5.00
25	Weapons of All Ages	1924	£2.00	—

DOBSON'S

20	The European War Series	1917	A	—

DOMINION TOBACCO CO. (1929) LTD.

25	Old Ships 1st Series	1934	80p	£20.00
25	Old Ships 2nd Series	1935	12p	£5.00
25	Old Ships 3rd Series	1936	12p	£5.00
25	Old Ships 4th Series	1936	40p	£10.00

JOSEPH W. DOYLE LTD.

F12	Beauties (Series CC.D)	1928	£20	—
F12	Beauties (Series CC.E)	1928	£20	—
XF18	Children	1928	£6.00	—
F12	Dirt Track Riders (Series CC.A)	1928	A	—
F12	Views (Series CC.B)	1928	A	—
F12	Views (Series CC.C)	1928	A	—

MAJOR DRAPKIN & CO.

Qty		Date	Odds	Sets
12	Actresses	1910	£2.50	—
8	Advertisement Cards	1926	£1.50	£12.00
50	Around Britain	1929	50p	£25.00
L50	Around Britain	1929	£1.00	—
50	Around the Mediterranean	1926	50p	£25.00
L50	Around the Mediterranean	1926	£1.00	—
F40	Australian and English Test Cricketers	1928	30p	£12.00
?100	Bandmaster Conundrums	1907	£2.00	—
25	British Beauties	1930	60p	£15.00
F36	Celebrities of the Great War	1916	30p	£11.00
F34	Celebrities of the Great War (Plain Backs)	1916	30p	£10.00
B96	Cinematograph Actors	1913	£2.50	—
15	Dogs and Their Treatment	1924	£1.00	£15.00
L15	Dogs and Their Treatment	1924	£1.00	£15.00
50	Girls of Many Lands	1929	£1.00	£50.00
M50	Girls of Many Lands	1929	12p	£5.00
25	How to Keep Fit	1912	£4.00	£100.00
54	Life at Whipsnade Zoo	1934	20p	£10.00
50	Limericks	1929	25p	£12.50
F36	National Types of Beauty	1928	30p	£11.00
25	Optical Illusions	1926	30p	£7.50
L25	Optical Illusions	1926	80p	£20.00
25	Palmistry	1927	40p	£10.00
L25	Palmistry	1927	60p	£15.00
48	Photogravure Masterpieces	1915	£2.50	—
25	Puzzle Pictures	1926	60p	£15.00
L25	Puzzle Pictures	1926	£1.00	£25.00
M40	Regimental Colours & Badges of the Indian Army (Silk)	1915	£1.50	£60.00
X22/25	Soldiers & Their Uniforms (cut-outs)	1914	40p	£8.00
25	Soldiers & Their Uniforms (cut-outs)	1914	—	£30.00
F35/36	Sporting Celebrities in Action	1930	30p	£10.50
40	The Game of Sporting Snap	1928	30p	£12.00
1	The Greys Advertisement Card	1935	—	£1.25
12	Views of the World	1910	£2.00	—
6	Warships	1912	£3.50	—

DRAPKIN & MILLHOFF

?40	Beauties "KEWA"	1899	C	—
25	Boer War Celebrities "PAM"	1901	£12.50	—
30	Colonial Troops	1902	£25.00	—
?25	Pretty Girl Series "BAGG"	1898	C	—

DU MAURIER CIGARETTES

X?50	Advertising Inserts	1931	£3.00	—

J. DUNCAN & CO. LTD.

47/50	Evolution of the Steamship	1925	25p	£12.00
48	Flags, Arms & Types of Nations	1911	£12.50	—
20	Inventors & Their Inventions	1915	B	—
30	Scottish Clans, Arms of Chiefs & Tartans	1912	£8.00	£240.00
L72	Scottish Gems (Coloured)	1912	£5.00	—
L50	Scottish Gems 2nd Series	1913	£5.00	—

J. DUNCAN & CO. LTD.—cont.

Qty		Date	Odds	Sets
L50	Scottish Gems 3rd Series	1914	£4.00	—
L50	Scottish Gems (Reprint, Black & White)	1925	30p	£15.00
25	Types of British Soldiers	1910	£25.00	—

GEO. DUNCOMBE

Qty		Date	Odds	Sets
30	Army Pictures, Cartoons, etc.	1916	B	—

EDWARD VII CIGARETTES

Qty		Date	Odds	Sets
40	Home & Colonial Regiments	1901	C	—

EDWARDS, RINGER & CO.

Qty		Date	Odds	Sets
X50	How To Count Cribbage Hands	1908	B	—

EDWARDS RINGER & BIGG

Qty		Date	Odds	Sets
25	Abbeys & Castles	1912	£5.00	£125.00
25	Alpine Views	1912	£5.00	£125.00
50	A Tour Round the World	1909	£3.50	—
12	Beauties "CERF"	1905	£20.00	—
25	Beauties "FECKSA"	1900	£15.00	—
50	Birds & Eggs	1906	£4.00	—
?25	Boer War Sketches	1901	C	—
25	Boer War Celebrities "STEW"	1901	£15.00	—
25	British Trees & Their Uses	1933	£1.20	£30.00
1	Calendar & Lighting up Table	1899	D	—
1	Calendar	1905	D	—
1	Calendar	1910	D	—
50	Celebrated Bridges	1924	£1.00	£50.00
50	Cinema Stars	1923	30p	£15.00
L25	Cinema Stars	1923	30p	£7.50
25	Coast and Country	1911	£5.00	£125.00
23	Dogs Series (Exmoor Hunt)	1908	£1.00	£23.00
23	Dogs Series (Klondyke)	1908	£3.00	—
3	Easter Manoeuvres of our Volunteers	1897	D	—
37	Flags of All Nations (various printings)	1907	£4.00	—
25	Garden Life	1934	£1.20	£30.00
25	How to Tell Fortunes	1929	£2.00	£50.00
50	Life on Board a Man Of War	1905	£5.00	—
1	Miners Bound for Klondyke	1897	D	—
50	Mining	1925	80p	£40.00
25	Musical Instruments	1924	£1.00	£25.00
25	Optical Illusions	1936	£1.00	£25.00
25	Our Pets A series	1926	£1.00	£25.00
25	Our Pets 2nd Series	1926	£1.20	£30.00
25	Past & Present	1928	£1.50	£37.50
10	Portraits of His Majesty the King	1902	£15.00	£150.00
25	Prehistoric Animals	1924	£1.50	£37.50
25	Sports & Games in Many Lands	1935	£1.00	£25.00
56	War Map, Western Front	1916	£3.00	—
54	War Map of the Western Front, Series 2	1917	£3.00	—

S. EISISKI

Qty		Date	Odds	Sets
?20	Actresses "ANGOOD"	1900	C	—
?20	Beauties "FENA"	1899	C	—
?40	Beauties "KEWA"	1900	C	—

EMPIRE TOBACCO CO.

Qty		*Date*	*Odds*	*Sets*
6	Franco British Exhibition	1907	C	—

ENCHANTERESSE EGYPTIAN CIG. CO.

20	Actresses "ANGOOD"	1898	C	—

THE EXPRESS TOBACCO CO. LTD

M50	How It Is Made (Motor Cars)	1939	£1.00	£50.00

L. & J. FABIAN

F24	The Elite Series	1932	A	—

FAIRWEATHER & SONS

50	Historic Buildings of Scotland	1914	£25.00	—

W. & F. FAULKNER

26	Actresses "FROGA"	1900	£25.00	—
25	Angling	1929	80p	£20.00
12	'Ation Series	1901	£7.50	—
25	Beauties (Coloured)	1898	£40.00	—
50	Beauties "FECKSA"	1901	£7.50	—
16	British Royal Family	1901	£15.00	—
50	Celebrated Bridges	1925	80p	£40.00
12	Coster Series	1900	£7.50	£90.00
20	Cricketers Series	1902	£45.00	—
12	Cricket Terms	1899	£12.50	—
12	Football Terms 1st Series	1900	£7.50	£90.00
12	Football Terms 2nd Series	1900	£7.50	£90.00
12	Golf Terms	1901	£20.00	—
12	Grenadier Guards	1899	£12.50	£150.00
40	Kings & Queens	1902	£7.50	—
12	Kipling Series	1900	£7.50	—
12	Military Terms 1st Series	1899	£7.50	£90.00
12	Military Terms 2nd Series	1899	£7.50	£90.00
12	Nautical Terms 1st Series	1900	£7.50	£90.00
12	Nautical Terms 2nd Series	1900	£7.50	£90.00
25	Old Sporting Prints	1930	50p	£12.50
25	Optical Illusions	1935	50p	£12.50
90	Our Colonial Troops	1900	£6.00	£550.00
20	Our Gallant Grenadiers	1902	£7.50	£150.00
40	Our Gallant Grenadiers (With I.T.C. Clause)	1903	£10.00	—
25	Our Pets	1926	80p	£20.00
25	Our Pets 2nd Series	1926	80p	£20.00
12	Policemen of the World	1899	£20.00	—
12	Police Terms	1899	£7.50	—
25	Prominent Racehorses of the Present Day	1923	60p	£15.00
25	Prominent Racehorses of the Present Day 2nd Series	1924	80p	£20.00
12	Puzzle Series	1898	£25.00	—
25	South African War Series	1901	£5.00	£125.00
12	Sporting Terms	1900	£10.00	—
12	Street Cries	1902	£7.50	—
12	The Language of Flowers	1900	£12.50	—

FINLAY & CO. LTD.

Qty		Date	Odds	Sets
?10	Our Girls	1910	C	—
30	World's Aircraft	1912	£20.00	—

FLYNN

26	Beauties "HOL"	1899	C	—

FRAENKEL BROS.

?20	Beauties—Don Jorge	1897	D	—
?20	Beauties—"FENA"	1899	£50.00	—
25	Beauties—"GRACC"	1898	C	—
24	Beauties—"HUMPS"	1899	C	—
26	Music Hall Artistes	1900	£40.00	—
25	Types of British & Colonial Troops	1900	£40.00	—

FRANKLYN DAVEY & CO.

12	Beauties "CERF"	1905	£25.00	—
50	Birds	1896	£30.00	—
10	Boer War Generals	1901	C	—
25	Boxing	1924	30p	£7.50
25	Ceremonial and Court Dress	1915	£4.00	—
50	Children of All Nations	1934	20p	£10.00
50	Football Club Colours	1909	£4.00	—
50	Historic Events	1924	80p	£40.00
25	Hunting	1925	24p	£6.00
50	Modern Dance Steps	1930	£2.00	—
50	Modern Dance Steps 2nd Series	1931	16p	£8.00
50	Naval Dress & Badges	1916	£3.50	—
50	Overseas Dominions (Australia)	1923	£1.00	—
25	Star Girls	1901	C	—
10	Types of Smokers	1898	£35.00	—
50	Wild Animals of the World	1902	£4.00	—

A. H. FRANKS & SONS

56	Beauties	1901	£20.00	—
24	Nautical Expressions	1902	B	—
25	Types of British & Colonial Troops	1900	£35.00	—

J. J. FREEMAN & CO.

12	Actresses "FRAN"	1915	B	—
33	Football Challenge	1969	A	—
B12	Manikin Cards	1915	B	—
12	Views of the World	1910	B	—

C. FRYER & SONS LTD.

25	Boer War & General Interest	1900	C	—
X50	Clan Sketches	1930	£5.00	£250.00
40	Naval & Military Phrases	1904	£30.00	—
?25	Vita Berlin Series	1901	C	—

FRYER & COULTMAN

X12	Almanack	1893	C	—

J. GABRIEL

10	Actresses "HAGG"	1900	B	—
25	Beauties "GRACC"	1898	C	—

J. GABRIEL—cont.

Qty		Date	Odds	Sets
20	Cricketers Series	1902	C	—
40	Home & Colonial Regiments	1902	£40.00	—
?50	Pretty Girl Series "BAGG"	1898	£35.00	—
25	Types of British & Colonial Troops	1899	£35.00	—

GALLAHER LTD.

Qty		Date	Odds	Sets
F110	Actors & Actresses	1901	£2.00	—
48	Aeroplanes	1939	12p	£6.00
25	Aesop's Fables (Series of 25)	1931	24p	£6.00
25	Aesop's Fables (Series of 50)	1931	24p	£6.00
100	Animals & Birds of Commercial Value	1921	25p	£25.00
48	Army Badges	1939	20p	£10.00
L24	Art Treasures of the World	1930	12p	£3.00
100	Association Football Club Colours	1910	£1.50	£150.00
52	Beauties (P/C Inset)	1905	£7.50	£400.00
52	Beauties (No Inset)	1905	£7.50	£400.00
MF48	Beautiful Scotland	1939	15p	£7.50
50	Birds & Eggs	1905	£5.00	—
100	Birds Nests & Eggs	1919	60p	£60.00
100	Boy Scout Series (Green back)	1911	75p	£75.00
100	Boy Scout Series (Brown back)	1922	60p	£60.00
48	British Birds	1937	12p	£3.50
100	British Birds by George Rankin	1923	30p	£30.00
75	British Champions of 1923	1924	50p	£37.50
50	British Naval Series	1914	£2.00	£100.00
48	Butterflies & Moths	1938	12p	£4.00
25	Champion Animals & Birds of 1923	1924	60p	£15.00
48	Champions A Series	1934	15p	£7.50
48	Champions 2nd Series	1935	12p	£6.00
48	Champions of Screen & Stage (Red back)	1934	12p	£4.00
48	Champions of Screen & Stage (Blue back)	1934	20p	£10.00
100	Cinema Stars	1926	50p	£50.00
MF48	Coastwise	1938	25p	—
24	Dogs (Caption in block)	1934	12p	£3.00
24	Dogs (Caption in script)	1934	40p	£10.00
L24	Dogs (Caption in block)	1934	12p	£3.00
L24	Dogs (Caption in script)	1934	40p	£10.00
48	Dogs A Series	1936	12p	£4.00
48	Dogs 2nd Series	1938	12p	£3.50
F100	English & Scotch Views	1910	£2.00	—
100	Fables & Their Morals (No. by caption)	1912	80p	£80.00
100	Fables & Their Morals (Thick numerals)	1922	35p	£35.00
100	Fables & Their Morals (Thin numerals)	1922	35p	£35.00
100	Famous Cricketers	1926	£1.00	£100.00
48	Famous Film Scenes	1935	12p	£4.00
50	Famous Footballers (Brown back)	1926	50p	£25.00
100	Famous Footballers (Green back)	1925	40p	£40.00
48	Famous Jockeys	1936	12p	£5.00
48	Film Episodes	1936	12p	£5.00
48	Film Partners	1935	12p	£5.00
M24	Flags (Silk)	1915	£3.50	—
MF48	Flying	1938	40p	—
50	Footballers (1-50)	1925	60p	£30.00
50	Footballers (51-100)	1925	80p	£40.00

GALLAHER LTD.—cont.

Qty		Date	Odds	Sets
50	Footballers in Action	1928	60p	£30.00
48	Garden Flowers	1938	12p	£3.00
100	How To Do It	1916	£1.25	£125.00
F100	Interesting Views (Black & White)	1923	75p	£75.00
F100	Interesting Views (Coloured)	1923	£1.00	—
400	Irish Views Scenery (Numbered on back) ...	1908	£1.25	—
F400	Irish View Scenery	1910	60p	£240.00
F200	Irish View Scenery (401-600)	1910	£1.00	—
LF48	Island Sporting Celebrities	1938	30p	£15.00
100	Kute Kiddies	1916	£1.25	£125.00
F50	Latest Actresses	1909	£5.00	—
50	Lawn Tennis Celebrities	1928	£1.00	£50.00
24	Motor Cars	1934	£1.25	£30.00
48	My Favourite Part	1939	12p	£3.50
MF48	Our Countryside	1938	30p	—
100	Plants of Commercial Value	1917	30p	£30.00
48	Portraits of Famous Stars	1935	12p	£3.50
48	Racing Scenes	1938	12p	£3.50
50	Regimental Colours & Standards	1899	£2.50	£125.00
100	Robinson Crusoe	1928	60p	£60.00
50	Royalty Series	1902	£2.50	£125.00
LF48	Scenes from the Empire	1939	12p	£5.00
48	Shots from Famous Films	1935	12p	£6.00
MF24	Shots from the Films	1936	60p	—
48	Signed Portraits of Famous Stars	1935	35p	£17.50
48	Sporting Personalities	1936	12p	£3.00
100	Sports Series	1912	£1.50	£150.00
100	Stage & Variety Celebrities	1899	£30.00	—
48	Stars of Screen & Stage (Brown back)	1935	25p	£12.50
48	Stars of Screen & Stage (Green back)	1935	12p	£3.50
25	The Allies Flags	1914	£2.50	£62.50
100	The Great War Series	1915	£1.00	£100.00
100	The Great War Second Series	1915	£1.00	£100.00
25	The Great War V.C. Heroes 1st Series	1915	£1.20	£30.00
25	The Great War V.C. Heroes 2nd Series	1915	£1.00	£25.00
25	The Great War V.C. Heroes 3rd Series	1915	£1.00	£25.00
25	The Great War V.C. Heroes 4th Series	1916	£1.00	£25.00
25	The Great War V.C. Heroes 5th Series	1916	£1.20	£30.00
25	The Great War V.C. Heroes 6th Series	1917	£1.00	£25.00
25	The Great War V.C. Heroes 7th Series	1917	£1.00	£25.00
25	The Great War V.C. Heroes 8th Series	1918	£1.00	£25.00
48	The Navy (Gallaher)	1937	15p	£7.50
48	The Navy (Park Drive)	1937	12p	£3.50
100	The Reason Why	1924	25p	£25.00
111	The South African Series	1901	£2.50	£280.00
100	The Zoo Aquarium	1924	50p	£50.00
48	Trains of the World	1937	20p	£10.00
100	Tricks & Puzzles Series (Green back)	1913	£1.50	£150.00
100	Tricks & Puzzles Series (Black back)	1933	12p	£10.00
50	Types of the British Army (Battle Honours) ...	1897	£5.00	£250.00
50	Types of the British Army (Green back)	1898	£5.00	£250.00
50	Types of the British Army (numbered 1-50) ...	1898	£4.00	£200.00
50	Types of the British Army (numbered 51-100)	1898	£4.00	£200.00
100	Useful Hints Series	1915	£1.25	£125.00

GALLAHER LTD.—cont.

Qty		Date	Odds	Sets
25	Views in North of Ireland	1912	£30.00	—
50	Votaries of the Weed	1916	£2.00	£100.00
100	Why Is It? (Brown back)	1915	£1.25	£125.00
100	Why Is It? (Green back)	1915	£1.25	£125.00
48	Wild Animals	1937	12p	£3.00
48	Wild Flowers	1939	12p	£3.00
100	Woodland Trees Series	1912	£1.25	£125.00
50	Zoo Tropical Birds 1st Series	1928	50p	£25.00
50	Zoo Tropical Birds 2nd Series	1929	50p	£25.00

GASPA

?20	Our Great Novelists	1930	A	—

SAMUEL GAWITH

X25	The English Lakeland	1926	£7.50	—

F. GENNARI

50	War Portraits	1916	B	—

LOUIS GERARD LTD.

50	Modern Armaments (Numbered)	1938	12p	£6.00
50	Modern Armaments (Unnumbered)	1938	15p	£7.50
24	Screen Favourites	1937	£1.25	—
48	Screen Favourites & Dancers	1937	40p	£20.00

GLASS & CO. LTD.

20	Actresses "BLARM"	1900	£25.00	—
10	Actresses "HAGG"	1900	£25.00	—
25	Beauties "FECKSA"	1903	B	—
20	Boer War Cartoons	1901	B	—
25	Boer War Celebrities "STEW"	1901	B	—
16	British Royal Family	1901	£30.00	—
20	Cricketers Series	1902	C	—
40	Naval & Military Phrases	1902	B	—
19	Russo Japanese Series	1903	£20.00	—

R. P. GLOAG & CO.

?25	Actresses "ANGLO"	1896	C	—
?50	Beauties "PLUMS" (Black & White) ...	1896	£35.00	—
?50	Beauties "PLUMS" (Brown)	1896	C	—
40	Home & Colonial Regiments	1900	£20.00	—
30	Proverbs	1901	B	—
25	Types of British & Colonial Troops	1900	£25.00	—

THE GLOBE CIGARETTE CO.

25	Actresses—French	1898	D	—

GOLDS LTD.

1	Advertisement Card	1905	D	—
18	Motor Cycle Series	1914	£12.50	—
L?15	Prints from Noted Pictures	1908	C	—

T. P. & R. GOODBODY

20	Actresses "ANGOOD"	1898	C	—
?50	Beauties "KEWA"	1898	C	—

T. P. & R. GOODBODY—cont.

Qty		Date	Odds	Sets
25	Boer War Celebrities	1901	£15.00	—
16	Boer War Celebrities	1901	£15.00	—
?50	Colonial Forces	1902	£35.00	—
B?50	Colonial Forces	1902	C	—
?50	Dogs	1903	£30.00	—
26	Eminent Actresses	1900	£15.00	—
20	Irish Scenery	1905	£25.00	—
?25	Pretty Girl Series "BAGG"	1898	C	—
50	Questions & Answers in Natural History ...	1924	80p	£40.00
25	Sports & Pastimes	1925	£1.50	£37.50
25	Types of Soldiers	1914	B	—
20	War Pictures	1915	£7.50	—
12	With the Flag to Pretoria	1901	B	—

GORDON'S

?4	Billiards	1912	C	—

GRAVESON

30	Army Pictures, Cartoons, etc.	1916	B	—

FRED GRAY

25	Types of British Soldiers	1914	B	—

GRIFFITHS BROS.

XF18	Children	1928	B	—

GUERNSEY TOBACCO CO. (Channel Isles)

49	And When Did You Last See Your Father? (Sect)	1936	50p	£25.00
K52	Miniature Playing Cards	1933	60p	—
48	The Laughing Cavalier (Sect)	1935	50p	£25.00
48	The Toast (Sect)	1935	50p	£25.00

HARRIS & SONS

26	Beauties "HOL"	1900	£10.00	—
30	Colonial Troops	1901	B	—
25	Star Girls	1899	C	—

JAS. H. HARRISON

18	Motor Cycle Series	1914	B	—

HARVEY & DAVEY

50	Birds & Eggs	1905	£2.00	£100.00
35	Chinese & South African Series	1901	C	—
30	Colonial Troops	1902	£30.00	—
25	Types of British & Colonial Troops	1901	B	—

W. HEATON

?6	Birkby Views	1912	C	—

HENLY & WATKINS LTD.

25	Ancient Egyptian Gods (Plain back)	1924	£1.20	£30.00
25	Ancient Egyptian Gods (Printed back)	1924	£1.20	£30.00

HIGNETT BROS & CO.

Qty		Date	Odds	Sets
50	Actors Natural & Character Studies	1938	12p	£6.00
26	Actors "FROGA"	1900	£30.00	—
25	Actresses, Photogravure	1900	£7.50	—
28	Actresses, PILPI I	1901	£12.50	—
F50	Actresses, PILPI II	1901	£7.50	—
50	A.F.C. Nicknames	1933	60p	—
50	Air Raid Precautions	1939	25p	£12.50
60	Animal Pictures	1899	£12.50	—
50	Arms & Armour	1924	£1.00	£50.00
25	Beauties "CHOAB"	1900	C	—
50	Beauties, Gravure	1898	£20.00	—
BF50	Beauties (Chess Cigarettes) (Set 1)	1927	50p	£25.00
BF50	Beauties (Chess Cigarettes) (Set 2)	1927	50p	£25.00
BF50	Beauties (No brand)	1927	60p	£30.00
50	British Birds & Their Eggs	1938	40p	—
50	Broadcasting	1935	50p	—
20	Cabinet 1900	1900	£40.00	—
25	Cathedrals & Churches	1909	£2.00	£50.00
50	Celebrated Old Inns	1925	£1.00	£50.00
50	Champions of 1936	1936	50p	£25.00
25	Common Objects of the Sea-Shore	1924	£1.00	£25.00
25	Company Drill	1915	£2.00	£50.00
50	Coronation Procession	1937	£1.00	—
50	Dogs	1936	25p	£12.50
50	Football Caricatures	1935	30p	—
50	Football Club Captains	1936	50p	—
25	Greetings of the World	1907	80p	£20.00
25	Historical London	1926	£1.00	£25.00
50	How to Swim	1935	15p	£7.50
50	Interesting Buildings	1905	£2.00	£100.00
25	International Caps and Badges	1924	£1.00	£25.00
25	Life In Pond & Stream	1925	£1.20	£30.00
40	Medals	1900	£10.00	—
25	Military Portraits	1914	£3.00	£75.00
50	Modern Railways	1936	£1.00	—
25	Modern Statesmen	1906	£3.00	£75.00
20	Music Hall Artistes	1898	£20.00	—
50	Ocean Greyhounds	1938	20p	—
25	Panama Canal	1914	£3.00	£75.00
12	Pretty Girl Series "RASH"	1900	£25.00	—
50	Prominent Cricketers of 1938	1938	75p	—
50	Prominent Racehorses of 1933	1933	30p	£15.00
50	Sea Adventure	1939	12p	£3.50
25	Ships, Flags & Cap Badges A Series	1926	80p	£20.00
25	Ships, Flags & Cap Badges 2nd Series	1927	£1.00	£25.00
50	Shots from the Films	1936	40p	—
25	The Prince of Wales Empire Tour	1924	60p	£15.00
50	Trick Billiards	1934	£1.50	—
25	Turnpikes	1927	80p	£20.00
25	V.C. Heroes	1901	£25.00	—
20	Yachts (Black back)	1898	£35.00	—
20	Yachts (White back)	1898	£35.00	—
50	Zoo Studies	1937	25p	—

R. & J. HILL LTD.

Qty		Date	Odds	Sets
25	Actresses—Belle of New York Series	1899	£7.50	—
20	Actresses—Chocolate	1917	£6.00	—
30	Actresses—Continental	1906	£6.00	£180.00
26	Actresses "FROGA"	1900	£25.00	—
?25	Actresses "HAGG"	1900	£15.00	—
20	Animal Series (Crowfoot Cigarettes)	1909	£7.50	—
20	Animal Series (Hill's)	1909	£10.00	—
20	Animal Series (Anonymous)	1909	£5.00	—
F25	Artistas Teatrais Portuguesos	1924	A	—
25	Aviation Series	1934	40p	£10.00
?15	Battleships	1908	C	—
25	Battleships & Crests	1901	£6.00	£150.00
12	Boer War Generals	1901	£20.00	£240.00
20	Breeds of Dogs	1914	£5.00	£100.00
L30	Britain's Stately Homes (Silk)	1917	£1.50	£45.00
?50	British Navy Series	1902	£10.00	—
L40	Canvas Masterpieces Series 1 (Silk)	1916	75p	£30.00
L40	Canvas Masterpieces Series 2 (Silk)	1916	£1.00	£40.00
X10	Canvas Masterpieces Series 2 (Silk)	1916	£1.00	—
50	Caricatures of Famous Cricketers	1926	60p	£30.0
L50	Caricatures of Famous Cricketers	1926	50p	£25.00
?	Celebrated Pictures	1905	C	—
50	Celebrities of Sport	1939	30p	£15.00
P4/5	Chinese Pottery & Porcelain (Silk)	1915	25p	£1.00
X11	Chinese Pottery & Porcelain Series 2 (Silk) ...	1915	£2.00	—
10	Chinese Series	1912	B	—
35	Cinema Celebrities	1936	16p	£5.50
50	Colonial Troops	1901	£10.00	—
40	Crystal Palace Souvenir Cards	1937	30p	£12.00
48	Decorations & Medals	1940	75p	£37.50
F48	Famous Cinema Celebrities	1931	£1.25	—
LF48	Famous Cinema Celebrities, Series A	1931	A	—
F50	Famous Cinema Celebrities, Series C	1932	£1.25	—
LF50	Famous Cinema Celebrities, Series D	1932	£1.25	—
28	Famous Cricketers Series (Blue back)	1912	£20.00	—
28	Famous Cricketers Series (Red back)	1912	£20.00	—
40	Famous Cricketers	1923	£1.25	£50.00
50	Famous Cricketers, including the S. Africa Test Team	1925	£1.50	£75.00
L50	Famous Cricketers, including the S. Africa Test Team	1925	£1.50	£75.00
50	Famous Dog Breeds	1952	£1.25	—
L30	Famous Engravings, Series 11	1910	£2.50	£75.00
40	Famous Film Stars	1938	40p	£16.00
40	Famous Film Stars (Arabic Text)	1938	30p	£12.00
20	Famous Footballers Series	1912	£6.00	£120.00
50	Famous Footballers (Brown)	1923	75p	£37.50
50	Famous Footballers (Coloured)	1939	40p	£20.00
25	Famous Footballers (51-75)	1939	50p	£12.50
25	Famous Pictures	1913	£2.00	£50.00
50	Famous Ships	1940	12p	£5.00
48	Film Stars and Celebrity Dancers	1935	40p	£20.00
30	Flags & Flags with Soldiers	1901	£12.50	—
24	Flags, Arms & Types of Nations	1910	£4.00	£100.00

Qty		Date	Odds	Sets
20	Football Captain Series	1906	£7.50	—
20	Fragments From France (Coloured)	1916	£7.50	£150.00
10	Fragments From France (Buff)	1916	£10.00	£100.00
10	Fragments From France (Black & White)	1916	£25.00	—
L23	Great War Leaders, Series 10 (Silk)	1917	£2.00	£46.00
50	Historic Places From Dickens' Classics	1926	20p	£10.00
L50	Historic Places From Dickens' Classics	1926	20p	£10.00
50	Holiday Resorts	1925	25p	£12.50
L50	Holiday Resorts	1925	30p	£15.00
20	Inventors and Their Inventions Series (1-20)	1907	£2.50	£50.00
20	Inventors & Their Inventions (Plain Back)	1934	30p	£6.00
20	Inventors and Their Inventions Series (21-40)	1908	£4.00	£80.00
15	Japanese Series (Black & White)	1904	£20.00	—
15	Japanese Series (Coloured)	1904	£35.00	—
30	Lighthouse Series	1903	£12.50	—
50	Magical Puzzles	1938	30p	£15.00
50	Modern Beauties	1939	30p	£15.00
30	Music Hall Celebrities—Past & Present	1930	40p	£12.00
L30	Music Hall Celebrities—Past & Present	1930	75p	£22.50
20	National Flag Series	1914	£4.00	£80.00
30	Nature Pictures	1930	40p	£12.00
30	Nautical Songs	1937	20p	£6.00
B25	Naval Series (Unnumbered)	1901	£25.00	—
30	Naval Series (Numbered)	1902	£7.50	—
30	Our Empire Series	1929	12p	£3.00
L30	Our Empire Series	1929	15p	£4.50
M30	Popular Footballers Series A	1935	75p	£22.50
M20	Popular Footballers Series B	1935	60p	£12.00
20	Prince of Wales Series	1911	£6.00	£120.00
L?15	Prints From Noted Pictures	1908	C	—
50	Public Schools and Colleges	1923	25p	£12.50
L50	Public Schools and Colleges	1923	30p	£15.00
75	Public Schools and Colleges	1923	30p	£22.50
L75	Public Schools and Colleges	1923	40p	£30.00
50	Puzzle Series	1937	16p	£8.00
42	Real Photographs Set 1	1930	75p	—
F42	Real Photographs Set 2	1930	£1.00	—
20	Rhymes	1904	£15.00	—
F50	Scenes from the Films	1934	75p	£37.50
40	Scenes from the Films	1938	12p	£5.00
35	Scientific Inventions and Discoveries (Black)	1929	30p	£10.50
35	Scientific Inventions and Discoveries (Coloured)	1929	30p	£10.50
L35	Scientific Inventions and Discoveries (Coloured)	1929	30p	£10.50
F50	Sports	1934	£1.00	—
28	Statuary Set 1	1908	£5.00	—
30	Statuary Set 2	1909	£2.50	£75.00
25	Statuary Set 3	1910	£7.50	—
X1	Sunripe Twins Bookmark	1925	—	£4.00
30	The All Blacks	1924	£1.50	£45.00
50	The Railway Centenary	1925	30p	£15.00
L50	The Railway Centenary	1925	50p	£25.00
25	The Railway Centenary 2nd Series	1925	80p	£20.00
L25	The Railway Centenary 2nd Series	1925	60p	£15.00

R. & J. HILL Ltd.—cont.

Qty		Date	Odds	Sets
25	The River Thames (1-25)	1924	£1.00	—
25	The River Thames (26-50)	1924	30p	£7.50
L50	The River Thames	1924	40p	£20.00
100	Transfers	1935	£2.00	—
20	Types of the British Army	1914	£15.00	—
LF48	Views of Interest 1st Series (Spinet)	1938	12p	£5.00
LF48	Views of Interest 1st Series (Sunripe)	1938	12p	£3.50
LF48	Views of Interest 2nd Series	1938	12p	£4.00
LF48	Views of Interest 3rd Series	1939	12p	£3.00
LF48	Views of Interest 4th Series	1939	12p	£6.00
LF48	Views of Interest 5th Series	1939	12p	£6.00
LF48	Views of Interest—Canada	1940	12p	£6.00
LF48	Views of Interest—India	1940	£1.25	£60.00
50	Views of London	1925	30p	£15.00
L50	Views of London	1925	40p	£20.00
L50	Views of the River Thames	1924	40p	£20.00
25	War Series	1915	£5.00	£125.00
50	Who's Who in British Films	1927	25p	£12.50
L50	Who's Who in British Films	1927	35p	£17.50
84	Wireless Telephony	1923	40p	£33.00
L20	Wireless Telephony—Broadcasting Series ...	1923	£1.00	£20.00
25	World's Masterpieces 2nd Series	1914	£1.00	£25.00
50	Zoological Series	1924	40p	£20.00
L50	Zoological Series	1924	40p	£20.00

J. W. HOBSON

18	Motor Cycle Series	1914	B	—

J. & T. HODGE

?2	Britain's Naval Crests	1896	D	—
16	British Royal Family	1901	C	—
?20	Scottish Views	1898	C	—

HOOK OF HOLLAND CIGARETTES

?15	Footballers	1900	D	—

HUDDEN & CO.

26	Actresses "FROGA"	1900	£30.00	—
25	Beauties "CHOAB"	1901	£15.00	—
?25	Beauties, Crown Seal	1898	C	—
24	Beauties "HUMPS" (blue back)	1899	£40.00	—
24	Beauties "HUMPS" (orange back)	1899	£20.00	—
24	Beauties "HUMPS" (type set back)	1899	D	—
?12	Comic Phrases	1900	£40.00	—
25	Famous Boxers	1927	A	—
25	Flags of All Nations	1904	£5.00	£125.00
48	Japanese Playing Cards	1900	C	—
18	Pretty Girl Series "RASH"	1900	£30.00	—
50	Public Schools & Colleges	1924	80p	£40.00
25	Soldiers of the Century	1903	£25.00	£625.00
25	Sports & Pastimes	1926	B	—
25	Star Girls	1900	£40.00	—
25	Types of Smokers	1903	£25.00	£625.00

HUDSON'S

Qty		Date	Odds	Sets
24	Beauties "BOCCA"	1900	D	—

HUNTER

?12	Footballers	1910	D	—

JAMES ILLINGWORTH LTD.

MF48	Beautiful Scotland	1939	40p	—
M25	Cavalry	1924	£2.00	£50.00
MF48	Coastwise	1938	25p	£12.50
25	Comicartoons of Sport	1927	£1.50	£37.50
MF48	Flying	1938	30p	—
25	Motor Car Bonnets	1925	£2.50	£62.50
25	Old Hostels	1926	£2.00	—
MF48	Our Countryside	1938	20p	—
MF24	Shots from the Films	1937	75p	—
?10	Views from the English Lakes	1895	D	—

IMPERIAL TOBACCO CO. LTD.

50	British Birds	1909	£2.00	£100.00
X1	Coronation Folder	1902	—	£35.00

INTERNATIONAL TOBACCO CO. LTD.

28	Domino Cards	1938	12p	£3.00
D50	Famous Buildings & Monuments (Metal) Series A	1934	20p	£10.00
D50	Famous Buildings & Monuments (Metal) Series B	1934	30p	£15.00
100	Film Favourites	1937	60p	—
D100	Gentlemen! The King! (black back)	1938	12p	£6.00
D100	Gentlemen! The King! (blue back)	1938	12p	—
50	International Code of Signals	1934	12p	£5.00
48	Screen Lovers (Summit)	unissued	60p	£30.00

PETER JACKSON

F28	Beautiful Scotland	1939	35p	£10.00
MF48	Beautiful Scotland	1939	25p	£12.00
F28	Coastwise	1938	35p	£10.00
MF48	Coastwise	1938	35p	—
F28	Famous Film Stars	1935	£1.00	£28.00
F27	Famous Films	1934	£1.00	£27.00
F28	Film Scenes	1936	50p	£14.00
LF28	Film Scenes (Different)	1936	80p	£22.50
F28	Flying	1938	75p	£21.00
LF28	Flying	1938	40p	—
D100	Gentlemen the King (Mixed Size)	1938	40p	—
F28	Life in the Navy	1937	40p	£11.00
LF28	Life in the Navy (Different)	1937	£1.00	£28.00
F28	Our Countryside	1938	30p	£8.50
MF48	Our Countryside	1938	40p	—
F28	Shots from the Films	1937	35p	£10.00
MF24	Shots from the Films	1937	50p	—
D250	Speed Through the Ages (Mixed Sizes) ...	1937	12p	£30.00
F28	Stars in Famous Films	1934	60p	—
D150	The Pageant of Kingship (Mixed Size)	1937	20p	£30.00

JACOBI BROS. & CO. LTD.

Qty		*Date*	*Odds*	*Sets*
?50	Boer War Celebrities "JASAS"	1901	C	—

JAMES & CO. (B'HAM) LTD.

20	Arms of Countries	1915	C	—

JAMES'S

?50	Pretty Girl Series "BAGG"	1898	D	—

JERSEY TOBACCO CO. LTD. (Channel Isles)

K53	Miniature Playing Cards	1933	40p	—

SOCIETE JOB

25	British Lighthouses	1925	£1.50	£37.50
B48	Cinema Stars (numbered)	1926	A	—
B48	Cinema Stars (unnumbered)	1926	20p	£15.00
48	Cinema Stars (numbered)	1926	£2.00	—
48	Cinema Stars (unnumbered)	1926	£1.50	—
25	Dogs	1911	£4.00	£100.00
25	Liners	1912	£12.50	—
K53	Miniature Playing Cards	1926	A	—
25	Orders of Chivalry	1924	£1.00	£25.00
25	Orders of Chivalry 2nd Series	1927	£1.00	£25.00
3	Orders of Chivalry (Unnumbered)	1927	£2.00	£6.00
25	Racehorses	1909	£4.00	£100.00

J. B. JOHNSON & CO.

25	National Flags, Flowers & Girls	1901	C	—

JONES BROS.

14/18	Spurs Footballers	1912	£2.00	—

A. I. JONES & CO. LTD.

B1	Advertisement Card	1901	D	—
12	Nautical Terms	1905	£15.00	£180.00

ALEX JONES & CO.

20	Actresses "ANGOOD"	1898	C	—
1	Diamond Jubilee 1897	1897	£60	—

A. S. JONES

30	Army Pictures, Cartoons, etc.	1916	B	—

T. E. JONES & CO.

?12	Conundrums	1900	C	—
50	Flags of All Nations	1899	C	—
?50	Footballers	1900	C	—
?12	Well-known Proverbs	1900	C	—

C. H. JORDEN LTD.

F12	Celebrities of the Great War	1915	B	—

J. & E. KENNEDY

Qty		Date	Odds	Sets
25	Beauties "FECKSA"	1902	£12.50	—

RICHARD KENNEDY

P?6	Army & Navy Cartoons	1906	C	—
50	War Portraits	1916	B	–

KINNEAR LTD.

13	Actresses	1899	£35.00	—
B1	A Gentleman in Kharki	1900	—	£20.00
15	Australian Cricket Team	1897	£50.00	—
?25	Cricketers	1898	D	—
X1	Cricket Fixture Folder	1903	D	—
25	Footballers & Club Colours	1898	£50.00	—
12	Jockeys, Set 1	1899	£15.00	£180.00
26	Jockeys (Different)	1900	£30.00	—
2	Prominent Personages	1902	D	—
13	Royalty	1897	£25.00	—
L1	The Four Generations	1900	D	—
K?25	Views	1898	D	—

B. KRIEGSFELD & CO.

1	Advertisement Card	1900	D	—
50	Beauties "KEWA"	1898	£40.00	—
?10	Celebrities	1901	C	—
50	Flags of All Nations	1899	£25.00	—
50	Phrases & Advertisements	1900	£30.00	—

A. KUIT LTD.

K?12	Arms of Cambridge Colleges	1914	B	—
K?12	Arms of Companies	1914	B	—
F30	British Beauties (Oval)	1914	£20.00	—
F?10	Crosmedo Bijou Cards	1915	C	—
25	Principal Streets of British Cities & Towns	1915	£50.00	—
F?50	Types of Beauty	1914	C	—

L. & Y. TOB. MFG. CO.

26	Actresses "FROGA"	1900	D	—

LAMBERT & BUTLER

10	Actresses & their Autographs (narrow)	1898	£40.00	—
10	Actresses & their Autographs (wide)	1898	£40.00	—
20	Actresses "BLARM"	1900	£6.00	£120.00
50	Admirals	1900	£6.00	—
1	Advertisement Card	1898	—	£150.00
50	Aeroplane Markings	1937	20p	£10.00
25	A History of Aviation (Brown Front)	1933	40p	£10.00
25	A History of Aviation (Green Front)	1932	30p	£7.50
40	Arms of Kings & Queens of England	1906	£2.00	£80.00
25	Aviation	1915	80p	£20.00
26	Beauties "HOL"	1899	£10.00	—
50	Birds & Eggs	1906	£1.20	£60.00
?25	Boer War & Boxer Rebellion—Sketches	1901	£10.00	—

LAMBERT & BUTLER—cont.

Qty		Date	Odds	Sets
20	Boer War Generals "CLAM"	1901	£10.00	—
10	Boer War Generals "FLAC"	1901	£10.00	—
25	British Trees & Their Uses	1937	80p	£20.00
1	Colonel R.S.S. Baden-Powell, King of Scouts	1901	D	—
25	Common Fallacies	1928	50p	£12.50
50	Conundrums (Blue Back)	1901	£7.50	—
50	Conundrums (Green Back)	1901	£5.00	—
12	Coronation Robes	1902	£7.50	£90.00
25	Dance Band Leaders	1936	80p	£20.00
28	Dominoes (Packets)	1955	60p	£15.00
50	Empire Air Routes	1936	25p	£12.50
25	Famous British Airmen & Airwomen	1935	30p	£7.50
25	Fauna of Rhodesia	1929	40p	£10.00
50	Find Your Way	1932	25p	£12.50
50	Footballers 1930-1	1931	£1.00	—
25	Garden Life	1930	24p	£6.00
25	Hints & Tips for Motorists	1929	80p	£20.00
50	Horsemanship	1938	40p	£20.00
25	How Motor Cars Work	1931	40p	£10.00
50	Interesting Customs & Traditions of the Navy, Army & Air Force	1939	20p	£10.00
25	Interesting Musical Instruments	1929	60p	£15.00
50	Interesting Sidelights on the Work of the G.P.O.	1939	25p	£12.50
20	International Yachts	1902	£30.00	—
25	Japanese Series	1904	£3.00	£75.00
4	Jockeys (no Frame)	1902	£12.50	£50.00
10	Jockeys (with Frame)	1902	£12.50	—
50	Keep Fit	1937	12p	£5.00
25	London Characters	1934	50p	£12.50
25	Motor Car Radiators	1928	£1.50	£37.50
25	Motor Cars A Series (Green Back)	1922	60p	£15.00
25	Motor Cars 2nd Series (26-50)	1923	80p	£20.00
50	Motor Cars 3rd Series	1926	£1.50	£75.00
25	Motor Cars (Grey Back)	1934	60p	£15.00
50	Motor Cycles	1923	£1.20	£60.00
50	Motor Index Marks	1926	75p	£37.50
25	Motors	1908	£8.00	£200.00
25	Naval Portraits (Series of 25)	1914	£1.50	£37.50
50	Naval Portraits (Series of 50)	1915	£1.50	£75.00
25	Pirates & Highwaymen	1926	24p	£6.00
25	Rhodesian Series	1928	40p	£10.00
50	The Thames From Lechlade to London	1907	£2.50	£125.00
25	Third Rhodesian Series	1930	16p	£4.00
4	Types of the British Army & Navy (Specialities)	1897	£20.00	£80.00
4	Types of the British Army & Navy (Viking)	1897	£25.00	—
25	Waverley Series	1904	£4.00	£100.00
25	Winter Sports	1914	£1.20	£30.00
25	Wireless Telegraphy	1909	£2.00	£50.00
25	Wonders of Nature	1924	20p	£5.00
25	World's Locomotives (Series of 25)	1912	£1.50	£37.50
50	World's Locomotives (Series of 50)	1912	£2.50	£125.00
25	World's Locomotives (Additional)	1913	£2.50	£62.50

LAMBERT & BUTLER—cont.

Qty		Date	Odds	Sets
Overseas Issues				
50	Actors & Actresses "WALP"	1908	£1.25	—
250	Actresses "ALWICS"	1908	£1.25	—
50	Beauties "LAWHA"	1908	£1.25	—
83	Danske Byvaabner	1912	£5.00	—
26	Etchings (Dogs)	1928	A	—
L26	Etchings (Dogs)	1928	A	—
25	Flag Girls of All Nations	1910	£4.00	—
F50	Homeland Events	1925	80p	£40.00
?2	Indian Women	1910	B	—
25	London Characters	1934	A	—
F50	London Zoo	1924	50p	£25.00
50	Merchant Ships of the World	1924	£1.00	£50.00
50	Music Hall Celebrities	1906	£1.50	—
F50	Popular Film Stars (Title in 1 Line)	1925	60p	£30.00
F50	Popular Film Stars (Title in 2 Lines)	1925	50p	£25.00
F50	Popular Film Stars (Varsity Cigarettes)	1925	£1.00	—
100	Royalty Notabilities & Events 1900-2	1902	£4.00	—
100	Russo Japanese Series	1903	£2.00	—
F50	The Royal Family at Home and Abroad	1928	40p	£20.00
F50	The World of Sport	1926	40p	£20.00
F50	Types of Modern Beauty	1927	40p	£20.00
F50	Who's Who in Sport (1926)	1926	40p	£20.00

LAMBKIN BROS.

36	Country Scenes (Ser. 1-6)	1924	£2.00	—
L36	Country Scenes (Ser. 7-12)	1926	£2.50	—
L?6	Lily of Killarney Views	1925	B	—

C. & J. LAW

25	Types of British Soldiers	1914	£10.00	—
50	War Portraits	1915	B	—

R. J. LEA LTD.

2	Advertisement Cards	1923	C	—
B12	Butterflies & Moths (Silk)	1924	30p	£3.50
L12	Butterflies & Moths (Silk)	1924	25p	£3.00
P6	Butterflies & Moths (Silk)	1924	50p	£3.00
12	Chairman Puzzles	1910	C	—
70	Cigarette Transfers (Locomotives)	1916	£2.00	£140.00
25	Civilians of Countries Fighting with the Allies	1914	£4.00	£100.00
F48	Coronation Souvenir (Glossy)	1937	12p	£6.00
48	Coronation Souvenir (Matt)	1937	16p	£8.00
LF48	Coronation Souvenir	1937	16p	£8.00
25	Dogs (1-25)	1923	£1.00	£25.00
25	Dogs (26-50)	1923	£2.50	—
25	English Birds	1922	£1.20	£30.00
F54	Famous Film Stars	1939	20p	£10.00
F48	Famous Racehorses of 1926	1927	60p	£30.00
MF48	Famous Racehorses of 1926	1927	£1.20	£60.00
F48	Famous Views (glossy)	1936	12p	£5.00
48	Famous Views (matt)	1936	25p	£12.50

R. J. LEA LTD.—cont.

Qty		*Date*	*Odds*	*Sets*
MF48	Famous Views	1936	12p	£5.00
F36	Film Stars 1st Series	1934	£1.00	—
F36	Film Stars 2nd Series	1934	60p	—
25	Fish	1926	30p	£7.50
50	Flowers to Grow—The Best Perennials	1913	£1.50	£75.00
F48	Girls from the Shows (glossy)	1935	30p	£15.00
48	Girls from the Shows (matt)	1935	40p	£20.00
50	Miniatures (No Border)	1912	£1.50	£75.00
50	Miniatures (Gold Border)	1912	£1.20	£60.00
50	Miniatures (51-100)	1912	£1.20	£60.00
46/50	Modern Miniatures	1913	50p	£23.00
12	More Lea's Smokers (green border)	1906	£30.00	—
12	More Lea's Smokers (red frame)	1906	£40.00	—
P24	Old English Pottery & Porcelain	1912	£4.00	£100.00
50	Old English Pottery & Porcelain	1912	£1.00	£50.00
50	Old Pottery & Porcelain 2nd Series (Chairman)	1912	80p	£40.00
50	Old Pottery & Porcelain 2nd Series (Recorder)	1912	£2.50	—
50	Old Pottery & Porcelain 3rd Series (Chairman)	1912	80p	£40.00
50	Old Pottery & Porcelain 3rd Series (Recorder)	1912	£2.50	—
50	Old Pottery & Porcelain 4th Series	1913	80p	£40.00
50	Old Pottery & Porcelain 5th Series	1913	80p	£40.00
54	Old Pottery (Silk)	1914	50p	£30.00
72	Old Pottery (Silk Different)	1914	60p	£45.00
F54	Radio Stars (glossy)	1935	50p	£27.00
54	Radio Stars (matt)	1935	50p	—
100	Regimental Crests & Badges (Silk)	1923	75p	£75.00
50	Roses	1924	35p	£17.50
50	Ships of the World	1925	60p	£30.00
25	The Evolution of the Royal Navy	1925	50p	£12.50
25	War Pictures	1915	£2.00	£50.00
25	War Portraits	1915	£3.00	£75.00
F48	Wonders of the World (glossy)	1938	20p	£10.00
48	Wonders of the World (matt)	1938	20p	£10.00
MF48	Wonders of the World	1938	15p	£7.50

J. LEES

21	Northampton Town Football Club	1915	£15.00	—

ALFRED L. LEAVER

B12	Manikin Cards	1915	B	—

LEON DE CUBA CIGARS

30	Colonial Troops	1902	C	—

A. LEWIS & CO. (WESTMINSTER) LTD.

52	Horoscopes	1938	20p	£10.00
50	War Portraits	1915	B	—

H. C. LLOYD & SONS LTD.

28	Academy Gems	1902	£25.00	—
26	Actresses & Boer War Celebrities	1901	£25.00	—
B18	Devon Footballers (with Frame line)	1902	C	—
B40	Devon Footballers & Boer War Celebrities	1902	£25.00	—

H. C. LLOYD & SONS LTD.—cont.

Qty		Date	Odds	Sets
25	Star Girls	1899	C	—
L36	War Pictures	1914	B	—

RICHARD LLOYD & SONS

20	Actresses, Celebrities & Yachts	1900	C	–
25	Atlantic Records	1936	40p	£10.00
25	Boer War Celebrities	1899	£12.50	—
F27	Cinema Stars (1-27)	1935	£1.50	£40.00
F27	Cinema Stars (28-54)	1935	15p	£4.00
F27	Cinema Stars, 3rd Series (55-81)	1936	£1.50	£40.00
25	Cinema Stars (Matt)	1937	30p	£7.50
25	Famous Cricketers Puzzle Series	1930	£2.00	£50.00
96	National Types, Costumes & Flags	1900	£15.00	—
25	Old English Inns	1923	30p	£7.50
25	Old Inns, Series 2	1924	£1.00	£25.00
50	Old Inns	1925	30p	£15.00
10	Scenes From San Toy	1905	£5.00	£50.00
25	Tricks & Puzzles	1935	12p	£3.00
25	Types of Horses	1926	60p	£15.00
25	Zoo Series	1926	24p	£6.00

LUSBY LTD.

25	Scenes from Circus Life	1902	£60.00	—

HUGH McCALL

1	RAF Recruiting Card	1924	C	—

D. & J. MACDONALD

10	Actresses "MUTA"	1901	£50.00	—
L?	Cricket & Football Teams	1902	C	—
25	Cricketers	1902	C	—
L1	Yorkshire County Team	1900	D	—

MACKENZIE & CO.

F50	Actors & Actresses	1902	£5.00	—
50	The Zoo	1910	£6.00	—
50	Victorian Art Pictures	1910	£5.00	—

WM. McKINNELL

20	The European War Series	1915	£35.00	—
50	War Portraits	1916	B	—

MACNAUGHTON JENKINS & CO. LTD.

B50	Castles of Ireland—Ancient & Modern	1924	£1.00	£50.00
50	Various Uses of Rubber	1924	70p	£35.00

A. McTAVISH

30	Army Pictures, Cartoons, etc.	1916	B	—

McWATTIE & SONS

30	Army Pictures, Cartoons, etc.	1916	B	—

THE MANXLAND TOB. CO.

Qty		*Date*	*Odds*	*Sets*
?	Views in the Isle of Man	1900	D	—

MARCOVITCH & CO.

F18	Beauties (Plain Back)	1932	12p	£2.00
L7	The Story in Red and White	1955	30p	£2.00

MARCUS'S

?25	Cricketers	1897	D	—
25	Footballers & Club Colours	1898	£50	—
L1	The Four Generations	1900	D	—

MARKHAM

M?25	Views of Bridgwater	1906	B	—

MARSUMA CO.

50	Famous Golfers & Their Strokes	1914	£5.00	£250.00

MARTINS LTD.

1	Arf A Mo Kaiserl	1915	—	£20.00
D?12	Carlyle Series	1923	B	—
P?750	The Performer Tobacco Fund Photographs ...	1916	£1.50	—
25	V.C. Heroes	1916	£7.50	—

R. MASON & CO.

30	Colonial Troops	1902	£35.00	—
40	Naval & Military Phrases	1904	£20.00	—

MASCOT CIGARETTES

?20	British Vlews	1925	B	—

JUSTUS VAN MAURIK

X12	Views of Holland	1915	C	—

MAY QUEEN VIRGINIA CIGARETTES

M10/12	Interesting Pictures	—	25p	£2.50

MENTORS LTD.

32	Views of Ireland	1912	£3.50	—

J. MILLHOFF & CO. LTD.

F54	Antique Pottery	1927	40p	£20.00
MF56	Antique Pottery	1927	50p	£28.00
30	Art Treasures	1927	25p	£7.50
L50	Art Treasures	1926	16p	£8.00
L25	Art Treasures 2nd Series (51-75)	1928	50p	£12.50
74	De Reszke Pictures (several printings)	1925	75p	—
L25	England Historic & Picturesque (1-25)	1928	30p	£7.50
L25	England Historic & Picturesque 2nd Series (26-50)	1928	20p	£5.00
F27	Famous Golfers	1928	£2.00	£55.00
F27	Famous Test Cricketers	1928	£1.50	£40.00
MF27	Famous Test Cricketers	1928	£1.50	£40.00
M25	Gallery Pictures	1929	40p	£10.00

J. MILLHOFF & CO. LTD.—cont.

Qty		Date	Odds	Sets
50	Geographia Map Series (Sect.)	1931	60p	£30.00
F36	In the Public Eye	1930	25p	£9.00
25	Men of Genius	1924	£1.60	£40.00
L25	Picturesque Old England	1931	36p	£9.00
F27	Real Photographs A Series (glossy)	1931	12p	£2.50
F27	Real Photographs A Series (matt)	1931	15p	£4.00
F27	Real Photographs 2nd Series	1931	12p	£3.00
F27	Real Photographs 3rd Series	1932	12p	£3.00
F27	Real Photographs 4th Series	1932	12p	£3.00
F27	Real Photographs 5th Series	1933	12p	£3.00
F27	Real Photographs 6th Series	1933	12p	£3.00
25	Reproductions of Celebrated Oil Paintings	1928	50p	£12.50
L25	Roses	1927	80p	£20.00
M?6	Theatre Advertisement Cards	1905	B	—
X?6	Theatre Advertisement Cards	1905	B	—
F54	The Homeland Series	1933	12p	£5.00
MF56	The Homeland Series	1933	12p	£6.00
50	Things to Make	1935	12p	£3.50
50	What the Stars Say	1934	12p	£5.00
F36	Zoological Studies	1929	15p	£5.00
Dutch Issues				
L40	Film Series 1	1924	A	—
L60	Film Series 1	1924	A	—
L60	Film Series 2	1925	A	—
L25	Film Series 3	1925	A	—
MF105	Film Series 4	1926	A	—
MF206	Film Series 4	1926	A	—
F?70	Sports Series	1925	A	—

MIRANDA LTD.

20	Dogs	1925	£1.50	—
25	Sports and Pastimes	1925	£1.25	—

STEPHEN MITCHELL

51	Actors & Actresses "FROGA" (Coloured)	1899	£8.00	—
26	Actors & Actresses "FROGA B" (Brown)	1899	£8.00	—
26	Actors & Actresses "FROGA C" (Coloured)	1899	£8.00	—
50	Actors & Actresses "FROGA D" (Brown)	1899	£8.00	—
1	Advertisement Card	1900	D	—
50	A Gallery of 1934	1935	50p	£12.50
50	A Gallery of 1935	1935	40p	£10.00
50	Air Raid Precautions	1938	25p	£12.50
30	A Model Army	1932	25p	£7.50
25	Angling	1928	80p	£20.00
50	Arms & Armour	1916	£1.50	£75.00
25	Army Ribbons & Buttons	1916	£1.50	£37.50
50	A Road Map of Scotland	1933	60p	£30.00
25	Boxer Rebellion—Sketches	1901	£10.00	—
25	British Warships (1-25)	1915	£2.00	£50.00
25	British Warships, 2nd Series (26-50)	1915	£2.00	£50.00
50	Clan Tartans A Series	1927	60p	£30.00
25	Clan Tartans 2nd Series	1927	16p	£4.00
25	Empire Exhibition, Scotland 1938	1938	15p	£3.75

STEPHEN MITCHELL—cont.

Qty		Date	Odds	Sets
25	Famous Crosses	1923	16p	£4.00
50	Famous Scots	1933	16p	£8.00
50	First Aid	1938	15p	£7.50
P3	Glasgow International Exhibition 1901	1901	£20.00	£60.00
50	Humorous Drawings	1924	75p	£37.50
50	Interesting Buildings	1905	£3.00	—
40	London Ceremonials	1928	40p	£16.00
25	Medals	1916	£2.50	£62.50
25	Money	1913	£2.00	£50.00
25	Old Sporting Prints	1930	16p	£4.00
50	Our Empire	1937	12p	£6.00
25	Regimental Crests & Collar Badges	1900	£5.00	£125.00
70	River & Coastal Steamers	1925	£1.20	£85.00
50	Scotland's Story	1929	75p	£37.50
25	Scottish Clan Series	1903	£4.00	£100.00
50	Scottish Footballers	1934	25p	£12.50
50	Scottish Football Snaps	1935	25p	£12.50
25	Seals	1911	£2.00	£50.00
25	Sports	1907	£3.00	£75.00
25	Stars of Screen & History	1939	30p	£7.50
25	Statues & Monuments	1914	£2.00	£50.00
50	The World of Tomorrow	1936	25p	£12.50
25	Village Models	1925	60p	£15.00
25	Village Models 2nd Series	1925	80p	£20.00
L25	Village Models	1925	£1.25	—
L25	Village Models 2nd Series	1925	£1.25	—
50	Wonderful Century	1937	12p	£5.00

MOORGATE TOBACCO CO. LTD.

D30	The New Elizabethan Age	1953	75p	£22.50

B. MORRIS & SONS LTD.

30	Actress (Black & White)	1898	60p	£30.00
26	Actresses "FROGA A"	1899	£12.50	—
L26	Actresses "FROGA B"	1899	D	—
50	Animals in the Zoo (Blue Back)	1924	20p	£10.00
50	Animals at the Zoo (Grey Back)	1924	16p	£8.00
35	At the London Zoo Aquarium	1928	12p	£3.00
25	Australian Cricketers	1925	80p	£20.00
M24	Battleship Crests (Silk)	1915	£10.00	—
50	Beauties "CHOAB"	1900	£15.00	—
50	Beauties Collotype	1897	C	—
21	Beauties "MOM"	1899	£12.50	—
20	Boer War 1900	1900	£12.50	—
25	Boer War Celebrities "PAM"	1901	£10.00	—
25	Captain Blood	1937	16p	£4.00
L25	English & Foreign Birds (Silk)	1915	£1.20	£30.00
L25	English Flowers (Silk)	1915	£1.50	£37.50
L50	English Flowers (Silk)	1915	£1.50	£75.00
50	Film Star Series	1923	£1.00	—
30	General Interest	1910	£3.00	£90.00
25	Golf Strokes Series	1923	60p	£15.00
12	Horoscopes	1936	12p	£1.50
25	How Films are Made	1934	15p	£3.75

B. MORRIS & SONS LTD.—cont.

Qty		Date	Odds	Sets
50	How to Sketch	1929	25p	£12.50
20	London Views	1904	£12.50	—
25	Marvels of the Universe Series	1912	£1.50	£37.50
25	Measurement of Time	1924	20p	£5.00
25	Motor Series	1922	£1.00	£25.00
50	National & Colonial Arms	1917	£3.00	£150.00
25	Racing Greyhounds	1939	16p	£4.00
L25	Regimental Colours (Silk)	1916	£1.00	£25.00
24	Shadowgraphs	1925	60p	£15.00
25	The Queen's Dolls House	1925	80p	£20.00
13	Treasure Island	1924	30p	£4.00
50	Victory Signs Series	1928	12p	£5.00
25	War Celebrities	1916	£3.00	£75.00
25	War Pictures	1915	£3.00	£75.00
25	Wax Art Series	1931	12p	£3.00
25	Whipsnade Zoo	1932	15p	£3.75
25	Wireless Series	1923	£1.00	£25.00

PHILIP MORRIS & CO. LTD.

50	British Views	1924	£1.00	—
L50	British Views	1924	£1.25	—

P. MOUAT & CO.

30	Colonial Troops	1902	C	—

MOUSTAFA LTD.

F50	Camera Studies	1923	£1.00	—
25	Cinema Stars	1924	£1.00	£25.00
40	Leo Chambers Dogs Heads	1924	50p	£20.00
25	Pictures of World Interest	1923	£1.00	£25.00
F25	Real Photos	1925	12p	£2.50

MUNRO

30	Colonial Troops	1902	C	—

B. MURATTI SONS & CO. LTD.

P?25	Actresses, Collotype	1899	C	—
26	Actresses "FROGA" (Cigarette Connoisseur)	1899	£10.00	—
26	Actresses "FROGA" (Zinnia)	1899	£15.00	—
P?50	Actresses & Beauties, Fancy Frames	1899	C	—
X?30	Advertisement Cards	1900	C	—
F24	Australian Racehorses	1931	15p	£3.50
25	Beauties "CHOAB"	1900	£15.00	—
L50	Beautiful Women	1900	£20.00	—
20	Boer War Generals "CLAM"	1901	£10.00	—
B15	Caricatures (Specialities)	1903	£7.50	—
B15	Caricatures (Vassos)	1903	B	—
B15	Caricatures (Zinnia)	1903	£7.50	—
L35	Crowned Heads	1912	£5.00	—
52	Japanese Series (P/C Inset) (printed back)	1904	£5.00	—
52	Japanese Series (P/C Inset) (plain back)	1904	£5.00	—
XF?	Post Card Series	1902	£5.00	—
19	Russo Japanese Series	1904	£6.00	£110.00

B. MURATTI SONS & CO. LTD.—cont.

Qty		Date	Odds	Sets
25	Star Girls	1899	C	—
50	Views of Jersey (printed back)	1913	£10.00	—
50	Views of Jersey (plain back)	1913	£7.50	—
25	War Series I	1916	£7.50	—
25	War Series II	1917	£5.00	£125.00
Silk Issues				
L40	Canvas Masterpieces Series M (small globe)	1916	£1.25	£50.00
L40	Canvas Masterpieces Series M (large globe)	1916	£4.00	—
P16	Canvas Masterpieces Series P	1916	£5.00	—
M25	Flags, Series A (26-50)	1914	£2.00	—
P3	Flags, Series A (1-3)	1914	£5.00	—
L1	Flags, Series B (No. 19)	1914	—	£3.00
M25	Flags, Series C (20-44)	1914	£1.60	£40.00
P18	Flags, Series C (1-18)	1914	£5.00	—
P3	Flags, Series D (45-47)	1914	£5.00	—
M25	Flags, Series E (48-72)	1914	£1.60	£40.00
P6	Flags, Series F (73-78)	1914	£4.00	—
P18	Great War Leaders, Series P	1916	£5.00	—
M25	Regimental Badges, Series A	1915	£2.00	—
L48	Regimental Badges, Series B	1915	£2.50	—
L18	Regimental Badges, Series B (Different) (4-18)	1915	£3.00	—
L16	Regimental Badges, Series G (79-94)	1915	£4.00	—
L25	Regimental Colours, Series CB	1915	£4.00	—
M72	Regimental Colours, Series RB	1915	£2.50	—
German Issues				
X216	Brennpunkte des Deutschen Sports Band 1	1935	30p	—
X288	Brennpunkte des Deutschen Sports Band 2	1936	30p	—
X216	Brennpunkte des Deutschen Sports Band 3	1936	30p	—

MURRAY, SONS & CO.

20	Actresses "BLARM"	1902	B	—
F22	Bathing Beauties	1929	£1.50	—
40	Bathing Belles	1939	12p	£2.00
15	Chess & Draughts Problems	1910	£20.00	—
F22	Cinema Scenes	1929	£1.50	—
20	Cricketers (black front)	1912	£20.00	—
20	Cricketers (brown front)	1912	£30.00	—
25	Crossword Puzzles	1923	B	—
F26	Dancers	1929	£1.50	—
F25	Dancing Girls	1929	80p	£20.00
F26	Dancing Girls (As Above)	1930	£1.20	—
25	Famous Works of Art	1910	£10.00	—
B16	Flags (Silk)	1910	£6.00	—
X3	Flags & Arms (Silk)	1910	B	—
34	Footballers, Series H	1912	£7.50	—
104	Footballers, Series J	1913	£5.00	—
?25	Football Colours (Shaped)	1905	B	—
25	Football Rules	1911	£10.00	—
25	High Class Works of Art	1909	£10.00	—
20	Holidays by the L.M.S.	1927	£4.00	—
20	Inventors Series	1924	£1.50	£30.00
25	Irish Scenery	1904	£10.00	—

MURRAY, SONS & CO.—cont.

Qty		Date	Odds	Sets
31	Orders of Chivalry (Silk)	1925	£6.00	—
25	Polo Pictures	1910	£7.00	—
50	Prominent Politicians (two strengths back) ...	1909	£1.00	£50.00
50	Prominent Politicians (without "in two strengths")	1909	£10.00	—
50	Puzzle Series	1929	£1.00	—
B25	Regimental Badges (Silk)	1910	£6.00	—
50	Stage and Film Stars	1926	£1.00	—
25	Steamships	1939	24p	£6.00
50	The Story of Ships	1940	12p	£2.50
25	Types of Aeroplanes	1929	20p	£5.00
20	Types of Dogs	1924	£1.00	£20.00
35	War Series K	1915	£10.00	—
25	War Series L	1916	£1.20	£40.00

H. J. NATHAN

40	Comic Military & Naval Pictures	1904	£35.00	—

JAMES NELSON

?20	Beauties "FENA"	1899	D	—

EDWD. J. NEWBEGIN

F50	Actors & Actresses	1901	£25.00	—
10	Actresses "HAGG"	1900	C	—
20	Cricketers Series	1902	C	—
1	Mabel Love Advertisement Card	1900	D	—
19	Russo Japanese Series	1904	C	—
16	Well-known Proverbs	1900	£40.00	—
24	Well-known Songs	1900	£40.00	—

W. H. NEWMAN LTD.

18	Motor Cycle Series	1914	B	—

THE NEW MOSLEM CIG. CO. LTD.

30	Proverbs	1903	C	—

THOS. NICHOLLS & CO.

50	Orders of Chivalry	1916	£2.50	£125.00

THE NILMA TOBACCO COY.

40	Home & Colonial Regiments	1903	B	—
30	Proverbs	1903	B	–

M. E. NOTARAS LTD.

B24	Chinese Scenes	1925	12p	£2.00
F36	National Types of Beauty	1925	20p	£7.50

OGDENS LTD.

25	ABC of Sport	1927	80p	£20.00
50	Actors, Natural & Character Studies	1938	12p	£3.00
25	Actresses (No Glycerine back)	1895	£35.00	—
?200	Actresses, Collotype	1894	£15.00	—
50	Actresses, Green Gravure	1898	£3.50	£175.00

Qty		Date	Odds	Sets
?1	Actresses, Green, green border	1898	D	—
200	Actresses, Woodburytype	1894	£15.00	—
F?573	Actresses, Guinea Gold Type	1900	£1.00	—
50	A.F.C. Nicknames	1933	60p	£30.00
50	Air Raid Precautions	1938	12p	£6.00
50	Applied Electricity	1928	40p	£20.00
192	Army Crests and Mottoes	1902	£1.50	—
36	Australian Test Cricketers	1928	£1.25	£45.00
28	Beauties "BOCCA"	1899	£12.50	—
50	Beauties "CHOAB"	1899	£15.00	—
26	Beauties "HOL"	1899	£7.50	£200.00
66	Beauties, Green Net Back (black & white)	1901	£4.00	£250.00
100	Beauties, Green Net Back (coloured)	1901	£6.00	—
52	Beauties, P/C Inset	1899	£12.50	£650.00
26	Beauties, As P/C Inset	1899	£15.00	—
52	Beauties & Military, P/C Inset	1898	£15.00	—
F50	Beauty Series (Unnumbered)	1900	£25.00	—
F50	Beauty Series (Numbered)	1900	£1.00	£50.00
50	Billiards by Tom Newman	1928	60p	£30.00
50	Birds Eggs	1908	80p	£40.00
50	Birds Eggs (Cut-Outs)	1923	30p	£15.00
F?141	Boer War & General Interest	1901	£1.50	—
LF?50	Boer War & General Interest	1901	A	—
50	Boxers	1915	£2.50	£125.00
25	Boxing	1914	£1.50	£37.50
50	Boy Scouts (Blue Back)	1911	£1.00	£50.00
50	Boy Scouts (Green Back)	1911	£2.00	—
50	Boy Scouts, 2nd Series (Blue Back)	1912	£1.20	£60.00
50	Boy Scouts, 2nd Series (Green Back)	1912	£2.00	—
50	Boy Scouts, 3rd Series (Blue Back)	1912	£1.20	£60.00
50	Boy Scouts, 3rd Series (Green Back)	1912	£2.00	—
50	Boy Scouts, 4th Series	1913	£1.50	£75.00
25	Boy Scouts, 5th Series	1914	£1.60	£40.00
50	Boy Scouts (Different)	1929	50p	£25.00
50	British Birds	1905	75p	£37.50
50	British Birds, 2nd Series	1909	£1.00	£50.00
50	British Birds (Cut-Outs)	1923	25p	£12.50
50	British Birds & Their Eggs	1939	30p	£15.00
50	British Costumes From 100 B.C. to 1904	1905	£2.00	£100.00
50	Broadcasting	1935	25p	£12.50
50	By the Roadside	1932	30p	£15.00
44	Captains of Association Football Clubs & Colours	1926	60p	£27.00
50	Cathedrals & Abbeys	1936	35p	£17.50
50	Champions of 1936	1937	15p	£7.50
50	Children of All Nations	1924	25p	£12.50
50	Club Badges	1914	£1.50	£75.00
50	Colour in Nature	1932	40p	£20.00
25	Comic Pictures	1897	D	—
50	Construction of Railway Trains	1930	80p	£40.00
50	Coronation Procession (Sect.)	1937	30p	£15.00
12	Cricketers & Footballers—Women	1896	D	—
50	Cricketers & Sportsmen	1898	£20.00	—
50	Cricket 1926	1926	£1.00	£50.00

Qty		Date	Odds	Sets
25	Derby Entrants 1926	1926	60p	£15.00
50	Derby Entrants 1928	1928	50p	£25.00
50	Derby Entrants 1929	1929	60p	£30.00
50	Dogs	1936	25p	£12.50
55	Dominoes	1909	80p	£44.00
112	Dominoes—Actress & Beauty Backs	1900	£10.00	—
25	Famous Dirt Track Riders	1929	£1.20	£30.00
50	Famous Footballers	1908	£1.00	£50.00
50	Famous Rugby Players	1926	40p	£20.00
50	Flags & Funnels of Leading Steamship Lines	1906	£1.50	£75.00
50	Football Caricatures	1935	40p	£20.00
43	Football Club Badges (Shaped)	1910	£2.50	—
50	Football Club Captains	1936	30p	£15.00
51	Football Club Colours	1906	80p	£40.00
50	Foreign Birds	1924	25p	£12.50
50	Fowls Pigeons & Dogs	1904	£1.00	£50.00
25	Greyhound Racing 1st Series	1927	£1.20	£30.00
25	Greyhound Racing 2nd Series	1928	£1.20	£30.00
1	History of the Union Jack (Folder)	1900	D	—
50	How to Swim	1935	12p	£5.00
50	Infantry Training	1915	£1.20	£60.00
50	Jockey and Owners Colours	1927	35p	£17.50
50	Jockeys 1930	1930	40p	£20.00
50	Leaders of Men	1924	75p	£37.50
MF?	Liners (Guinea Gold Type)	1901	B	—
25	Marvels of Motion	1928	60p	£15.00
K154	Miniature Playing Cards (Actress/Beauty Back)	1900	£1.25	—
K52	Miniature Playing Cards (Coolie)	1904	£1.00	£52.00
K52	Miniature Playing Cards (Tabs)	1909	£1.25	—
50	Modern British Pottery	1925	30p	£15.00
50	Modern Railways	1936	50p	£25.00
50	Modern War Weapons	1915	£1.00	£50.00
25	Modes of Conveyance	1927	£1.00	£25.00
50	Motor Races 1931	1931	80p	£40.00
50	Ocean Greyhounds	1938	25p	£12.50
25	Optical Illusions	1923	80p	£20.00
50	Orders of Chivalry	1907	£1.50	£75.00
25	Owners Racing Colours & Jockeys (Green Back)	1914	£1.50	£37.50
50	Owners Racing Colours & Jockeys (Blue Back)	1906	£1.00	£50.00
25	Picturesque People of the Empire	1927	30p	£7.50
50	Picturesque Villages	1936	35p	£17.50
25	Poultry (Ogdens On Front) (1-25)	1915	£1.00	£25.00
25	Poultry (No Ogdens On Front) (1-25)	1915	£1.50	£37.50
25	Poultry 2nd Series (26-50)	1916	£1.00	£25.00
25	Poultry Alphabet	1924	£1.00	£25.00
25	Poultry Rearing & Management 1st Series	1922	60p	£15.00
25	Poultry Rearing & Management 2nd Series	1923	60p	£15.00
50	Prominent Cricketers of 1938	1938	40p	£20.00
50	Prominent Racehorses of 1933	1934	30p	£15.00
50	Pugilists & Wrestlers A Series (1-50)	1908	£1.50	£75.00
25	Pugilists & Wrestlers 2nd Series (51-75)	1909	£2.00	£50.00
50	Pugilists in Action	1928	40p	£20.00
50	Racehorses	1907	80p	£40.00
50	Racing Pigeons	1931	40p	£20.00

Qty		Date	Odds	Sets
25	Records of the World	1908	£1.50	£37.50
50	Royal Mail	1909	£2.00	£100.00
50	Sea Adventure	1939	12p	£2.50
50	Sectional Cycling Map	1910	£1.50	£75.00
50	Shakespeare Series (numbered)	1905	£7.50	£375.00
50	Shakespeare Series (unnumbered)	1905	£7.50	£375.00
50	Shots from the Films	1936	30p	£15.00
25	Sights of London	1923	60p	£15.00
50	Smugglers and Smuggling	1932	40p	£20.00
50	Soldiers of the King	1909	£2.50	£125.00
50	Steeplechase Celebrities	1931	30p	£15.00
50	Steeplechase Trainers and Owners Colours	1927	30p	£15.00
50	Swimming Diving and Life Saving	1931	20p	£10.00
25	Swiss Views 1-25	1910	£1.00	£25.00
25	Swiss Views 26-50	1910	£2.50	£62.50
50	The Blue Riband of the Atlantic	1929	£1.00	£50.00
50	The Story of Sand	1935	25p	£12.50
25	Trainers and Owners Colours 1st Series	1925	40p	£10.00
25	Trainers and Owners Colours 2nd Series	1926	70p	£17.50
50	Trick Billiards	1934	30p	£15.00
50	Turf Personalities	1929	40p	£20.00
48	Victoria Cross Heroes	1901	£7.50	£360.00
25	Whaling	1927	70p	£17.50
50	Yachts & Motor Boats	1930	60p	£30.00
50	Zoo Studies	1937	15p	£7.50

Guinea Gold Issues

LF1	Actresses Base C	1899	—	£7.50
F374	Actresses Base D	1900	50p	—
LF423	Actresses Base D	1900	75p	—
F40	Actresses Base E	1900	£1.25	—
F662	Actresses Base I	1899	50p	—
LF21	Actresses Base I	1899	£20.00	—
F30	Actresses Base J	1899	£2.00	—
F238	Actresses Base K	1899	75p	—
F215	Actresses Base L	1899	75p	—
F113	Actresses & Miscellaneous Base I	1900	50p	£56.00
F2974	Actresses & Miscellaneous Base M	1900	50p	—
LF403	Actresses & Miscellaneous Base M	1900	75p	—
F58	Boer War & Actresses Base F	1901	40p	£24.00
F186	Boer War & Miscellaneous Base D	1901	30p	—
LF153	Boer War & Miscellaneous Base D	1900	60p	—
F312	Continental Actresses Base B	1899	£1.00	—
LF71	Continental Actresses Base B	1899	£7.50	—
F11	Cricketers Base I	1901	£6.00	£66.00
F77	Cricketers Base M	1899	£6.00	—
F57	Cyclists Base M	1899	£3.00	—
F58	Denumbered Group Base D	1900	60p	—
LF50	Denumbered Group Base D	1900	£1.00	£50.00
F176	Footballers Base M	1899	£3.00	—
F320	General Interest (White Panel) Base D	1900	50p	£160.00
F200	General Interest Numbered 1-200	1899	25p	£50.00
F300	General Interest Numbered 201-500	1900	60p	—
F395/397	General Interest Numbered 501-898	1900	40p	£160.00

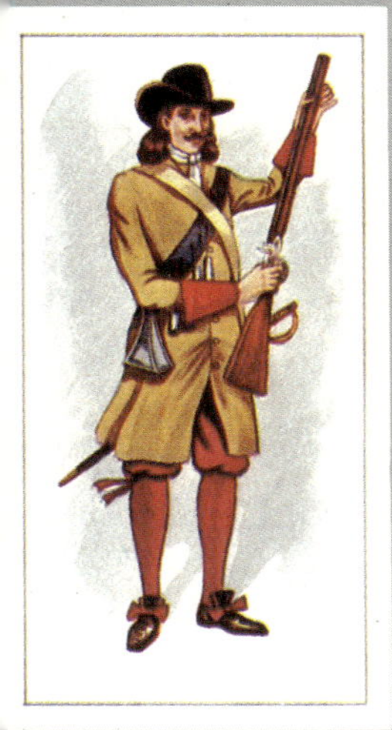

Regimental Uniforms of the Past (Badshah or Rington)

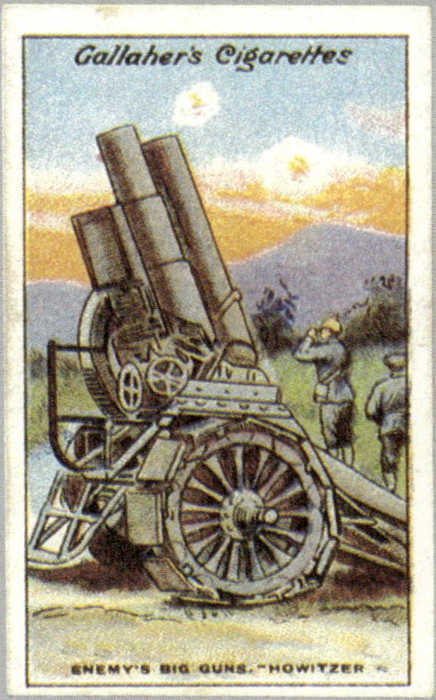

The Great War Series. Gallaher

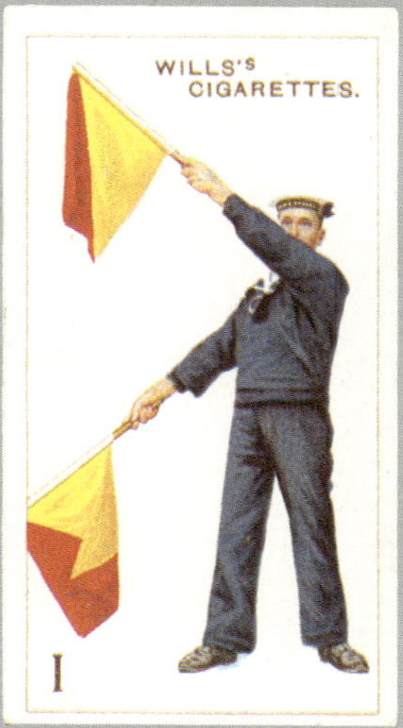

Signalling Series. Wills (also Player)

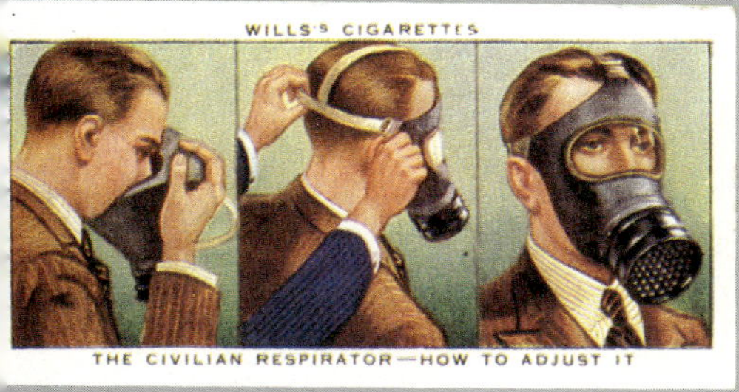

Air Raid Precautions. Wills (also Hignett, Mitchell or Ogden)

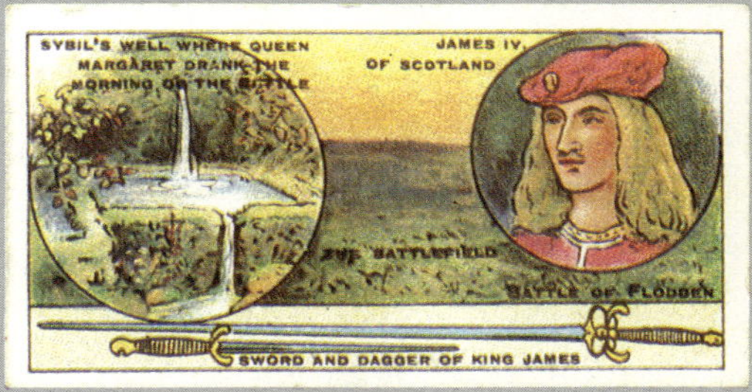

Battlefields of Great Britain. Smith

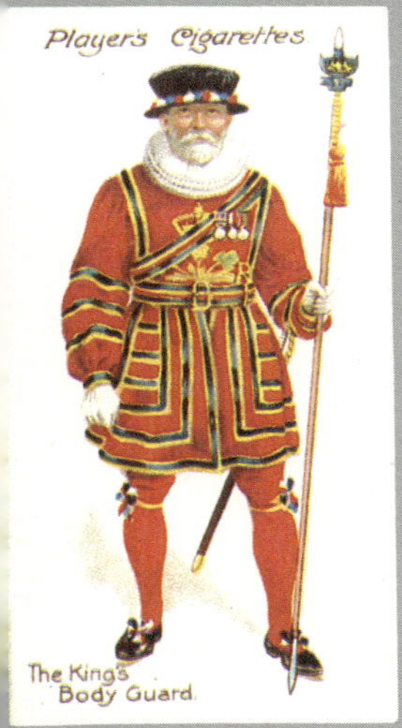

Ceremonial & Court Dress. Player

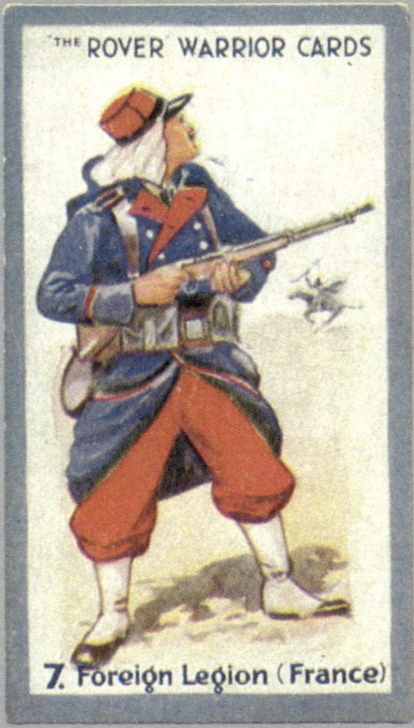

Warrior Cards. Thomson

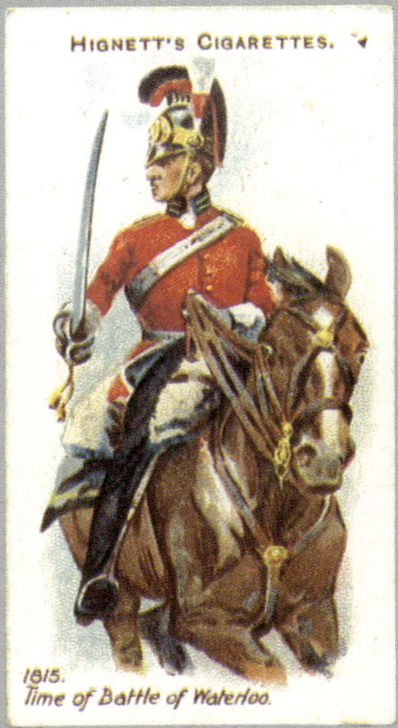

Arms & Armour. Hignett (also Mitchell, Player or Wills)

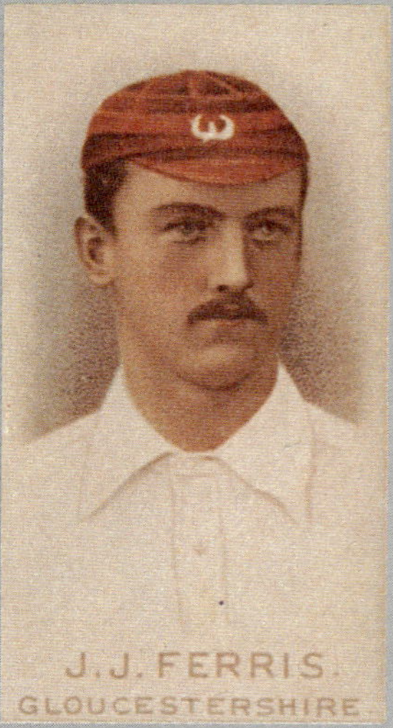

Cricketers, 1896. Wills

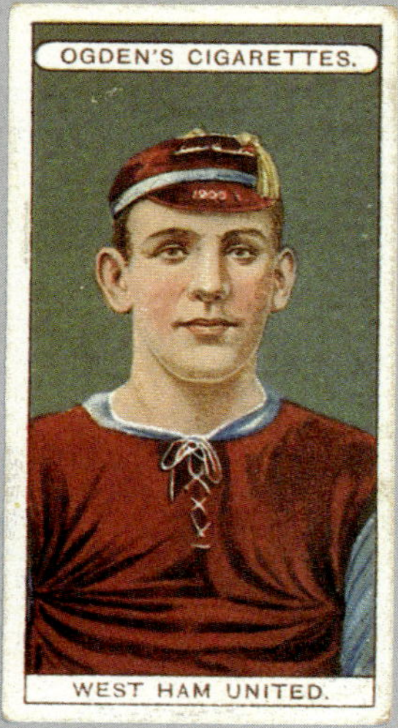

Football Club Colours. Ogden

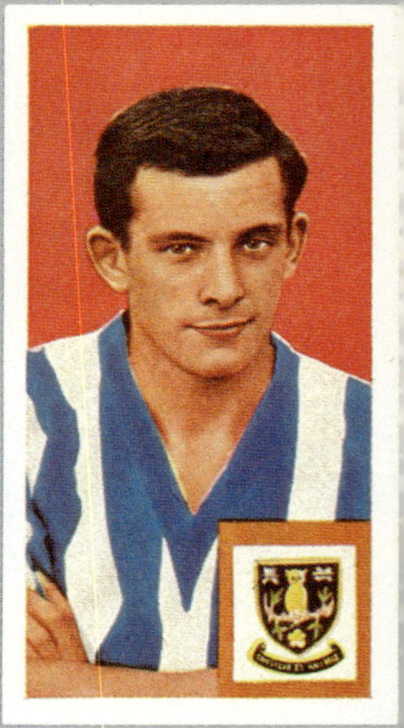
Footballers & Club Colours. Cadet

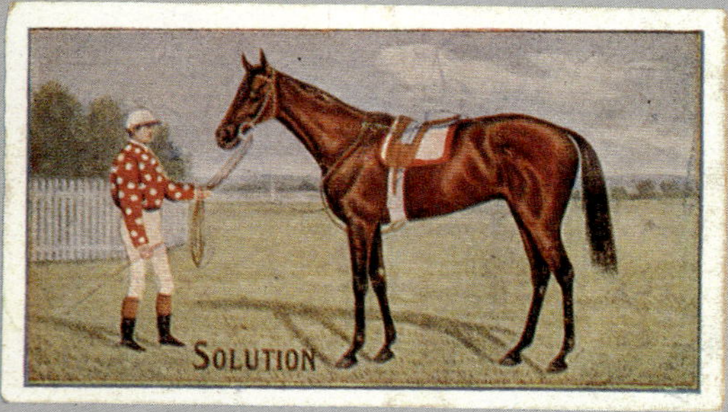

Australian Racehorses. Sniders & Abrahams

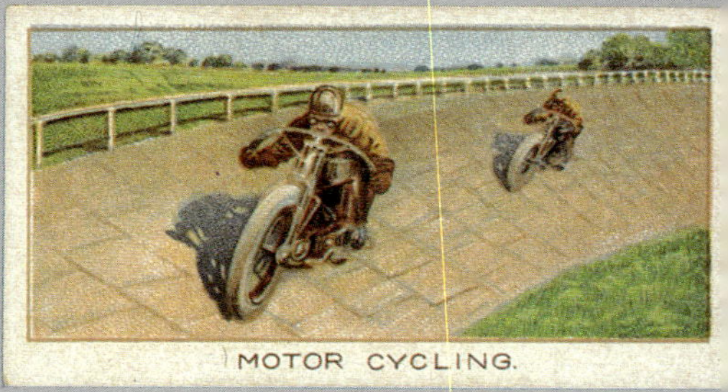

Sports Records. Boguslavsky

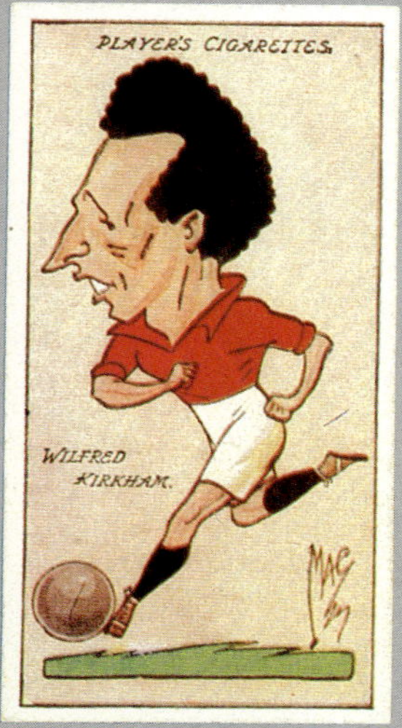

Football Caricatures by MAC.
Player

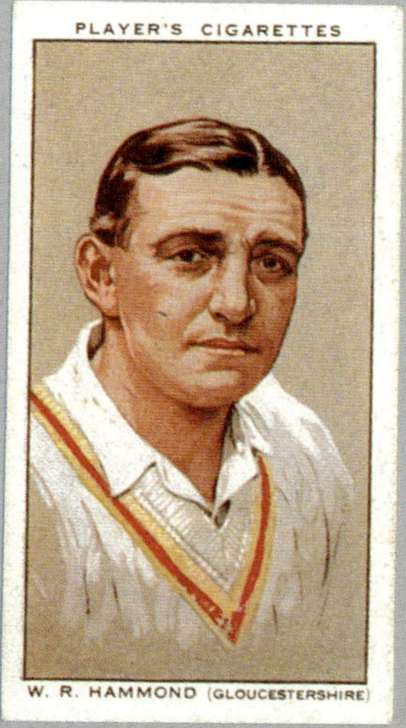

Cricketers, 1934. Player

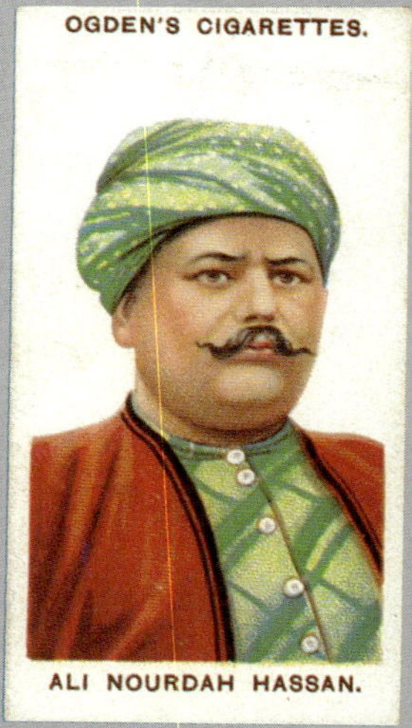

Pugilists & Wrestlers. Ogden

OGDENS LTD.—cont.

Qty		Date	Odds	Sets
F180/200	General Interest Numbered 899-1098	1901	75p	—
F50	General Interest Numbered 1099-1148 ...	1901	50p	£25.00
F18	Golf Base I	1901	£6.00	£100.00
F14	London Street Scenes Base I	1901	£1.25	£17.50
F400	New Series 1	1902	60p	£240.00
F400	New Series B	1902	60p	£240.00
F300	New Series C	1902	50p	£150.00
F46	Pantomime & Theatre Artistes Base D	1899	£1.25	£60.00
LF45	Pantomime & Theatre Artistes Base D	1899	£1.50	£67.50
F50	Pantomime & Theatre Artistes Base M	1899	£1.25	£62.50
F60/62	Politicians, Base D	1900	40p	£24.00
F3	Royalty Base M	1899	£1.00	£3.00
F32	Turner Paintings Base I	1901	75p	£24.00
F10	Views & Scenes Abroad Base I	1901	60p	£6.00
Tabs Type Issues				
75	Actresses (numbered 126-200)	1900	£4.00	—
?200	Actresses (Plain Back)	1900	£1.00	—
200	Actresses & Foreign Views	1900	75p	£150.00
1	General de Wet	1901	—	75p
1	General Interest (Unnumbered)	1901	—	£2.50
?33	General Interest (no Labour clause)	1900	A	—
150	General Interest A Series	1901	30p	£45.00
200	General Interest B Series	1901	30p	£60.00
200	General Interest C Series (1-200)	1902	30p	£60.00
100	General Interest C Series (201-300)	1902	£1.00	—
50	General Interest C Series (301-350)	1902	40p	£20.00
200	General Interest D Series	1903	30p	£60.00
120	General Interest E Series	1903	50p	£60.00
320	General Interest F Series (1-320)	1904	50p	£160.00
100	General Interest F Series (321-420)	1904	£1.25	—
120	General Interest (1-120)	1902	50p	£60.00
196	General Interest (Item 95)	1902	50p	£100.00
100	General Interest (Item 96)	1903	50p	£50.00
100	General Interest (Item 97-1)	1902	75p	£75.00
200	General Interest (Item 97-2)	1902	50p	£100.00
?107	General Interest (Oblong back)	1902	£4.00	—
17	Heroes of the Ring	1901	£2.50	£42.50
1	H.M. The Queen	1901	—	£1.25
2	H.R.H. The Prince of Wales	1901	£1.00	£2.00
14	Imperial Interest	1901	50p	£7.00
106	Imperial or International Interest	1901	40p	£40.00
3	International Interest	1901	50p	£1.50
14	International Interest or a Prominent British Officer	1901	50p	£7.00
71	Leading Artistes of the Day	1901	60p	£42.50
?24	Leading Artistes of the Day (no Labour clause)	1901	A	—
?82	Leading Artistes of the Day (non descriptive)	1901	£4.00	—
22	Leading Athletes	1901	75p	£17.50
15	Leading Favourites of the Turf	1901	£1.25	£19.00
54	Leading Generals at the War	1901	50p	—
25	Leading Generals at the War (Different)	1901	60p	—
47	Leading Generals at the War (Non-Descriptive)	1901	50p	£23.50
25	Leading Generals at the War (Lucky Star) ...	1901	£2.00	—

OGDENS LTD.—cont.

Qty		Date	Odds	Sets
2	Members of Parliament	1901	£1.00	£2.00
11	Notable Coursing Dogs	1901	£1.50	£16.50
12	Our Leading Cricketers	1901	£6.00	£72.00
17	Our Leading Footballers	1901	£1.50	£25.00
37	Prominent British Officers	1901	50p	£18.50
50	Stage Artistes & Celebrities	1900	£1.00	£50.00
1	The Yacht "Columbia"	1901	—	£2.00
1	The Yacht "Shamrock"	1901	—	£2.00

Australian Issues (Tabs Type, Guinea Gold Brand)

1	Christian de Wet	1901	A	—
1	Corporal G. E. Nurse, V.C.	1901	A	—
14	English Cricketer Series	1901	£20.00	—
400	General Interest (Numbered)	1901	£1.50	—
?84	General Interest (Unnumbered)	1901	£2.50	—
1	Imperial Interest	1901	A	—
21	Imperial or International Interest	1901	A	—
4	International Interest	1901	A	—
1	Lady Sarah Wilson	1901	A	—
29	Leading Generals at the War	1901	A	—
8	Prominent British Officers	1901	A	—

Other Overseas Issues

51	Actresses, Black & White (Polo)	1906	£1.50	—
30	Actresses, Brown (Polo)	1908	£1.00	£30.00
17	Animals (Polo)	1916	£6.00	—
60	Animals (Ruler)	1912	£1.50	£90.00
60	Animals (Tabs)	1912	£1.50	£90.00
50	Aviation Series (Tabs)	1912	£1.50	—
45	Beauties—Picture Hats (Polo)	1911	£3.00	—
50	Best Dogs of Their Breed (Polo blue)	1916	£3.00	—
50	Best Dogs of Their Breed (Polo pink)	1916	£3.00	—
52	Birds of Brilliant Plumage, P/C Inset (Ruler)	1914	£1.25	£65.00
25	British Trees & Their Uses (Guinea Gold)	1927	80p	£20.00
25	China's Ancient Warriors (Ruler)	1913	£1.50	£37.50
25	Famous Railway Trains (Guinea Gold)	1928	£1.00	£25.00
20	Flowers (Polo)	1915	£3.00	—
25	Indian Women (Polo)	1919	£2.50	£62.50
30	Music Hall Celebrities (Polo)	1911	£2.00	—
50	Music Hall Celebrities (Tabs)	1911	£2.00	—
52	Playing Cards (Polo)	1922	A	—
50	Riders of the World (Polo)	1911	£1.50	£75.00
50	Russo Japanese Series	1904	A	—
36	Ships & Their Pennants (Polo)	1911	£2.50	—
32	Transport of the World (Polo)	1917	£2.50	—

THE ORLANDO CIGARETTE & CIGAR CO.

40	Home & Colonial Regiments	1901	D	—

W. T. OSBORNE & CO.

40	Naval & Military Phrases	1904	£20.00	—

OSBORNE TOBACCO CO.

Qty		Date	Odds	Sets
50	Modern Aircraft (Blue Front)	1952	—	£1.50
50	Modern Aircraft (Brown Front)	1952	—	£3.50

J. A. PATTREIOUEX LTD.

Early Photographic Sets, Mainly with Serial Letters

Qty		Date	Odds	Sets
F96	Animals (CA1-96)	1926	40p	—
LF50	Animals & Scenes (Unnumbered)	1924	50p	—
LF50	Animals & Scenes (1-50)	1925	50p	—
F192	Animals & Scenes (250-441)	1925	40p	—
F96	Animals & Scenes (CC1-96)	1926	40p	—
LF50	Animals & Scenes (I1-50)	1927	50p	—
F96	Animals & Scenes (JS1-96A)	1928	40p	—
LF100	Animal Studies (A42-141)	1925	40p	—
LF50	Animal Studies (A151-200)	1925	40p	—
LF30	Beauties (JM1-30)	1928	£1.00	—
LF50	British & Egyptian Scenes (CM1-50A)	1927	50p	—
LF50	British Empire Exhibition (JM1-50B)	1928	80p	£40.00
XF100	Cathedrals, Abbeys & Castles (SJ1-100)	1928	£1.00	—
LF30	Child Studies (JM No. 1-30)	1928	£1.00	—
F96	Famous Cricketers (C1-96, plain back)	1926	£5.00	—
F96	Famous Cricketers (C1-96, printed back)	1926	£5.00	—
F192	Famous Footballers (F1-192)	1927	£1.25	—
LF50	Famous Statues (JCM1-50C)	1928	75p	—
F96	Footballers (FA1-96)	1927	£1.25	£120.00
F96	Footballers (FB1-96)	1928	£1.25	£120.00
F96	Footballers (FC1-96)	1928	£1.25	£120.00
LF50	Football Teams (F193-242)	1927	£2.50	—
F96	Natives & Scenes (1-96B)	1926	40p	—
F36	Natives & Scenes (1-36B) (As Above)	1926	40p	—
F96	Natives & Scenes (CB1-96)	1926	40p	—
F96	Natives & Scenes (JS1-96) (As Above)	1926	40p	—
F96	Overseas Scenes (1-96C)	1926	40p	—
LF50	Overseas Scenes (CM1-50B)	1926	50p	—
LF50	Overseas Scenes (JM1-50) (As Above)	1928	50p	£25.00
LF50	Overseas Scenes (CM1-50S)	1927	50p	—
LF50	Overseas Scenes (S101-150) (As Above)	1929	50p	—
F96	Overseas Scenes (1-96D)	1927	40p	—
LF50	Overseas Scenes (1-50E)	1928	50p	—
LF50	Overseas Scenes (1-50F)	1928	60p	—
LF50	Overseas Scenes (JM1-50A)	1928	50p	£25.00
LF50	Scenes (201-250)	1925	50p	£25.00
LF50	Scenes (G1-50)	1927	60p	—
LF50	Scenes (1-50H)	1927	50p	—
LF50	Scenes (JCM1-50D)	1927	50p	—
LF100	Scenes (S1-100)	1928	50p	—
LF4	Scenes (V1-4)	1928	£2.00	—

Other Series

Qty		Date	Odds	Sets
F28	Beautiful Scotland	1939	20p	£5.50
MF48	Beautiful Scotland	1939	12p	£4.00
MF48	Britain from the Air	1939	12p	£3.50
50	British Empire Exhibition Series	1929	80p	£40.00
MF48	British Railways	1938	12p	£6.00
50	Builders of the British Empire	1929	£1.00	£50.00

J. A. PATTREIOUEX LTD.—cont.

Qty		*Date*	*Odds*	*Sets*
50	Celebrities in Sport	1930	80p	£40.00
F28	Coastwise	1939	20p	£5.50
MF48	Coastwise	1939	12p	£3.00
75	Cricketers Series	1928	£2.50	—
50	Dirt Track Riders	1929	£2.00	—
F54	Dirt Track Riders	1935	£2.50	—
MF48	Dogs	1939	12p	£3.00
30	Drawing Made Easy	1930	£1.00	£30.00
F28	Flying	1938	80p	£22.50
MF48	Flying	1938	16p	£8.00
F78	Footballers in Action	1934	£1.00	£78.00
100	Footballers Series	1927	£1.50	—
MF48	Holiday Haunts by the Sea	1938	12p	£3.50
X24	Jackpot Jigsaws	1969	A	—
25	King Lud Problems	1936	£7.50	—
26	Maritime Flags	1931	£5.00	£130.00
F28	Our Countryside	1938	20p	£5.50
MF48	Our Countryside	1938	12p	£3.00
25	Photos of Football Stars	1929	£10.00	—
50	Railway Posters by Famous Artists	1930	£2.50	—
F54	Real Photographs of London	1936	75p	£40.00
F28	Shots from the Films	1938	60p	£16.50
MF48	Sights of Britain	1936	12p	£4.00
MF48	Sights of Britain 2nd Series	1936	12p	£3.00
MF48	Sights of Britain 3rd Series	1937	12p	£4.00
MF48	Sights of London 1st Series	1935	25p	£12.50
MF12	Sights of London—Suplementary Series	1935	40p	£5.00
F54	Sporting Celebrities	1935	£1.00	£55.00
MF96	Sporting Events and Stars	1935	20p	£20.00
50	Sports Trophies	1931	£1.00	£50.00
MF48	The Bridges of Britain	1938	12p	£3.50
52	The English & Welsh Counties	1928	£1.00	£52.00
MF48	The Navy	1937	12p	£5.00
B24	Treasure Isle	1968	A	—
F51	Views	1933	70p	£35.00
F54	Views of Britain	1937	£1.00	£55.00
MF48	Winter Scenes	1937	12p	£3.00

W. PEPPERDY

30	Army Pictures, Cartoons, etc.	1916	B	—

M. PEZARO & SON

25	Armies of the World	1900	C	—
?25	Song Titles Illustrated	1900	C	—

GODFREY PHILLIPS LTD.

50	Actresses (Oval)	1916	£4.00	—
50	Actresses (Oval, Anonymous)	1916	£2.00	£100.00
25	Actresses, C Series (Ball of Beauty)	1900	C	—
25	Actresses, C Series (Carriage)	1900	£15.00	—
25	Actresses, C Series (Derby)	1900	C	—
25	Actresses, C Series (Horseshoe)	1900	£10.00	—
25	Actresses, C Series (Teapot)	1900	C	—
25	Actresses, C Series (Volunteer)	1900	C	—

GODFREY PHILLIPS LTD.—cont.

Qty		Date	Odds	Sets
2	Advertisement Cards	1934	£6.00	£12.00
50	Aircraft	1938	50p	£25.00
54	Aircraft Series No. 1 (matt)	1938	20p	£10.00
54	Aircraft Series No. 1 (varnished)	1938	£2.00	—
40	Animal Series	1903	£3.00	£120.00
M30	Animal Studies	1936	12p	£2.50
50	Annuals	1939	12p	£3.00
L25	Arms of the English Sees	1924	£2.00	£50.00
48	A Selection of BDV Wonderful Gifts	1930	25p	£12.50
48	A Selection of BDV Wonderful Gifts	1931	20p	£10.00
48	A Selection of BDV Wonderful Gifts	1932	15p	£7.50
24	Beauties "HUMPS"	1898	£35.00	—
24	Beauties "HUMPS" (Plums front)	1898	D	—
30	Beauties, Nymphs	1896	£35.00	—
?50	Beauties, Plums (black & white)	1897	C	—
50	Beauties, Plums (green front)	1897	£15.00	—
50	Beauties, Plums (plum front)	1897	£15.00	—
25	Beauties (Numbered 801-825)	1902	£5.00	£125.00
30	Beauties, Oval (Plain Backs)	1914	£1.20	£36.00
44	Beauties of To-day	1937	30p	£13.50
50	Beauties of To-day	1938	12p	£6.00
36	Beauties of To-day 2nd Series	1940	12p	£3.50
F54	Beauties of To-day	1939	25p	£13.50
LF36	Beauties of To-day	1938	£1.00	—
XF36	Beauties of To-day (Unnumbered)	1937	60p	£21.00
XF36	Beauties of To-day 2nd Series	1938	40p	£15.00
XF36	Beauties of To-day 3rd Series	1938	30p	£11.00
XF36	Beauties of To-day 4th Series	1938	40p	£15.00
XF36	Beauties of To-day 5th Series	1938	20p	£7.00
XF36	Beauties of To-day 6th Series	1939	20p	£7.00
XF36	Beauties of To-day 7th Series	1939	20p	£7.00
XF36	Beauties of To-day (B.D.V. Back)	1939	12p	£3.50
36	Beauties of the World	1931	40p	£15.00
36	Beauties of the World Series No. 2	1933	60p	£22.00
50	Beautiful Women (I.F. Series)	1908	£3.50	£175.00
50	Beautiful Women (W.I. Series)	1908	£3.50	£175.00
L50	Beautiful Women	1908	£6.00	£300.00
P30	Beauty Spots of the Homeland	1938	16p	£5.00
50	Bird Painting	1938	12p	£6.00
25	Boxer Rebellion	1904	£10.00	—
50	British Beauties (Photogravure)	1916	£2.00	£100.00
K76	British Beauties	1916	£1.50	£115.00
F54	British Beauties (1-54)	1914	£1.25	£65.00
F54	British Beauties (55-108)	1915	£1.25	£65.00
108	British Beauties (Plain Back)	1914	£1.50	—
50	British Birds and Their Eggs	1936	20p	£10.00
30	British Butterflies, No. 1 Issue	1911	£2.00	£60.00
25	British Butterflies	1927	20p	£5.00
25	British Butterflies (Transfers)	1936	16p	£4.00
25	British Orders of Chivalry & Valour (De Reszke)	1939	80p	£20.00
25	British Orders of Chivalry & Valour (Phillips)	1939	80p	£20.00
25	British Warships	1915	£3.00	£75.00
L25	British Warships	1915	£20.00	—

Qty		*Date*	*Odds*	*Sets*
F80	British Warships	1916	£6.00	—
50	Busts of Famous People (brown back)	1907	£5.00	—
50	Busts of Famous People (green back)	1907	£2.50	£125.00
M36	Characters Come to Life	1938	12p	£3.00
25	Chinese Series (English text)	1910	£2.50	£62.50
25	Chinese Series (Volunteer Cigarettes)	1910	£3.00	£75.00
M25	Cinema Stars (Circular)	1924	40p	£10.00
F52	Cinema Stars (Set 1)	1923	£1.00	£50.00
30	Cinema Stars (Brown)	1924	£1.00	£30.00
30	Cinema Stars (Black & White)	1925	60p	£18.00
32	Cinema Stars (Black & White)	1930	40p	£12.50
32	Cinema Stars (Brown, Hand Coloured)	1934	60p	£20.00
30	Cinema Stars (Plain Back)	1935	16p	£5.00
50	Colonial Troops	1902	£12.50	—
50	Coronation of Their Majesties	1937	12p	£3.00
M36	Coronation of Their Majesties	1937	12p	£2.50
P24	Coronation of Their Majesties	1937	40p	£10.00
KF198	Cricketers (Pinnace)	1924	£1.50	—
F192	Cricketers (Brown Back)	1924	£1.50	—
LF25	Cricketers (Brown Back)	1924	£3.00	£75.00
LF?75	Cricketers (Pinnace)	1924	A	—
1	Cricket Fixture Card	1936	—	£2.00
25	Derby Winners & Jockeys	1923	80p	£20.00
30	Eggs, Nests & Birds (Numbered)	1912	£2.50	£75.00
30	Eggs, Nests & Birds (Unnumbered)	1912	£2.50	£75.00
25	Empire Industries	1927	30p	£7.50
49/50	Evolution of the British Navy	1930	30p	£15.00
25	Famous Boys	1924	80p	£20.00
32	Famous Cricketers	1926	£1.25	£40.00
25	Famous Crowns	1938	12p	£3.00
50	Famous Footballers	1936	35p	£17.50
M36	Famous Love Scenes	1939	12p	£4.00
50	Famous Minors	1936	12p	£3.50
P26	Famous Paintings	1936	80p	£21.00
25	Feathered Friends	1928	50p	£12.50
50	Film Favourites	1934	12p	£4.00
50	Film Stars	1934	15p	£7.50
P24	Film Stars (Series of Cards) (Vivid Fronts)	1934	30p	£7.50
P24	Film Stars (Series of 24 Cards)	1934	30p	£7.50
P24	Film Stars, 2nd (25-48)	1934	80p	£20.00
50	First Aid	1923	40p	£20.00
25	First Aid Series	1914	£2.50	£62.50
25	Fish	1924	60p	£15.00
M30	Flower Studies	1937	12p	£2.50
P30	Flower Studies	1937	25p	£7.50
KF940	Footballers (Pinnace 1-940)	1922	30p	—
KF1522	Footballers (Pinnace 941-2462)	1923	60p	—
LF2462	Footballers (Pinnace)	1923	75p	—
P30	Garden Studies	1938	15p	£4.50
13	General Interest	1899	£20.00	£260.00
90	Guinea Gold Series (Numbered)	1900	£2.00	£180.00
100	Guinea Gold Series	1900	£2.00	£200.00
160	Guinea Gold Series	1900	£1.50	£240.00
100	Guinea Gold Series (Brown)	1900	£3.50	—

Qty		Date	Odds	Sets
25	Home Pets	1924	60p	£15.00
25	How to Build a Two Valve Set	1929	30p	£7.50
25	How To Do It Series	1913	£3.00	£75.00
25	How to Make a Valve Amplifier	1924	80p	£20.00
25	How to Make Your Own Wireless Set	1923	50p	£12.50
25	Indian Series	1908	£5.00	£125.00
54	In the Public Eye	1935	12p	£3.50
50	International Caps	1936	20p	£10.00
35/37	Kings & Queens of England	1925	60p	£21.00
25	Lawn Tennis	1930	50p	£12.50
K52	Miniature Playing Cards (Red back)	1906	B	—
K53	Miniature Playing Cards (Blue Design)	1934	25p	£12.50
K53	Miniature Playing Cards (Buff)	1932	25p	£12.50
K53	Miniature Playing Cards (White)	1933	30p	—
K53	Miniature Playing Cards (Yellow)	1933	30p	—
25	Model Railways	1927	80p	£20.00
30	Morse Signalling	1916	£3.00	£90.00
50	Motor Cars at a Glance	1924	£1.20	£60.00
20	Novelty Series	1924	£4.00	£80.00
25	Old Favourites	1924	60p	£15.00
M36	Old Masters	1939	16p	£6.00
36	Olympic Champions, Amsterdam 1928	1928	40p	£15.00
25	Optical Illusions	1927	50p	£12.50
36	Our Dogs	1939	35p	£12.50
M30	Our Dogs	1939	12p	£3.00
P30	Our Dogs	1939	£1.25	£37.50
M48	Our Favourites	1935	12p	£3.00
P30	Our Glorious Empire	1939	25p	£7.50
M30	Our Puppies	1936	12p	£3.00
P30	Our Puppies	1936	20p	£6.00
25	Personalities of To-day	1932	30p	£7.50
25	Popular Superstitions	1930	30p	£7.50
25	Prizes for Needlework	1925	70p	£17.50
25	Railway Engines	1934	80p	£20.00
KF27	Real Photo Series (War Leaders)	1916	£5.00	£135.00
1	Real Stamp Card	1928	—	35p
25	Red Indians	1927	60p	£15.00
20	Russo Japanese War Series	1905	C	—
25	School Badges	1927	30p	£7.50
48	Screen Stars A	1936	12p	£6.00
48	Screen Stars B (different)	1936	12p	£6.00
48	Screen Stars (not embossed)	1936	15p	£7.50
30	Semaphore Signalling	1916	£3.00	£90.00
25	Ships and their Flags	1924	£1.20	£30.00
M36	Ships that have Made History	1938	12p	£3.00
M48	Shots from the Films	1934	12p	£4.00
50	Soccer Stars	1936	20p	£10.00
36	Soldiers of The King	1939	20p	£7.50
M20	Special Jubilee Year Series	1935	12p	£2.50
P12	Special Jubilee Year Series	1935	75p	£9.00
30	Speed Champions	1930	30p	£9.00
36	Sporting Champions	1929	30p	£11.00
25	Sporting Series	1910	£5.00	—
25	Sports	1923	£1.20	£30.00

Qty		Date	Odds	Sets
50	Sportsmen—Spot the Winner	1937	12p	£3.50
35	Stage & Cinema Beauties A	1933	15p	£5.00
35	Stage & Cinema Beauties B (Different)	1933	20p	£7.00
50	Stage & Cinema Beauties (Different)	1935	40p	£20.00
54	Stars of the Screen	1934	40p	£22.00
48	Stars of the Screen (Different)	1936	12p	£5.00
25	Statues & Monuments (brown back)	1907	B	—
25	Statues & Monuments (green back)	1907	£3.00	£75.00
25	Territorial Series (Motors Back)	1908	£10.00	£250.00
25	The 1924 Cabinet	1924	60p	£15.00
48	The "Old Country"	1935	25p	£12.50
50	This Mechanized Age 1st Series (adhesive)	1936	12p	£3.00
50	This Mechanized Age 1st Series (non-adhesive)	1936	12p	£5.00
50	This Mechanized Age 2nd Series	1937	15p	£7.50
25	Types of British & Colonial Troops	1899	£25.00	—
25	Types of British Soldiers (M651-M675)	1900	£7.00	£175.00
F63	War Photos	1916	£3.00	—
X20	Wrestling Holds	1930	A	—
XS30	Zoo Studies—Come to Life Series	1939	50p	£15.00
X1	Zoo Studies Viewer	1939		50p
BDV Package Issues				
17	Boxers	1932	75p	—
53	Cricketers	1932	£1.50	—
67	Film Stars	1932	50p	—
132	Footballers	1932	60p	—
19	Jockeys	1932	60p	—
21	Speedway Riders	1932	£1.25	—
38	Sportsmen	1932	60p	—
"Sports" Package Issues				
50	All Sports 1st	1948	60p	—
25	All Sports 2nd	1949	60p	—
25	All Sports 3rd	1953	60p	£15.00
25	All Sports 4th	1954	60p	—
25	Cricketers 1st	1948	£2.00	—
25	Cricketers 2nd	1951	£2.00	£50.00
25	Footballers 1st	1948	75p	—
50	Footballers 2nd	1950	75p	—
25	Footballers 3rd	1951	75p	—
25	Jockeys	1952	60p	—
25	Radio Stars	1949	60p	—
25	Rugby & Association Footballers	1952	60p	—
Overseas Issues				
50	Animal Studies	1930	£1.00	£50.00
50	Annuals	1939	40p	£20.00
X32	Australian Birds (Cartons)	1968	—	£2.50
X24	Australian Scenes (Cartons)	1965	—	£2.50
50	Australian Sporting Celebrities	1932	80p	£40.00
X32	Australian Wild Flowers (Cartons)	1967	A	—
50	Film Stars	1934	80p	£40.00
G16	Gemstones (Cartons)	1970	—	£2.50
50	Stars of British Films	1934	80p	£40.00
38	Test Cricketers	1932	£1.00	£38.00

Qty		Date	Odds	Sets
X32	The Barrier Reef (Cartons)	1968	—	£2.50
50	Victorian Footballers	1933	80p	—
75	Victorian Footballers	1933	£1.00	—
50	Victorian League and Association Footballers	1934	80p	—
100	Who's Who in Australian Sport	1933	75p	£75.00
Silk Issues				
M62	Arms of Countries & Territories	1912	£1.00	—
B32	Beauties—Modern Paintings	1910	£2.50	—
P32	Beauties—Modern Paintings	1910	£12.50	—
B100	Birds	1920	75p	—
M12	Birds of the Tropics	1913	£3.00	—
L12	Birds of the Tropics	1913	£3.50	—
P12	Birds of the Tropics	1913	£6.00	—
X24	British Admirals	1916	£2.00	—
D50	British Butterflies & Moths	1922	75p	—
M108	British Naval Crests (Anon)	1918	40p	—
M108	British Naval Crests (B.D.V.)	1918	50p	—
B23	Butterflies	1911	£4.00	—
B47	Ceramic Art	1925	40p	£20.00
M47	Ceramic Art	1925	40p	£20.00
L47	Ceramic Art	1925	60p	—
B65	Clan Tartans	1922	30p	—
M65	Clan Tartans (B.D.V.)	1922	40p	£26.00
M49	Clan Tartans (Anon)	1922	50p	£25.00
L56	Clan Tartans	1922	£2.00	—
P12	Clan Tartans	1922	£1.50	£18.00
M108	Colonial Army Badges	1913	75p	—
M17	County Cricket Badges (Anon)	1921	£5.00	—
M17	County Cricket Badges (BDV)	1921	£5.00	—
M108	Crests & Badges of the British Army (Anon, Numbered)	1914	40p	£40.00
M108	Crests & Badges of the British Army (Anon, Unnumbered)	1914	50p	£54.00
M108	Crests & Badges of the British Army (BDV)	1914	40p	£40.00
L108	Crests & Badges of the British Army (Anon)	1914	75p	—
L108	Crests & Badges of the British Army (BDV)	1914	60p	—
M143	Flags, Set 4 (Short)	1913	40p	—
L142	Flags, Set 4 (Long)	1913	£1.25	—
M24	Flags, Set 5 (With Caption)	1913	40p	£10.00
M12	Flags, Set 5 (No Caption)	1913	50p	£6.00
G8	Flags, Set 5	1913	£5.00	—
M18	Flags, Set 6	1913	40p	£7.00
M20	Flags, Set 7	1913	60p	£12.00
M50	Flags, 5th Series	1914	60p	—
M120	Flags, 7th Series	1914	30p	£36.00
L120	Flags, 10th Series	1915	40p	—
M120	Flags, 12th Series	1915	50p	—
L65	Flags, 15th Series	1916	75p	—
L64	Flags, 16th Series	1916	75p	£48.00
M132	Flags, 20th Series	1917	50p	—
M126	Flags, 25th Series	1917	40p	£50.00
L62	Flags, 25th Series	1917	£1.50	—
M112	Flags, 26th Series	1918	35p	—

Qty		*Date*	*Odds*	*Sets*
M70	Flags, 28th Series	1918	30p	£21.00
P18	Flags, Set 13	1914	60p	£10.50
G23	Flags, Set 13 (Anon)	1914	60p	£14.00
G27	Flags, Set 13 (BDV)	1914	60p	£16.00
M21	Football Colours (Anon)	1920	£1.50	—
M86	Football Colours (BDV)	1920	75p	—
P78	Football Colours	1920	75p	—
M126	G.P. Territorial Badges	1913	50p	—
L25	Great War Leaders (Sepia)	1915	£1.25	—
M3	Great War Leaders & Celebrities (Anon)	1916	£2.00	£6.00
M4	Great War Leaders & Celebrities (BDV)	1916	£2.00	£8.00
L3	Great War Leaders & Celebrities (Anon)	1916	£2.00	£6.00
L2	Great War Leaders & Celebrities (BDV)	1916	£2.00	£4.00
P18	Great War Leaders & Celebrities (BDV)	1916	£1.25	—
G30	Great War Leaders & Celebrities (Anon)	1916	£1.25	—
G47	Great War Leaders & Celebrities (BDV)	1916	£1.25	—
M51	Great War Leaders & Warships	1914	£2.00	—
B25	Heraldic Series	1924	40p	£10.00
M25	Heraldic Series	1924	40p	£10.00
L25	Heraldic Series	1924	£1.50	—
X12	Heraldic Series	1924	£1.50	£18.00
M26	House Flags	1920	£3.00	—
M10	Irish Patriots	1919	£4.00	—
X10	Irish Patriots	1919	£5.00	—
P10	Irish Patriots	1919	£5.00	—
M1	Irish Republican Stamp	1925	—	75p
M1	Let 'Em All Come	1920	—	£2.00
M54	Naval Badges of Rank & Military Headdress	1917	£2.00	—
G1	Nelson's Signal at Trafalgar	1921	A	—
G40	Old Masters, Set 1	1911	£10.00	£400.00
G20	Old Masters, Set 2 (Anon)	1912	£2.00	£40.00
G20	Old Masters, Set 2 (BDV)	1912	£1.50	£30.00
M85	Old Masters, Set 3 (Anon)	1912	75p	—
M40	Old Masters, Set 3 (BDV)	1912	£1.00	—
M120	Old Masters, Set 4	1913	60p	£72.00
M20	Old Masters, Set 5 (Anon, Unnumbered)	1915	£1.50	—
M20	Old Masters, Set 5 (Anon, 101-120)	1915	50p	£10.00
M60	Old Masters, Set 5 (BDV 1-60)	1915	30p	—
M20	Old Masters, Set 5 (BDV 101-120)	1915	50p	£10.00
B50	Old Masters, Set 6	1924	40p	—
M50	Old Masters, Set 7 (301-350)	1916	£1.25	—
M50	Orders of Chivalry (Anon)	1920	75p	—
M24	Orders of Chivalry (BDV, 1-24)	1920	60p	£15.00
M24	Orders of Chivalry (GP401-424)	1920	75p	—
M25	Pilot & Signal Flags (Anon)	1921	75p	—
M25	Pilot & Signal Flags (BDV)	1921	60p	£15.00
L72	Regimental Colours	1918	£1.50	—
M50	Regimental Colours, Series 12	1918	60p	£30.00
M120	Regimental Colours & Crests (Anon)	1918	60p	—
M120	Regimental Colours & Crests (BDV)	1918	60p	—
G120	Regimental Colours & Crests (Anon)	1918	£3.00	—
G120	Regimental Colours & Crests (BDV)	1918	£2.50	—
M10	Religious Pictures	1911	£5.00	—
X10	Religious Pictures	1911	£5.00	—

GODFREY PHILLIPS LTD.—cont.

Qty		Date	Odds	Sets
G10	Religious Pictures	1911	£6.00	—
B1	The Allies Flags	1916	—	£4.00
G2	The Allies Flags (Anon)	1916	£3.00	—
G2	The Allies Flags (BDV)	1916	£3.00	—
M75	Town & City Arms	1918	40p	—
L75	Town & City Arms	1918	60p	—
M25	Victoria Cross Heroes I	1915	£3.00	—
M25	Victoria Cross Heroes II (With Flags)	1915	£5.00	—
M90	War Pictures	1915	£2.00	—

JOHN PLAYER & SONS

25	Actors & Actresses	1898	£12.00	£300.00
50	Actresses	1897	£12.00	£600.00
8	Advertisement Cards	1894	D	—
1	Advertisement Card—Sailor	1929	—	£2.00
L1	Advertisement Card—Sailor	1929	—	£7.50
L1	Advertisement Card—Wants List	1936	—	60p
50	Aeroplanes (Eire)	1935	30p	£15.00
50	Aeroplanes (Civil)	1935	12p	£6.00
50	Aircraft of the Royal Air Force	1938	12p	£6.00
X10	Allied Cavalry	1914	£4.00	£40.00
L24	A Nature Calendar	1930	75p	£18.00
50	Animals of the Countryside	1939	12p	£3.50
50	Animals of the Countryside (Eire)	1939	30p	—
L25	Aquarium Studies	1932	50p	£12.50
L25	Architectural Beauties	1927	50p	£12.50
50	Arms & Armour (blue back)	1909	£1.25	£62.50
50	Army Corps & Divisional Signs (1-50)	1924	12p	£3.50
100	Army Corps & Divisional Signs 2nd (51-150)	1925	12p	£10.00
25	Army Life	1910	30p	£7.50
X12	Artillery in Action	1917	£2.00	£24.00
50	A Sectional Map of Ireland	1932	75p	£37.50
50	Association Cup Winners	1930	20p	£10.00
50	Aviary and Cage Birds	1933	12p	£6.00
50	Aviary and Cage Birds (Transfers)	1933	12p	£5.00
L25	Aviary & Cage Birds	1935	50p	£12.50
50	Badges & Flags of British Regiments (Green)	1903	£1.00	£50.00
50	Badges & Flags of British Regiments (Brown back, Numbered)	1904	£1.00	£50.00
50	Badges & Flags of British Regiments (Brown back, Unnumbered)	1904	£1.25	£62.50
50	Birds & Their Young	1937	12p	£3.00
50	Birds & Their Young (Eire) (adhesive)	1937	40p	—
50	Birds & Their Young (Eire) (non-adhesive)	1937	40p	—
25	Birds & Their Young (non adhesive)	Unissued	12p	£1.25
25	Birds & Their Young 2nd (non adhesive)	Unissued	12p	£1.25
CF10	Bookmarks (Authors)	1900	£30.00	£300.00
25	Boxing (Eire)	1934	£1.00	£25.00
50	Boy Scouts & Girl Guide	1933	12p	£4.00
50	Boy Scouts & Girl Guide (Transfers)	1933	12p	£5.00
L25	British Butterflies	1934	50p	£12.50
50	British Empire Series	1904	40p	£20.00
25	British Live Stock	1915	35p	£9.00

Qty		Date	Odds	Sets
X25	British Live Stock (Blue Back)	1923	50p	£12.50
X25	British Live Stock (Brown Back)	1916	£1.50	£37.50
L25	British Naval Craft	1939	12p	£3.50
X20	British Pedigree Stock	1925	75p	£15.00
L25	British Regalia	1937	30p	£7.50
50	Butterflies	1932	25p	£12.50
50	Butterflies (Transfers)	1932	12p	£5.00
50	Butterflies & Moths	1904	£1.00	£50.00
25	Bygone Beauties	1914	40p	£10.00
X10	Bygone Beauties	1916	£1.00	£10.00
G?30	Cabinet Size Pictures	1896	£40.00	—
20	Castles & Abbeys (no border)	1895	£15.00	£300.00
20	Castles & Abbeys (white border)	1895	£15.00	£300.00
L24	Cats	1936	£1.50	£36.00
50	Celebrated Bridges	1903	£1.20	£60.00
50	Celebrated Gateways	1909	50p	£25.00
25	Ceremonial and Court Dress	1911	25p	£6.25
L25	Championship Golf Courses	1936	50p	£12.50
25	Characters from Dickens A Series (1-25)	1912	30p	£7.50
25	Characters from Dickens 2nd Series (26-50)	1912	30p	£7.50
50	Characters from Dickens (Reprint)	1923	50p	£12.50
X10	Characters from Dickens	1914	75p	£7.50
L25	Characters from Fiction	1933	60p	£15.00
25	Characters from Thackeray	1913	25p	£6.25
50	Cities of the World	1900	£2.00	£100.00
L20	Clocks—Old & New	1928	£1.50	£30.00
25	Colonial & Indian Army Badges	1917	20p	£5.00
50	Coronation Series—Ceremonial Dress	1937	12p	£4.50
25	Counties and Their Industries (Numbered)	1914	40p	£10.00
25	Counties and Their Industries (Unnumbered)	1914	40p	£10.00
50	Countries Arms &Flags	1905	16p	£8.00
50	Country Seats and Arms (1-50)	1909	30p	£15.00
50	Country Seats and Arms 2nd Series (51-100)	1910	30p	£15.00
50	Country Seats and Arms 3rd Series (101-150)	1910	30p	£15.00
L25	Country Sports	1930	40p	£10.00
50	Cricketers 1930	1930	25p	£12.50
50	Cricketers 1934	1934	12p	£6.00
50	Cricketers 1938	1938	12p	£5.00
50	Cricketers, Caricatures by "RIP"	1926	50p	£25.00
25	Cries of London A Series	1913	60p	£15.00
X10	Cries of London A Series	1912	£1.50	£15.00
X10	Cries of London 2nd Series	1914	£1.00	£10.00
25	Cries of London 2nd Series	1916	25p	£6.25
50	Curious Beaks	1929	12p	£5.00
50	Cycling	1939	12p	£5.00
50	Cycling (Eire) (adhesive)	1939	40p	—
50	Cycling (Eire) (non-adhesive)	1939	40p	—
50	Dandies	1932	12p	£5.00
L25	Dandies	1932	20p	£5.00
50	Decorations & Medals	Unissued	1.00	£50.00
50	Derby and Grand National Winners	1933	25p	£12.50
50	Derby and Grand National Winners (Transfers)	1933	12p	£5.00
50	Dogs (Scenic Background)	1925	15p	£7.50
X12	Dogs (Scenic Background)	1924	40p	£5.00

JOHN PLAYER & SONS—cont.

Qty		Date	Odds	Sets
50	Dogs, by Wardle (Full Length)	1931	12p	£5.00
50	Dogs, by Wardle (Transfers)	1931	12p	£5.00
L25	Dogs, by Wardle (Full Length)	1933	50p	£12.50
50	Dogs, by Wardle (Heads)	1929	12p	£5.00
L20	Dogs, by Wardle A Series (Heads)	1926	75p	£15.00
L20	Dogs, by Wardle 2nd Series (Heads)	1928	60p	£12.00
25	Dogs, by Wardle (Eire) A Series (Heads)	1927	60p	£15.00
25	Dogs, by Wardle 2nd Series (Eire) (Heads)	1929	60p	£15.00
50	Dogs Heads by Biegel	Unissued	12p	£4.00
L25	Dogs (Heads)	Unissued	30p	£7.50
50	Dogs' Heads (Silver Background, Eire)	1940	60p	£30.00
50	Drum Banners & Cap Badges	1924	16p	£8.00
25	Egyptian Kings & Queens and Classical Deities	1912	25p	£6.25
X10	Egyptian Sketches	1915	£2.00	£20.00
25	England's Military Heroes (Narrow)	1898	£12.50	—
25	England's Military Heroes (Wide)	1898	£20.00	—
25	England's Naval Heroes (Non-Descriptive Narrow)	1897	£10.00	—
25	England's Naval Heroes (Non-Descriptive Wide)	1897	£20.00	—
25	England's Naval Heroes (Descriptive, Narrow)	1898	£10.00	—
25	England's Naval Heroes (Descriptive, Wide)	1898	£20.00	—
25	Everyday Phrases by Tom Browne	1901	£8.00	£200.00
L25	Fables of Aesop	1927	80p	£20.00
20	Famous Authors & Poets (Narrow)	1900	£7.50	£150.00
20	Famous Authors & Poets (Wide)	1900	£10.00	£200.00
L25	Famous Beauties	1937	20p	£5.00
50	Famous Irish Bred Horses	1936	60p	£30.00
50	Famous Irish Greyhounds	1935	80p	£40.00
X10	Famous Paintings	1913	£2.00	£20.00
50	Film Stars	1934	25p	£12.50
50	Film Stars Second Series	1934	12p	£6.00
50	Film Stars Second Series (Eire)	1934	50p	—
50	Film Stars Third Series	1938	12p	£5.00
L25	Film Stars	1934	80p	£20.00
L25	Film Stars (Eire)	1934	A	—
50	Firefighting Appliances	1930	20p	£10.00
50	Fishes of the World	1903	80p	£40.00
50	Flags of the League of Nations	1928	12p	£4.00
50	Football Caricatures by "MAC"	1927	12p	£6.00
50	Footballers, Caricatures by "RIP"	1926	12p	£6.00
50	Footballers 1928	1928	15p	£7.50
25	Footballers 1928-9, 2nd Series	1929	20p	£5.00
50	Fresh-water Fishes (pink back)	1933	20p	£10.00
50	Fresh-water Fishes (white back)	1934	30p	£15.00
L25	Fresh-water Fishes	1935	50p	£12.50
L25	Fresh-water Fishes (Eire, non-adhesive)	1935	£2.00	—
25	From Plantation to Smoker	1926	12p	£3.00
50	Gallery of Beauty Series	1896	£12.50	£625.00
50	Game Birds and Wild Fowl	1927	20p	£10.00
L25	Game Birds & Wild Fowl	1928	£1.00	£25.00
25	Gems of British Scenery	1917	16p	£4.00
50	Gilbert and Sullivan	1925	16p	£8.00
X25	Gilbert & Sullivan	1926	80p	£20.00

JOHN PLAYER & SONS—cont.

Qty		Date	Odds	Sets
50	Gilbert and Sullivan 2nd Series	1927	12p	£6.00
L25	Gilbert & Sullivan 2nd Series	1928	80p	£20.00
L25	Golf	1939	50p	£12.50
25	Hidden Beauties	1929	12p	£2.50
25	Highland Clans	1907	£1.20	£30.00
50	Hints on Association Football	1934	12p	£6.00
X10	Historic Ships	1910	£2.00	£20.00
50	History of Naval Dress	1930	20p	£10.00
L25	History of Naval Dress	1929	70p	£17.50
50	International Air Liners	1936	12p	£5.00
50	International Air Liners (Eire)	1936	35p	—
25	Irish Place Names A Series	1927	60p	£15.00
25	Irish Place Names 2nd Series	1929	60p	£15.00
M5	Jubilee Issue	1960	50p	£2.50
50	Kings & Queens of England	1935	25p	£12.50
L50	Kings & Queens of England	1935	60p	£30.00
50	Life on Board a Man Of War in 1805 and 1905	1905	£1.00	£50.00
25	Live Stock	1925	£1.00	—
50	Military Head-dress	1931	25p	£12.50
50	Military Series	1900	£8.00	£400.00
50	Military Uniforms of the British Empire Overseas	1938	12p	£6.00
25	Miniatures	1923	12p	£3.00
50	Modern Naval Craft	1939	12p	£3.00
50	Modern Naval Craft (Eire)	1939	25p	—
50	Motor Cars A Series	1936	25p	£12.50
50	Motor Cars (Eire) A Series	1936	50p	—
50	Motor Cars 2nd Series	1937	25p	£12.50
L20	Mount Everest	1925	£1.00	£20.00
25	Napoleon	1916	40p	£10.00
50	National Flags and Arms	1936	12p	£3.50
50	National Flags and Arms (Eire)	1936	30p	—
50	Natural History	1924	12p	£4.00
X12	Natural History	1924	40p	£5.00
X12	Natural History, 2nd Series	1924	40p	£5.00
50	Nature Series	1909	50p	£25.00
X10	Nature Series (Birds)	1908	£6.00	£60.00
X10	Nature Series (Mammals)	1913	£2.50	£25.00
50	Old England's Defenders	1898	£8.00	£400.00
L25	Old Hunting Prints	1938	50p	£12.50
L25	Old Naval Prints	1936	80p	£20.00
X25	Old Sporting Prints	1924	80p	£20.00
L25	Picturesque Bridges	1929	60p	£15.00
L25	Picturesque Cottages	1929	60p	£15.00
L25	Picturesque London	1931	80p	£20.00
25	Players Past & Present	1916	25p	£6.25
25	Polar Exploration A Series	1915	30p	£7.50
25	Polar Exploration, 2nd Series	1916	30p	£7.50
L25	Portals of the Past	1930	50p	£12.50
50	Poultry	1931	16p	£8.00
50	Poultry (Transfers)	1931	12p	£5.00
25	Products of the World	1908	20p	£5.00
50	Products of the World (Different)	1928	12p	£3.50
25	Racehorses	1926	£1.20	£30.00

JOHN PLAYER & SONS—cont.

Qty		*Date*	*Odds*	*Sets*
40	Racing Caricatures	1925	20p	£10.00
L25	Racing Yachts	1938	25p	£6.25
50	R.A.F. Badges (No Motto)	1937	12p	£4.50
50	R.A.F. Badges (With Motto)	1937	12p	£6.00
50	Regimental Colours & Cap Badges (Regulars)	1907	40p	£20.00
50	Regimental Colours & Cap Badges (Territorials, Blue Back)	1910	40p	£20.00
50	Regimental Colours & Cap Badges (Territorials, Brown Back)	1910	40p	£20.00
50	Regimental Standards and Cap Badges	1930	20p	£10.00
50	Regimental Uniforms (Blue)	1912	50p	£25.00
50	Regimental Uniforms (Brown)	1914	60p	£30.00
X10	Regimental Uniforms (Different)	1914	£4.00	£40.00
50	Regimental Uniforms 2nd Series (51-100)	1913	50p	£25.00
50	Riders of the World	1905	50p	£25.00
P30	Rulers & Views	1902	£35.00	—
50	Sea Fishes	1935	12p	£3.50
50	Sea Fishes (Eire)	1935	40p	—
50	Screen Celebrities (Eire)	1938	50p	—
25	Shakespearean Series	1917	25p	£6.25
L20	Ship-Models	1926	£1.00	£20.00
50	Shipping	Unissued	—	£40.00
25	Ships' Figure-heads	1912	40p	£10.00
L25	Ships' Figure-heads	1931	60p	£15.00
L8	Snap Cards	1930	£5.00	£40.00
50	Speedway Riders	1937	25p	£12.50
S150	Stereoscopic Series	1904	£15.00	—
50	Straight Line Caricatures	1926	16p	£8.00
25	Struggle for Existence	1923	12p	£3.00
50	Tennis	1936	12p	£4.00
116	The Corsair Game (Eire)	1965	A	—
L25	The Nation's Shrines	1929	60p	£15.00
X1	The Royal Family	1937	—	75p
P6	The Royal Family	1901	£15.00	£90.00
25	Those Pearls of Heaven	1916	20p	£5.00
66	Transvaal Series	1902	£2.00	—
L25	Treasures of Britain	1931	40p	£10.00
25	Treasures of Ireland	1930	60p	£15.00
L25	Types of Horses	1939	60p	£15.00
50	Uniforms of the Territorial Army	1939	12p	£6.00
50	Useful Plants & Fruits	1902	£1.00	£50.00
25	Victoria Cross	1914	40p	£10.00
90	War Decorations & Medals	1927	25p	£22.50
50	Wild Animals' Heads	1931	12p	£4.00
50	Wild Animals' Heads (Transfers)	1931	12p	£5.00
L25	Wild Animals (Heads) A Series	1927	80p	£20.00
L25	Wild Animals (Heads) 2nd Series	1932	60p	£15.00
45	Wild Animals of the World (Narrow) (no Ltd)	1901	£3.00	—
45	Wild Animals of the World (Narrow) (with Ltd)	1901	£3.00	—
50	Wild Animals of the World (Wide) (no Ltd)	1901	£1.50	£75.00
50	Wild Animals of the World (Wide) (with Ltd)	1901	£1.50	£75.00
50	Wild Birds	1932	12p	£4.00
50	Wild Birds (Transfers)	1932	12p	£5.00
L25	Wild Birds	1934	50p	£12.50

Qty		Date	Odds	Sets
L25	Wildfowl	1937	60p	£15.00
50	Wonders of the Deep	1904	80p	£40.00
25	Wonders of the World (Blue Back)	1916	20p	£5.00
25	Wonders of the World (Grey Back, Eire)	1926	30p	£7.50
X10	Wooden Walls	1908	£2.00	£20.00
25	Wrestling & Ju-Jitsu (Blue Back)	1913	30p	£7.50
25	Wrestling & Ju-Jitsu (Grey Back, Eire)	1925	40p	£10.00
26	Your Initials (Transfers)	1932	20p	£5.00
L25	Zoo Babies	1938	15p	£3.75
Overseas Issues				
50	Aeroplane Series	1926	80p	£40.00
50	Aircraft of the Royal Air Force	1938	30p	£15.00
50	Animals of the Countryside	1939	20p	£10.00
50	Arms & Armour (grey back)	1926	£1.20	£60.00
F50	Beauties	1925	75p	£37.50
BF50	Beauties (Coloured)	1925	80p	£40.00
F50	Beauties 2nd Series	1925	75p	£37.50
50	Birds & Their Young	1937	20p	£10.00
52	Birds of Brilliant Plumage	1927	£2.00	—
25	"Bonzo" Dogs	1923	£1.20	£30.00
50	Boy Scouts	1924	£1.00	£50.00
L25	British Live Stock	1924	£3.00	£75.00
50	Butterflies (girls)	1928	£1.50	£75.00
50	Coronation Series Ceremonial Dress	1937	20p	£10.00
50	Cricketers 1938	1938	50p	£25.00
50	Cycling	1939	25p	£12.50
25	Dogs (Heads)	1927	24p	£6.00
32	Drum Horses	1911	£3.00	—
L25	Famous Beauties	1937	60p	—
50	Film Stars Third Series	1938	25p	—
25	Flag Girls of All Nations	1908	£3.00	—
L25	Golf	1939	30p	£7.50
50	Household Hints	1928	60p	—
50	International Air Liners	1936	25p	£12.50
50	Lawn Tennis	1928	£1.00	£50.00
50	Leaders of Men	1925	80p	£40.00
50	Military Uniforms of the British Empire Overseas (adhesive)	1938	25p	£12.50
50	Military Uniforms of the British Empire Overseas (non-adhesive)	1938	30p	£15.00
50	Modern Naval Craft	1939	20p	£10.00
50	Motor Cars A Series	1936	50p	£25.00
50	Motor Cars 2nd Series	1937	40p	£20.00
50	National Flags and Arms	1936	20p	£10.00
L25	Old Hunting Prints	1938	80p	£20.00
M22	Old Masters	1966	30p	—
L25	Old Naval Prints	1936	£1.20	£30.00
48	Pictures of the East	1931	£1.00	—
25	Picturesque People of the Empire	1938	£1.20	£30.00
B53	Playing Cards	1929	75p	—
50	Pugilists in Action	1928	£1.00	—
L25	Racing Yachts	1938	60p	£15.00
50	R.A.F Badges	1937	25p	£12.50

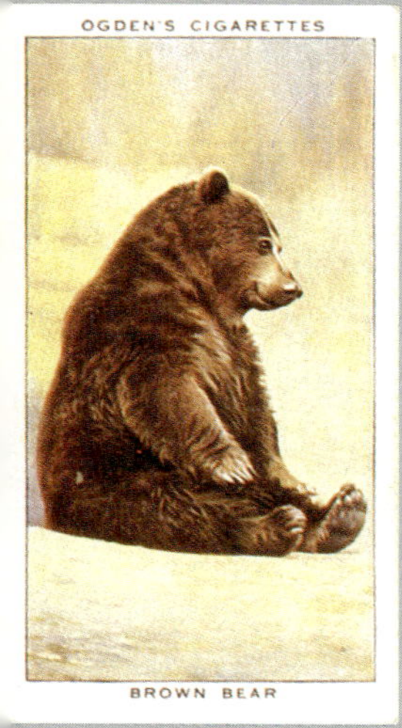

Zoo Babies. Ogden. Also Hignett

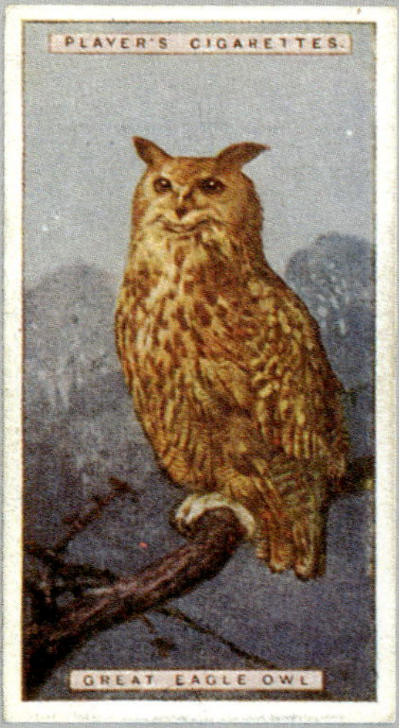

Natural History. Player

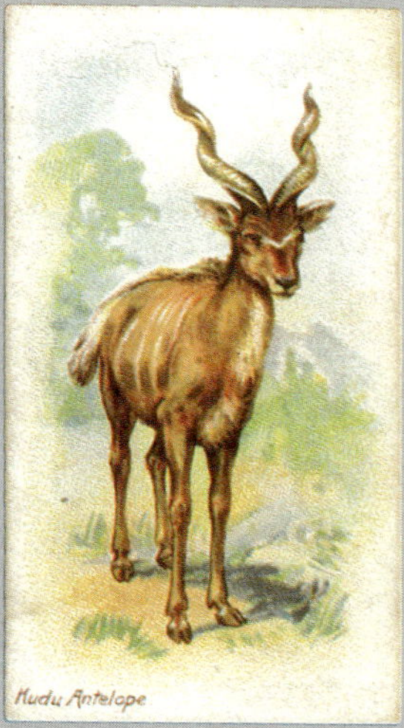

Wild Animals of the World. Adkin, Churchman, Franklyn Davey, Player and Wills

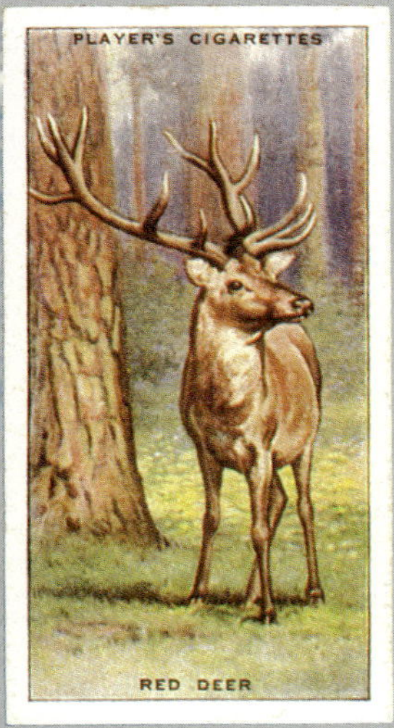

Animals of the Countryside. Player

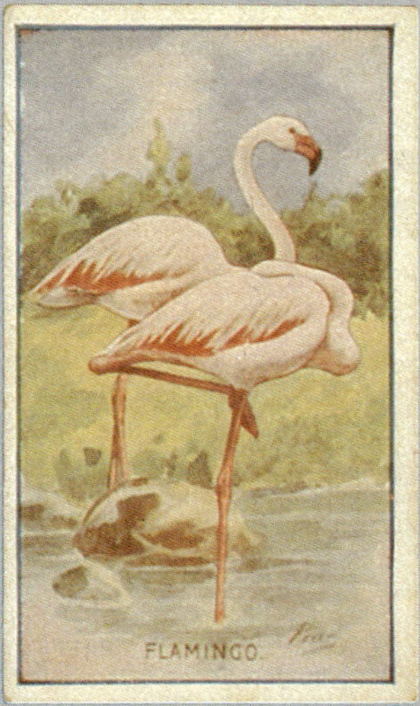

Animals & Birds. Sniders & Abrahams

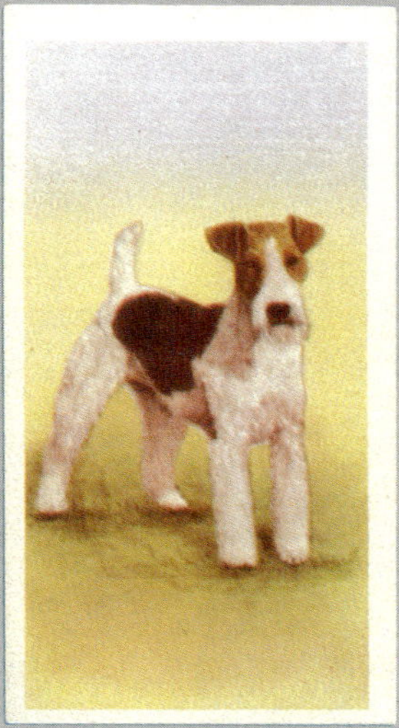

Dogs. Priory Tea

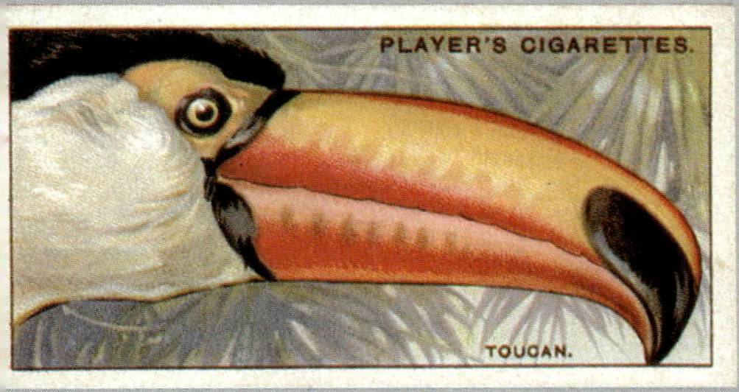

Curious Beaks. Player

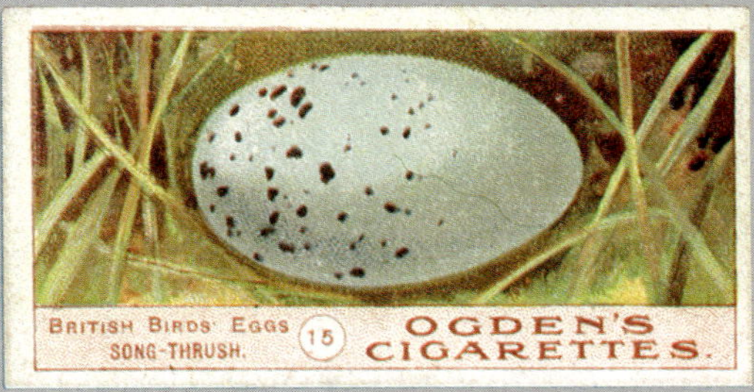

Birds Eggs (1908). Ogden

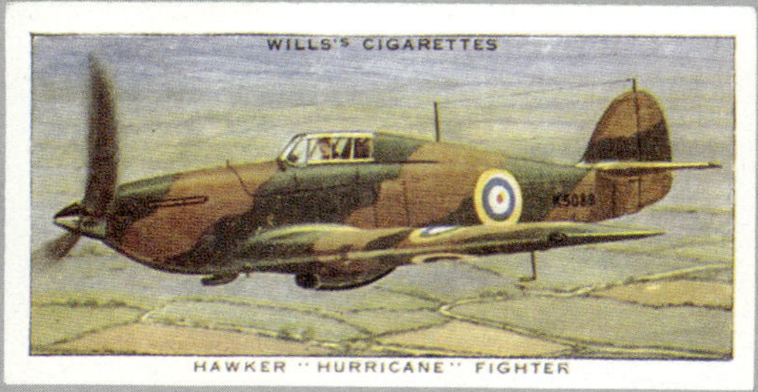

Speed, 1938. Wills

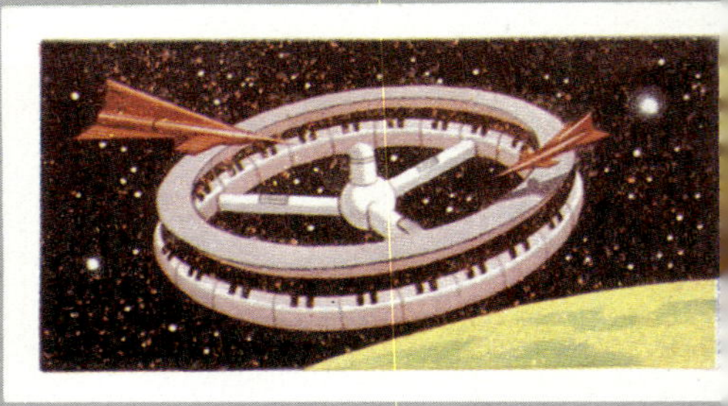

Transport, Present and Future. Edwards

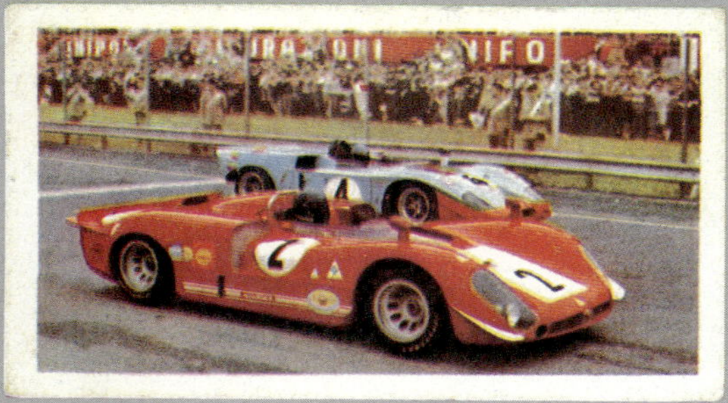

Auto Sprint. Candy Gum

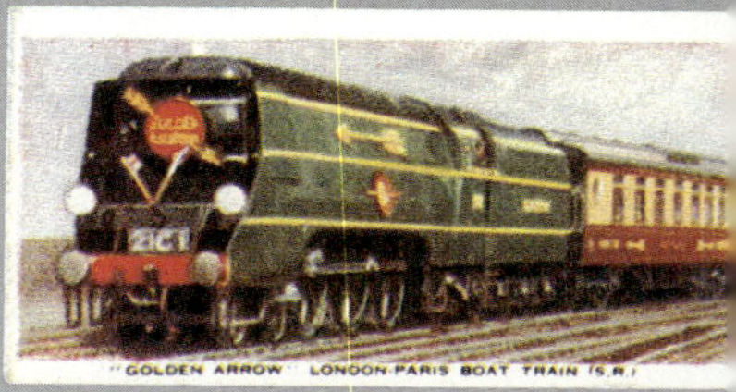

British Locomotives. British Automatic Co.

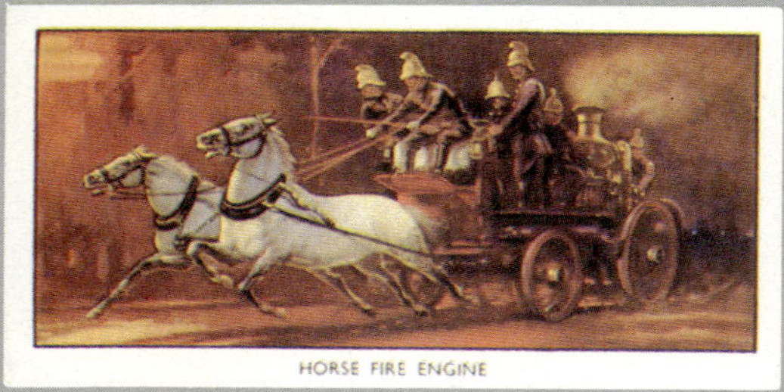

Transport Then & Now. Teofani

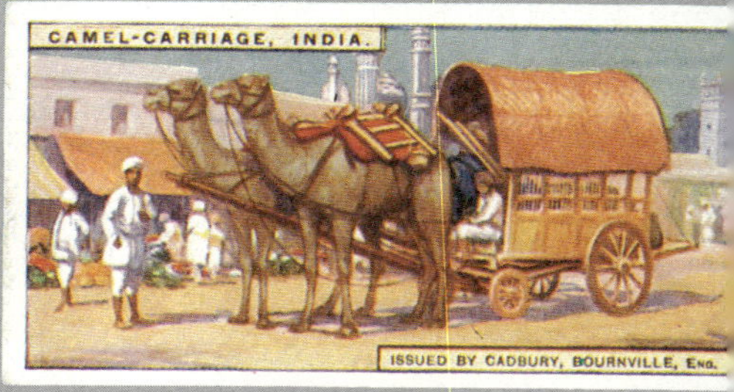

Transport. Cadbury

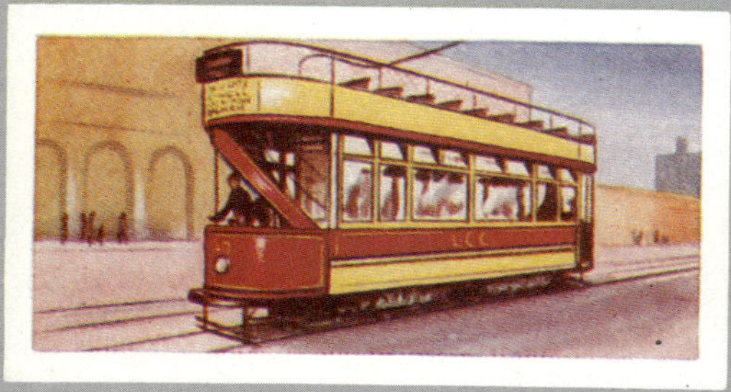

Transport through the Ages. Clover or Ewbanks

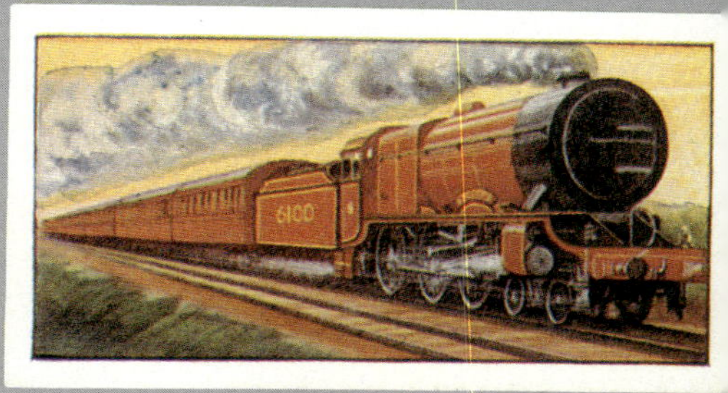

History of the Railways. Browne, Empson, Glengettie or Northern Co-op

JOHN PLAYER & SONS—cont.

Qty		*Date*	*Odds*	*Sets*
50	Railway Working	1926	80p	£40.00
50	Sea Fishes	1935	20p	£10.00
50	Ships' Flags & Cap Badges	1930	80p	£40.00
50	Signalling Series	1926	80p	£40.00
F50	The Royal Family at Home & Abroad	1927	80p	—
L25	Types of Horses	1939	£1.00	—
25	Whaling	1930	80p	£20.00
L25	Zoo Babies	1937	60p	—
Modern Issues (Doncella)				
T30	British Mammals	1983	16p	£5.00
T32	Country Houses and Castles	1981	12p	£3.00
T24	Golden Age of Flying	1977	12p	£2.50
T24	Golden Age of Motoring	1975	12p	£1.50
T24	Golden Age of Sail	1978	12p	£2.50
T24	Golden Age of Steam	1976	12p	£1.50
T24	History of the V.C.	1980	20p	£5.00
T24	Napoleonic Uniforms	1980	12p	£2.50
Modern Issues (Grandee)				
T32	British Birds	1980	15p	£5.00
T32	British Butterflies	1983	15p	—
T30	British Mammals	1982	15p	£5.00
T28	Famous M.G. Marques	1981	12p	£2.50
T25	Top Dogs	1979	24p	£6.00
T6	World of Gardening	1976	A	—
Modern Issues (Panama)				
T7	Limericks	1977	A	—
T7	Panama Puzzles	1976	A	—
T6	Play Ladbroke Spot Ball	1975	£1.25	£7.50
T6	Play Panama Spot Six	1977	£1.50	—
Modern Issues (Tom Thumb)				
L32	Exploration of Space	1982	15p	£5.00
L32	Myths & Legends	1981	15p	£5.00

JAMES PLAYFAIR & CO.

25	How To Keep Fit	1912	£25.00	—

PREMIER TOBACCO MFRS. LTD.

50	Eminent Stage & Screen Personalities	1936	80p	£40.00
K52	Miniature Playing Cards	1935	A	—
100	Stage & Screen Personalities	1936	60p	£60.00

PRITCHARD & BURTON

51	Actors & Actresses "FROGA"	1899	£10.00	—
15	Beauties "PAC"	1899	£25.00	—
20	Boer War Cartoons	1900	B	—
30	Flags & Flags with Soldiers (masts draped)	1902	£5.00	£150.00
15	Flags & Flags with Soldiers (masts undraped)	1902	£7.50	—
25	Holiday Resorts & Views	1902	£6.00	£150.00
40	Home & Colonial Regiments	1901	£25.00	—
25	Royalty Series	1902	£8.00	—
25	South African Series	1901	£6.00	£150.00
25	Star Girls	1900	C	—

G. PRUDHOE

Qty		Date	Odds	Sets
30	Army Pictures, Cartoons, etc.	1916	B	—

JAS. QUINTON LTD

26	Actresses "FROGA"	1899	C	—

Q.V. CIGARS

B?10	Barnum & Bailey's Circus Performers	1900	C	—

RAY & CO. LTD.

K6	Flags of the Allies (shaped)	1916	A	—
25	War Series (1-25)	1915	£6.00	—
75	War Series (26-100)	1915	£4.00	—
25	War Series (101-125)	1916	£10.00	—

RAYMOND REVIEWBAR

BF25	Striptease Artistes	1960	£3.00	—

RECORD CIGARETTE CO.

X36	The Talkie Cigarette Card (Real Records)	1934	£20.00	—

REDFORD & CO.

20	Actresses "BLARM"	1900	B	—
25	Armies of the World	1901	£35.00	—
25	Beauties "GRACC"	1899	C	—
30	Colonial Troops	1902	£30.00	—
24	Nautical Expressions	1900	C	—
40	Naval & Military Phrases	1904	£20.00	—
25	Picture Series	1906	B	—
25	Sports & Pastimes	1906	B	—
50	Stage Artistes of the Day	1908	£4.00	—

RELIANCE TOBACCO MFG. CO.

24	British Birds	1934	£1.50	—
35	Famous Stars	1934	£1.50	—

A. S. RICHARDSON

B12	Manikin Cards	1915	B	—

RICHMOND CAVENDISH CO. LTD.

26	Actresses "FROGA"	1900	£12.50	—
28	Actresses "PILPI I"	1902	£6.00	£165.00
F50	Actresses "PILPI II"	1903	£4.00	£200.00
?229	Actresses, Gravure	1904	£3.00	—
14	Beauties "AMBS"	1899	£20.00	—
52	Beauties P/C Inset	1899	£20.00	—
28	Chinese Actors & Actresses	1923	£1.50	£42.00
F50	Cinema Stars	1927	£1.00	—
40	Medals	1900	£7.50	£300.00
20	Music Hall Artistes	1901	£12.50	£250.00
12	Pretty Girl Series "RASH"	1899	£15.00	£180.00
20	Yachts (black back)	1900	£25.00	—
20	Yachts (white back)	1900	£30.00	—

ROBERTS & SONS

Qty		*Date*	*Odds*	*Sets*
26	Actresses "FROGA"	1899	B	–
25	Armies of the World (plain back)	1900	£15.00	—
25	Armies of the World (printed back)	1900	£20.00	—
50	Beautiful Women	1898	C	—
50	Beauties "CHOAB"	1900	C	—
50	Colonial Troops	1902	£12.50	—
B28	Dominoes	1905	B	—
K52	Miniature Playing Cards	1905	B	—
24	Nautical Expressions	1902	£35.00	—
70	Stories without Words	1904	£20.00	—
25	Types of British & Colonial Troops	1900	£25.00	—

ROBINSON & BARNSDALE LTD.

B25	Actresses, Colin Campbell	1898	£50.00	—
?14	Actresses, Cupola	1898	C	—
1	Advertisement Card, Colin Campbell	1897	–	£50.00
?13	Beauties, Collotype	1895	C	—
B?4	Beauties, Highest Honors	1895	D	—

E. ROBINSON & SONS

10	Beauties	1900	£30.00	—
?24	Derbyshire and The Peak	1903	C	—
25	Egyptian Studies	1914	£7.50	—
25	King Lud Problems	1934	£7.50	—
?10	Medals & Decorations	1902	C	—
40	Nature Studies	1914	£7.50	—
25	Regimental Mascots	1916	£30.00	—
25	Wild Flowers	1915	£6.00	£150.00

ROMAN STAR CIGARS

26	Actresses "FROGA"	1899	C	—
24	Beauties "BOCCA"	1899	C	—

ROTHMANS LTD.

40	Beauties of the Cinema	1939	25p	£10.00
L24	Beauties of the Cinema (Circular)	1939	40p	£10.00
X25	Canterbury Bankstown District Rugby League Football Club (New Zealand)	1980	A	—
24	Cinema Stars	1925	30p	£7.50
L25	Cinema Stars	1925	12p	£3.00
P30	Country Living Cards	1974	—	£6.50
36	Landmarks in Empire History	1936	30p	£7.50
50	Modern Inventions	1935	30p	£15.00
LF54	New Zealand	1933	40p	£20.00
24	Prominent Screen Favourites	1934	25p	£6.00
F50	Punch Jokes	1935	12p	£5.00
5	Rare and Historic Banknotes	1970	75p	—

WM. RUDDELL LTD.

?	Couplet Cards	1924	A	—
25	Grand Opera Series	1924	£2.00	—
25	Rod & Gun	1924	£2.00	—
50	Songs That Will Live For Ever	1924	£1.50	£75.00

I. RUTTER & CO.

Qty		*Date*	*Odds*	*Sets*
15	Actresses (printed back)	1900	£15.00	—
15	Actresses (rubber stamped back)	1900	£20.00	—
1	Advertisement Card	1899	D	—
7	Boer War Celebrities	1901	£15.00	£120.00
54	Comic Phrases	1905	£6.00	—
20	Cricketers Series	1902	B	—
30	Flags & Flags with Soldiers	1901	£10.00	—
24	Girls, Flags & Arms of Countries	1900	£15.00	—
25	Proverbs	1904	£15.00	—
25	Shadowgraphs	1903	£15.00	—

S.D.V. TOBACCO CO. LTD.

16	British Royal Family	1901	C	—

SACCONE & SPEED

F55	Beauties	1912	£1.50	—
F55	Beauties (red overprint)	1912	£1.50	—

ST. PETERSBURG CIGARETTE CO. LTD.

?	Footballers	1904	D	—

SALMON & GLUCKSTEIN LTD.

X1	Advertisement Card (Snake Charmer)	1897	D	—
15	Billiard Terms	1905	£15.00	—
12	British Queens	1902	£15.00	—
X30	Castles, Abbeys & Houses (brown back)	1906	£7.50	£225.00
X30	Castles, Abbeys & Houses (red back)	1906	£12.50	—
32	Characters from Dickens	1903	£10.00	£320.00
25	Coronation Series	1911	£4.00	£100.00
L25	Famous Pictures (Brown)	1912	£3.00	£75.00
L25	Famous Pictures (Green, Different)	1912	£2.50	£62.50
6	Her Most Gracious Majesty Queen Victoria	1897	£12.50	£75.00
40	Heroes of the Transvaal War	1901	£4.00	£250.00
25	Magical Series	1923	£1.20	£30.00
30	Music Hall Celebrities	1902	£12.50	—
?25	Occupations	1898	D	—
20	Owners & Jockeys Series	1900	£15.00	—
L50	Pottery Types (Silk)	1916	£1.50	£75.00
6	Pretty Girl Series "RASH"	1900	£25.00	—
22	Shakespearian Series	1902	£8.00	£175.00
25	Star Girls	1899	£35.00	—
50	The Great White City	1908	£3.00	£150.00
48	The Post in Various Countries	1900	£12.50	£600.00
25	Traditions of the Army & Navy	1917	£4.00	£100.00
25	Wireless Explained	1923	£1.20	£30.00

W. SANDORIDES & CO. LTD.

25	Aquarium Studies from the London Zoo	1925	£1.00	£25.00
L25	Aquarium Studies from the London Zoo	1925	£1.20	£30.00
25	Cinema Celebrities	1924	£1.00	£25.00
X25	Cinema Celebrities	1924	£1.20	—
25	Cinema Stars (As Above)	1924	A	—

W. SANDORIDES & CO. LTD.—cont.

Qty		Date	Odds	Sets
X25	Cinema Stars (As Above)	1924	60p	£15.00
50	Famous Racecourses	1926	80p	£40.00
L50	Famous Racecourses	1926	£1.20	£60.00
50	Famous Racehorses	1923	60p	£30.00
25	Sports & Pastimes	1924	A	—

SANSOM'S CIGAR STORES

?	London Views	1905	C	—

NICHOLAS SARONY & CO.

25	A Day on the Airway	1928	20p	£5.00
L25	A Day on the Airway	1928	24p	£6.00
50	Around the Mediterranean	1926	25p	£12.50
L50	Around the Mediterranean	1926	30p	£15.00
?	Boer War Scenes	1901	D	—
100	Celebrities and Their Autographs	1923	20p	£20.00
L100	Celebrities and Their Autographs	1923	25p	£25.00
50	Cinema Stars	1933	20p	£10.00
P38	Cinema Stars	1930	£3.00	—
P42	Cinema Stars, 2nd Series	1930	75p	—
P50	Cinema Stars, 3rd Series	1930	75p	—
P42	Cinema Stars, 4th Series	1930	75p	—
P25	Cinema Stars, 5th Series	1930	75p	—
25	Cinema Studies	1929	20p	£5.00
F54	Life at Whipsnade Zoo	1934	20p	£10.00
50	Links with the Past	1925	16p	£8.00
L50	Links with the Past	1925	16p	£8.00
25	Links with the Past (Australia)	1926	30p	—
L25	Links with the Past (Australia)	1926	35p	—
25	Links with the Past (New Zealand)	1926	30p	£7.50
L25	Links with the Past (New Zealand)	1926	24p	£6.00
L25	Links with the Past (Presentation Issue)	1926	£1.00	—
25	Museum Series	1927	12p	£3.00
L25	Museum Series	1927	12p	£3.00
L25	Museum Series (Australia)	1927	30p	—
25	Museum Series (New Zealand)	1927	20p	£5.00
L25	Museum Series (New Zealand)	1927	30p	—
L25	Museum Series (Presentation Issue)	1927	30p	£7.50
F36	National Types of Beauty	1928	15p	£5.50
MF36	National Types of Beauty	1928	15p	£5.50
15	Origin of Games	1923	£1.00	£15.00
L15	Origin of Games	1923	£1.20	£18.00
50	Saronicks	1929	12p	£3.00
M50	Saronicks	1929	12p	£3.50
50	Ships of All Ages	1929	12p	£5.00
M50	Ships of All Ages	1929	12p	£6.00
25	Tennis Strokes	1923	60p	£15.00

T. S. SAUNT

30	Army Pictures, Cartoons, etc.	1916	B	—

SCOTTISH C.W.S.

Qty		*Date*	*Odds*	*Sets*
25	Burns	1924	30p	£7.50
20	Dogs	1925	£2.50	—
25	Dwellings of All Nations	1924	80p	£20.00
L25	Famous Pictures	1924	£2.00	—
L25	Famous Pictures—Glasgow Galleries (Adhesive)	1927	50p	£12.50
L25	Famous Pictures—Glasgow Galleries (Non-Adhesive)	1927	70p	£17.50
L25	Famous Pictures—London Galleries (Adhesive)	1927	50p	£12.50
L25	Famous Pictures—London Galleries (Non-Adhesive)	1927	70p	£17.50
50	Feathered Favourites (Adhesive)	1926	50p	£25.00
50	Feathered Favourites (Non-Adhesive)	1926	60p	£30.00
25	Racial Types	1925	£2.50	£62.50
50	Triumphs of Engineering	1926	£1.00	£50.00
50	Wireless	1924	£1.00	£50.00

SELBY

B12	Manikin Cards	1915	B	—

SHARPE & SNOWDEN

?	Views of England	1905	C	—
?	Views of London	1905	C	—

W. J. SHEPHERD

25	Beauties "FECKSA"	1901	B	—

SHORTS

L?20	House Views	1924	A	—

SIMONETS LTD. (Channel Isles)

MF36	Beautiful Women	1928	£1.50	—
F24	Cinema Scenes Series	1926	£1.25	£30.00
F27	Famous Actors & Actresses	1929	£1.00	£27.00
50	Local Footballers	1925	£1.50	£75.00
25	Picture Series	1925	£1.50	—
F27	Sporting Celebrities	1929	£1.50	£40.00
LF50	Views of Jersey (Plain Back)	1926	75p	—

JOHN SINCLAIR LTD.

B?65	Actresses	1902	B	—
F48	Birds (numbered)	1924	£1.00	£50.00
F48	Birds ("specimen cigarette card")	1924	£2.00	—
LF50	Birds	1924	£1.50	—
50	British Sea Dogs	1928	£1.20	£60.00
F54	Champion Dogs	1938	12p	£4.00
LF52	Champion Dogs	1938	12p	£5.00
F54	Champion Dogs, 2nd Series	1939	50p	—
LF52	Champion Dogs, 2nd Series	1939	50p	£26.00
F50	English & Scottish Football Stars	1935	12p	£6.00
F54	Film Stars (Series of 54 Real Photos)	1934	30p	£15.00
F54	Film Stars (Series of Real Photos)	1937	25p	£12.50
F54	Film Stars (55-108)	1937	12p	£6.00

JOHN SINCLAIR LTD.—cont.

Qty		*Date*	*Odds*	*Sets*
M12	Flags (Numbered, Silk) (25-36)	1914	£6.00	—
M24	Flags (Unnumbered Silk, blue captions)	1914	£4.00	—
M24	Flags (Unnumbered, Silk, myrtle green captions)	1914	£4.00	—
M24	Flags (Unnumbered, Silk, olive green captions)	1914	£4.00	—
M24	Flags (Unnumbered, Silk, grey captions) ...	1914	£4.00	—
M24	Flags (Unnumbered, Silk, red captions)	1914	£4.00	—
M50	Flags, 4th Series (Silk)	1914	£3.00	—
M50	Flags, 5th Series (Silk)	1914	£3.00	—
D50	Flags, 6th Series (Silk)	1914	£4.00	—
G10	Flags, 7th Series (Silk)	1914	A	—
F96	Flowers & Plants (numbered)	1924	£1.00	£100.00
F96	Flowers & Plants ("specimen cigarette card")	1924	£2.00	—
F50	Football Favourites	1906	£15.00	—
4	North Country Celebrities	1904	£20.00	—
F?81	Northern Gems	1902	£25.00	—
50	Picture Puzzles & Riddles Series	1916	£7.50	—
F54	Radio Favourites	1935	40p	£20.00
L50	Regimental Badges (Silk)	1915	£1.50	—
D24	Regimental Colours (Silk) (38-61)	1914	£6.00	—
K53	Rubicon Cards (Miniature P/C)	1934	A	—
G1	The Allies Flags (No. 37, Silk)	1915	A	—
50	Trick Series	1916	£10.00	—
50	Well Known Footballers—N.E. Counties ...	1938	12p	£5.00
50	Well Known Footballers—Scottish	1938	12p	£4.00
50	World's Coinage	1914	£6.00	—

ROBERT SINCLAIR TOBACCO CO. LTD.

X4	Battleships & Crests (Silk)	1915	£15.00	—
10	Billiards, 1st Set	1928	£1.25	£12.50
15	Billiards, 2nd Set	1928	£1.25	£20.00
3	Billiards, 3rd Set	1928	£2.50	—
28	Dominoes	1902	B	—
M9	Flags (Silk)	1915	£10.00	—
?3	Footballers	1900	C	—
P6	Great War Area (Silk)	1915	£10.00	—
M10	Great War Heroes (Silk)	1915	£10.00	—
12	Policemen of the World	1899	C	—
X1	Red Cross Nurse (Silk)	1915	B	—
M5	Regimental Badges (Silk)	1915	£10.00	—
12	The Smiler Series	1924	£1.50	£18.00
L12	The Smiler Series	1924	£3.00	—

J. SINFIELD

24	Beauties "HUMPS"	1899	D	—

SINGLETON & COLE LTD.

50	Atlantic Liners	1910	£8.00	£400.00
25	Bonzo Series	1928	£1.50	£37.50
50	Celebrities—Boer War Period	1901	£6.00	—
110	Crests & Badges of the British Army (Silk) ...	1915	£2.50	—
35	Famous Boxers	1930	£2.00	—
25	Famous Film Stars	1930	£1.50	—
35	Famous Officers	1915	£5.00	£225.00

SINGLETON & COLE LTD.—cont.

Qty		*Date*	*Odds*	*Sets*
50	Footballers	1905	£20.00	—
40	Kings & Queens	1902	£7.50	£300.00
B12	Manikin Cards	1915	B	–
25	Maxims of Success	1906	£7.50	—
8	Orient Royal Mail Line	1904	£15.00	—
25	The Wallace-Jones Keep Fit System	1910	£6.00	—

F. & J. SMITH

24	Advertisement Cards	1899	£75.00	—
50	A Tour Round the World (Postcard Backs)	1901	£25.00	—
50	A Tour Round the World (Script Backs)	1901	£10.00	£500.00
50	A Tour Round the World (Descriptive)	1906	£3.00	£150.00
50	Battlefields of Great Britain	1913	£3.50	£175.00
25	Boer War Series (Black & White)	1901	£20.00	—
50	Boer War Series (Coloured)	1901	£15.00	£750.00
50	Champions of Sport (Blue Back)	1902	£15.00	—
50	Champions of Sport (Red Back)	1902	£12.50	—
25	Cinema Stars	1920	£1.50	£37.50
50	Cricketers (1-50)	1912	£4.00	£200.00
20	Cricketers, 2nd Series (51-70)	1912	£10.00	£200.00
50	Derby Winners	1913	£2.50	£125.00
50	Famous Explorers	1911	£3.00	£150.00
50	Football Club Records	1917	£2.50	£125.00
50	Football Club Records (Different)	1922	£2.50	£125.00
120	Footballers (Brown Back)	1906	£8.00	—
100	Footballers (Blue Back, No Series Title)	1908	£2.50	£250.00
150	Footballers (Titled)	1912	£2.00	£300.00
50	Fowls, Pigeons & Dogs	1908	£2.50	£125.00
25	Holiday Resorts	1925	£2.00	—
50	Medals (Numbered Smith back)	1902	£3.00	£150.00
50	Medals (Numbered, Imperial Tobacco Co. back)	1903	£12.50	—
50	Medals (Numbered, Imperial Tobacco Company)	1906	£3.00	£150.00
20	Medals (Unnumbered)	1905	£4.00	£80.00
50	Nations of the World	1923	£1.20	£60.00
50	Naval Dress & Badges (descriptive back)	1911	£3.00	—
50	Naval Dress & Badges (non-descriptive)	1914	£3.00	—
50	Phil May Sketches (Brown Back)	1924	£1.50	£75.00
50	Phil May Sketches (Grey Back)	1908	£3.00	£150.00
25	Prominent Rugby Players	1924	£2.00	—
40	Races of Mankind (no series title)	1900	£35.00	—
40	Races of Mankind (with series title)	1900	£25.00	—
25	Shadowgraphs	1915	£3.00	£75.00
25	War Incidents	1914	£2.50	£62.50
25	War Incidents 2nd Series	1915	£2.50	£62.50

SNELL & CO.

25	Boer War Celebrities "STEW"	1901	C	—

SOROKO

6	Jubilee Series	1935	A	—
L6	Jubilee Series	1935	A	—

S. E. SOUTHGATE & SON

Qty		*Date*	*Odds*	*Sets*
25	Types of British & Colonial Troops	1900	C	—

SOUTH WALES TOB. MFG. CO. LTD.

30	Army Pictures, Cartoons, etc.	1915	B	—
?91	Game of Numbers	1912	B	—
25	Views of London	1912	£6.00	—

T. SPALTON

30	Army Pictures, Cartoons, etc.	1916	B	—

SPIRO VALLERI & CO.

?15	Noted Footballers	1905	D	—

G. STANDLEY

B12	Manikin Cards	1915	B	—

STAPLETON

B12	Manikin Cards	1915	B	—

STAR OF THE WORLD

20	Boer War Cartoons	1901	C	—
?50	Boer War Celebrities "JASAS"	1901	C	—
30	Colonial Troops	1901	£40.00	—

H. STEVENS & CO.

20	Dogs	1923	£1.50	—
25	Zoo Series	1926	£1.25	—

A. STEVENSON

50	War Portraits	1916	B	—

ALBERT STOCKWELL

30	Army Pictures, Cartoons, etc.	1916	B	—

STRATHMORE TOBACCO CO.

M25	British Aircraft	1938	20p	£5.00

SWEET ALVA CIGARETTES

?50	Boer War Celebrities "JASAS"	1901	C	—

T.S.S.

24	Nautical Expressions	1900	B	—

TADDY & CO.

72	Actresses, Collotype	1897	£40.00	—
25	Actresses with Flowers	1899	£50.00	£1250.00
37	Admirals & Generals—The War	1914	£6.00	—
25	Admirals & Generals—The War (South Africa)	1914	£20.00	—
1	Advertisement Card	1900	D	—

TADDY & CO.—cont.

Qty		Date	Odds	Sets
25	Autographs	1912	£6.00	£150.00
20	Boer Leaders	1901	£7.50	£150.00
50	British Medals & Decorations, Series 2	1912	£5.00	£250.00
50	British Medals & Ribbons	1912	£5.00	£250.00
20	Clowns & Circus Artistes	—	D	—
30	Coronation Series	1902	£8.00	£240.00
238	County Cricketers	1907	£12.50	—
50	Dogs	1900	£7.50	£375.00
5	English Royalty	1897	D	—
25	Famous Actors/Famous Actresses	1903	£6.00	£150.00
50	Famous Horses and Cattle	1908	B	—
25	Famous Jockeys (No Frame)	1910	£10.00	—
25	Famous Jockeys (With Frame)	1910	£6.00	£150.00
50	Footballers (New Zealand)	1900	B	—
25	Heraldry Series	1911	£6.00	£150.00
25	Honours & Ribbons	1906	£8.00	£200.00
10	Klondyke Series	1900	£25.00	—
60	Leading M.L.A.'s (South Africa)	1900	D	—
25	Natives of the World	1899	£30.00	£750.00
25	Orders of Chivalry	1911	£6.00	£150.00
25	Orders of Chivalry 2nd Series	1912	£12.50	—
595	Prominent Footballers (No Footnote)	1907	£2.50	—
400	Prominent Footballers (With Footnote)	1908	£2.50	—
?350	Prominent Footballers (London Mixture)	1913	£10.00	—
20	Royalty, Actresses & Soldiers	1898	£100.00	—
25	Royalty Series	1903	£5.00	£125.00
25	Russo Japanese War (1-25)	1904	£5.00	£125.00
25	Russo Japanese War (26-50)	1904	£10.00	£250.00
16	South African Cricket Team, 1907	1907	£25.00	—
26	South African Football Team, 1906-7	1906	£10.00	—
25	Sports & Pastimes	1912	£6.00	£150.00
25	Territorial Regiments	1908	£10.00	£250.00
25	Thames Series	1903	£20.00	—
20	Victoria Cross Heroes (1-20)	1901	£17.50	£350.00
20	Victoria Cross Heroes (21-40)	1901	£17.50	£350.00
20	VC Heroes—Boer War (41-60)	1902	£6.00	£120.00
20	VC Heroes—Boer War (61-80)	1902	£6.00	£120.00
20	VC Heroes—Boer War (81-100)	1902	£8.00	£160.00
25	Victoria Cross Heroes (101-125)	1904	£35.00	—
2	Wrestlers	1908	£100.00	£200.00

TADDY (re-registered, no connection with earlier Co.)

8	Advertisement Cards	1980	25p	£2.00
26	Motor Cars (Clown Cigarettes)	1980	—	£1.50
26	Motor Cars (Myrtle Grove Cigarettes)	1980	—	£1.50
26	Railway Locomotives (Clown Cigarettes)	1980	—	£1.50
26	Railway Locomotives (Myrtle Grove Cigs.)	1980	—	£1.50

W. & M. TAYLOR

8	The European War Series	1915	£25.00	—
25	War Series	1915	£5.00	£125.00

TAYLOR WOOD

Qty		Date	Odds	Sets
18	Motor Cycle Series	1914	B	—

TEOFANI & CO. LTD.

25	Aquarium Studies from the London Zoo ...	1925	A	—
50	Cinema Celebrities	1926	£1.25	—
25	Cinema Stars	1924	£2.00	—
X25	Cinema Stars	1924	£3.00	—
25	Famous Boxers	1925	£2.50	£62.50
F32	Famous British Ships & Officers	1934	£1.00	£32.00
12	Film Actors & Actresses (Plain Back)	1936	15p	£2.00
20	Great Inventors	1924	£3.00	—
20	Head-dress of all Nations (Plain back)	1926	£5.00	£100.00
LF50	Icelandic Employees	1926	£2.00	—
12	London Views (Plain Back)	1936	15p	£2.00
48	Modern Movie Stars & Cinema Celebrities ...	1934	12p	£6.00
50	Natives in Costume (Plain back)	1926	£5.00	—
24	Past & Present "A"—The Army	1938	20p	£5.00
24	Past & Present "B"—Weapons of War	1938	12p	£3.00
4	Past & Present "C"—Transport	1939	£1.25	£5.00
50	Public Schools & Colleges	1923	£2.50	£125.00
50	Ships and Their Flags	1925	£1.00	£50.00
25	Sports & Pastimes (Plain Back)	1924	£1.00	£25.00
25	Sports & Pastimes (Printed Back)	1924	A	—
22	Teofani Gems	1925	50p	—
28	Teofani Gems	1925	40p	—
36	Teofani Gems	1925	50p	—
48	Transport Then & Now	1939	12p	£5.00
50	Views of London	1925	£1.50	—
F36	Views of the British Empire	1927	30p	£10.00
24	Well Known Racehorses	1923	£2.50	—
50	Worlds Smokers (Plain back)	1926	£5.00	—
50	Zoological Studies	1924	£2.50	—
L50	Zoological Studies	1924	A	—

TETLEY & SONS

1	The Allies	1915	D	—
50	War Portraits	1916	B	—
25	World's Coinage	1914	£20.00	—

THEMANS & CO.

?10	Anecdotes & Riddles	1913	C	—
55	Dominoes	1913	B	—
18	Motor Cycle Series	1914	B	—
50	War Portraits	1915	£25.00	—
10	War Posters	1916	C	—

THOMSON & PORTEOUS

50	Arms of British Towns	1905	£3.00	—
25	Boer War Celebrities "STEW"	1901	£25.00	—
25	Shadowgraphs	1902	£20.00	—
20	The European War Series	1915	£5.00	£100.00
41	V.C. Heroes	1916	£3.50	£150.00

TOPSY CIGARETTES

Qty		Date	Odds	Sets
F?10	Actresses	1896	D	—

TURKISH MONOPOLY CIGARETTE CO. LTD.

X?12	Boer War Scenes	1901	C	—

UNITED KINGDOM TOBACCO CO. LTD.

50	Aircraft	1933	30p	£15.00
P48	Beautiful Britain	1929	50p	£25.00
P48	Beautiful Britain 2nd Series	1929	50p	£25.00
25	British Orders of Chivalry & Valour	1936	16p	£4.00
24	Chinese Scenes	1933	12p	£2.00
32	Cinema Stars	1933	25p	£8.00
50	Cinema Stars	1934	30p	£15.00
36	Officers Full Dress	1936	35p	£12.50
?50	Soldiers (Metal)	1935	£5.00	—
36	Soldiers of the King	1937	30p	£11.00

UNITED SERVICES MFG. CO. LTD.

50	Ancient Warriors	1938	40p	£20.00
25	Ancient Warriors	1957	£1.00	—
50	Bathing Belles	1939	12p	£6.00
100	Interesting Personalities	1935	£1.00	£100.00
50	Popular Footballers	1936	£1.25	£62.50
50	Popular Screen Stars	1937	£1.00	£50.00

UNITED TOBACCONISTS ASSOCIATION LTD.

10	Actresses "MUTA"	1901	C	—
12	Pretty Girl Series "RASH"	1900	C	—

WALKERS TOBACCO CO. LTD. (W.T.C.)

60	British Beauty Spots	1924	A	—
28	Dominoes (Old Monk)	1908	B	—
28	Dominoes (W.T.C.)	1924	£1.00	—
F31/32	Film Stars (Tatleys)	1936	25p	£7.50
F48	Film Stars (Walkers)	1935	£1.00	—

WALTERS TOBACCO CO. LTD.

L6	Angling Information	1939	30p	£2.00

E. T. WATERMAN

30	Army Pictures, Cartoons, etc.	1916	B	—

WEBB & RASSELL

50	War Portraits	1916	B	—

HENRY WELFARE & CO.

?25	Prominent Politicians	1912	£30.00	—

WESTMINSTER TOBACCO CO. LTD.

Qty		Date	Odds	Sets
F36	Australia, 1st Series	1932	12p	£2.50
F36	Australia, 2nd Series (Plain Back)	1933	12p	£2.00
F48	British Royal and Ancient Buildings (Unnumbered)	1925	30p	£15.00
F48	British Royal and Ancient Buildings (Numbered)	1925	25p	£12.50
F48	British Royal and Ancient Buildings 2nd Series	1926	12p	£6.00
F36	Canada 1st Series	1926	25p	£9.00
F36	Canada 2nd Series	1928	25p	£9.00
F48	Indian Empire 1st Series	1925	15p	£7.50
F48	Indian Empire 2nd Series	1926	15p	£7.50
F36	New Zealand 1st Series	1928	20p	£7.50
F36	New Zealand 2nd Series	1929	12p	£4.00
F36	South Africa 1st Series	1928	20p	£7.50
F36	South Africa 2nd Series	1928	20p	£7.50

Overseas Issues

Qty		Date	Odds	Sets
L?200	Adamson's Oplevelser	1926	A	—
MF50	Beauties	1924	£1.00	—
MF100	Beautiful Women	1915	75p	—
M50	Birds, Beasts & Fishes	1923	£1.25	—
B100	British Beauties (Hand coloured)	1915	£1.00	—
B102	British Beauties (Uncoloured)	1915	£1.00	—
F48	British Royal and Ancient Buildings	1925	40p	£20.00
B50	Butterflies & Moths	1920	£1.50	—
F36	Canada 1st Series	1926	50p	—
F36	Canada 2nd Series	1928	50p	—
30	Celebrated Actresses	1921	£2.50	£75.00
100	Cinema Artistes (Green Back)	1928	60p	—
50	Cinema Artistes (Grey Back)	1931	60p	—
48	Cinema Celebrities (C)	1935	£1.00	—
F50	Cinema Stars	1927	A	—
MF50	Cinema Stars (Coloured)	1926	£1.00	—
MF50	Cinema Stars (Uncoloured)	1930	£1.25	—
B27	Dancing Girls	1917	£2.00	£50.00
50	Do You Know?	1922	£1.00	—
24	Fairy Tales (Booklets)	1926	A	—
M100	Famous Beauties (Blue Caption)	1916	£1.00	—
M100	Famous Beauties (Brown Caption)	1916	£1.00	—
MF52	Film Favourites (Coloured)	1927	75p	—
MF52	Film Favourites (Uncoloured)	1927	75p	—
M50	Film Personalities	1931	£1.00	—
M50	Garden Flowers of the World	1917	£1.00	£50.00
M50	Garden Flowers of the World (Silk)	1913	£1.50	£75.00
F48	Indian Empire, 1st Series	1925	60p	—
F48	Indian Empire 2nd Series	1926	60p	—
MF50	Islenzkar Eimskipamyndir	1931	£1.25	£62.50
MF50	Islenzkar Landslagsmyndir	1928	£1.25	£62.50
MF50	Islenzkar Landslagsmyndir Nr2	1929	£1.25	£62.50
40	Merrie England Studies	1914	£2.50	—
X?	Miniature Rugs	1924	A	—
36	Modern Beauties	1938	A	—
MF52	Movie Stars	1925	£1.00	—
F36	New Zealand 1st Series	1928	60p	—

WESTMINSTER TOBACCO CO. LTD.—cont.

Qty		Date	Odds	Sets
F36	New Zealand 2nd Series	1929	60p	—
55	Playing Cards	1934	60p	—
M55	Playing Cards (blue back)	1934	60p	—
M55	Playing Cards (red back)	1934	60p	—
F50	Popular Film Stars	1926	75p	—
L?200	Skjeggen's Oplevelser	1926	A	—
F36	South Africa, 1st Series	1928	60p	—
F36	South Africa, 2nd Series	1928	60p	—
M49	South African Succulents	1937	12p	£4.00
M100	Stage & Cinema Stars (Black Caption)	1921	60p	£60.00
M100	Stage & Cinema Stars (Grey Caption)	1921	75p	—
MF50	Stars of Filmland	1927	75p	£37.50
50	Steamships of the World	1920	£3.00	—
40	The Great War Celebrities	1914	£3.00	—
50	The World of Tomorrow	1938	25p	£12.50
M50	Uniforms of All Ages	1917	£4.00	—
F50	Views of Malaya	1930	£3.00	—
25	Wireless	1923	£1.25	—
M50	Women of Nations	1922	£1.50	—

WHALE & COMPANY

?12	Conundrums	1900	C	—

M. WHITE & CO.

20	Actresses "BLARM"	1900	C	—

WHITFORD & SONS

20	Inventors	1924	A	—

WHOLESALE TOBACCO CO.

25	Armies of the World	1903	£35	—
40	Army Pictures	1902	B	—

P. WHYTE

30	Army Pictures, Cartoons, etc.	1916	B	—

W. WILLIAMS & CO.

30	Aristocrats of the Turf A Series	1924	£2.00	—
36	Aristocrats of the Turf 2nd Series	1924	A	—
25	Boer War Celebrities "STEW"	1901	£25.00	—
25	Boxing	1923	£2.00	—
50	Interesting Buildings	1912	£4.00	—
12	Views of Chester	1912	£8.00	—
12	Views of Chester, 2nd Series (As it Was)	1913	£10.00	—

W. D. & H. O. WILLS LTD.

?	Actresses (typeset back)	1895	D	—
52	Actresses (Brown Back, P/C Inset)	1898	£7.00	£350.00
52	Actresses (Grey Back, P/C Inset)	1897	£8.00	£400.00
52	Actresses (Grey Back, No Inset)	1897	£8.00	£400.00
25	Actresses, Collotype (Wills')	1894	£35.00	—
50	Actresses & Celebrities, Collotype (Wills's)	1894	£40.00	—

Qty		*Date*	*Odds*	*Sets*
1	Advertisement Card (Serving Maid)	1890	D	—
4	Advertisement Cards (Cigarette Packets)	1891	D	—
11	Advertisement Cards (Tobacco Packings)	1891	D	—
3	Advertisement Cards (Showcards)	1893	£100.00	—
6	Advertisement Cards (Showcards)	1893	£100.00	—
1	Advertisement Card—Three Castles	1965	—	50p
L1	Advertisement Card—Wants List	1935	—	15p
50	Air Raid Precuations	1938	12p	£4.50
40	Air Raid Precautions (Eire)	1938	30p	£12.00
50	Allied Army Leaders	1917	50p	£25.00
50	Alpine Flowers	1913	20p	£10.00
49	And When Did You Last See Your Father? (Sect.)	1932	40p	£20.00
50	Animals & Birds (Descriptive)	1900	£5.00	—
50	Animals & Birds in Fancy Costume	1896	£25.00	£1250.00
48	Animalloys (Sect.)	1929	12p	£5.00
L25	Animals and Their Furs	1929	50p	£12.50
50	Arms of Companies	1913	20p	£10.00
50	Arms of Foreign Cities	1912	20p	£10.00
L42	Arms of Oxford & Cambridge Colleges	1922	60p	£25.00
L25	Arms of Public Schools 1st Series	1933	40p	£10.00
L25	Arms of Public Schools 2nd Series	1934	40p	£10.00
50	Arms of the Bishopric	1907	30p	£15.00
50	Arms of the British Empire	1910	20p	£10.00
L25	Arms of the British Empire 1st Series	1933	40p	£10.00
L25	Arms of the British Empire 2nd Series	1933	40p	£10.00
L25	Arms of Universities	1923	50p	£12.50
50	Association Footballers (Frame on back)	1935	16p	£8.00
50	Association Footballers (No Frame on back)	1939	16p	£8.00
50	Association Footballers (Eire)	1939	30p	—
L25	Auction Bridge	1926	50p	£12.50
50	Aviation	1910	60p	£30.00
?100	Beauties, Collotype	1894	B	—
K52	Beauties, Playing Card Inset	1896	£10.00	—
52	Beauties, Playing Card Insets	1897	£8.00	£400.00
?	Beauties (No inset, scroll back)	1897	C	—
?	Beauties (No inset, type set back)	1897	C	—
?	Beauties, Girl Studies	1895	D	—
L25	Beautiful Homes	1930	60p	£15.00
48	Between Two Fires (Sect.)	1930	12p	£5.00
50	Billiards	1909	40p	£20.00
K9	Boer War Medallions	1900	£25.00	—
50	Borough Arms (Scroll Back, Numbered)	1903	£4.00	£200.00
50	Borough Arms (Scroll Back, Unnumbered)	1903	40p	£20.00
50	Borough Arms (1-50 descriptive)	1904	50p	£25.00
50	Borough Arms Second Edition (1-50)	1906	25p	£12.50
50	Borough Arms 2nd Series (51-100)	1904	20p	£10.00
50	Borough Arms Second Edition (51-100)	1906	20p	£10.00
50	Borough Arms 3rd Series (101-150 Red Print)	1905	25p	£12.50
50	Borough Arms 3rd Series (101-150 Grey Print)	1905	30p	£15.00
50	Borough Arms Second Edition (101-150)	1906	20p	£10.00
50	Borough Arms 4th Series (151-200)	1905	20p	£10.00
24	Britain's Part in the War	1917	30p	£7.50
50	British Birds	1915	40p	£20.00

Qty		*Date*	*Odds*	*Sets*
50	British Butterflies	1927	25p	£12.50
L25	British Castles	1925	60p	£15.00
L25	British School of Painting	1927	40p	£10.00
M48	British Sporting Personalities	1937	15p	£7.50
50	Builders of the Empire	1898	£3.00	£150.00
L40	Butterflies & Moths	1938	20p	£8.00
1	Calendar for 1911	1910	—	£7.50
1	Calendar 1912	1911	—	£4.00
L25	Cathedrals	1933	80p	£20.00
L25	Celebrated Pictures A Series	1916	50p	£12.50
L25	Celebrated Pictures 2nd Series	1916	60p	£15.00
50	Celebrated Ships	1911	40p	£20.00
25	Cinema Stars 1st Series	1928	40p	£10.00
25	Cinema Stars 2nd Series	1928	24p	£6.00
50	Cinema Stars 3rd Series	1931	40p	£20.00
P12	Cities of Britain	1929	£2.50	£30.00
25	Conundrums (no album clause)	1898	£3.00	£75.00
25	Conundrums (with album clause)	1898	£3.00	£75.00
60	Coronation Ser. (narrow arrows)	1902	£2.50	£150.00
60	Coronation Ser. (wide arrows)	1902	£2.00	£120.00
50	Cricketers	1896	£30.00	£1500.00
50	Cricketer Series 1901	1901	£8.00	£400.00
25	Cricketers (WILLS'S)	1908	£2.50	£62.50
50	Cricketers (WILLS's)	1908	£2.50	£125.00
50	Cricketers, 1928	1928	35p	£17.50
50	Cricketers 2nd Series	1929	30p	£15.00
50	Dogs	1937	12p	£6.00
50	Dogs (Eire)	1937	30p	—
L25	Dogs A Series	1914	60p	£15.00
L25	Dogs 2nd Series	1915	60p	£15.00
50	Double Meaning	1898	£3.50	£175.00
52	Double Meaning (P/C Inset)	1898	£3.50	£180.00
50	Do You Know A Series	1922	12p	£5.00
50	Do You Know 2nd Series	1924	12p	£4.00
50	Do You Know 3rd Series	1926	12p	£4.00
50	Do You Know 4th Series	1933	16p	£8.00
50	Engineering Wonders	1927	12p	£6.00
50	English Period Costumes	1929	30p	£15.00
L25	English Period Costumes	1927	50p	£12.50
L40	Famous British Authors	1937	30p	£12.00
L30	Famous British Liners A Series	1934	£1.20	£36.00
L30	Famous British Liners 2nd Series	1935	60p	£18.00
L25	Famous Golfers	1930	£1.00	£25.00
50	Famous Inventions	1915	25p	£12.50
50	First Aid (No Album Clause)	1913	20p	£10.00
50	First Aid (With Album Clause)	1913	20p	£10.00
50	Fish & Bait	1910	25p	£12.50
25	Flags of the Empire A Series	1926	25p	£6.25
25	Flags of the Empire 2nd Series	1929	25p	£6.25
50	Flower Culture in Pots	1925	12p	£4.00
L30	Flowering Shrubs	1934	35p	£10.50
50	Flowering Trees & Shrubs	1924	12p	£6.00
66	Football Series	1902	£2.00	£130.00
50	Garden Flowers	1933	12p	£5.00

W. D. & H. O. WILLS LTD.—cont.

Qty		*Date*	*Odds*	*Sets*
50	Garden Flowers by Sudell	1939	12p	£2.50
50	Garden Flowers by Sudell (Eire)	1939	12p	£6.00
L40	Garden Flowers—New Varieties A Series	1938	12p	£2.50
L40	Garden Flowers—New Varieties 2nd Series	1939	12p	£2.50
50	Garden Hints	1938	12p	£2.50
50	Garden Hints (Eire)	1938	12p	£6.00
50	Gardening Hints	1923	12p	£3.50
50	Garden Life	1914	15p	£7.50
50	Gems of Belgian Architecture	1915	20p	£10.00
50	Gems of French Architecture	1916	50p	£25.00
F50	Gems of Italian Architecture (Reproduction)	—	—	£4.00
50	Gems of Russian Architecture	1917	20p	£10.00
L25	Golfing	1924	£1.00	£25.00
X32	Happy Families	1939	—	£65.00
L25	Heraldic Signs & Their Origin	1925	50p	£12.50
50	Historic Events	1912	35p	£17.50
F54	Homeland Events	1932	12p	£4.00
50	Household Hints	1927	12p	£4.00
50	Household Hints 2nd Series	1930	15p	£7.50
50	Household Hints (Different)	1936	12p	£2.50
50	Household Hints (Eire)	1936	12p	£5.00
50	Hurlers (Eire)	1927	30p	£15.00
2	Indian Series	1900	C	—
P12	Industries of Britain	1930	£2.50	£30.00
25	Irish Beauty-Spots	1924	£2.00	£50.00
25	Irish Holiday Resorts	1924	£2.00	£50.00
50	Irish Industries	1937	30p	£15.00
25	Irish Rugby Internationals	1926	£2.00	—
50	Irish Sportsmen	1936	60p	£30.00
50	Japanese Series	1900	£20.00	£1000.00
50	Kings & Queens (Short Card, Brown Back)	1898	£6.00	£300.00
50	Kings & Queens (Short Card, Grey Back)	1898	£2.00	£100.00
50/51	Kings & Queens (Long Card, "Wills" at Base)	1902	£2.00	£100.00
50	Kings & Queens (Long Card, "Wills" at Top)	1902	£5.00	—
L25	Lawn Tennis, 1931	1931	60p	£15.00
50	Life in the Hedgerow	Unissued	—	£7.50
50	Life in the Royal Navy	1939	12p	£3.50
50	Life in the Treetops	1925	12p	£5.00
50	Life of King Edward VIII	Unissued	A	—
50	Locomotives & Rolling Stock (No Clause)	1901	£3.00	£150.00
50	Locomotives & Rolling Stock (With ITC Clause)	1902	£3.00	£150.00
50	Lucky Charms	1923	12p	£5.00
100	Maori Series	1900	B	—
50	Medals	1906	£1.20	£60.00
50	Merchant Ships of the World	1924	30p	£15.00
50	Military Motors (Not Passed by Censor)	1916	40p	£20.00
50	Military Motors (Passed by Censor)	1916	40p	£20.00
52	Miniature Playing Cards (Blue Back, Numbered)	1931	25p	£12.50
52	Miniature Playing Cards (Blue Back, Unnumbered)	1931	25p	£12.50
52	Miniature Playing Cards (Blue Back, Red Overprints)	1931	25p	£12.50

W. D. & H. O. WILLS LTD.—cont.

Qty		Date	Odds	Sets
52	Miniature Playing Cards (Pink Back)	1931	40p	£20.00
52	Miniature Playing Cards (Eire)	1931	75p	—
50	Mining	1916	20p	£10.00
L25	Modern Architecture	1931	50p	£12.50
L30	Modern British Sculpture	1928	40p	£12.00
48	Mother & Son (Sect.)	1931	12p	£5.00
50	Musical Celebrities	1912	60p	£30.00
50	Musical Celebrities 2nd Series	1914	£1.00	£50.00
25	National Costumes	1895	D	—
?	National Types	1893	D	—
50	Naval Dress & Badges	1909	80p	£40.00
50	Nelson Series	1905	£1.00	£50.00
50	Old English Garden Flowers	1910	20p	£10.00
50	Old English Garden Flowers 2nd Series	1913	20p	£10.00
L25	Old Furniture 1st Series	1923	60p	£15.00
L25	Old Furniture 2nd Series	1924	60p	£15.00
L40	Old Inns A Series	1936	65p	£26.00
L40	Old Inns 2nd Series	1939	40p	£16.00
L25	Old London	1929	70p	£17.50
L30	Old Pottery & Porcelain	1934	35p	£10.50
L25	Old Silver	1924	60p	£15.00
L25	Old Sundials	1928	60p	£15.00
20	Our Gallant Grenadiers	1902	£12.50	£250.00
50	Our King & Queen	1937	10p	£3.50
50	Overseas Dominions (Australia)	1915	16p	£8.00
50	Overseas Dominions (Canada)	1914	16p	£8.00
50	Physical Culture	1914	25p	£12.50
25	Pond & Aquarium 1st Series	Unissued	—	£4.00
25	Pond & Aquarium 2nd Series	Unissued	—	£5.00
50	Portraits of European Royalty (1-50)	1908	40p	£20.00
50	Portraits of European Royalty (51-100)	1908	50p	£25.00
L25	Public Schools	1927	50p	£12.50
L25	Punch Cartoons 1st Series	1916	£1.20	£30.00
L25	Punch Cartoons 2nd Series	1917	£7.50	—
L40	Racehorses & Jockeys 1938	1939	25p	£10.00
50	Radio Celebrities A Series	1934	20p	£10.00
50	Radio Celebrities A Series (Eire)	1934	50p	—
50	Radio Celebrities 2nd Series	1934	16p	£8.00
50	Radio Celebrities 2nd Series (Eire)	1934	50p	—
50	Railway Engines	1924	30p	£15.00
50	Railway Engines (adhesive)	1936	25p	£12.50
50	Railway Engines (Eire)	1936	50p	—
50	Railway Equipment	1938	12p	£3.00
50	Railway Locomotives	1930	50p	£25.00
12	Recruiting Posters	1915	£2.00	£24.00
L25	Rigs of Ships	1929	60p	£15.00
50	Romance of the Heavens	1928	20p	£10.00
50	Roses A Series (1-50)	1912	20p	£10.00
50	Roses Second Series (51-100)	1913	20p	£10.00
50	Roses (Different)	1926	12p	£6.00
L40	Roses (Different)	1936	25p	£10.00
M48	Round Europe	1936	12p	£6.00
50	Rugby Internationals	1929	20p	£10.00
50	Safety First	1934	12p	£5.00

Qty		Date	Odds	Sets
50	Safety First (Eire)	1934	30p	—
50	School Arms	1906	20p	£10.00
50	Seaside Resorts	1899	£4.00	£200.00
40	Shannon Electric Power Scheme (Eire)	1931	65p	£20.00
25	Ships (Three Castles Back)	1895	£15.00	—
25	Ships (No "Wills" on Front)	1895	£15.00	£375.00
50	Ships (With "Wills" on Front)	1896	£8.00	£400.00
100	Ships (Brownish Card)	1897	£10.00	—
50	Ships' Badges	1925	12p	£5.00
50	Signalling Series	1911	25p	£12.50
50	Soldiers & Sailors (Blue Back)	1894	£25.00	£1250.00
50	Soldiers & Sailors (Grey back)	1894	£25.00	£1250.00
100	Soldiers of the World (Ltd. back)	1895	£4.00	£400.00
100/101	Soldiers of the World (no Ltd. on back)	1895	£4.00	£400.00
52	Soldiers of the World (P/C Inset)	1896	£15.00	£750.00
100	South African Personalities (Collotype)	1901	£40.00	—
50	Speed	1930	40p	£20.00
50	Speed (Different)	1938	12p	£4.00
50	Speed (Eire)	1938	20p	£10.00
50	Sports of All Nations	1901	£2.50	£125.00
50	Strange Craft	1931	16p	£8.00
48	The Boyhood of Raleigh (Sect.)	1931	15p	£7.50
P12	The British Empire	1929	£2.50	£30.00
50	The Coronation Series	1911	30p	£15.00
L40	The King's Art Treasures	1938	12p	£5.00
48	The Laughing Cavalier (Sect.)	1931	15p	£7.50
48	The Laughing Cavalier (Sect. Eire)	1931	75p	—
50	The Reign of King George V	1935	12p	£6.00
50	The Sea Shore	1938	12p	£3.00
50	The Sea Shore (Eire)	1938	15p	£7.50
48	The Toast (Sect.)	1931	12p	£6.00
48	The Toast (Sect., Eire)	1931	75p	—
25	The World's Dreadnoughts	1910	60p	£15.00
50	Time & Money in different Countries	1908	60p	£30.00
50	Transvaal Series (Black Border)	1901	£5.00	—
66	Transvaal Series (White Border)	1901	75p	£50.00
66	Transvaal Series (Non Descriptive Back)	1902	£2.00	£130.00
L40	Trees	1937	30p	£12.00
L25	University Hoods & Gowns	1926	80p	£20.00
50	Vanity Fair Series (Unnumbered)	1902	£1.50	£75.00
50	Vanity Fair 1st Series	1902	£1.50	£75.00
50	Vanity Fair 2nd Series	1902	£1.50	£75.00
50	Waterloo	Unissued	£40.00	—
50	Wild Animals of the World (Green Scroll Back)	1900	£2.50	£125.00
15	Wild Animals of the World (Grey Descriptive Back)	1902	£20.00	£300.00
52	Wild Animals of the World (P/C Inset)	1900	£5.00	£260.00
50	Wild Flowers	1923	12p	£4.00
50	Wild Flowers A Series (adhesive)	1936	12p	£3.00
50	Wild Flowers (Eire)	1936	15p	£7.50
50	Wild Flowers 2nd Series	1937	12p	£2.50
50	Wild Flowers 2nd Series (Eire)	1937	15p	£7.50
50	Wonders of the Past	1926	20p	£10.00

Qty		*Date*	*Odds*	*Sets*
50	Wonders of the Sea	1928	16p	£8.00
MODERN ISSUES (EMBASSY)				
M36	World of Firearms	1982	12p	£2.00
M36	World of Speed	1981	12p	£2.00
AUSTRALIAN ISSUES				
100	Actresses	1903	£1.25	—
1	Advertisement Card (Capstan)	1902	C	—
60	Animals (cut-outs)	1916	30p	£18.00
60	Animals (cut-outs Havelock)	1916	75p	—
50	Arms & Armour	1910	60p	£30.00
50	Arms & Armour (Havelock)	1910	£1.25	—
50	Arms of the British Empire	1910	20p	£10.00
50	Arms of the British Empire (Havelock)	1910	50p	—
M50	Arms of the British Empire (Silk)	1910	£1.00	£50.00
50	A Tour Round the World	1907	£1.00	£50.00
25	Australian & English Cricketers (Numbered)	1903	£5.00	£125.00
25	Australian & English Cricketers (Blue/Red Frame)	1909	£5.00	£125.00
59	Australian & English Cricketers (Titled)	1911	£5.00	£300.00
50	Australian & English Cricketers (Havelock)	1911	£12.50	—
24	Australian & South African Cricketers (dark background—SA only)	1910	£7.50	—
60	Australian & South African Cricketers (light background)	1910	£6.00	£360.00
60	Australian & South African Cricketers (Havelock)	1910	£15.00	—
M50	Australian Butterflies (Silk)	1914	£1.00	£50.00
40/46	Australian Club Cricketers	1905	£6.00	—
MF100	Australian Scenic Series	1925	25p	£25.00
50	Australian Wild Flowers	1913	25p	£12.50
50	Australian Wild Flowers (Havelock)	1913	75p	—
75	Aviation (Black Back)	1910	60p	£45.00
75	Aviation (Black Back, Havelock)	1910	£1.25	—
75	Aviation (Green Back)	1910	75p	—
75	Aviation (Green Back, Havelock)	1910	£1.50	—
85	Aviation	1910	80p	£68.00
50	Best Dogs of their Breed	1914	£1.25	£62.50
50	Best Dogs of Their Breed (Havelock)	1914	£2.50	—
M50	Birds and Animals of Australia (Silk)	1915	£1.00	£50.00
100	Birds of Australasia (Green Back)	1912	35p	£35.00
100	Birds of Australasia (Green Back, Havelock)	1912	75p	—
100	Birds of Australasia (Yellow Back)	1912	30p	£30.00
100	Birds of Australasia (Yellow Back, Havelock)	1912	75p	—
50	Britain's Defenders (1-50)	1914	40p	£20.00
50	Britain's Defenders (Havelock)	1914	£1.00	£50.00
8	Britain's Defenders (51-8)	1914	£4.00	—
50	British Empire Series	1912	25p	£12.50
50	British Empire Series (Havelock)	1912	75p	£37.50
M68	Crests and Colours of Australian Universities Colleges and Schools	1929	15p	£10.00
M50	Crests and Colours of Australian Universities Colleges and Schools (Silk)	1929	£1.00	£50.00

Qty		*Date*	*Odds*	*Sets*
M1	Crests and Colours of Australian Schools (Silk, Unnumbered)	1929	A	—
50	Cricketers (Grey Scroll Back, No Frame)	1901	£35.00	—
25	Cricketers (Grey Scroll Back, Fancy Frame)	1902	£35.00	—
F63	Cricketers (Plain Back)	1926	£2.00	£130.00
F40/48	Cricket Season, 1928-29	1929	75p	£30.00
L20	Dogs A Series	1927	35p	£7.00
L20	Dogs 2nd Series	1928	35p	£7.00
L25	English Period Costumes	1929	40p	£10.00
100	Famous Film Stars	1930	20p	£20.00
M100	Famous Film Stars	1933	30p	£30.00
MF100	Famous Film Stars	1933	60p	£60.00
B20	Fiestas (Cartons)	1968	65p	—
50	Fish of Australasia	1912	25p	£12.50
50	Fish of Australasia (Havelock)	1912	75p	—
50	Flag Girls of All Nations	1908	£1.00	£50.00
8	Flags (Shaped, Metal)	1915	£3.00	—
M13	Flags (Lace)	1916	£2.00	£26.00
28	Flags of the Allies (Silk)	1915	50p	£15.00
25	Flags of the Empire	1926	A	—
28	Football Club Colours & Flags	1913	£1.50	—
28	Football Club Colours & Flags (Havelock)	1913	£2.50	—
200	Footballers 1933	1933	25p	£50.00
M200	Footballers 1933	1933	40p	—
?6	Footballers (Shaped)	1910	B	—
?	Football Pennants (Shaped)	1905	B	—
?	Football Pennants (Shaped Havelock)	1905	B	—
50	Girls of All Nations	1908	£1.00	£50.00
X?	Havelock Comics	1904	C	—
50	Historic Events	1913	25p	£12.50
50	Historic Events (Havelock)	1913	80p	£40.00
L25	History of Naval Dress	1929	A	—
50	Horses of Today	1906	60p	£30.00
50	Horses of Today (Havelock)	1906	£1.25	—
50	Interesting Buildings	1905	60p	£30.00
5	Islands of the Pacific	1917	C	—
38	Kings & Queens of England (Silk)	1910	£1.50	£60.00
45	Melbourne Cup Winners	1906	£2.00	—
40	Merrie England Studies	1916	£2.00	£80.00
50	Modern War Weapons	1915	50p	£25.00
50	Modern War Weapons (Havelock)	1915	£1.00	—
50	Past & Present Champions	1908	£2.00	£100.00
M50	Popular Flowers (Silk)	1913	£1.50	£75.00
L70	Practical Wireless	1923	60p	£42.00
50	Prominent Australian & English Cricketers (1-50)	1907	£5.00	£250.00
23	Prominent Australian & English Cricketers (51-73)	1907	£5.00	£115.00
10	Recruiting Posters (Anon back)	1915	£3.00	£30.00
50	Riders of the World	1913	60p	£30.00
50	Riders of the World (Havelock)	1913	£1.25	—
50	Royal Mail	1913	50p	£25.00
50	Royal Mail (Havelock)	1913	£1.00	—
50	Signalling Series	1912	20p	£10.00
50	Signalling Series (Havelock)	1912	60p	£30.00

Qty		*Date*	*Odds*	*Sets*
40	Sketches in Black & White	1905	£1.00	—
50	Soldiers of the World	1902	£2.50	£125.00
25	Sporting Terms	1905	£3.00	—
50	Sports of the World	1917	£1.50	—
50	Stage & Music Hall Celebrities (Oval Frame)	1904	80p	£40.00
50	Stage & Music Hall Celebrities (Havelock)	1904	£2.00	—
50	Stage & Music Hall Celebrities (Square Frame)	1904	80p	£40.00
L25	The Nation's Shrines	1928	40p	£10.00
25	The World's Dreadnoughts	1910	40p	£10.00
50	Time & Money in Different Countries	1908	30p	£15.00
50	Time & Money in Different Countries (Havelock)	1908	80p	£40.00
50	Types of the British Army	1912	£1.00	£50.00
50	Types of the Commonwealth Forces	1910	£1.25	£62.50
50	Types of the Commonwealth Forces (Havelock)	1910	£2.50	—
P1	Union Jack (Silk)	1915	—	£5.00
25	United States Warships	1911	80p	£20.00
25	United States Warships (Havelock)	1911	£2.00	—
25	Victoria Cross Heroes	1915	80p	£20.00
25	Victoria Cross Heroes (Havelock)	1915	£2.00	£50.00
29	Victorian Football Pennants	1910	£1.50	—
29	Victorian Football Pennants (Havelock)	1910	£3.00	—
FS165	Views of the World	1908	30p	£50.00
50	War Incidents	1915	40p	£20.00
50	War Incidents (Havelock)	1915	£1.00	—
50	War Incidents, 2nd Series	1915	50p	£25.00
50	War Incidents 2nd Series (Havelock)	1915	£1.50	—
L67	War Medals (Silk)	1916	£1.50	£100.00
50	War Pictures	1915	40p	£20.00
50	War Pictures (Havelock)	1915	£1.00	£50.00
50	Wild Animals (Heads)	1934	15p	£7.50
M25	Wild Animals (Heads)	1934	30p	£7.50
50	Wild Animals of the World	1906	£1.25	£62.50
LF50	Zoological Series	1922	60p	£30.00

BRAND ISSUES

(A) Autocar Cigarettes

40	Chinese Trades	1905	£2.50	—

(B) Flag Cigarettes

67	International Footballers, Season 1909-1910	1910	£2.50	—
50	Jiu Jitsu	1911	£2.00	—
50	Types of the British Army	1912	£2.00	—

(C) Four Aces Cigarettes

52	Birds of Brilliant Plumage (P/C Inset)	1924	£1.25	£65.00
75	Film Favourites	1928	60p	£45.00
25	Modes of Conveyance	1928	60p	£15.00
50	Stage & Film Stars (numbered)	1926	50p	£25.00
50	Stage & Film Stars (unnumbered)	1926	60p	£30.00
F52	Stars of the Cinema	1926	£1.00	—

Qty		Date	Odds	Sets
(D)	**Pirate Cigarettes**			
G?	Advertisement Cards	1910	£30.00	—
?100	Baseball Series	1912	A	—
52	Birds of Brilliant Plumage (P/C Inset frame line)	1914	£1.50	—
52	Birds of Brilliant Plumage (P/C Inset no frame)	1914	£1.50	£78.00
100	China's Ancient Warriors	1911	50p	£50.00
28	Chinese Actors & Actresses	1907	80p	£22.50
50	Chinese Beauties	1907	50p	£25.00
50	Chinese Costumes	1928	£1.25	—
P25	Chinese Pagodas	1911	A	—
50	Chinese Proverbs (Brown)	1928	60p	£30.00
50	Chinese Proverbs (Coloured)	1914	60p	£30.00
33	Houses of Parliament	1914	50p	£16.50
50	Products of the World	1913	60p	£30.00
(E)	**Purple Mountain Cigarettes**			
20	Flowers (Numbered)	1914	A	—
100	Flowers (Unnumbered)	1915	A	—
25	Roses	1912	£2.00	£50.00
(F)	**Ruby Queen Cigarettes**			
30	Birds & Animals	1911	£1.00	—
50	Birds of the East	1912	40p	£20.00
30	Chinese Children's Games	1911	60p	—
50	Chinese Proverbs	1927	50p	—
50	Chinese Transport	1914	75p	—
(G)	**Scissors Cigarettes**			
50	Actresses (Black & White)	1904	A	—
50	Actresses (Four Colour Surround)	1904	A	—
30	Actresses (Green Surround)	1905	£2.50	—
30	Actresses (Mauve Surround)	1916	60p	£18.00
30	Actresses (Orange Surround)	1916	£1.00	£30.00
30	Actresses (Purple Brown, Brown Back)	1908	£1.00	£30.00
30	Actresses (Purple Brown, Red Back)	1908	60p	£18.00
30	Actresses (Purple Brown, Long Card)	1909	60p	£18.00
25	Army Life	1914	80p	£20.00
30	Beauties (Green Surround)	1921	£2.50	—
52	Beauties (P/C Inset) (lattice background)	1911	£1.25	£65.00
52	Beauties (P/C Inset, no lattice on back)	1911	£2.50	—
32	Beauties (Picture Hat)	1914	£1.25	£40.00
40	Beauties (Brown Tint)	1913	60p	£24.00
30	Beauties & Children	1910	£1.20	£40.00
36	Boxers	1911	£2.50	£90.00
50	Britain's Defenders (Green Back)	1914	60p	£30.00
50	Britain's Defenders (Red Back & Front)	1914	50p	£25.00
50	Britain's Defenders (Red Back, Blue Front)	1914	50p	£25.00
43	British Army Boxers	1913	£1.25	£55.00
25	Cinema Stars	1916	60p	£15.00
F50	Cinema Stars	1926	A	—
27	Dancing Girls (Series of 27)	1915	£1.25	£35.00
27/28	Dancing Girls (Series of 28)	1915	£1.25	£35.00
25	Derby Day Series	1914	£1.00	£25.00
25	Derby Day Series A (no series title)	1914	£2.50	—

Qty		Date	Odds	Sets
32	Drum Horses (Horizontal back)	1909	£3.00	£96.00
32	Drum Horses (Vertical back)	1909	£4.00	—
50	Famous Footballers	1914	£1.20	£60.00
25	Flag Girls of All Nations	1908	A	—
50	Football Club Colours	1907	£2.00	£100.00
25	Governors-General of India	1912	£3.00	£75.00
30	Heroic Deeds	1913	80p	£24.00
50	Indian Regiments Series	1912	£3.00	£150.00
67	International Footballers, Season 1909-1910	1910	£2.50	—
50	Jiu Jitsu	1910	£2.50	—
53	Jockeys & Owners Colours (P/C Inset)	1914	£3.00	—
25	Military Portraits	1917	£2.50	£62.50
50	Music Hall Celebrities	1911	£2.50	£125.00
K52	Playing Cards	1906	A	—
25	Puzzle Series (United Service Backs)	1910	£3.00	—
50	Regimental Colours & Cap Badges	1907	60p	£30.00
33	Regimental Pets	1911	£2.50	£85.00
30	Sporting Girls	1913	£2.50	—
50	Types of the British Army	1908	£2.00	£100.00
25	Victoria Cross Heroes	1915	£1.00	£25.00
50	War Incidents	1915	60p	£30.00
30	What It Means	1916	50p	£15.00
F50	"Zoo"	1927	A	—

(H) United Service Cigarettes

50	Arms & Armour	1910	£1.00	£50.00
32	Drum Horses	1909	£3.00	£96.00
25	Flag Girls of All Nations	1908	£1.00	£25.00
67	International Footballers, Season 1909-1910	1910	£2.50	—
	Puzzle Series—See Scissors Cigarettes			
50	Regimental Colours & Cap Badges (Blue Back)	1907	40p	£20.00
50	Regimental Colours & Cap Badges (Red Back)	1907	50p	£25.00

(I) Wild Woodbine Cigarettes

50	British Army Uniforms	1909	£2.50	£125.00

CHANNEL ISLANDS ISSUES (Similar to British Sets)

50	Air Raid Precautions	1938	25p	£12.50
50	Association Footballers	1935	35p	£17.50
50	Dogs	1937	25p	£12.50
50	Garden Flowers by Sudell	1939	12p	£6.00
50	Garden Hints	1938	12p	£6.00
50	Household Hints	1936	12p	£6.00
50	Life in the Royal Navy	1939	12p	£6.00
50	Our King & Queen	1937	16p	£8.00
50	Railway Equipment	1938	16p	£8.00
50	Speed	1938	16p	£8.00
50	The Sea Shore	1938	12p	£6.00
50	Wild Flowers A Series	1936	25p	£12.50
50	Wild Flowers 2nd Series	1937	16p	£8.00

NEW ZEALAND ISSUES

F50	A Sporting Holiday in New Zealand	1928	15p	£7.50
LF50	A Sporting Holiday in New Zealand (Different)	1928	35p	£17.50

Qty		Date	Odds	Sets
F50	Beautiful New Zealand	1928	12p	£3.50
50	Birds, Beasts and Fishes	1924	25p	£12.50
F48	British Royal and Ancient Buildings	1925	15p	£7.50
45	British Rugby Players	1930	50p	£22.50
50	Children of All Nations	1925	15p	£7.50
50	Coaches and Coaching Days	1925	40p	£20.00
50	Dogs	1926	12p	£6.00
F25	English Cricketers	1926	60p	£15.00
26	Etchings (Dogs)	1925	24p	£6.00
L26	Etchings (Dogs)	1925	40p	£10.00
50	Famous Inventions	1926	25p	£12.50
L25	Heraldic Signs & Their Origin	1925	40p	£10.00
F50	Homeland Events	1927	12p	£4.00
50	Household Hints	1927	12p	£5.00
50	Lighthouses	1926	12p	£3.50
50	Merchant Ships of the World	1925	20p	£10.00
48	Motor Cars	1923	60p	£30.00
F50	Motor Cars	1926	40p	£20.00
50	Motor Cycles	1926	60p	£30.00
50	New Zealand Birds	1925	30p	£15.00
F50	New Zealand—Early Scenes & Maori Life	1926	15p	£7.50
F50	New Zealand Footballers	1927	12p	£6.00
50	New Zealand Racehorses	1928	30p	£15.00
50	N.Z. Butterflies, Moths & Beetles	1925	20p	£10.00
25	Past & Present	1929	30p	£7.50
25	Picturesque People of the Empire	1928	24p	£6.00
25	Pirates & Highwaymen	1925	24p	£6.00
50	Products of the World	1929	15p	£7.50
50	Railway Engines	1925	25p	£12.50
50	Railway Working	1927	75p	£37.50
50	Regimental Standards and Cap Badges	1928	15p	£7.50
50	Riders of the World	1931	25p	£12.50
50	Romance of the Heavens	1928	40p	—
50	Safety First	1935	30p	£15.00
F50	Ships and Shipping	1928	12p	£5.00
50	Ships' Badges	1925	40p	£20.00
F50	The Royal Family at Home & Abroad	1927	30p	£15.00
F50	The Royal Navy	1929	75p	—
F50	Units of the British Army and R.A.F.	1928	12p	£5.00
50	U.S.S. Co's. Steamers	1930	75p	—
50	V.C's.	1926	50p	£25.00
25	Village Models Series	1925	40p	£10.00
L25	Village Models Series	1925	A	—
50	Warships	1926	50p	£25.00
25	Wonders of the World	1926	20p	£5.00
F50	"Zoo"	1926	12p	£4.00

OTHER OVERSEAS ISSUES

50	Actors & Actresses "WALP"	1905	£1.00	£50.00
250	Actresses "ALWICS"	1905	80p	£200.00
25	Actresses, Tabs Type (101-125)	1902	£5.00	£125.00
50	Actresses, Four Colour Surround	1904	£1.00	£50.00
50	Aeroplanes	1926	75p	—
50	Animals & Birds (With Series Title)	1912	£1.20	£60.00

W. D. & H. O. WILLS LTD.—cont.

Qty		Date	Odds	Sets
50	Animals & Birds (No Series Title)	1909	£1.20	£60.00
50	Arms of the British Empire	1911	30p	£15.00
50	Art Photogravures—Set 1	1912	15p	£7.50
B50	Art Photogravures—Set 1	1912	20p	£10.00
50	Art Photogravures—Set 2	1913	15p	£7.50
50	Aviation Series	1911	80p	£40.00
50	Beauties "LAWHA" (Red Tinted)	1905	80p	£40.00
40	Beauties (Brown Tinted)	1913	£1.25	—
52	Beauties (P/C Inset)	1911	£2.00	—
32	Beauties—Picture Hats	1914	£2.00	—
M72	Beauties	1923	£4.00	—
BF50	Beauties (Hand Coloured)	1925	75p	—
F25	Beauties	1925	£1.00	—
F50	Beauties, 2nd Series	1925	£1.00	—
52	Birds of Brilliant Plumage (P/C Inset)	1914	£2.00	—
36	Boxers	1911	£3.00	£108.00
50	Britain's Defenders	1914	£1.00	£50.00
101	British Beauties	1915	75p	£75.00
50	British Costumes from 100 BC to 1904	1905	B	—
50	Chateaux	1925	£1.50	£75.00
50	Conundrums	1903	£3.50	£175.00
25	Derby Day Series	1914	£3.00	—
32	Drum Horses	1909	£3.00	£96.00
26	Etchings (Dutch Text)	1925	£1.50	—
50	Famous Footballers	1914	£2.00	—
25	Flag Girls of All Nations	1908	80p	£20.00
126	Flags & Ensigns	1904	50p	£60.00
6	Flags of the Allies (Shaped)	1915	£5.00	£30.00
50	Girls of All Nations	1908	£1.25	—
32	Houses of Parliament	1912	60p	£20.00
50	Indian Regiments Series	1912	£3.50	—
24	Merveilles Du Monde	1927	£3.00	—
M25	Miniatures (Metal)	1914	£25.00	£625.00
F48	Movie Stars	1927	A	—
50	National Flags and Arms	1936	60p	—
FS50	Nature Studies	1928	60p	£30.00
25	Police of the World	1910	£2.50	£62.50
25	Products of the World	1913	60p	—
50	Races of Mankind	1911	£5.00	£250.00
100	Royalty, Notabilities & Events, 1900-2	1902	80p	£80.00
27	Rulers of the World	1911	£2.50	£70.00
100	Russo Japanese Series (black front)	1905	60p	£60.00
50	Russo Japanese Series (red front)	1905	£3.00	—
LF48	Scenes from the Empire	1939	60p	—
30	Semaphore Signalling	1910	75p	£22.50
36	Ships & Their Pennants	1913	£1.50	—
75	Soldiers of the World	1903	£4.00	—
F52	Stars of the Cinema	1926	A	—
25	The Evolution of the British Navy	1915	80p	£20.00
25	The World's Dreadnoughts	1910	50p	£12.50
50	Wild Animals of the World (Star, Circle & Leaves)	1906	£2.50	—

WILSON & CO.

50	War Portraits	1916	B	—

W. WILSON

Qty		Date	Odds	Sets
30	Army Pictures, Cartoons, etc.	1916	B	—

A. & M. WIX

D250	Cinema Cavalcade	1936	16p	£40.00
D250	Cinema Cavalcade, Volume 2	1937	15p	£37.50
100	Film Favourites	1930	£1.00	—
100	Film Favourites, 2nd Series	1931	75p	—
100	Film Favourites, 3rd Series	1932	35p	£35.00
L?23	Maxims of Max (Package Issue)	1952	A	—
X100	Men of Destiny	1934	£2.00	—
D250	Speed—Through the Ages	1938	20p	£50.00
D250	This Age of Power & Wonder	1935	15p	£37.50

J. WIX & SONS LTD.

F?	Animals	1928	B	—
P80	Bridge Favours & Place Cards	1937	A	—
P50	Bridge Hands	1937	A	—
L48	British Empire Flags (Silk)	1938	25p	£12.00
L48	British Empire Flags (Silk, Printed in U.S.A.)	1938	25p	£12.00
50	Builders of Empire	1937	12p	£5.00
42	Card Tricks	1938	£1.00	—
M42	Card Tricks	1938	£1.25	—
50	Coronation (Kensitas)	1937	12p	£5.00
50	Coronation (Wix)	1937	12p	£5.00
L50	Henry	1935	15p	£7.50
P25	Henry	1935	60p	£15.00
L50	Henry, 2nd Series	1936	40p	£20.00
P25	Henry, 2nd Series	1936	60p	£15.00
L50	Henry, 3rd Series	1936	15p	£7.50
L50	Henry, 4th Series	1936	12p	£5.00
L50	Henry, 5th Series	1937	12p	£3.50
L182	Jenkynisms (Yellow)	1932	30p	—
?150	Jenkynisms (Red Borders)	1931	A	—
L?150	Jenkynisms (Red Borders)	1931	A	—
P96	Ken-Cards	1969	20p	£20.00
60	Kensitas Flowers (Silk, plain back)	1923	40p	£24.00
60	Kensitas Flowers (Silk, printed back)	1923	40p	£24.00
L60	Kensitas Flowers (Silk, plain back)	1923	75p	£45.00
L60	Kensitas Flowers (Silk, printed back)	1923	75p	£45.00
P30	Kensitas Flowers (Silk)	1923	£6.00	—
40	Kensitas Flowers 2nd Series (Silk)	1924	£1.00	£50.00
L40	Kensitas Flowers 2nd Series (Silk)	1924	£1.25	£65.00
25	Love Scenes from Famous Films, 1st Series	1932	80p	£20.00
L25	Love Scenes from Famous Films, 1st Series	1932	£1.00	£25.00
P25	Love Scenes from Famous Films, 1st Series	1932	£1.50	—
25	Love Scenes from Famous Films, 2nd Series	1932	80p	—
L25	Love Scenes from Famous Films, 2nd Series	1932	£1.00	—
P25	Love Scenes from Famous Films, 2nd Series	1932	£1.50	—
K53	Miniature Playing Cards (Blue Scroll)	1938	12p	£5.00
K53	Miniature Playing Cards (Red Scroll)	1938	12p	£5.00
K53	Miniature Playing Cards (Revenge)	1938	12p	£6.50
K53	Miniature Playing Cards (Victory)	1938	12p	£6.50
L60	National Flags (Silk)	1939	30p	£18.00
F24	Royal Tour in New Zealand	1928	£5.00	—

J. WIX & SONS LTD.—cont.

Qty		Date	Odds	Sets
25	Scenes from Famous Films	1932	80p	£20.00
P25	Scenes from Famous Films	1932	£1.50	—

T. WOOD & SONS

30	Army Pictures, Cartoons, etc.	1916	B	—

WOOD BROS.

28	Dominoes	1910	B	—

JOHN J. WOODS

?	Views of London	1905	C	—

W. H. & J. WOODS LTD.

25	Aesop's Fables	1932	50p	£12.50
F50	Modern Motor Cars	1936	£1.25	—
25	Romance of the Royal Mail	1931	20p	£5.00
25	Types of Volunteer & Yeomanry	1902	£12.00	£300.00

J. & E. WOOLF

50	Beauties "KEWA"	1898	D	—

M. H. WOOLLER

24	Beauties "BOCCA"	1899	D	—

T. E. YEOMANS & SONS LTD.

M72	Beauties	1900	C	—
50	War Portraits	1916	B	—

JOHN YOUNG & SONS LTD.

12	Naval Skits	1904	£75.00	—
12	Russo Japanese Series	1904	£35.00	—

A. ZICALIOTTI

1	Milly-Totty Advertisement Card	1900	D	—

Part 2

OVERSEAS TOBACCO MANUFACTURERS

AFRICAN TOBACCO MANUFACTURERS (S. Africa)

Qty		*Date*	*Odds*	*Sets*
L18	All Blacks South African Tour, 1928	1928	A	—
60	Animals	1922	£2.00	—
MF48	British Aircraft	1926	£1.50	—
50	Chinese Transport	1923	£2.00	—
MF48	Cinema Artistes	1926	£1.00	—
50	Cinema Stars "OMBI", 1st Series	1923	75p	—
50	Cinema Stars "OMBI", 2nd Series	1923	75p	—
B50	Famous & Beautiful Women	1938	75p	—
L50	Famous & Beautiful Women	1938	75p	—
33	Houses of Parliament	1923	£2.50	—
?60	Miniatures	1924	£4.00	—
MF48	National Costumes	1926	£1.00	—
53	Playing Cards (MP)	1929	50p	—
53	Playing Cards (OK)	1929	50p	—
53	Playing Cards (Scots)	1929	50p	—
MF48	Popular Dogs	1926	£1.25	—
B100	Postage Stamps—Rarest Varieties	1930	50p	£50.00
B80	Prominent N.Z. & Australian Rugby Players and Springbok 1937 Touring Team	1937	50p	—
L80	Prominent N.Z. & Australian Rugby Players and Springbok 1937 Touring Team	1937	40p	£40.00
29	S.A. Rugby Football Team, 1912-13	1912	A	—
L30	Some Beautiful Roses (Silk)	1928	£4.00	£120.00
?115	S. African Members of the Legislative Assembly	1919	A	—
25	The Arcadia Fair	1923	£4.00	—
25	The Racecourse	1923	£3.00	—
B100	The World of Sport	1939	50p	—
L100	The World of Sport	1939	50p	—
L25	Types of British Birds (Silk)	1928	£5.00	£125.00
L20	Types of British Butterflies (Silk)	1928	£5.00	—
L25	Types of Railway Engines (Silk)	1928	£10.00	—
L25	Types of Sea Shells (Silk)	1928	£6.00	—

ALLEN & GINTER (U.S.A.)

50	American Editors	1887	£7.50	£375.00
X50	American Editors	1887	£12.50	—
50	Arms of All Nations	1887	£6.00	£300.00
50	Birds of America	1890	£3.50	£175.00
X50	Birds of America	1890	£8.00	£400.00
50	Birds of the Tropics	1889	£4.00	£200.00
X50	Birds of the Tropics	1889	£8.00	—
50	Celebrated American Indian Chiefs	1888	£5.00	£250.00
50	City Flags	1888	£4.00	£200.00
50	Fans of the Period	1886	£8.00	£400.00
50	Fish from American Waters	1889	£4.00	£200.00
X50	Fish from American Waters	1889	£8.00	—
48	Flags of All Nations, 1st Series	1887	£3.00	£150.00
50	Flags of All Nations, 2nd Series	1890	£4.00	£200.00
47	Flags of The States & Territories	1890	£4.00	£190.00
50	Fruits	1891	£7.50	£375.00
50	Game Birds	1889	£4.00	£200.00
X50	Game Birds	1889	£8.00	—
50	General Government & State Capitol Buildings	1889	£4.00	£200.00
50	Great Generals	1886	£12.50	—

ALLEN & GINTER (U.S.A.)—cont.

Qty		Date	Odds	Sets
50	Natives in Costume	1886	£12.50	—
50	Naval Flags	1887	£5.00	£250.00
50	Parasol Drill	1888	£7.50	£375.00
F?	Photographic Cards (Many Types)	1885	From £1.00	
50	Pirates of the Spanish Main	1888	£8.00	—
50	Prize & Game Chickens	1892	£4.00	£200.00
50	Quadrupeds	1889	£5.00	£250.00
X50	Quadrupeds	1889	£8.00	—
50	Racing Colours of the World (no border)	1888	£6.00	£300.00
50	Racing Colours of the World (white border)	1888	£5.00	£250.00
50	Song Birds of the World	1890	£4.00	£200.00
X50	Song Birds of the World	1890	£8.00	—
X50	The American Indian	1888	£10.00	£500.00
50	The World's Beauties, 1st Series	1888	£7.50	—
50	The World's Beauties, 2nd Series	1888	£7.50	—
50	The World's Champions, 1st Series	1888	£4.00	—
50	The World's Champions, 2nd Series	1889	£5.00	—
X50	The World's Champions, 2nd Series	1889	£10.00	—
50	The World's Decorations	1890	£4.00	£200.00
X50	The World's Decorations	1890	£8.00	£400.00
50	The World's Racers	1888	£7.50	—
50	Types of All Nations	1887	£7.50	£375.00
50	Wild Animals of the World	1888	£5.00	£250.00
50	World's Dudes	1888	£6.00	£300.00
50	World's Smokers	1888	£6.00	£300.00
50	World's Sovereigns	1887	£10.00	—
Printed Albums (exchanged for coupons)				
	American Editors	1887	—	£50.00
	Birds of America	1890	—	£35.00
	Birds of the Tropics	1889	—	£35.00
	Celebrated American Indian Chiefs	1888	—	B
	City Flags	1888	—	£50.00
	Decorations of Principal Orders	1890	—	£45.00
	Fish from American Waters	1889	—	£35.00
	Flags of All Nations	1890	—	£40.00
	Game Birds	1889	—	£35.00
	General Government & State Capitol Buildings of the United States	1889	—	£35.00
	George Washington	1889	—	£50.00
	Napoleon	1889	—	£50.00
	Our Navy	1889	—	£45.00
	Paris Exhibition 1889	1889	—	£40.00
	Quadrupeds	1889	—	£50.00
	Racing Colours of the World	1888	—	£40.00
	Song Birds of the World	1890	—	£35.00
	With the Poets in Smokeland	1890	—	£40.00
	World's Beauties, 1st Series	1888	—	£40.00
	World's Beauties, 2nd Series	1888	—	£50.00
	World's Champions, 1st Series	1888	—	B
	World's Champions, 2nd Series	1889	—	B
	World's Inventors	1888	—	£40.00
	World's Racers	1888	—	B

ALLEN TOBACCO CO. (U.S.A.)

X?300	Views & Art Studies	1912	£1.50	—

AMERICAN CIGARETTE CO. (China)

Qty		*Date*	*Odds*	*Sets*
10	Admirals & Generals	1900	£25.00	—
25	Beauties (Black Back)	1902	£6.00	—
?25	Beauties (Green Back)	1901	£10.00	—
52	Beauties, Playing Card Inset	1901	£15.00	—
?	Chinese Girls	1900	B	—
50	Flowers	1902	£6.00	—

AMERICAN EAGLE TOBACCO CO. (U.S.A.)

36	Flags of All Nations	1890	£12.50	—
36	Flags of States	1890	£12.50	—
50	Occupations for Women	1892	£20.00	—
F?	Photographic Cards	1886	£2.50	—
LF?	Photographic Cards	1886	A	—
23	Presidents of U.S.	1890	£12.50	—

AMERICAN TOBACCO CO. (U.S.A.)

Early Issues

F100	Actresses (Black Back)	1901	£1.00	—
F300	Actresses (Blue Back)	1901	£1.00	—
44	Australian Parliament	1901	£1.50	£66.00
25	Battle Scenes	1901	£4.00	£100.00
177	Beauties (Typeset Back)	1901	75p	—
350	Beauties (Old Gold Back)	1901	75p	—
101	Beauties (Label Back)	1901	£1.00	—
?500	Beauties (Green Net Back)	1901	75p	—
?75	Beauties (Blue Net Back)	1901	£3.00	—
24	Beauties (Plain Back, Carton)	1901	£1.25	£30.00
25	Beauties, Black Background	1900	£4.00	£100.00
25	Beauties, Blue Frame Line	1900	£10.00	—
25	Beauties, Curtain Background	1900	£3.00	£75.00
28	Beauties, Domino Girls	1900	£10.00	—
25	Beauties, Flower Girls	1900	£3.00	£75.00
25	Beauties, Flowers Inset	1900	£3.00	£75.00
25	Beauties, International Code of Signals, 1st ...	1900	£2.50	£62.50
25	Beauties, International Code of Signals, 2nd ...	1900	£3.00	£75.00
50	Beauties, Marine & Universe Girls	1900	£4.00	£200.00
25	Beauties, Numbered	1900	£7.50	—
25	Beauties, Orange Framelines	1900	£12.50	—
25	Beauties, Palette Girls	1900	£4.00	£100.00
F?	Beauties, Photographic	1894	£7.50	—
52	Beauties, Playing Card Inset, Set 1	1900	£4.00	£100.00
52	Beauties, Playing Card Inset, Set 2	1900	£3.00	£150.00
53	Beauties, Playing Card Superimposed, Set 3 ...	1900	£3.00	£150.00
25	Beauties, Star Girls	1900	£7.50	—
25	Beauties, Star Series	1900	£7.50	—
25	Beauties, Stippled Background	1900	£3.00	£75.00
100	Beauties, Thick Borders	1895	A	—
25	Boer War, Series A	1901	£1.20	£30.00
22	Boer War, Series B	1901	£1.50	£35.00
50	Butterflies	1895	£10.00	—
32	Celebrities	1900	£2.00	£65.00
25	Chinese Girls	1900	£5.00	£125.00
1	Columbian & Other Postage Stamps	1895	—	£4.00
25	Comic Scenes	1900	£3.00	£75.00

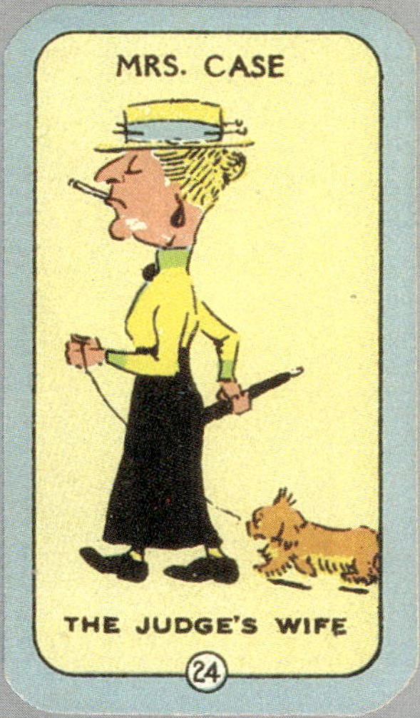

Happy Family. Carreras

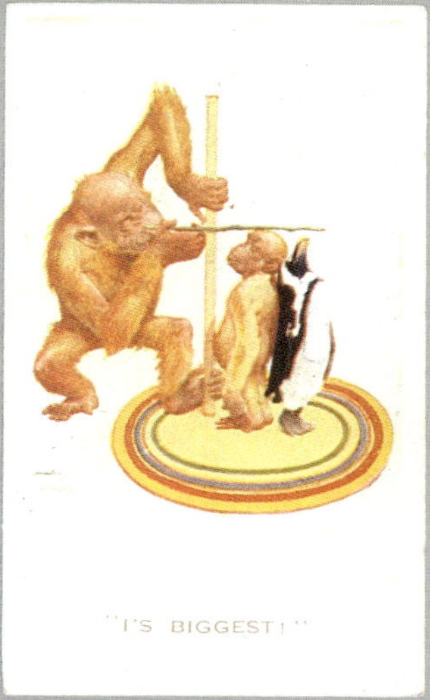

Gran-pop. Carreras

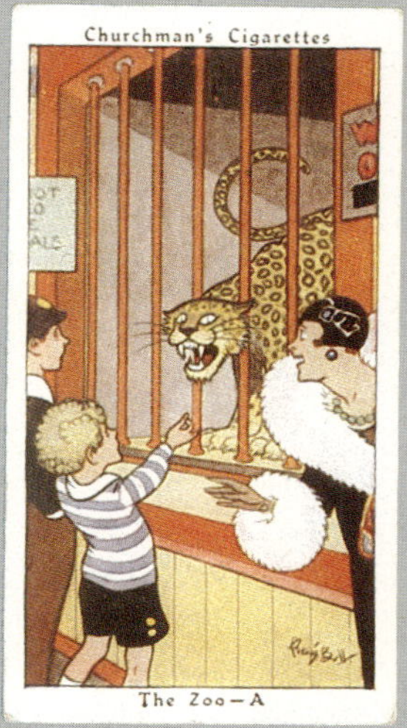

Howlers. Churchman

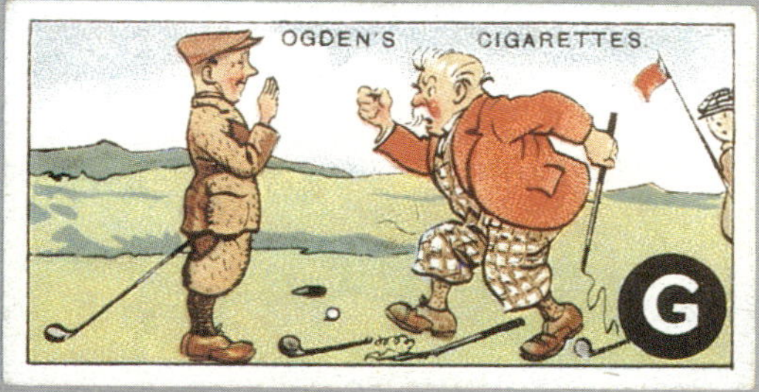

A.B.C. of Sport. Ogden

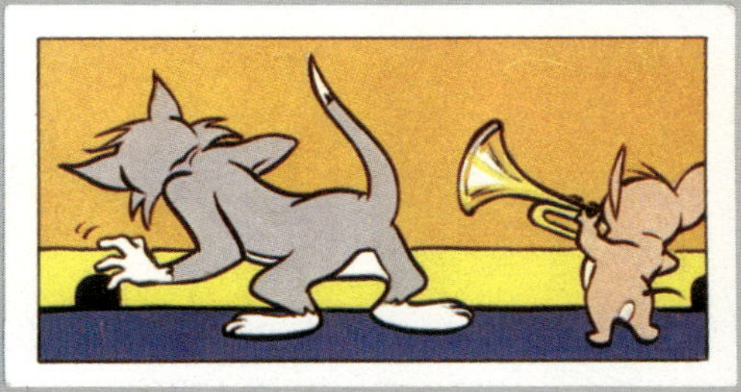
Tom & Jerry. Barratt

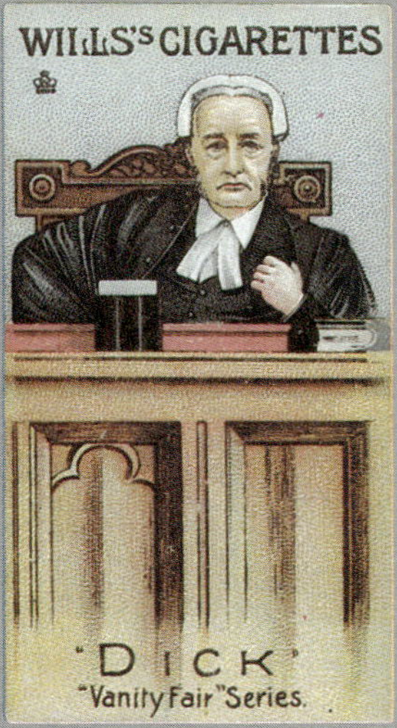

Vanity Fair Series. Wills

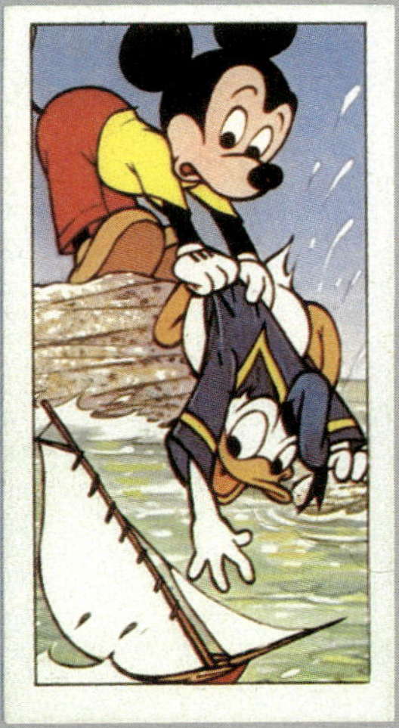
Disney—Health & Safety. Bassett

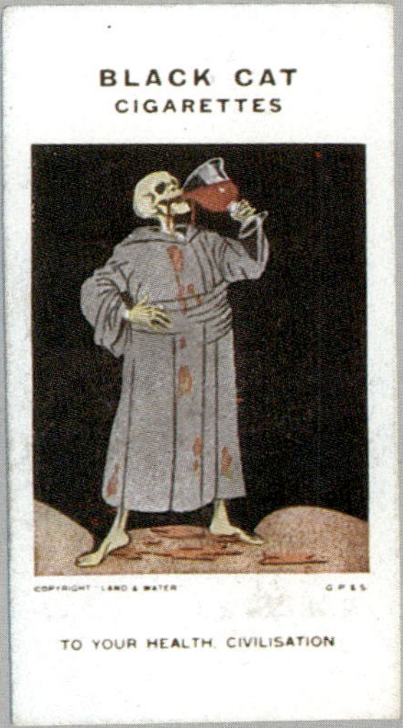

Raemaekers War Cartoons. Carreras

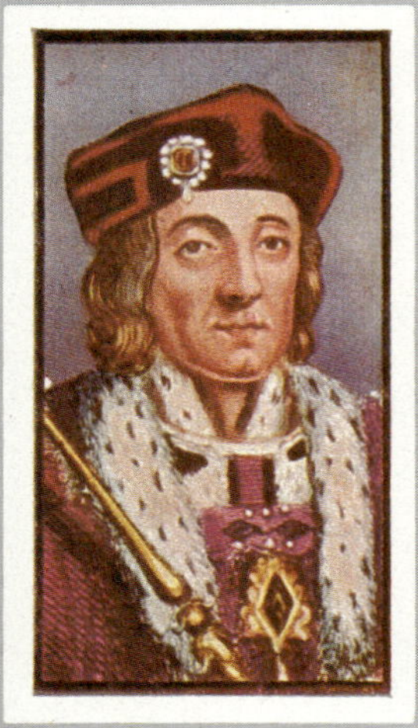

Kings & Queens. Gaycon, Gee, Kane, Kings or Queens

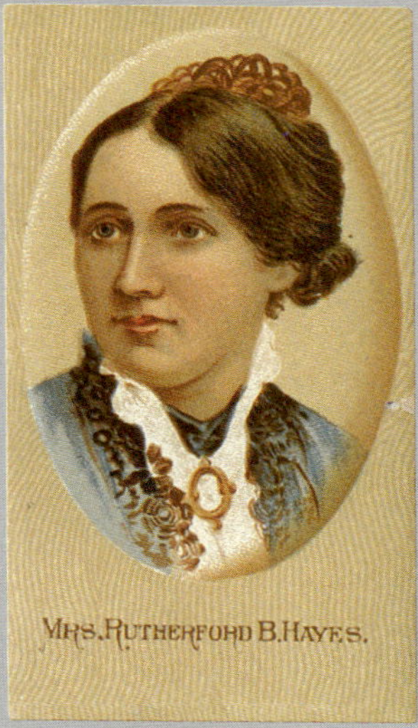

Ladies of the White House. Consolidated

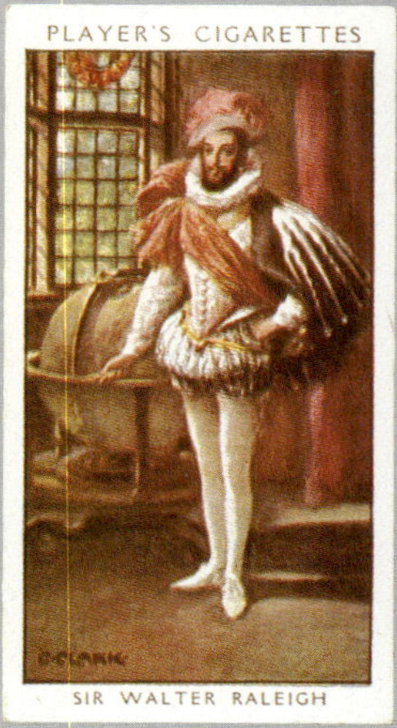

Dandies. Player

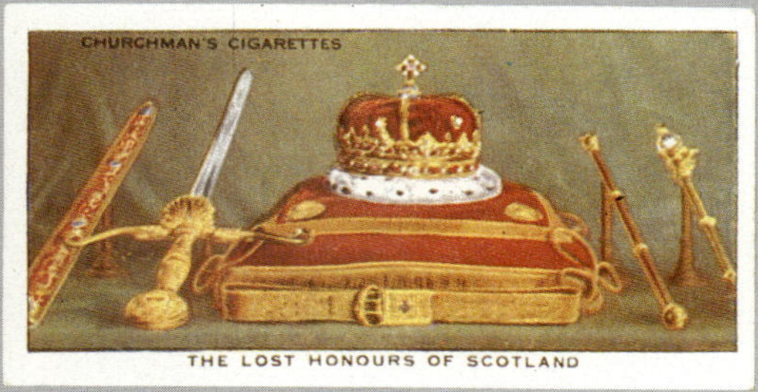

The King's Coronation. Churchman

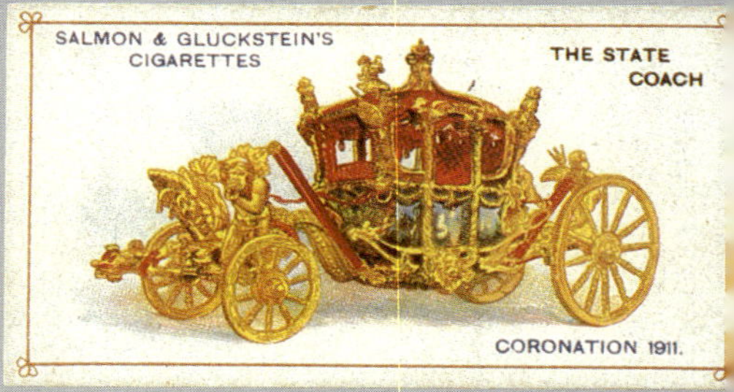

Coronation Series. Salmon & Gluckstein

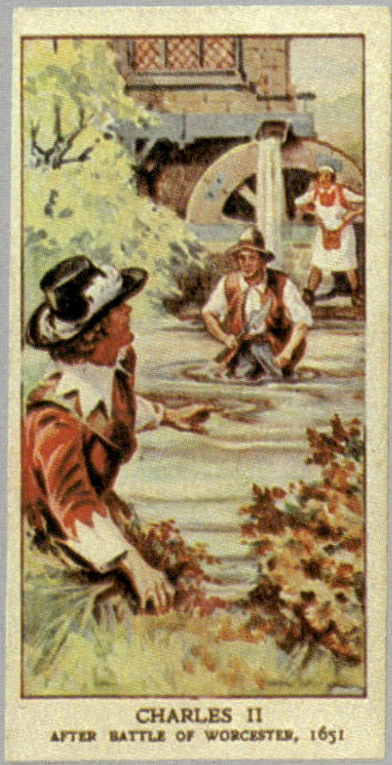

Famous Escapes. Mars

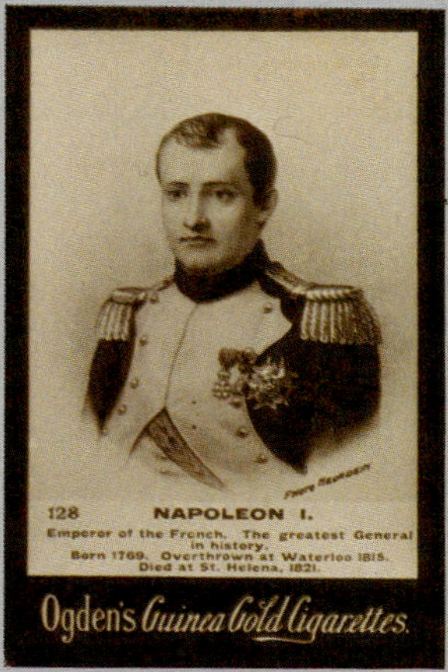

Guinea Gold General Interest. Ogden

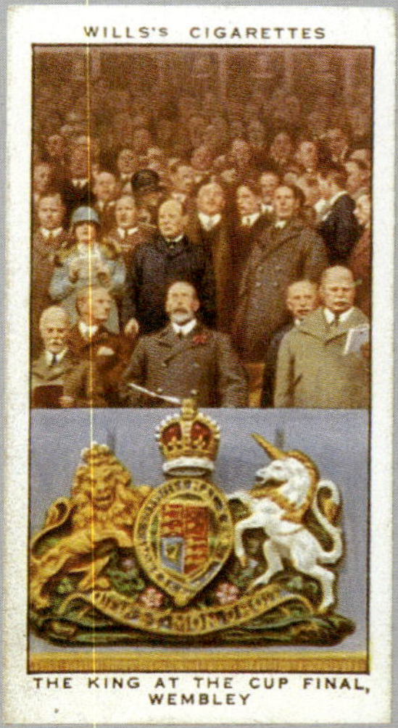

The Reign of King George V. Wills

Qty		Date	Odds	Sets
50	Congress of Beauty, World's Fair	1893	£7.50	—
25	Dancers	1895	£4.00	—
50	Dancing Women	1895	£7.50	—
50	Fancy Bathers	1895	£7.50	—
25	Fish From American Waters (Green Net)	1900	£2.50	£62.50
50	Fish From American Waters (List Back)	1895	£3.00	—
28	Flags, Dominoes Superimposed (Carton)	1900	£1.50	£50.00
50	Flags of All Nations	1895	£4.00	—
50	Heroes of The Spanish American War (Carton)	1900	£1.50	£75.00
?36	Japanese Girls	1900	A	—
25	Military Uniforms, A	1900	£6.00	—
25	Military Uniforms, B	1900	£4.00	£100.00
27	Military Uniforms, C (Green Net)	1900	£1.50	£40.00
27	Military Uniforms, C (Typeset)	1900	£2.00	£55.00
25	Military Uniforms, D	1900	£5.00	£125.00
50	Musical Instruments	1895	£7.50	—
50	National Flags & Arms	1895	£2.00	—
25	National Flags & Flower-Girls	1900	£7.50	—
25	Old Ships, 1st Series	1900	£1.00	£25.00
25	Old Ships, 2nd Series	1900	£2.00	£50.00
50	Savage & Semi Barbarous Chiefs & Rulers	1895	£7.50	—
25	Songs A	1900	£4.00	£100.00
25	Songs B	1900	£4.00	£100.00
25	Songs C, 1st Group	1900	£2.00	£50.00
25	Songs C, 2nd Group	1900	£3.00	—
25	Songs D	1900	£2.00	£50.00
27	Songs E	1900	£4.00	—
25	Songs F	1900	£4.00	—
25	Songs G	1900	£3.00	£75.00
25	Songs H	1900	£6.00	—
25	Songs I	1900	£7.50	—
F150	Views	1901	£1.00	—
Later Issues				
L50	Actors	1907	£1.00	£50.00
L50	Actresses "Between The Acts"	1902	£3.00	—
G25	Actresses "Turkish Trophies" (Premiums)	1902	£4.00	£100.00
B85	Actress Series	1904	£2.00	—
L80	Animals	1912	60p	£50.00
L25	Arctic Scenes	1916	80p	£20.00
M15	Art Gallery Pictures	1904	£1.50	£22.50
M50	Art Reproductions	1904	A	—
21	Art Series (Grand Duke)	1902	£5.00	—
P10	Artistic Pictures	1910	A	—
18	Ask Dad	1905	A	—
L50	Assorted Standard Bearers of Different Countries	1910	£2.50	£125.00
B25	Auto-Drivers	1908	£2.50	£62.50
M50	Automobile Series	1908	£2.50	£125.00
L50	Baseball Folders	1907	£3.00	—
M121	Baseball Series (T204)	1907	A	—
208	Baseball Series (T205, Gold Borders)	1907	£2.50	—
522	Baseball Series (T206, White Borders)	1907	£2.00	—
200	Baseball Series (T207, Brown Background)	1907	A	—
?578	Baseball Series (T210, Red Borders)	1907	A	—
75	Baseball Series (T211, Southern Association)	1907	A	—

AMERICAN TOBACCO CO. (U.S.A.)—cont.

Qty		*Date*	*Odds*	*Sets*
376	Baseball Series (T212, "Obak")	1907	A	—
180	Baseball Series (T213, "Coupon")	1907	A	—
?90	Baseball Series (T214, Victory Tobacco) ...	1907	A	—
159	Baseball Series (T215, Red Cross)	1907	A	—
L76	Baseball Triple Folders	1907	A	—
50	Bird Series (Gold Borders)	1912	50p	£25.00
50	Bird Series (White Border)	1912	50p	£25.00
30	Bird Series (Fancy Gold Frame)	1911	60p	£18.00
M361	Birthday Horoscopes	1910	60p	—
P80	Bridge Favors & Place Cards	1938	£1.25	—
P100	Bridge Game Hands	1938	£2.00	—
M24	British Buildings	1937	60p	£15.00
M42	British Sovereigns	1939	60p	£25.00
M50	Butterfly Series	1908	£1.20	£60.00
L153	Champion Athlete & Prizefighter Series	1910	40p	£60.00
X50	Champion Athlete & Prizefighter Series (Prizefighters Only)	1910	£1.00	£50.00
L50	Champion Pugilists	1908	£2.00	—
X100	Champion Women Swimmers	1906	£2.50	—
M150	College Series	1914	40p	£60.00
G25	College Series (Premiums)	1904	£4.00	£100.00
M50	Costumes and Scenery for All Countries of The World	1912	£1.00	£50.00
X49	Cowboy Series	1914	£1.00	£50.00
M?38	Cross Stitch	1906	A	—
L?17	Embarrassing/Emotional Moments	1906	A	—
M50	Emblem Series	1908	75p	£37.50
L100	Fable Series	1913	50p	£50.00
PF?53	Famous Baseball Players, American Athletic Champions & Photoplay Stars	1910	A	—
100	Fish Series	1909	50p	£50.00
200	Flags of All Nations Series	1909	50p	£100.00
L100	Flags of All Nations Series (Red Cross) ...	1904	A	—
50	Foreign Stamp Series	1906	£2.00	—
L505	Fortune Series	1907	60p	—
G12	Hamilton King Girls (1-12 Sketches)	1902	£5.00	—
G12	Hamilton King Girls (13-24 Girls)	1902	£4.00	£50.00
G12	Hamilton King Girls (25-36 Bathing Girls) ...	1902	£4.00	£50.00
G25	Hamilton King Girls (37-61 Period Gowns) ...	1902	£4.00	£100.00
G25	Hamilton King Girls (62-86 Flag Girls)	1902	£4.00	£100.00
G25	Hamilton King Girls (1-25)	1913	£5.00	—
L?3	Helmar Girls	1902	A	—
M79	Henry	1937	50p	—
X50	Heroes of History	1912	80p	£40.00
M50	Historic Homes	1913	60p	£30.00
X25	Historical Events Series	1911	£1.00	£35.00
M25	Hudson-Fulton Series	1908	£1.20	£30.00
45	Imitation Cigar Bands	1909	40p	—
L50	Indian Life in The 60's	1914	£1.00	£50.00
L221	Jig Saw Puzzle Pictures	1910	£1.50	—
L50	Lighthouse Series	1912	£1.00	£50.00
X50	Men of History	1912	80p	£40.00
B100	Military Series (White Borders)	1908	£1.50	£150.00
50	Military Series (Gold Borders)	1908	£2.00	£100.00

Qty		Date	Odds	Sets
50	Military Series (Recruit)	1908	£1.50	£75.00
50	Movie Stars	1915	60p	—
L100	Movie Stars	1915	60p	—
B15	Moving Picture Stars Series	1915	A	—
X50	Murad Post Card Series	1905	£2.50	—
100	Mutt & Jeff Series (Black & White)	1908	£1.50	—
100	Mutt & Jeff Series (Coloured)	1908	£2.00	—
F16	National League & American League Teams	1910	A	—
G126	Prominent Base Ball Players & Athletes (Premium)	1911	A	—
50	Pugilistic Subjects	1908	A	—
X18	Puzzle Picture Series	1904	A	—
L200	Riddle Series	1907	60p	—
X?60	Royal Bengal Souvenir Cards	1906	£2.50	—
M150	Seals of The United States & Coats of Arms	1912	50p	£75.00
L25	Series of Champions	1906	A	—
X50	Sights & Scenes of The World	1912	75p	£37.50
X50	Silhouettes	1908	£2.00	—
L25	Song Bird Series	1905	A	—
32	Sports Champions	1908	A	—
45	Stage Stars (Transfers)	1910	A	—
B25	State Girl Series	1910	£2.00	—
L50	Theatres Old & New Series	1912	£1.00	£50.00
L25	The World's Greatest Explorers	1914	80p	£20.00
L50	Toast Series (Sultan)	1910	A	—
M550	Toast Series (Mogul)	1910	50p	—
M25	Toasts	1910	A	—
50	Types of Nations	1912	80p	£40.00
M25	Up To Date Baseball Comics	1908	£3.00	—
L26	Up To Date Comics	1908	£2.00	—
F?500	World Scenes & Portraits	1910	£1.00	—
250	World War I Scenes	1916	60p	£150.00
X50	World's Champion Athletes	1909	£1.25	

Silk Issues

Qty		Date	Odds	Sets
M111	Actresses	1910	£1.00	—
X2	Actresses	1910	B	—
L15	Animals	1910	£2.50	—
P250	Athlete and College Seal	1910	£1.50	—
G250	Athlete and College Seal	1910	£2.50	—
B?6	Automobile Pennants	1910	B	—
M?100	Baseball—Actress Series	1910	£3.00	—
M?100	Baseball Players	1910	£5.00	—
G25	Baseball Players	1910	B	—
M25	Bathing Beach Girls	1910	£4.00	£100.00
G6	Bathing Girls	1910	£7.50	£45.00
X50	Birds, Set 1	1910	£2.00	—
B26	Birds, Set 2	1910	£2.00	—
B30	Birds, Set 3	1910	£2.00	—
L20	Birds in Flight	1910	£2.00	—
L25	Breeds of Dogs	1910	£3.50	—
L10	Breeds of Fowls	1910	£2.50	—
P6	Butterflies	1910	£6.00	£36.00
L50	Butterflies & Moths, Set 1	1910	£1.00	—
L50	Butterflies & Moths, Set 2	1910	£1.00	—

AMERICAN TOBACCO CO. (U.S.A.)—cont.

Qty		Date	Odds	Sets
L25	Butterflies & Moths, Set 3	1910	£1.50	—
B77	City Seals	1910	75p	—
G50	College Flag, Seal, Song, Yell	1910	A	—
X24	College Pennants	1910	A	—
B145	College Seals	1910	75p	—
G?7	College Yells	1910	A	—
L10	Comics	1910	£3.00	—
M25	Domestic Animals' Heads	1910	£3.00	£75.00
G6	Domestic Animals' Heads	1910	£6.00	£36.00
M50	Emblem Series	1910	£2.00	—
L15	Famous Queens	1910	£3.00	—
L11	Feminine Types	1910	£3.00	£30.00
D322	Flags & Arms (Woven)	1910	75p	—
P24	Flag Girls of Nations	1910	£3.00	£75.00
G24	Flag Girls of Nations	1910	£4.00	—
X50	Flowers, Set 1	1910	£2.00	—
M25	Flowers, Set 2	1910	£2.00	—
L50	Flowers, Set 2	1910	£2.00	—
L52	Flowers, Set 3	1910	£2.00	—
L10	Fruits	1910	£2.00	—
G5	Generals	1910	B	—
M10	Girls (Portrait in Circle)	1910	A	—
L10	Girls (Portrait in Circle)	1910	B	—
G10	Girls (Portrait in Circle)	1910	B	—
G?50	Hatbands	1910	£6.00	—
M50	Indian Portraits	1910	£2.00	—
G6	Indian Portraits	1910	£7.50	£45.00
L25	Indian Portraits & Scenes	1910	£3.00	—
P10	Indian Portraits & Scenes	1910	£5.00	—
G12	King Girls	1910	A	—
G20	Kink Series	1910	B	—
B51	Military & Lodge Medals	1910	£1.50	—
L?5	Miniature National Flags	1910	A	—
L10	Mottoes & Quotations	1910	£2.50	—
L25	National Arms (Silko)	1910	£2.00	—
B42	National Arms (Woven)	1910	£1.50	£65.00
L154	National Flags	1910	60p	—
G?150	National Flags (Many Styles)	1910	£2.00	—
L25	National Flags & Arms	1910	£1.00	—
X40	National Flags & Arms	1910	£1.00	—
P53	National Flags & Arms (Many Styles)	1910	£1.50	—
X27	National Flags, Song & Flower	1910	£1.50	—
P20	National Flags, Song & Flower	1910	£2.00	—
G17	National Flags, Song & Flower	1910	£4.00	—
M?37	Orders & Military Medals	1910	A	—
B24	Presidents of U.S.	1910	£3.00	£75.00
P27	Ruler With Flags	1910	£5.00	—
P24	Ruler With National Arms	1910	£4.00	—
P10	Rulers of The Balkans & Italy	1910	£4.00	—
L120	Silk National Flags	1910	75p	—
M36	State Flags	1910	£1.50	—
B?11	State Flowers	1910	A	—
M25	State Flowers	1910	£3.00	—
L25	State Girl & Flower	1910	£4.00	—

Qty		Date	Odds	Sets
M50	State Maps & Maps of Territories	1910	£3.00	—
M48	State Seals	1910	£1.00	—
X?75	Twelfth Night Miscellany	1910	A	—
M25	Women of Ancient Egypt	1910	£3.00	—
L10	Zira Girls	1910	£3.00	£30.00
Blanket Issues				
P?	Animal Pelts	1908	£3.00	—
G90	Baseball Players	1908	A	—
P?	Butterflies	1908	£1.00	—
G?	Butterflies	1908	£1.25	—
P135	College Athlete, Pennant, Seals	1908	£1.00	—
G10	College Pennants	1908	A	—
G53	College Seals	1908	£1.25	—
X?	Conventional Rug Designs	1908	50p	—
P?	Conventional Rug Designs	1908	75p	—
G?	Conventional Rug Designs	1908	£1.00	—
X5	Domestic Pets	1908	£3.00	—
P?	Miniature Indian Blankets	1908	75p	—
G?	Miniature Indian Blankets	1908	£1.00	—
E6	National Arms	1908	£2.00	—
P45	National Flags	1908	50p	—
G71	National Flags	1908	75p	—
E31	National Flags	1908	£1.25	—
G?	National Flags and Arms	1908	£1.50	—
X9	Nursery Rhymes	1908	A	—
X13	Soldiers	1908	£4.00	—
Leather Issues				
B15	Breeds of Dogs	1908	£3.00	—
X97	College Building, Shield, Etc.	1908	£2.00	—
P19	College Buildings	1908	£2.00	—
M14	College Fraternity Seals	1908	A	—
M159	College Pennants	1908	50p	—
M112	College Pennants (Shaped)	1908	75p	—
X23	College Pennant, Yell, Emblem	1908	£2.50	—
M144	College Seals	1908	50p	—
M122	College Seals (Shaped)	1908	75p	—
M29	College Seals (Card Suit Shaped)	1908	£1.50	—
M19	Comic Designs	1908	£1.50	—
B23	Flowers	1908	£2.00	—
B9	Girls	1908	£2.50	—
M26	Girls (Alphabet Background)	1908	£3.50	—
M94	Mottoes & Quotations	1908	£1.50	—
M5	Movie Film Personalities	1908	A	—
M21	National Flags	1908	A	—
M45	Nursery Rhymes Illustrated	1908	£2.50	—
M56	State Seals	1908	60p	—
M18	State Seals (Pennant Shaped)	1908	75p	—
Celluloid Buttons & Pins				
K245	Actresses	1901	75p	—
K152	Baseball Players	1901	A	—
K8	Boer War Leaders	1901	B	—
K362	Comic Pictures	1901	£1.50	—
K425	Comic Sayings	1901	£1.50	—

AMERICAN TOBACCO CO. (U.S.A.)—cont.

Qty		Date	Odds	Sets
K14	Cricketers	1901	B	—
K125	Flags	1901	£1.25	—
K48	Girls' Heads	1901	A	—
K25	Jockeys	1901	A	—
K48	State Arms	1901	£1.50	—
K187	Yellow Kid Designs	1901	A	—

AMERICAN TOBACCO CO. OF NEW SOUTH WALES (Australia)

25	Beauties, Group 1	1902	£3.00	£75.00
25	Beauties, Group 2	1902	£3.00	—

AMERICAN TOBACCO COMPANY OF VICTORIA LTD. (Australia)

100?	Beauties	1902	£4.00	—

ATLAM CIGARETTE FACTORY (Malta)

150	Beauties	1924	A	—
B65	Beauties	1924	75p	—
B519	Celebrities	1924	40p	—
L50	Views of Malta	1924	A	—
B128	Views of The World	1924	A	—

BANNER TOBACCO CO. (U.S.A.)

X25	Beauties	1890	£10.00	—

AUG. BECK & CO. (U.S.A.)

24	Actors & Actresses	1885	B	—
?	Beauties—Burdick 488	1888	£20.00	—
25	National Dances	1889	B	—
F?	Photographic Cards	1886	£3.00	—
?	Picture Cards	1888	A	—
24	Presidents of U.S.A.	1890	B	—
?	State Seals	1887	B	—

DE BEER & CO. (Australia)

20	Admirals & Warships of U.S.A	1908	£25.00	—

BOOKER TOBACCO CO. (U.S.A.)

35	Indian Series	1906	£15.00	—
?20	U.S. Battleships	1906	£15.00	—

BRITISH AMERICAN TOBACCO CO. LTD. (B.A.T.)

(1) SERIES WITH FIRM'S NAME

48	A Famous Picture Series, The Toast (Sect.)	1931	£1.50	—
BF50	Beauties	1925	50p	—
BF40	Beauties	1925	50p	—
25	Beauties, Art Series	1903	£5.00	—
25	Beauties, Black Background	1903	£4.00	£100.00
25	Beauties, Blossom Girls	1903	£15.00	—
25	Beauties, Flower Girls	1903	£3.00	£75.00
25	Beauties, Fruit Girls	1903	£5.00	£125.00
25	Beauties, Girls in Costumes	1903	£4.00	£100.00
20	Beauties, Group 1	1903	£3.00	£60.00
25	Beauties, Lantern Girls	1903	£3.00	£75.00
50	Beauties, Marine & Universe Girls	1903	£4.00	£200.00

Qty		Date	Odds	Sets
25	Beauties, Numbered	1903	£7.50	—
25	Beauties, Palette Girls	1903	£4.00	£100.00
25	Beauties, Palette Girls (Red Border)	1903	£6.00	—
53	Beauties, Playing Cards	1903	£3.00	£150.00
24	Beauties, Smoke Girls	1903	£7.50	—
25	Beauties, Star Girls	1903	£6.00	—
25	Beauties, Stippled Background	1903	£3.00	£75.00
25	Beauties, Water Girls	1903	£3.00	£75.00
M50	Birds, Beasts & Fishes	1934	60p	—
50	Buildings	1905	£3.00	—
25	Chinese Girls "A"	1904	£3.00	—
25	Chinese Girls "B"	1904	£3.00	—
25	Chinese Girls "C"	1904	£3.00	—
25	Chinese Girls "D"	1904	£3.00	—
25	Chinese Girls "E"	1904	£3.00	—
25	Chinese Girls "F1"	1904	£3.00	—
25	Chinese Girls "F2"	1904	£3.00	—
50	Chinese Girls "F3"	1904	£3.00	—
40	Chinese Trades	1904	£2.00	—
50	Danish Athletes	1906	£3.00	—
28	Dominoes	1908	£2.00	—
48	Fairy Tales	1928	A	—
25	New York Views	1908	£3.00	—
53	Playing Cards	1908	£3.00	—
M50	Wild Animals	1930	50p	—

(2) SERIES WITH BRAND NAMES

(A) Albert Cigarettes (Belgium Etc.)

Qty		Date	Odds	Sets
L50	Aeroplanes (Civils)	1935	A	—
50	Artistes De Cinema (1-50)	1932	A	—
50	Artistes De Cinema (51-100)	1933	60p	—
50	Artistes De Cinema (101-150)	1934	A	—
M48	Beauties	1928	A	—
M75	Belles Vues De Belgique	1926	A	—
M50	Birds, Beasts & Fishes	1934	A	—
M50	Butterflies (Girls)	1926	A	—
M50	Cinema Stars, Set 1 (Brown)	1927	A	—
M100	Cinema Stars, Set 2	1928	£1.00	—
M208	Cinema Stars, Set 3 (Unnumbered)	1928	A	—
M100	Circus Scenes	1930	A	—
M100	Famous Beauties	1916	A	—
M100	La Faune Congolaise	1934	75p	—
M50	L'Afrique Equatoriale De L'est A L'ouest	1932	A	—
M50	Les Grandes Paquebots Du Monde	1924	A	—
M50	Merveilles du Monde	1927	A	—
M50	Women of Nations	1922	£1.50	—

(B) Atlas Cigarettes (China)

Qty		Date	Odds	Sets
50	Buildings	1907	£3.00	—
25	Chinese Beauties	1912	80p	£20.00
50	Chinese Trades, Set 4	1908	60p	£30.00
85	Chinese Trades, Set 6	1912	A	—

(C) Battle Ax Cigarettes

Qty		Date	Odds	Sets
M100	Famous Beauties	1916	£1.00	—
M50	Women of Nations	1922	£2.00	—

Qty		Date	Odds	Sets
(D)	**Copain Cigarettes (Belguim)**			
52	Birds of Brilliant Plumage (P/C Inset)	1927	£2.50	—
(E)	**Domino Cigarettes (Mauritius)**			
25	Animaux et Reptiles	1961	—	£1.00
25	Coursaires et Boucaniers	1961	—	50p
25	Figures Historiques, 1st Serie	1961	—	£1.25
25	Figures Historiques, 2nd Serie	1961	—	£3.50
25	Fleures De Culture	1961	—	50p
25	Les Oiseaux et L'art Japonais	1961	—	£5.00
25	Les Produits Du Monde	1961	—	50p
50	Voitures Antiques	1961	—	£15.00
(F)	**Eagle Bird Cigarettes (China & Siam)**			
50	Animal & Birds	1909	75p	£37.50
50	Aviation Series	1912	75p	—
25	Birds of the East	1912	60p	—
25	China's Famous Warriors	1911	75p	—
25	Chinese Beauties, 1st Series	1908	75p	—
25	Chinese Beauties, 2nd Series	1909	A	—
50	Chinese Trades	1908	60p	—
25	Cock Fighting	1911	£1.20	£30.00
60	Flags & Pennons	1926	50p	£30.00
50	Romance of the Heavens	1929	£1.50	—
50	Siamese Alphabet	1922	50p	£25.00
50	Siamese Dreams & Their Meaning	1923	50p	£25.00
50	Siamese Horoscopes	1916	40p	£20.00
50	Siamese Play—Inao	1916	40p	—
50	Siamese Play—Khun Chang Khun Phaen 1st	1917	40p	£20.00
50	Siamese Play—Khun Chang Khun Phaen 2nd	1917	50p	£25.00
36	Siamese Play—Phra Aphai, 1st	1918	40p	£15.00
36	Siamese Play—Phra Aphai, 2nd	1919	40p	£15.00
50	Siamese Play—Ramakien I	1913	50p	£25.00
50	Siamese Play—Ramakien II	1914	50p	£25.00
50	Siamese Uniforms	1915	75p	£37.50
50	Views of Bangkok	1928	50p	£25.00
50	Views of Siam	1928	40p	£20.00
30	War Weapons	1914	75p	£22.50
(G)	**Gold Dollar Cigarettes (Germany)**			
M270	Auf Deutscher Scholle	1934	30p	—
M270	Der Weltkrieg	1933	30p	—
M270	Deutsche Kolonien	1931	30p	—
M270	Die Deutsche Wehrmacht	1935	30p	—
?50	Do You Know?	1928	£1.00	—
B100	Filmbilder	1935	50p	£50.00
B100	Im Prarie Und Urwald	1930	40p	£40.00
100	Wild-West	1932	50p	£50.00
(H)	**Kong Beng Cigarettes (China)**			
50	Animals	1912	A	—
(I)	**Mascot Cigarettes (Germany)**			
100	Cinema Stars	1931	£2.00	—
M208	Cinema Stars	1924	£1.00	—
(J)	**Motor Cigarettes (Denmark)**			
50	Aviation Series	1911	A	—

Qty		Date	Odds	Sets
50	Butterflies & Moths	1911	A	—
50	Flag Girls of All Nations	1908	A	—
50	Girls of All Nations	1908	A	—
(K)	**Pedro Cigarettes (India)**			
50	Actors & Actresses	1906	A	—
37	Nautch Girls (Red Border)	1907	75p	—
40	Nautch Girls (Coloured)	1907	£1.00	—
52	Nautch Girls (P/C) Inset)	1907	£1.25	—
(L)	**Pinhead Cigarettes (China)**			
50	Chinese Modern Beauties	1912	75p	£37.50
33	Chinese Heroes, Set 1	1912	75p	—
50	Chinese Heroes, Set 2	1913	75p	—
50	Chinese Trades, Set III	1908	60p	£30.00
50	Chinese Trades, Set IV	1909	60p	£30.00
50	Chinese Trades, Set V	1910	50p	£25.00
50	Types of the British Army	1909	£2.00	—
(M)	**Railway Cigarettes (India)**			
37	Nautch Girls Series	1907	75p	£28.00
(N)	**Shantung Cigarettes (China)**			
50	Chinese Curios	1928	£2.50	—
(O)	**Sunflower Cigarettes (China)**			
50	Chinese Trades	1906	£3.00	—
(P)	**Teal Cigarettes (Siam)**			
30	Chinese Beauties	1917	A	—
50	Cinema Stars	1930	75p	£37.50
30	Fish Series	1916	75p	£22.50
50	War Incidents	1916	£1.00	£50.00
(Q)	**Tiger Cigarettes (India)**			
52	Nautch Girl Series (P/C Inset)	1911	£1.00	—
(3)	**SERIES WITH PRINTED BACK, NO MAKER'S NAME OR BRAND (See also Imperial Tobacco Co. (Canada & India), United Tobacco Co.)**			
250	Actresses "ALWICS" (Design Back)	1906	£1.00	—
50	Aeroplanes (Gilt Border)	1926	75p	£37.50
50	Aeroplanes of Today	1936	25p	£12.50
25	Angling	1930	60p	—
L25	Arabic Proverbs (Silk)	1913	£6.00	—
50	Arms & Armour	1910	£2.00	—
L50	Arms of the British Empire (Silk)	1911	£1.00	—
25	Army Life	1908	£3.00	—
50	Art Photogravures	1912	60p	—
1	Australia Day	1915	—	£3.00
L50	Australian Wild Flowers (Silk)	1913	£1.00	—
75	Aviation	1910	£1.50	—
50	Aviation Series	1911	£1.00	£50.00
50	Beauties, Red Tinted (Design Back)	1906	75p	—
52	Beauties, Tobacco Leaf Back (P/C Inset)	1908	£1.00	£50.00
52	Beauties, Tobacco Leaf Back (No Inset)	1908	£2.50	—
F50	Beauties, Set 1	1925	50p	—
BF50	Beauties, Set 1 (Hand Coloured)	1925	60p	—
F50	Beauties, 2nd Series	1926	25p	£12.50
F50	Beauties, 3rd Series	1926	25p	£12.50

Qty		*Date*	*Odds*	*Sets*
F50	Beauties of Great Britain	1930	25p	£12.50
F50	Beautiful England	1928	15p	£7.50
50	Best Dogs of their Breed	1916	80p	£40.00
L50	Best Dogs of their Breed (Silk)	1913	£1.25	£62.50
50	Billiards	1929	75p	—
50	Birds Beasts & Fishes	1937	15p	£7.50
M50	Birds Beasts & Fishes	1937	60p	—
24	Birds of England	1924	£1.00	—
50	Boy Scouts	1930	80p	£40.00
50	Britain's Defenders (Blue Front)	1914	60p	—
50	Britain's Defenders (Mauve Front)	1914	50p	£25.00
50	British Butterflies	1930	30p	£15.00
50	British Empire Series	1913	£1.00	—
25	British Trees & Their Uses	1930	60p	—
50	British Warships and Admirals	1915	£1.50	£75.00
50	Butterflies & Moths	1911	75p	—
50	Butterflies (Girls)	1928	£1.00	£50.00
M50	Butterflies (Girls)	1928	£1.25	£62.50
M50	Celebrities of Film and Stage	1930	40p	—
LF48	Channel Islands, Past & Present	1939	12p	£3.00
38/40	Characters from the Works of Charles Dickens	1919	15p	£6.00
50	Cinema Artistes (Black & White 1-50)	1928	40p	—
50	Cinema Artistes (Black & White 101-150)	1930	40p	—
60	Cinema Artistes, Set 1 (Brown)	1929	40p	—
50	Cinema Artistes, Set 2 (Brown)	1931	40p	—
L42	Cinema Artistes, Set 3	1932	50p	—
48	Cinema Celebrities (C)	1935	20p	£10.00
L48	Cinema Celebrities (C)	1935	25p	£12.50
L56	Cinema Celebrities (D)	1937	A	—
50	Cinema Favourites	1929	£1.50	—
50	Cinema Stars, Set 2 (1-50)	1928	25p	—
50	Cinema Stars, Set 3 (51-100)	1930	25p	—
50	Cinema Stars, Set 4 (101-150)	1932	25p	—
100	Cinema Stars (Coloured)	1931	£1.00	—
F50	Cinema Stars, Set 1	1924	30p	—
F50	Cinema Stars, Set 2	1924	20p	£10.00
F50	Cinema Stars, Set 3	1925	30p	—
MF52	Cinema Stars, Set 4	1925	A	—
MF52	Cinema Stars, Set 5	1926	A	—
MF52	Cinema Stars, Set 6	1927	A	—
LF48	Cinema Stars, Set 7	1927	A	—
F50	Cinema Stars, Set 8	1928	40p	—
F50	Cinema Stars, Set 9 (51-100)	1929	40p	—
F50	Cinema Stars, Set 10 (101-150)	1930	40p	—
F50	Cinema Stars, Set 11	1931	30p	—
110	Crests & Badges of the British Army (Silk)	1915	£1.00	—
M108	Crests & Badges of the British Army (Silk)	1915	£1.00	
M50	Crests & Colours of Australian Universities, Colleges & Schools (Silk)	1916	£1.00	—
25	Derby Day Series	1914	£3.00	—
50	Do You Know?	1923	20p	£10.00
50	Do You Know? 2nd Series	1931	12p	£5.00
25	Dracones Posthistorici	1938	£2.50	—
?50	Dutch Footballers	1913	£3.00	—

Qty		Date	Odds	Sets
25	Dutch Scenes	1928	£1.20	£30.00
50	Engineering Wonders	1930	15p	£7.50
40	English Costumes of Ten Centuries	1919	60p	£24.00
F25	English Cricketers	1926	60p	£15.00
26	Etchings (of Dogs)	1926	20p	£5.00
F50	Famous Bridges	1935	30p	£15.00
50	Famous Footballers, Set 1	1923	60p	£30.00
50	Famous Footballers, Set 2	1924	60p	£30.00
50	Famous Footballers, Set 3	1925	60p	£30.00
25	Famous Racehorses	1926	60p	£15.00
25	Famous Railway Trains	1929	75p	—
50	Favourite Flowers	1923	30p	£15.00
50	Film and Stage Favourites	1926	40p	—
75	Film Favourites	1928	50p	—
50	Flags of the Empire	1928	40p	£20.00
50	Foreign Birds	1930	20p	£10.00
50	Game Birds & Wild Fowl	1929	40p	—
LF45	Grace & Beauty (1-45)	1938	12p	£4.00
LF45	Grace & Beauty (46-90)	1939	12p	£3.00
LF48	Guernsey, Alderney & Sark, 1st Series	1937	12p	£5.00
LF48	Guernsey, Alderney & Sark, 2nd Series	1938	12p	£3.50
L80	Guernsey Footballers, Priaulx League	1938	12p	£10.00
F52	Here There & Everywhere	1929	12p	£6.00
25	Hints & Tips for Motorists	1929	50p	—
F50	Homeland Events	1928	35p	—
50	Horses of Today	1906	£2.00	—
32	Houses of Parliament (Red Back)	1912	60p	£18.00
32	Houses of Parliament (Brown, Back with Verse)	1912	A	—
50	Indian Chiefs	1930	£1.20	£60.00
50	Indian Regiments Series	1912	£3.00	—
50	International Air Liners	1937	25p	£12.50
25	Java Scenes	1929	A	—
LF48	Jersey Then & Now, 1st Series	1935	20p	£10.00
LF48	Jersey Then & Now, 2nd Series	1937	12p	£4.00
50	Jiu Jitsu	1911	£1.00	—
50	Keep Fit	1939	20p	£10.00
M?48	La Belgique Monumentale et Pittoresque	1926	£1.50	—
50	Leaders of Men	1929	£1.25	—
50	Life in the Treetops	1931	20p	£10.00
50	Lighthouses	1926	40p	£20.00
40	London Ceremonials	1929	60p	—
F50	London Zoo	1927	40p	—
50	Lucky Charms	1930	£1.00	—
25	Marvels of the Universe Series	1925	£1.00	£25.00
45	Melbourne Cup Winners	1906	£1.20	£55.00
50	Merchant Ships of the World	1925	£1.50	—
25	Merchant Ships of the World	1925	£1.50	—
25	Military Portraits	1917	80p	£20.00
LF36	Modern Beauties	1939	12p	£3.00
XF36	Modern Beauties	1936	35p	£12.50
36	Modern Beauties 1st Series	1938	12p	£3.00
MF54	Modern Beauties 1st Series	1937	12p	£3.00
36	Modern Beauties 2nd Series	1938	12p	£1.50
MF54	Modern Beauties 2nd Series	1938	12p	£3.00

Qty		*Date*	*Odds*	*Sets*
XF36	Modern Beauties 2nd Series	1936	20p	£7.50
MF36	Modern Beauties 3rd Series	1938	12p	£2.00
XF36	Modern Beauties 3rd Series	1936	12p	£3.50
MF36	Modern Beauties 4th Series	1939	12p	£2.00
XF36	Modern Beauties 4th Series	1937	12p	£3.00
XF36	Modern Beauties 5th Series	1938	12p	£3.00
XF36	Modern Beauties 6th Series	1938	12p	£3.00
XF36	Modern Beauties 7th Series	1938	12p	£3.00
LF36	Modern Beauties 8th Series	1939	12p	£3.50
LF36	Modern Beauties 9th Series	1939	12p	£3.50
50	Modern Warfare	1936	20p	£10.00
25	Modes of Conveyance	1928	60p	£15.00
48	Motor Cars (Coloured)	1926	£1.50	—
36	Motor Cars (Brown)	1929	£1.25	—
50	Motor Cycles	1927	£1.25	£62.50
F50	Native Life in Many Lands	1932	30p	£15.00
F50	Natural & Man Made Wonders of the World ...	1937	20p	£10.00
F50	Nature Studies	1928	30p	£15.00
50	Naval Portraits	1917	80p	£40.00
25	Notabilities	1917	80p	£20.00
25	Past & Present	1929	60p	—
FS48	Pictures of the East	1930	20p	£10.00
M48	Picturesque China	1925	40p	£20.00
B53	Playing Cards	1940	12p	£2.50
36	Popular Stage, Cinema & Society Celebrities	1928	£1.50	—
25	Prehistoric Animals	1931	60p	£15.00
50	Prominent Australian & English Cricketers ...	1911	£7.50	—
25	Puzzle Series	1916	£2.00	—
50	Railway Working	1927	75p	£37.50
33	Regimental Pets	1911	£2.50	£80.00
50	Regimental Uniforms	1936	60p	£30.00
50	Romance of the Heavens	1929	25p	£12.50
FS50	Round the World in Pictures	1931	30p	—
50	Royal Mail	1912	£2.00	—
27	Rulers of the World	1911	£3.00	—
40	Safety First	1931	25p	£10.00
25	Ships' Flags & Cap Badges, 1st Series ...	1930	50p	£12.50
25	Ships' Flags & Cap Badges, 2nd Series ...	1930	50p	£12.50
F50	Ships & Shipping	1928	30p	£15.00
50	Signalling Series	1913	£1.25	—
100	Soldiers of the World (Tobacco Leaf Back) ...	1902	£5.00	—
50	Speed	1938	30p	£15.00
25	Sports & Games in Many Lands	1930	60p	—
50	Stage & Film Stars	1926	75p	—
M50	Stars of Filmland	1927	75p	—
F50	The Royal Navy	1930	£1.25	—
F50	The World of Sport	1927	50p	£25.00
32	Transport of the World	1911	A	—
20	Types of North American Indians	1931	£2.50	—
F50	Types of the World	1936	30p	£15.00
F52	Ur Ollum Attum	1930	£1.50	—
FS270	Views of the World	1908	A	—
25	Warriors of All Nations (Gold Panel)	1937	50p	£12.50
50	War Incidents (Blue Back)	1915	50p	£25.00

BRITISH AMERICAN TOBACCO CO. LTD. (B.A.T.)—cont.

Qty		Date	Odds	Sets
50	War Incidents (Brown Back)	1916	60p	£30.00
50	Warships	1926	£1.00	—
25	Whaling	1930	60p	£15.00
F50	Who's Who in Sport	1927	60p	£30.00
50	Wild Animals of the World (Tobacco Leaf back)	1903	£2.50	—
25	Wireless	1923	80p	£20.00
50	Wonders of the Past	1930	40p	£20.00
50	Wonders of the Sea	1929	35p	£17.50
25	Wonders of the World	1928	20p	£5.00
40	World Famous Cinema Artistes	1933	35p	£14.00
L40	World Famous Cinema Artistes	1933	40p	£16.00
50	World's Products	1929	20p	£10.00
F50	Zoo	1935	35p	—
50	Zoological Studies	1928	25p	£12.50

(4) SERIES WITH PLAIN BACKS

Qty		Date	Odds	Sets
50	Actors & Actresses "WALP"	1906	75p	£37.50
50	Actresses "ALWICS"	1907	£1.00	—
50	Actresses, Four Colours Surround	1905	75p	£37.50
30	Actresses, Unicoloured (Light Brown)	1910	25p	£7.50
30	Actresses, Unicoloured (Purple Brown)	1910	40p	£12.00
50	Animals & Birds	1912	75p	£37.50
60	Animals—Cut-Outs	1912	60p	—
50	Art Photogravures	1912	60p	—
50	Aviation Series	1911	£1.25	—
40	Beauties (Brown Tinted)	1913	75p	—
50	Beauties, Coloured Backgrounds	1911	£1.00	—
50	Beauties, "LAWHA"	1906	80p	—
32	Beauties, Picture Hats I	1914	60p	£20.00
45	Beauties, Picture Hats II	1914	60p	£27.00
30	Beauties & Children	1912	A	—
52	Birds of Brilliant Plumage (P/C Inset)	1914	£1.00	£50.00
25	Bonzo Series	1923	£1.20	£30.00
30	Boys Scouts Signalling	1922	£1.00	£30.00
50	Butterflies & Moths	1910	60p	—
50	Cinema Artistes	1930	25p	—
50	Cinema Stars (1-50)	1927	30p	£15.00
50	Cinema Stars (51-100)	1928	40p	—
50	Cinema Stars (101-150)	1930	40p	—
100	Cinema Stars (201-300)	1932	30p	—
50	Cinema Stars, "FLAG"	1929	50p	—
27	Dancing Girls	1913	60p	£16.00
32	Drum Horses	1910	£2.00	£65.00
50	English Period Costumes	1929	40p	£20.00
50	Flag Girls of All Nations	1911	75p	£37.50
165	Flags, Pennons & Signals	1907	25p	—
20	Flowers	1915	35p	£7.00
50	Girls of All Nations	1908	75p	£37.50
30	Heroic Deeds	1913	60p	£18.00
25	Hindoo Gods	1909	A	—
32	Houses of Parliament	1914	£2.00	—
25	Indian Mogul Paintings	1909	A	—
53	Jockeys & Owners Colours (P/C Inset)	1914	£1.00	£50.00
K36	Modern Beauties, 1st Series	1938	£1.00	—

BRITISH AMERICAN TOBACCO CO. LTD. (B.A.T.)—cont.

Qty		*Date*	*Odds*	*Sets*
36	Modern Beauties, 2nd Series	1939	60p	—
F48	Movie Stars	1928	40p	—
F50	New Zealand, Early Scenes & Maori Life	1929	60p	—
50	Poultry & Pigeons	1926	75p	—
25	Products of the World	1914	50p	—
50	Royal Mail	1912	A	—
36	Ships & Their Pennants	1913	60p	£20.00
75	Soldiers of the World	1904	£2.50	—
30	Sporting Girls	1913	60p	£18.00
50	Sports of the World (Brown)	1917	A	—
50	Sports of the World (Coloured)	1917	60p	—
B50	Stars of Filmland	1927	60p	—
32	Transport of the World	1917	30p	£10.00
50	Types of the British Army (Numbered)	1908	£1.00	—
50	Types of the British Army (Unnumbered)	1908	£1.00	—
F50	Types of the World	1936	A	—
F50	Units of the British Army & R.A.F.	1930	A	—
FS50	Views of the World	1908	75p	—
M50	Women of Nations (Flag Girls)	1922	£1.20	—

BRITISH-AUSTRALIAN TOBACCO CO. (Australia)

?100	Flags of All Nations	1910	£3.00	—

BROWN & WILLIAMSON TOBACCO CORP. (U.S.A.)

B50	Modern American Warplanes Series A	1941	60p	£30.00
B50	Modern American Warplanes Series B	1941	60p	£30.00
B50	Modern American Warplanes Series C	1941	60p	£30.00
50	Movie Stars	1940	£1.50	—

D. BUCHNER & CO. (U.S.A.)

B45	Actors	1888	£8.00	—
X?100	Actresses	1888	£12.50	—
X?60	American Scenes with Policeman	1888	£20.00	—
B120	Baseball Players	1888	B	—
X?10	Butterflies & Bugs	1888	B	—
P200	Defenders & Offenders	1888	£15.00	—
B31	Jockeys	1888	£10.00	—
X52	Morning Glory Maidens	1888	20.00	—
X31	Morning Glory Maidens & American Flowers	1888	B	—
X25	Musical Instruments	1888	£25.00	—
X25	New York City Scenes	1888	£20.00	—
B101	Police Inspectors	1888	£7.50	—
X100	Police Inspectors & Captains	1888	£7.50	—
X12	Presidential Puzzle Cards	1888	B	—
X25	Yacht Club Colours	1888	£25.00	—

CALCUTTA CIGARETTE CO. (India)

25	Actresses (Blue Front)	1906	£6.00	—
25	Actresses (Brown Front)	1906	£10.00	—

A. G. CAMERON & SIZER (U.S.A.)

24	Occupations for Women	1890	£20.00	—
F?	Photographic Cards	1890	£2.00	—
25	The New Discovery	1890	£10.00	

V. CAMILLERI (Malta)

Qty		Date	Odds	Sets
BF104	Popes of Rome	1922	60p	£60.00

CAMLER TOBACCO COY. (Malta)

F250	Footballers	1926	£1.50	—
B96	Maltese Families' Coats of Arms	1925	35p	£35.00

CASTELANO BROS. (INDIA)

52	Beauties, Playing Card Inset	1899	£15.00	—

C. COLOMBOS (Malta)

MF?200	Actresses	1902	£1.00	—
BF?25	Actresses	1902	A	—
50	Actresses (Coloured)	1900	£4.00	—
BF?25	Celebrities	1900	£5.00	—
F136	Dante's Divine Comedy	1914	75p	£100.00
MF72	Famous Oil Paintings, Serie A	1910	40p	£30.00
MF108	Famous Oil Paintings, Serie B	1911	40p	£43.00
MF240	Famous Oil Paintings, Serie C	1912	40p	£96.00
MF100	Famous Oil Paintings, Serie D	1913	40p	£40.00
XF100	Famous Oil Paintings	1911	£2.50	—
BF100	Life of Napoleon Bonaparte	1914	60p	£60.00
BF70	Life of Nelson	1914	60p	£42.00
BF70	Life of Wellington	1914	60p	£42.00
MF100	National Types and Costumes	1908	75p	£75.00
F?25	Opera Singers	1899	A	—
120	Paintings and Statues	1913	30p	£36.00
B112	Royalty and Celebrities	1908	£1.00	£110.00

COLONIAL TOBACCOS (PTY.) LTD. (South Africa)

X150	World's Fairy Tales	1930	75p	—

CONSOLIDATED CIGARETTE CO. (U.S.A.)

25	Ladies of the White House	1893	£12.00	£300.00
B14	Ladies of the White House	1898	£15.00	£200.00
B25	Turn Cards	1894	£20.00	—
M25	Turn Cards	1894	B	—

A. G. COUSIS & CO. (Malta)

254	Actors & Actresses	1924	20p	—
KF100	Actors & Actresses (Hand Coloured)	1906	50p	—
F100	Actors & Actresses (Hand Coloured)	1906	60p	—
KF100	Actresses Serie I	1907	40p	—
KF80	Actresses Serie II	1907	40p	—
F1900	Actresses Serie I to Serie XIX	1907	40p	—
KF?2000	Actresses (Unnumbered)	1905	20p	—
F?1300	Actresses (Unnumbered)	1905	25p	—
MF?150	Actresses (White Border)	1902	A	—
KF100	Actresses, Partners & National Costumes (Cousis')	1906	50p	—
KF200	Actresses, Partners & National Costumes (Cousis's)	1906	60p	—
F100	Actresses, Partners & National Costumes ...	1906	50p	—
50	Beauties, Couples & Children (Red Back) ...	1923	50p	£25.00
MF50	Beauties, Couples & Children, Collection No. 1	1908	60p	
MF50	Beauties, Couples & Children, Collection No. 2	1908	60p	—
MF50	Beauties, Couples & Children, Collection No. 3	1908	60p	—

A. G. COUSIS & CO. (Malta)—cont.

Qty		Date	Odds	Sets
F402	Celebrities (Numbered)	1906	25p	—
KF?2156	Celebrities (Unumbered)	1905	15p	—
F?2156	Celebrities (Unnumbered)	1905	15p	—
XF?30	Celebrities & Warships (White Border)	1902	A	—
MF72	Grand Masters of the Order of St. John	1909	60p	—
F100	National Costumes	1908	60p	—
MF100	Paris Exhibition, 1900	1900	A	—
MF102	Paris Series	1902	A	—
MF182	Popes of Rome (To A.D. 1241)	1904	30p	£55.00
MF81	Popes of Rome (Dubec, After A.D. 1241)	1904	60p	—
F100	Statues & Monuments (Numbered)	1905	60p	—
F100	Statues & Monuments (Unnumbered)	1905	60p	—
KF127	Views of Malta	1903	35p	—
F?100	Views of Malta (Numbered)	1903	30p	—
BF?127	Views of Malta (Numbered)	1903	30p	—
BF?65	Views of Malta (Unnumbered)	1903	30p	—
F?30	Views of the Mediterranean	1903	A	—
BF?100	Views of the Mediterranean	1903	A	—
F?555	Views of the World	1903	30p	—
BF?555	Views of the World	1903	30p	—
F99	Warships (White Border)	1910	75p	—
KF850	Warships	1904	35p	—
BF850	Warships	1904	60p	—
BF?75	Warships & Liners (Dubec)	1904	£1.00	—
BF?25	Warships & Liners (Excelsior)	1904	£1.00	—
MF?50	Warships & Liners (Superior)	1904	£1.25	—

CROWN TOBACCO CO. (India)

X24	Actresses	1900	B	—
96	National Types, Costumes & Flags	1900	£15.00	—
B96	National Types, Costumes & Flags	1900	B	—
?	Photo Series	1900	B	—

CHARLES C. DAVIS (U.S.A.)

?15	Actresses	1890	£20.00	—

DIXSON (Australia)

50	Australian M.P.s & Celebrities	1900	£4.00	—

DOMINION TOBACCO CO. (CANADA)

100	Photos (Actresses)	1905	£15.00	—
50	The Smokers of the World	1904	£25.00	—

DOMINION TOBACCO CO. LTD (New Zealand)

50	Coaches & Coaching Days	1927	75p	£37.50
50	People & Places Famous in New Zealand History	1925	£1.00	—
50	Products of the World	1929	30p	£15.00
50	USS Co's Steamers	1928	£1.00	—

DRUMMOND TOBACCO CO. (U.S.A.)

?20	Actresses	1895	B	—
?50	Bathing Girls	1895	B	—
50	Beauties "CHOAB"	1897	C	—
X?25	Girls	1896	£30.00	—

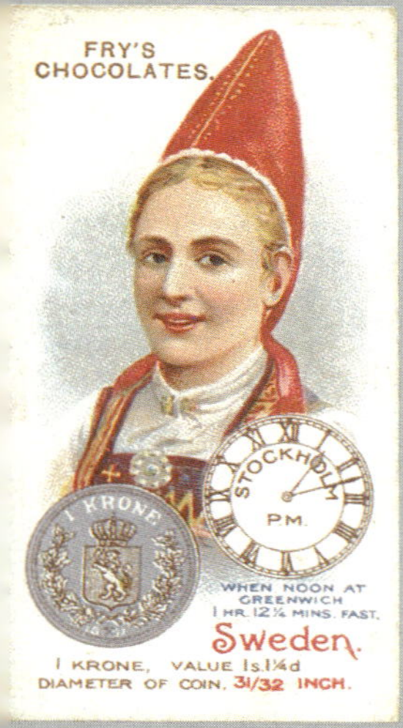

Time & Money. Fry (also Smith. Wills)

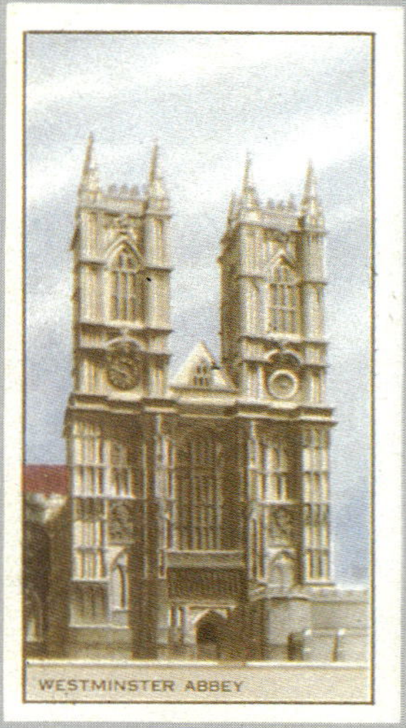

Marvels of the World. Beaulah or Wright

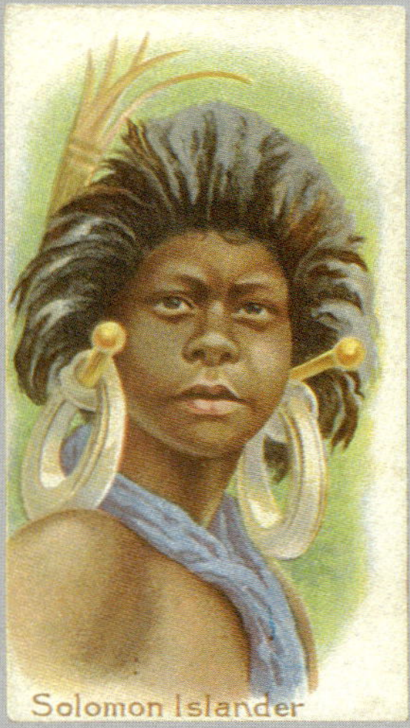

Natives of the World. Taddy or Sniders & Abrahams

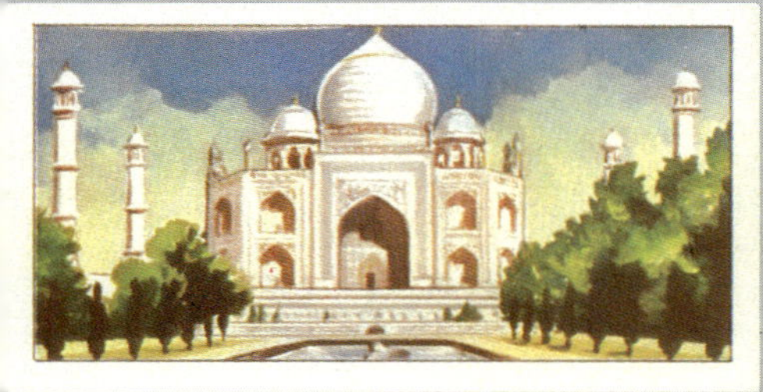

Wunders der Welt. Barratt

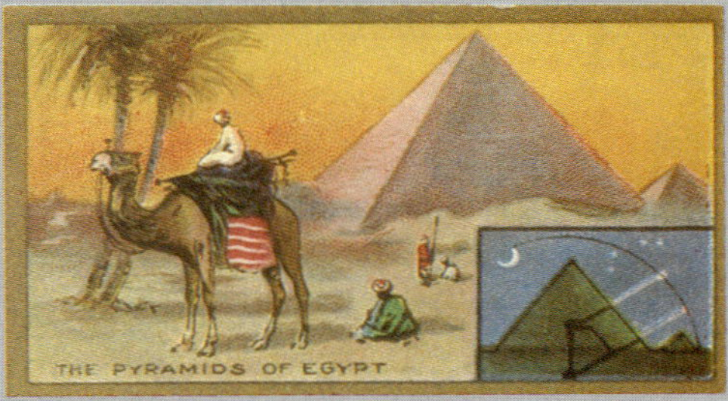

Wonders of the World. Cohen Weenen

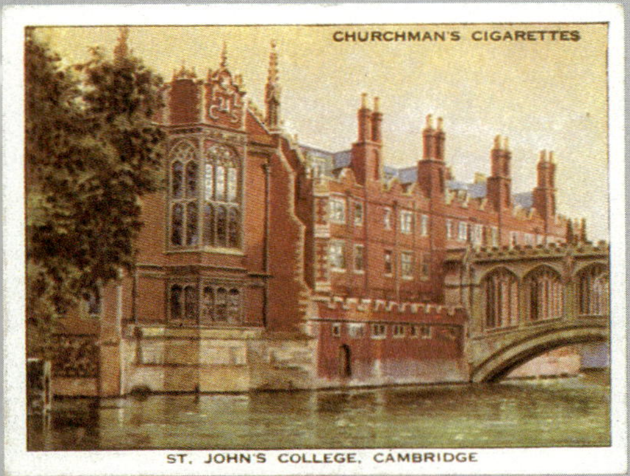

Holidays in Britain. Churchman

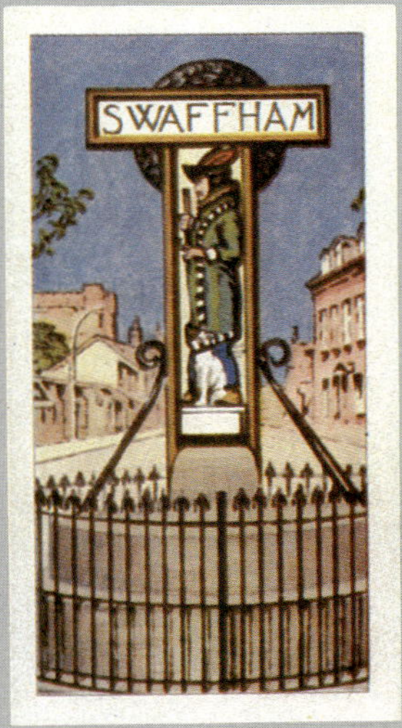

Historic East Anglia. Lambert

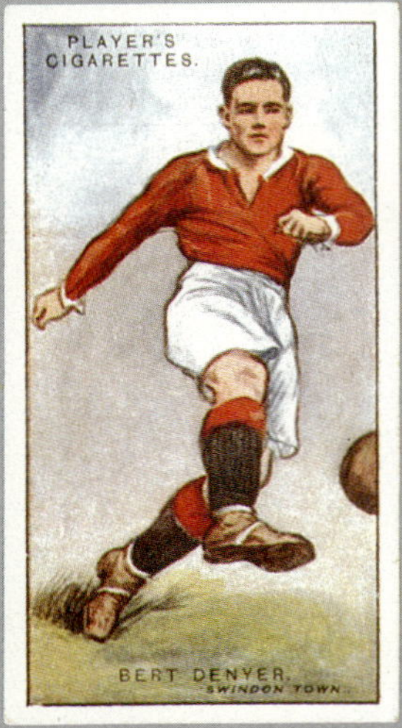

Footballers, 1928. Player

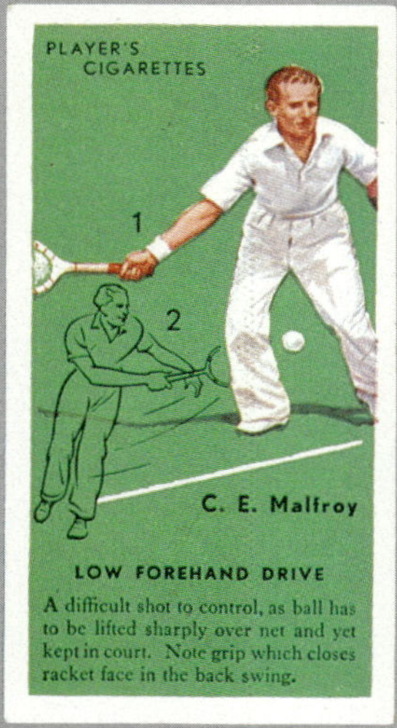

Tennis. Player

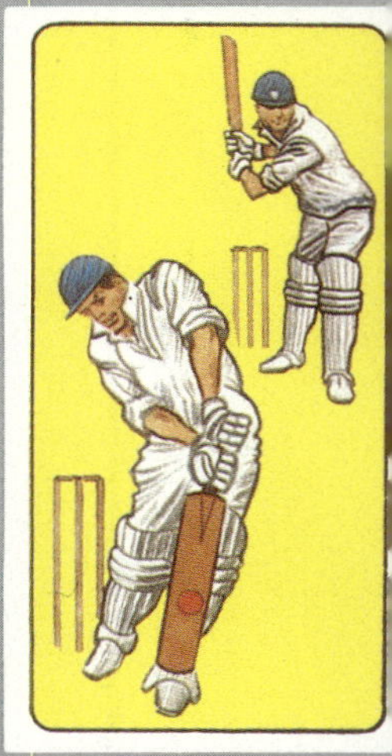
Play Cricket. Bassett

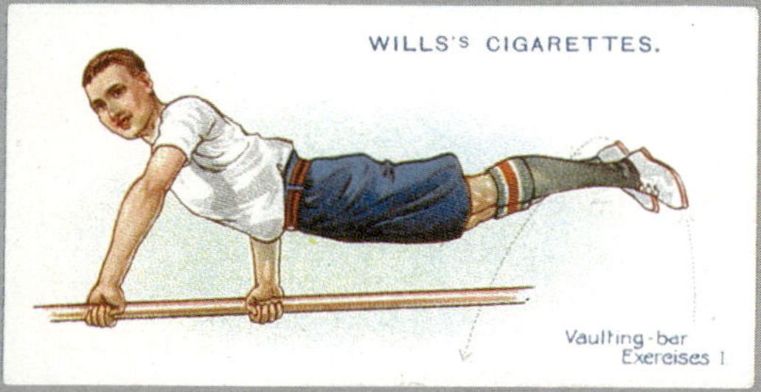

Physical Culture. Wills

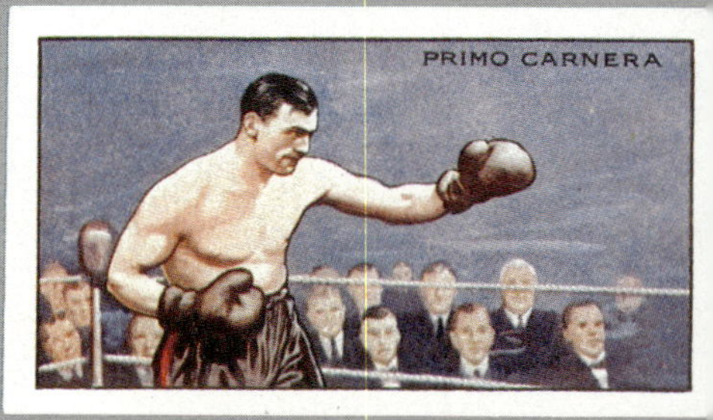

Champions. Gallaher

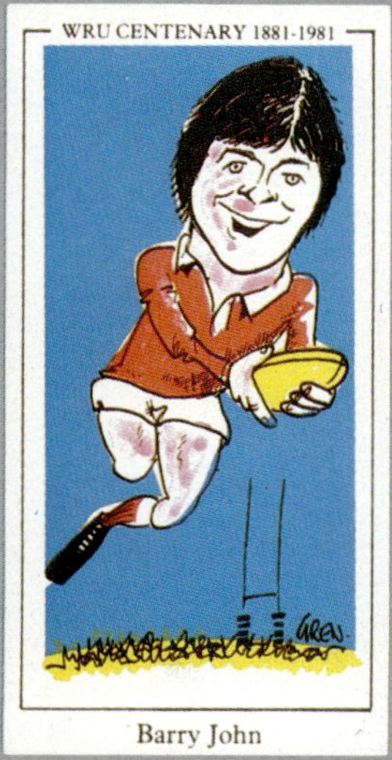

Great Welsh Rugby Players.
Welsh Rugby Union

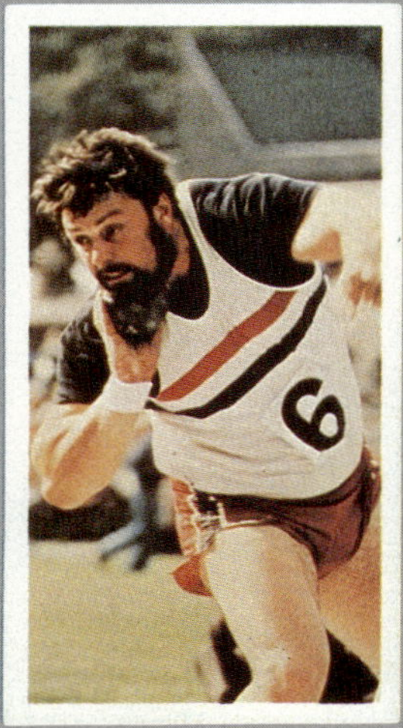

Athletes of the World. Bassett

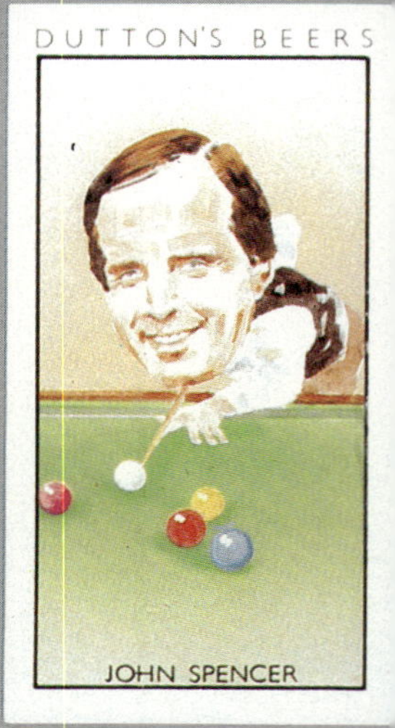

Team of Sporting Heroes. Dutton

DUDGEON & ARNELL (Australia)

Qty		*Date*	*Odds*	*Sets*
B16	1934 Australian Test Team	1934	£2.00	£30.00
B55	Famous Ships	1933	£1.00	—

W. DUKE & SONS LTD. (U.S.A.)

50	Actors & Actresses, Series 1	1889	£4.00	£200.00
B50	Actors & Actresses, Series 1	1889	A	—
50	Actors & Actresses, Series 2	1889	£4.00	£200.00
B50	Actors & Actresses, Series 2	1889	A	—
X30	Actors & Actresses (As Above)	1889	£8.00	—
X25	Albums of American Stars	1886	£12.50	—
X25	Battle Scenes	1887	£8.00	—
X25	Beauties, Black Border	1886	£8.00	£200.00
X25	Beauties, Folders	1886	£15.00	—
X25	Bicycle & Trick Riders	1891	£10.00	—
X25	Breeds of Horses	1892	£10.00	£250.00
X25	Bridges	1888	£7.50	£187.00
X25	Burlesque Scenes	1887	£8.00	—
50	Coins of All Nations	1889	£5.00	£250.00
X25	Comic Characters	1887	£7.00	£175.00
X25	Cowboy Scenes	1888	£10.00	—
X50	Fairest Flowers of the World	1887	£8.00	—
F45	Famous Ships	1884	A	—
50	Fancy Dress Ball Costumes	1887	£5.00	£250.00
B50	Fancy Dress Ball Costumes	1887	A	—
X50	Fancy Dress Ball Costumes	1887	£8.00	—
50	Fishers & Fish	1888	£5.00	£250.00
X25	Fishers & Fish	1888	£8.00	—
X25	Flags & Costumes	1892	£10.00	£250.00
50	Floral Beauties & Language of Flowers	1893	£4.00	£200.00
X25	French Novelties	1892	£8.00	—
X25	Gems of Beauty	1884	£8.00	—
50	Great Americans	1888	£5.00	£250.00
X16	Great Americans	1888	£10.00	—
25	Gymnastic Exercises	1887	£10.00	£250.00
X25	Habitations of Man	1890	£7.00	£175.00
X50	Histories of Generals	1888	£8.00	—
50	Histories of Generals (Booklets)	1888	£6.00	£300.00
50	Histories of Poor Boys & Other Famous People	1888	£7.00	£350.00
50	Holidays	1890	£5.00	£250.00
X25	Illustrated Songs	1893	£8.00	—
X25	Industries of States	1889	£12.50	—
50	Jokes	1890	£6.00	—
X25	Jokes	1890	£8.00	—
X25	Lighthouses (Die Cut)	1890	£8.00	£200.00
X25	Miniature Novelties	1891	£7.00	£175.00
50	Musical Instruments	1888	£7.50	—
X25	Musical Instruments of the World	1888	£10.00	—
36	Ocean & River Steamers	1887	£7.50	£270.00
F?	Photographic Cards	1885	50p	—
MF?	Photographic Cards	1885	£1.00	—
XF?	Photographic Cards	1885	75p	—
53	Playing Cards	1887	£5.00	£250.00
50	Popular Songs & Dancers	1894	£7.50	—
50	Postage Stamp Cards	1888	£6.00	£300.00

W. DUKE & SONS LTD. (U.S.A.)—cont.

Qty		*Date*	*Odds*	*Sets*
X25	Presidential Possibilities	1888	£7.00	£175.00
X15	Puzzles	1887	£10.00	—
50	Rulers, Flags & Arms (Folders)	1889	£5.00	£240.00
X50	Rulers, Flags & Arms	1889	£7.00	—
50	Scenes of Perilous Occupations	1888	£7.50	—
X25	Sea Captains	1887	£10.00	—
50	Shadows	1890	£5.00	£250.00
X25	Snapshots from "Puck"	1889	£7.00	£175.00
X25	Stars of the Stage, 1st Series	1891	£7.50	£187.50
X25	Stars of the Stage, 2nd Series	1891	£10.00	£250.00
X25	Stars of the Stage, 3rd Series	1892	£7.50	£187.50
X25	Stars of the Stage, 4th Series (Die Cut)	1893	£8.00	£200.00
48	State Governors, Arms & Maps (Folders) ...	1889	£5.00	£240.00
X48	State Governors, Arms & Maps	1889	£7.50	—
X25	Talk of the Diamond	1893	£12.50	—
50	The Terrors of America & Their Doings	1890	£5.00	£250.00
M50	The Terrors of America & Their Doings	1890	A	—
X50	The Terrors of America & Their Doings	1890	£10.00	—
50	Tinted Photos	1887	£10.00	—
X25	Transparencies	1888	£20.00	—
X24	Tricks with Cards	1887	£12.50	—
X25	Types of Vessels (Die Cut)	1889	£8.00	£200.00
50	Vehicles of the World	1888	£8.00	—
X50	Yacht Club Colors of the World	1890	£7.50	—
50	Yacht Colors of the World	1890	£5.00	£250.00
B50	Yacht Colors of the World	1890	A	—

Printed Albums (exchanged for coupons)

		Date	*Odds*	*Sets*
	Costumes of All Nations (3 Sets)	1890	—	£40.00
	Governors, Coats of Arms, etc.	1889	—	£35.00
	Postage Stamp Album	1888	—	£40.00
	Shadows	1890	—	£35.00
	Sporting Girls	1888	—	C
	The Heroes of the Civil War	1889	—	£40.00
	The Rulers, Flags, Coats of Arms	1889	—	£40.00
	The Terrors of America	1890	—	£35.00
	Yacht Colors of the World (3 Sets)	1890	—	£40.00

EGYPTIAN CIGARETTE COY. (Malta)

F120	Actresses	1906	£2.00	—
LF?150	Actresses	1906	A	—
264	Decorations & Medals	1908	£3.00	—
F100	Maltese Band Players	1910	£4.00	

EGYPTIAN CIGARETTES MFG. CO. (China)

?50	Actresses	1900	£15.00	—
25	Armies of the World	1900	£25.00	—
?	Beauties	1900	B	—
30	Beauties "Nymphs"	1900	£25.00	—
?30	Chinese & South African Series	1900	B	—
25	National Flags & Flowers—Girls	1900	B	—
30	Old Masters	1900	£20.00	—
?55	Russo-Japanese War Series	1903	B	—
25	Types of British & Colonial Troops	1900	£25.00	—
25	Warships	1900	£15.00	—

H. ELLIS & CO. (U.S.A.)

Qty		*Date*	*Odds*	*Sets*
25	Breeds of Dogs	1890	£10.00	£250.00
25	Costumes of Women	1890	B	—
25	Generals of the Late Civil War	1890	£20.00	—
F?	Photographic Cards	1887	£3.00	—

D. FANCIULLI & CO. (Malta)

50	Il Paradiso Perduta	1906	£2.50	—

JOHN FINZER & BROS. (U.S.A.)

X10	Inventors & Inventions	1891	£12.50	£125.00

G. W. GAIL & AX (U.S.A.)

X25	Battle Scenes	1891	£10.00	—
X25	Bicycle & Trick Riders	1891	£15.00	—
X25	French Novelties	1891	£12.50	—
X25	Industries of States	1891	£12.50	—
X25	Lighthouses (Die Cut)	1891	£15.00	—
X25	Novelties (Die Cut)	1890	£15.00	—
XF?	Photographic Cards	1885	£1.50	—
X25	Stars of the Stage	1891	£12.50	—

GOODWIN & CO. (U.S.A.)

50	Champions	1888	£8.00	£400.00
50	Dogs of the World	1890	£5.00	£250.00
50	Flowers	1890	£6.00	—
50	Games & Sports Series	1889	£10.00	£500.00
50	Holidays	1889	A	—
50	Occupations for Women	1887	£30.00	—
F?	Photographic Cards	1886	75p	—
50	Vehicles of the World	1888	A	—

Printed Albums (exchanged for coupons)

	Champions	1888	—	C
	Floral Album	1890	—	£50.00
	Games & Sports	1889	—	C

L. O. GROTHE LTD. (Canada)

52	Bridge Hands	1927	£1.50	—

THOS. W. HALL (U.S.A.)

B155	Actors & Actresses (Dull Background)	1881	£3.00	—
B142	Actors & Actresses (Black Background)	1882	£4.00	—
B?200	Actors & Actresses (Fancy Corners)	1884	£7.50	—
B?150	Actors & Actresses (Sun's Rays)	1890	£6.00	—
B?50	Actresses (Tiled Wall)	1888	£10.00	—
B?50	Actresses (No Borders)	1892	£15.00	—
X20	Actresses (Ours All)	1885	£25.00	—
B12	Athletes	1881	£20.00	—
B8	Presidential Candidates & Actresses	1880	£40.00	—
B22	Presidents of the United States	1884	£12.50	—
25	Theatrical Types	1890	£15.00	—

HARTLEY'S TOBACCO CO. (S. Africa)

L19	South African English Cricket Tour 1929	1929	£15.00	—

S. F. HESS & CO. (U.S.A.)

Qty		Date	Odds	Sets
F?	Photographic Cards	1885	£4.00	—
55	Poker Puzzle Cards	1890	£20.00	
25	Terms of Poker Illustrated	1890	£20.00	—

HILSON CO. (U.S.A.)

X25	Battleships & Signal Flags	1901	£6.00	£150.00
X25	National Types	1901	£6.00	—

IMPERIAL CIGARETTE & TOBACCO CO. (CANADA)

?24	Actresses	1900	£25.00	—

IMPERIAL TOBACCO CO. OF INDIA LTD. (India)

25	Indian Historical Views	1910	80p	£20.00
40	Nautch Girl Series (Pedro Cigs.)	1908	£1.00	£40.00
40	Nautch Girl Series (Railway Cigs.)	1908	£1.00	£40.00
52	Nautch Girl Series (P/C Inset, Pedro)	1908	£1.20	£62.50
52	Nautch Girl Series (P/C Inset, Railway)	1908	£1.20	£62.50
K52	Miniature Playing Cards	1933	50p	—
52	Playing Cards	1919	£1.25	—

IMPERIAL TOBACCO CO. OF CANADA LTD. (Canada)

50	Actresses, Framed Border (Plain Back)	1910	£1.50	—
L66	Aircraft Spotter Series (Packets)	1941	25p	£16.50
60	Animals (Millbank)	1916	40p	£24.00
L50	Animal With Flag (Silk)	1915	£1.25	£62.50
50	Arms of the British Empire	1911	£1.00	—
50	Around the World	1912	£2.00	—
50	Aviation Series	1910	£1.25	—
100	Baseball Series	1912	A	—
30	Beauties—Art Series (Plain Back)	1911	£4.00	—
25	Beauties—Girls in Costume	1904	£12.50	—
24	Beauties—Smoke Girls	1904	£12.50	—
M50	Birds, Beasts & Fishes	1924	£1.00	—
30	Bird Series	1910	£1.00	—
X100	Birds of Canada	1924	£1.25	—
X100	Birds of Canada (Western Canada)	1925	£1.50	—
50	Boy Scouts	1911	£2.00	—
50	British Birds	1923	30p	£15.00
50	British Man of War Series (Plain Back)	1910	£3.00	£150.00
50	Buildings (Plain Back)	1902	£3.00	—
50	Butterflies & Moths	1911	£1.00	—
L24	Canada's Corvettes 1st Series	1943	A	—
L24	Canada's Corvettes 2nd Series	1944	A	—
50	Canadian Historical Portraits	1913	A	—
48	Canadian History Series	1926	40p	£20.00
50	Canadian History Series (Anon)	1926	50p	—
P50	Canadian History Series (Silk)	1914	£5.00	—
M118	Canadian Miscellany (Silk)	1912	£2.00	—
50	Children of All Nations	1924	30p	£15.00
23	Dogs Series	1924	40p	£10.00
50	Dogs 2nd Series	1925	30p	£15.00
50	Famous English Actresses	1924	50p	£25.00
50	Film Favourites	1926	A	—
50	Fish & Bait	1924	50p	—

IMPERIAL TOBACCO CO. OF CANADA LTD. (Canada)—cont.

Qty		Date	Odds	Sets
50	Fishes of the World	1924	60p	—
50	Fish Series	1912	75p	—
50	Flower Culture in Pots	1925	30p	£15.00
50	Fowls, Pigeons & Dogs	1911	£1.00	—
30	Game Bird Series	1925	40p	£12.00
L55	Garden Flowers (Silk)	1913	£1.00	£55.00
G5	Garden Flowers (Silk)	1913	£7.50	—
50	Gardening Hints	1923	25p	£12.50
L25	Heraldic Signs & Their Origin	1925	60p	—
45	Hockey Players	1912	£2.00	—
50	How To Do It	1911	£1.50	—
50	How to Play Golf	1925	£2.00	—
50	Infantry Training	1915	£1.00	£50.00
100	Lacrosse Series Set 1	1910	£1.50	—
100	Lacrosse Series Set 2	1911	£1.50	—
50	Lacrosse Series Set 3	1912	£1.50	—
50	L'Histoire Du Canada	1914	60p	—
B48	Mail Carriers and Stamps	1903	£7.50	—
50	Merchant Ships of the World	1924	40p	£20.00
25	Military Portraits	1914	£1.00	—
50	Modern War Weapons	1915	£2.50	—
56	Motor Cars	1921	75p	£40.00
50	Movie Stars	1925	50p	—
50	Music Hall Artistes (Plain Back)	1911	75p	—
50	Naval Portraits	1915	£1.00	—
25	Notabilities	1915	£1.00	—
L55	Orders & Military Medals (Silk)	1915	£1.25	—
L50	Pictures of Canadian Life	1912	£3.00	—
52	Poker Hands	1924	50p	£26.00
25	Poultry Alphabet	1924	60p	£15.00
50	Prominent Men of Canada	1912	£1.50	—
50	Railway Engines	1924	50p	£25.00
L55	Regimental Uniforms of Canada (Silk)	1914	£1.25	£70.00
127	Smokers Golf Cards	1926	£1.00	—
50	The Reason Why	1924	50p	£25.00
25	The World's Dreadnoughts	1910	£1.00	—
50	Types of Nations	1910	£1.00	—
25	V.C. Heroes (Blue Back)	1915	80p	£20.00
L45	Views of the World	1912	£2.00	—
B144	World War I Scenes & Portraits	1916	80p	—
49	Yacht Pennants & Views (Silk)	1915	£1.25	£62.00

IMPERIAL TOBACCO CO. (NFLD.) LTD. (Canada)

B52	Playing Cards	1930	£2.00	—

JACK & JILL CIGARS (U.S.A.)

X25	Actresses "JAKE"	1890	£15.00	—

JAMAICA TOBACCO CO.

F?100	Miniature Post Card Series	1915	£2.00	—

KENTUCKY TOBACCOS (PTY.) LTD. (S. Africa)

L120	The March of Mankind	1940	75p	—

KEY WEST FAVORS (U.S.A.)

Qty		*Date*	*Odds*	*Sets*
X50	Actresses "JAKE"	1892	£15.00	—

KHEDIVIAL COMPANY (U.S.A.)

B10	Aeroplane Series No. 103	1912	£4.00	£40.00
B10	Prize Dog Series No. 102	1911	£4.00	£40.00
M25	Prize Fight Series No. 101	1910	£4.00	—
M25	Prize Fight Series No. 102	1911	£4.00	—

WM. S. KIMBALL & CO. (U.S.A.)

?25	Actresses, Collotype	1887	£25.00	—
72	Ancient Coins	1888	£12.50	—
48	Arms of Dominions	1888	£8.00	—
50	Ballet Queens	1889	£7.50	£375.00
X20	Beautiful Bathers	1889	£12.00	—
52	Beauties, Playing Card Insets	1895	£8.00	£420.00
50	Butterflies	1888	£7.50	—
50	Champions of Games & Sports	1888	£10.00	£500.00
50	Dancing Girls of the World	1889	£6.00	£300.00
50	Dancing Women	1889	£6.00	£300.00
50	Fancy Bathers	1889	£6.00	£300.00
X25	French Novelties	1891	£15.00	
X25	Gems of Beauty	1891	£15.00	—
50	Goddesses of the Greeks & Romans	1889	£8.00	—
X25	Household Pets	1891	£12.00	—
X15	National Flags	1887	£16.00	—
F?	Photographic Cards	1886	£1.25	—
XF?	Photographic Cards	1886	£2.00	—
X20	Pretty Athletes	1890	£12.00	—
50	Savage & Semi Barbarous Chiefs & Rulers	1890	£8.00	—
L?25	Wellstood Etchings	1887	B	—

Printed Albums (exchanged for coupons)

	Ancient Coins	1888	—	C
	Ballet Queens	1889	—	£60.00
	Champions of Games & Sports	1888	—	C
	Dancing Girls of the World	1889	—	C
	Dancing Women	1889	—	C
	Fancy Bathers	1889	—	C
	Goddesses of the Greeks & Romans	1889	—	C
	Savage & Semi Barbarous Chiefs & Rulers	1890	—	C

KINNEY BROS. (U.S.A.)

25	Actresses "Set 1"	1891	£3.00	£75.00
25	Actresses "Set 2"	1891	£5.00	—
50	Actresses (Group 2)	1891	£2.00	£100.00
50	Actresses (Group 3)	1892	£2.00	£100.00
50	Actresses (Group 4, Coloured)	1893	£2.00	—
150	Actresses (Group 4, Sepia)	1893	£1.00	—
25	Animals	1890	£6.00	£150.00
10	Butterflies of the World (White)	1888	£6.00	£60.00
50	Butterflies of the World (Gold)	1888	£5.00	£250.00
25	Famous Gems of the World	1889	£5.00	£125.00
25	Famous Running Horses (American)	1890	£4.00	£100.00
25	Famous Running Horses (English)	1890	£3.00	£75.00

KINNEY BROS. (U.S.A.)—cont.

Qty		Date	Odds	Sets
F45	Famous Ships	1887	A	—
25	Great American Trotters	1890	£7.50	—
52	Harlequin Cards, 1st Series	1888	£7.00	£365.00
53	Harlequin Cards, 2nd Series	1888	£7.00	£370.00
L?4	Inaugural Types	1888	B	—
L50	International Cards	1888	£12.50	—
K25	Jocular Oculars	1887	£15.00	—
25	Leaders	1889	£5.00	£125.00
50	Magic Changing Cards	1888	£7.50	—
622	Military Series	1887	£1.50	—
50	National Dances (white border)	1889	£5.00	£250.00
25	National Dances (no border)	1889	£6.00	£150.00
25	Naval Vessels of the World	1889	£6.00	£150.00
50	New Year 1890 Cards	1889	£8.00	—
K25	Novelties (Circular, Thick Cards)	1888	£12.50	—
K50	Novelties (Circular, Thin Cards)	1888	£4.00	£200.00
75	Novelties (Die Cut)	1888	£3.00	£225.00
14	Novelties (Oval)	1888	£15.00	—
45	Novelties (Rectangular)	1888	£5.00	£225.00
F?	Photographic Cards	1886	25p	—
LF?	Photographic Cards	1886	75p	—
50	Surf Beauties	1889	£6.00	£300.00
1	Sweet Caporal Calendar	1890	—	£40.00
52	Transparent Playing Cards	1888	£8.00	£415.00
25	Types of Nationalities (Folders)	1890	£10.00	—
Printed Albums (exchanged for coupons)				
	Butterflies	1889	—	£60.00
	Celebrated American & English Running Horses	1890	—	C
	Leaders	1889	—	£45.00
	Liberty Album	1889	—	£35.00
	National Dances	1889	—	C
	Natural History	1890	—	£35.00
	Reigning Beauties	1889	—	£50.00
	Singers & Opera Houses	1889	—	£60.00
	Surf Beauties	1889	—	C

KRAMERS TOBACCO CO. (PTY.) LTD. (S. Africa)

50	Badges of South African Rugby Football Clubs	1933	£1.50	—

LA FAVORITA (Canary Islands)

M30/58	Flags & Soldiers (Silk)	1915	30p	£9.00

LEWIS & ALLEN CO. (U.S.A.)

X120	Views & Art Studies	1912	£1.50	—

LONE JACK CIGARETTE CO. (U.S.A.)

25	Inventors & Inventions	1887	A	—
50	Language of Flowers	1888	£12.50	—
F?	Photographic Cards	1886	£2.50	—

P. LORILLARD CO. (U.S.A.)

25	Actresses (Coloured)	1888	£10.00	£250.00
B20	Actresses (Irregular Gold Frame)	1889	£10.00	—
B?150	Actresses (Fancy Surrounds)	1889	£6.00	—

P. LORILLARD CO. (U.S.A.)—cont.

Qty		Date	Odds	Sets
B75	Actresses (Plain Surrounds)	1890	£7.50	—
X25	Actresses (Burdick 263)	1889	£7.50	£185.00
X25	Actresses (Burdick 264-1)	1890	£7.50	£185.00
X25	Actresses (Burdick 264-2)	1890	£7.50	—
X25	Actresses (Burdick 264-3, Grey Border)	1890	£7.50	—
X25	Actresses in Opera Rules	1892	£12.50	—
X25	Ancient Mythology Burlesqued	1893	£6.00	£150.00
X50	Beautiful Women	1893	£6.00	£300.00
X25	Boxing Positions & Boxers	1887	£15.00	—
M?10	Busts of Girls (Die Cut)	1886	B	—
X25	Circus Scenes	1888	£20.00	—
X?10	Everyday Annoyances	1886	B	—
25	National Flags	1888	£12.50	—
X52	Playing Card Inset Girls	1893	£10.00	—
X50	Prizefighters	1887	A	—
X?15	Song Album	1887	A	—
X25	Types of Flirtation	1892	£20.00	—
X25	Types of the Stage	1893	£6.00	£150.00

W. C. MACDONALD INC. (Canada)

?350	Aeroplanes & Warships	1940	30p	—
53	Playing Cards (Many Printings)	1927	15p	—

B. & J. B. MACHADO (Jamaica)

25	British Naval Series	1916	£5.00	—
F50	Popular Film Stars	1926	£1.25	—
F50	Stars of the Cinema	1926	A	—
50	The Great War—Victoria Cross Heroes	1916	£5.00	—
F50	The Royal Family at Home & Abroad	1927	£1.25	—
F50	The World of Sport	1928	£1.25	—

MACLIN–ZIMMER (U.S.A.)

X53	Playing Cards (Actresses)	1892	£7.50	—

H. MANDELBAUM (U.S.A.)

20	Comic Types of People	1890	£20.00	—
36	Flags of Nations	1890	£20.00	—

MASPERO FRERES LTD. (Palestine)

50	Birds, Beasts & Fishes	1925	£1.50	—

S. MATTINNO & SONS (Malta)

X36	Britain Prepared Series	1940	£1.00	—

P. H. MAYO & BROTHER (U.S.A.)

B25	Actresses (Fancy Frame)	1890	£6.00	£150.00
?25	Actresses (Sepia)	1886	£25.00	—
M25	Actresses (Black Border)	1890	£10.00	—
L12	Actresses (Diagonal)	1888	£25.00	—
?50	Actresses (Burdick 488)	1888	£12.50	—
X25	Actresses	1887	A	—
28	Baseball Game (Die Cut)	1890	B	—
40	Baseball Players	1892	A	—
35	College Football Stars	1892	£12.50	—

P. H. MAYO & BROTHER (U.S.A.)—cont.

Qty		Date	Odds	Sets
20	Costumes & Flowers	1892	£10.00	£200.00
19	Costumes of Warriors & Soldiers	1892	£15.00	—
25	Headdresses of Various Nations	1890	£15.00	—
?100	National Dances (Die Cut)	1890	A	—
M25	National Flowers (Girl & Scene)	1891	£12.50	—
20	Naval Uniforms	1892	£12.50	—
F?	Photographic Cards	1887	A	—
24	Presidents of U.S.	1888	A	—
35	Prizefighters	1890	£10.00	—
20	Shakespeare Characters	1891	£12.50	£250.00
X12	The Seasons	1888	B	—
X15	Wings of Birds of Plumage	1888	B	—

M. MELACHRINO & CO. (Malta)

52	Peuples Exotiques "1 Serie"	1925	30p	—
52	Peuples Exotiques "2 Serie"	1925	30p	—
52	Peuples Exotiques "3 Serie"	1925	16p	£8.00

MIFSUD & AZZOPARDI (Malta)

KF59	First Maltese Parliament	1922	£1.50	—

MRS. G. B. MILLER & CO. (U.S.A.)

X?	Actresses & Celebrities	1885	B	—
X?	Alphabet Cards	1887	£25.00	—
22	Photographs of all the Presidents	1888	B	—

L. MILLER & SONS (U.S.A.)

49	Animals & Birds	1900	B	—
X25	Battleships	1900	£12.50	—
X100	Beauties "THIBS"	1900	B	—
X25	Generals & Admirals (Spanish War)	1900	£10.00	—
X24	Presidents of U.S.	1900	£10.00	—
X50	Rulers of the World	1900	£10.00	—

CHAS. J. MITCHELL (Canada)

26	Actresses "FROGA" (Brown Back)	1900	£15.00	—
26	Actresses "FROGA" (Green Back)	1900	£15.00	—

MOORE & CALVI (U.S.A.)

X53	Beauties, Playing Card Inset, Set 1	1888	£10.00	£500.00
X53	Beauties, Playing Card Inset, Set 2	1889	£8.00	£400.00
X53	Beauties, Playing Card Inset, Set 3	1890	£6.00	£300.00
X10	Rope Knots	1888	£25.00	—

MURAI BROS. (Japan)

?	Actresses "ALWICS"	1910	£2.00	—
50	Beauties	1902	£5.00	£250.00
50	Dancing Girls of the World	1900	£10.00	—
32	Flowers	1900	£10.00	
50	World's Smokers	1900	£10.00	—

NATIONAL CIGARETTE & TOBACCO CO. (U.S.A.)

25	National Types (Sailor Girls)	1890	£8.00	£200.00
F?	Photographic Cards	1888	£2.00	

NATIONAL TOBACCO WORKS (U.S.A.)

Qty		*Date*	*Odds*	*Sets*
G?	Actresses, etc. (Newsboy)	1900	£7.50	—
G100	Actresses (Coloured)	1900	£15.00	—

OLD FASHION FINE CUT (U.S.A.)

FX?	Photographic Cards	1890	£4.00	—

OMEGA CIGARETTE FACTORY (Malta)

KF100	Cinema Stars	1936	50p	—

PENINSULAR TOBACCO CO. LTD. (India)

50	Animals and Birds	1910	£1.00	—
52	Birds of Brilliant Plumage (P/C Inset)	1916	£1.50	—
25	Birds of the East, 1st Series	1912	60p	£15.00
25	Birds of the East, 2nd Series	1912	60p	£15.00
25	China's Famous Warriors	1912	60p	£15.00
50	Chinese Heroes	1913	£1.00	—
50	Chinese Modern Beauties	1912	A	—
50	Chinese Trades Set 3	1912	60p	—
50	Chinese Trades Set 5	1913	60p	—
30	Fish Series	1916	£1.00	—
25	Hindoo Gods	1909	80p	£20.00
37	Nautch Girl Series	1910	A	—
25	Products of the World	1915	50p	£12.50

PIZZUTO (Malta)

50	Milton's "Paradise Lost"	1910	£1.25	—

THE PLANTERS STORES (India)

50	Actresses "FROGA"	1900	£10.00	—
25	Beauties "FECKSA"	1900	£10.00	—

POLICANSKY BROS. (South Africa)

M50	Birds, Beasts & Fishes (Nassa Cigs)	1924	£1.50	—
50	South African Fauna	1925	£2.00	—

RED MAN CHEWING TOBACCO (U.S.A.)

X40	American Indian Chiefs	1952	£1.50	£60.00

D. RITCHIE & CO. (Canada)

30	Actresses "RITAN"	1887	£15.00	—
52	Beauties P/C Inset	1888	£15.00	—
52	Playing Cards	1888	£12.50	—

D. E. ROSE & CO. (U.S.A.)

G28	Imperial Cards	1890	£15.00	£420.00

RUGGIER BROS. (Malta)

M50	Story of the Knights of Malta	1924	£1.50	£75.00

JOHN SCERRI (Malta)

147/150	Beauties & Children (Black & White)	1930	30p	£45.00
45	Beauties & Children (Coloured)	1930	30p	—
BF50	Beautiful Women	1931	50p	—
BF480	Cinema Artists	1931	50p	—

JOHN SCERRI (Malta)—cont.

Qty		Date	Odds	Sets
BF180	Cinema Stars	1931	50p	—
B50	Famous London Buildings	1934	£1.25	—
60	Film Stars (First Serie)	1931	60p	—
60	Film Stars (Second Serie)	1931	60p	—
52	Interesting Places of the World	1934	20p	£10.00
F25	International Footballers	1933	£1.00	£25.00
401	Malta Views	1928	20p	—
B51	Members of Parliament—Malta	1928	12p	£6.00
146	Prominent People	1930	40p	—
BF100	Scenes from Films	1932	40p	—
XF100	Talkie Stars	1932	75p	—
B100	World's Famous Buildings	1931	25p	£25.00

J. J. SCHUH TOBACCO CO. (Australia)

Qty		Date	Odds	Sets
60	Australian Footballers A (½ Length)	1920	£2.00	£120.00
40	Australian Footballers B (Rays)	1921	£2.50	—
60	Australian Footballers C (Oval Frame)	1922	£4.00	—
60	Australian Jockeys	1921	£2.00	£120.00
F72	Cinema Stars (Black & White)	1924	75p	£54.00
60	Cinema Stars (Coloured)	1924	75p	£45.00
L12	Maxims of Success	1917	B	—
F72	Official War Photographs	1918	£1.50	£100.00
F96	Portraits of our Leading Footballers	1920	£1.50	£150.00

G. SCLIVAGNOTI (Malta)

Qty		Date	Odds	Sets
50	Actresses & Cinema Stars	1923	50p	£25.00
MF71	Grand Masters of the Order of Jerusalem ...	1898	£2.50	—
F102	Opera Singers	1898	£2.00	—
M100	Opera Singers	1898	£2.00	£200.00
B?47	Scenes with Girls	1905	B	—

SNIDERS & ABRAHAMS PTY. LTD. (Australia)

Qty		Date	Odds	Sets
31	Actresses	1905	£3.00	£100.00
20	Admirals & Warships of the USA	1908	£3.00	—
2	Advertisement Cards	1905	A	—
60	Animals (Green, Descriptive Backs)	1912	75p	£45.00
60	Animals & Birds	1912	75p	£45.00
15	Australian Cricket Team	1905	£6.00	—
16	Australian Football—Incidents in Play	1906	£3.00	£50.00
74	Australian Footballers—Series A (Full Length)	1904	£5.00	—
76	Australian Footballers—Scales B (½ Length)	1906	£4.00	—
76	Australian Footballers—Series C (½ Length) ...	1907	£4.00	—
56	Australian Footballers—Series D (Head/Shoulders)	1908	£3.00	—
140	Australian Footballers—Series D (Head/Shoulders)	1909	£3.00	—
60	Australian Footballers—Series E (Head in Oval)	1910	£3.00	—
60	Australian Footballers—Series F (Head in Rays)	1911	£3.00	—
60	Australian Footballers—Series G (With Pennant)	1912	£2.50	—
60	Australian Footballers—Series H (Head in Star)	1913	£2.00	—
60	Australian Footballers—Series I (Head in Shield)	1914	£2.00	—
56	Australian Footballers—Series J (½–¾ Length)	1910	£3.00	—

SNIDERS & ABRAHAMS PTY. LTD. (Australia)—cont.

Qty		Date	Odds	Sets
48	Australian Jockeys (Blue Back)	1907	£1.50	£75.00
83	Australian Jockeys (Brown Back)	1908	£2.00	—
56	Australian Racehorses (Horizontal Back)	1906	£1.50	£85.00
56	Australian Racehorses (Vertical Back)	1907	£1.50	£85.00
40	Australian Racing Scenes	1911	£1.50	£60.00
132	Australian V.C.'s and Officers	1917	£2.50	—
12	Billiard Tricks	1908	£4.00	—
60	Butterflies & Moths (Captions in Capitals)	1914	75p	£45.00
60	Butterflies & Moths (Captions in Small Letters)	1914	75p	£45.00
60	Cartoons & Caricatures	1907	£3.00	—
12	Coin Tricks	1908	£3.00	—
64	Crests of British Warships	1915	£2.00	—
40	Cricketers in Action	1906	£6.00	£240.00
12	Cricket Terms	1905	£5.00	£60.00
32	Dickens Series	1909	£2.00	£65.00
16	Dogs	1910	£2.50	£40.00
6	Flags (Shaped Metal)	1915	£1.00	—
6	Flags (Shaped Card)	1915	£1.00	—
60	Great War Leaders & Warships	1915	£1.50	£90.00
30	How to Keep Fit	1907	£3.00	—
60	Jokes	1906	£1.50	—
12	Match Puzzles	1908	£3.00	—
48	Medals & Decorations	1915	£3.00	—
M45	Melbourne Buildings	1914	£4.00	—
25	Natives of the World	1904	£4.00	£100.00
12	Naval Terms	1905	£3.00	£36.00
30	Oscar Asche, Lily Brayton & Lady Smokers	1911	£3.00	£100.00
40	Shakespeare Characters	1909	£2.50	£100.00
30	Signalling Series	1916	£3.00	—
?14	Statuary	1905	£4.00	—
60	Street Criers in London, 1707	1914	£4.00	—
32	Views of Victoria in 1857	1906	£3.00	—
FS?200	Views of the World	1908	£1.00	—

SPAULDING & MERRICK (U.S.A.)

B24	Animals	1890	£12.50	—

STAR TOBACCO CO. (India)

52	Beauties (P/C Inset)	1898	£15.00	—
52	Indian Native Types (P/C Inset)	1898	£15.00	—

SURBRUG CO. (U.S.A.)

B10	Aeroplane Series No. 103	1912	£4.00	—
B10	Prize Dog Series No. 102	1911	£4.00	—
M25	Prize Fight Series No. 101	1910	£4.00	—
M25	Prize Fight Series No. 102	1911	£4.00	—

TOBACCO PRODUCTS CORPORATION (Canada & U.S.A.)

?45	Canadian Sports Champions	1917	A	—
60	Do You Know?	1918	£2.50	—
60	Hockey Players	1918	A	—
220	Movie Stars	1915	75p	—
120	Movie Stars (Portrait in Oval)	1915	75p	—
L?50	Movie Stars	1915	£1.00	—
L?100	Movie Stars, Series No. 3	1916	£1.00	—
?180	Movie Stars, Series No. 4	1916	A	—
L100	Movie Stars, Series No. 5	1916	A	—

TUCKETT LTD. (Canada)

Qty		Date	Odds	Sets
B52	Aeroplane Series	1930	£2.00	—
25	Autograph Series	1913	£10.00	—
?50	Beauties & Scenes	1910	A	—
25	Boy Scout Series	1914	A	—
7	British Gravures	1923	A	—
L7	British Gravures	1923	A	—
F50	British Views	1912	75p	—
F?250	British Views	1912	75p	—
F80	British Warships	1914	£2.50	—
F?100	Canadian Scenes	1912	75p	—
?50	Card Trick Series	1928	£2.50	—
B52	Tucketts Auction Bridge Series	1930	A	—

U.S. TOBACCO CO. (U.S.A.)

X25	Actresses	1890	£15.00	—

UNITED CIGAR STORES (U.S.A.)

L25	The Aviators	1911	£5.00	£125.00

UNITED TOBACCO COMPANIES (SOUTH) LTD. (South Africa)

50	Aeroplanes of Today	1936	50p	—
50	African Fish	1937	60p	£30.00
50	Animals & Birds	1923	30p	—
L24	Arms & Crests of Universities & Schools	1930	40p	£10.00
FS50	Beauties of Great Britain	1930	50p	—
L52	Boy Scout, Girl Guide & Voortrekker Badges	1932	50p	£26.00
B50	British Aeroplanes	1933	75p	£37.50
L20	British Butterflies (Silk)	1924	£4.00	—
L30	British Roses (Silk)	1924	£3.50	£100.00
L62	British Rugby Tour of South Africa	1938	35p	£22.00
X25	Champion Dogs	1934	60p	—
50	Children of All Nations	1928	60p	—
50	Cinema Stars (Flag Cigarettes)	1922	60p	—
60	Do You Know?	1930	30p	—
50	Do You Know? 2nd Series	1930	35p	£17.50
50	Do You Know? 3rd Series	1931	35p	£17.50
30	Do You Know? (Different)	1933	35p	£10.00
50	Eminent Film Personalities	1930	75p	—
50	English Period Costumes	1932	20p	£20.00
L50	Exercises for Men & Women	1932	25p	£12.50
24	Fairy Tales	1926	40p	—
25	Famous Figures from South African History	1932	75p	—
L100	Famous Works of Art	1939	12p	£6.00
L120	Farmyards of South Africa	1934	15p	£18.00
L65	Flags of All Nations (Silk)	1910	£1.50	—
25	Flowers of South Africa	1932	75p	—
FS52	Here There & Everywhere	1930	30p	—
L50	Household Hints	1926	60p	—
B50	Humour in Sport	1929	80p	£40.00
25	Interesting Experiments	1930	50p	£12.50
L100	Medals & Decorations of the British Commonwealth of Nations	1941	30p	£30.00
50	Merchant Ships of the World	1925	50p	—
50	Motor Cars	1928	£1.50	£75.00
FS48	Nature Studies	1930	40p	—

UNITED TOBACCO COMPANIES (SOUTH) LTD. (South Africa)—cont.

Qty		*Date*	*Odds*	*Sets*
M25	Old Masters (Silk)	1926	£4.00	—
L100	Our Land	1938	12p	£6.00
B150	Our South African Birds	1942	12p	£15.00
L150	Our South African Birds	1942	12p	£12.50
B100	Our South African Flora	1940	12p	£6.00
L100	Our South African Flora	1940	12p	£4.00
B100	Our South African National Parks	1941	12p	£7.50
L100	Our South African National Parks	1941	12p	£6.00
L200	Our South Africa—Past & Present	1938	12p	£12.00
L24	Pastel Plates	1930	50p	£12.00
L88	Philosophical Sayings	1938	60p	—
L50	Pictures of South Africa's War Effort	1940	12p	£6.00
FS48	Pictures of the East	1930	30p	£15.00
25	Picturesque People of the Empire	1929	50p	£12.50
L50	Pottery Types (Silk)	1926	£3.00	—
M50	Pottery Types (Silk)	1926	£4.00	—
L50	Racehorses—South Africa (Set 1)	1929	40p	£20.00
L52	Racehorses—South Africa (Set 2)	1930	40p	£20.00
50	Regimental Uniforms	1937	60p	£30.00
50	Riders of the World	1931	60p	—
50	Safety First	1936	30p	—
B40	Ships of All Times	1931	60p	£24.00
25	South African Birds 1st Series	1927	60p	£15.00
25	South African Birds 2nd Series	1927	60p	£15.00
L52	South African Butterflies	1937	25p	£13.00
L52	South African Coats of Arms	1931	20p	£10.00
L17	South African Cricket Touring Team	1929	£4.00	£70.00
B100	South African Defence	1941	12p	£5.00
L52	South African Flora	1935	15p	£7.50
L100	South African Flowers (Silk)	1913	£1.50	£150.00
L50	South African Places of Interest	1934	15p	£7.50
L65	South African Rugby Football Clubs	1933	30p	£20.00
L52	Sports & Pastimes of South Africa	1936	40p	£20.00
L47	Springbok Rugby & Cricket Teams	1931	50p	£25.00
FS50	Stereoscopic Photographs, Assorted Subjects	1928	30p	—
FS50	Stereoscopic Photographs of South Africa	1929	35p	—
25	Studdy Dogs (Bonzo)	1925	£2.00	—
B50	Tavern of the Seas	1939	12p	£4.00
50	The Story of Sand	1934	40p	—
50	The World of Tomorrow	1938	30p	—
L40	Views of South African Scenery, 1st Series	1918	£1.25	—
L36	Views of South African Scenery, 2nd Series	1920	£1.25	—
25	Warriors of the World (Crossed Swords)	1937	60p	£15.00
25	What's This—Troublesome Things & Their Remedy	1929	75p	—
50	Wild Animals of the World	1932	50p	£25.00
25	Wild Flowers of South Africa 1st Series	1925	60p	£15.00
25	Wild Flowers of South Africa 2nd Series	1926	60p	£15.00
B40	Wonders of the World	1931	40p	£16.00
B100	World Famous Boxers	1939	50p	—

UNIVERSAL TOBACCO CO. (India)

F50	Actresses	1900	£10.00	—

UNIVERSAL TOBACCO CO. (PTY.) LTD. (S. Africa)

Qty		*Date*	*Odds*	*Sets*
835	Flags of All Nations	1935	40p	—

S. W. VENABLE TOBACCO CO. (U.S.A.)

Qty		*Date*	*Odds*	*Sets*
X?56	Actresses	1888	£15.00	—
X8	Baseball Scenes	1888	B	—
X?2	Sea Shore Scenes	1888	B	—

GEO. F. YOUNG (U.S.A.)

Qty		*Date*	*Odds*	*Sets*
X?76	Actresses	1889	£12.50	—
X8	Baseball Scenes	1888	B	—
X10	National Sports—Girls	1887	B	—
X?	Photographic Cards	1886	£2.00	—
X2	Seashore Scenes	1888	B	—

INDEX OF BRANDS (Non-Tobacco)

Part 3

NON-TOBACCO ISSUES

A-1 DAIRIES LTD. (Tea)

Qty		Date	Odds	Sets
25	Birds and Their Eggs	1965	—	—
25	Butterflies & Moths	1964	—	50p
25	The Story of Milk	1967	—	£1.00

A-1 DOLLISDALE TEA

25	Do You Know About Shipping & Trees?	1963	—	50p

A. B. C. (Cinemas)

10	Animals	1952	75p	£7.50
10	An Adventure in Space	1950	£1.00	—
10	Birds	1958	—	£3.00
10	Birds & Birdwatching	1953	75p	—
10	British Athletes	1955	—	£2.50
20	British Soldiers (Black Back)	1949	12p	—
20	British Soldiers (Brown Back)	1949	10p	£2.00
10	Colorstars 1st	1962	—	75p
10	Colorstars 2nd	1962	—	—
10	Colorstars 3rd	1962	—	—
10	Dogs	1957	—	£3.00
L15	Film Stars	1935	£1.50	—
10	Film Stars	1948	30p	£3.00
10	Horses	1958	—	£3.00
10	Interesting Buildings	1956	—	£2.50
10	Journey by Land	1954	75p	—
10	Journey by Water	1954	75p	—
10	Journey to the Moon	1955	—	£3.00
10	Parliament Buildings	1957	—	£4.00
10	Railway Engines	1951	£1.50	£15.00
10	Scenes from Films	1953	75p	—
10	Sea Exploration	1957	—	£2.50
10	Sea Scenes	1958	—	£2.50
10	Sports on Land	1956	—	£3.00
12	Star Series	1936	£2.00	—
10	Travel of the Future	1956	—	£2.50
10	Water Sports	1956	—	£2.50

A. H. C. (Confectionery)

25	Tropical Birds (Anon.)	1955	—	50p
25	Wonders of the Universe	1955	—	£1.00

A. & B. C. GUM

M120	All Sports Series	1954	£1.00	—
X55	Batman (Numbered Pink Back)	1966	50p	£27.50
X55	Batman (Numbered on Front)	1966	50p	£27.50
X44	Batman (1A-44A)	1966	50p	£22.00
X44	Batman (1B-44B)	1966	75p	—
X38	Batman (Black Back)	1966	40p	£15.00
X73	Battle Cards	1966	35p	£25.00
X66	Battle of Britain	1970	25p	£16.50
X60	Bazooka Joe and his Gang	1968	£1.50	—
X60	Beatles (Black & White)	1964	60p	£36.00
X45	Beatles, 2nd Series	1965	£1.25	—
X40	Beatles (Coloured)	1965	£1.50	—
X45	Champions	1969	20p	—
X15	Civil War Banknotes	1965	60p	£9.00

A. & B. C. GUM—cont.

Qty		*Date*	*Odds*	*Sets*
X88	Civil War News	1965	40p	£35.00
X42	Comic Book Foldees	1968	75p	—
X48	Cricketers	1959	£1.00	£48.00
X48	Cricketers 1961 Test Series	1961	£1.00	£48.00
X66	Elvis Presley Series	1956	£2.00	—
X36	Exploits of William Tell	1960	40p	£15.00
22	Famous Indian Chiefs	1968	75p	—
X54	Fantastic Twisters	1972	60p	—
M48	Film & TV Stars	1953	£1.00	—
M48	Film & TV Stars No. 2 Series (49-96)	1953	£1.00	—
M48	Film & TV Stars No. 3 Series (97-144)	1953	£1.00	—
X48	Film Stars (Plain Back)	1954	60p	£30.00
X80	Flags of the World	1959	12p	£10.00
X46	Footballers (Planet, 1-46)	1958	6p	£2.50
X46	Footballers (Planet, 47-92)	1958	£1.00	—
X49	Footballers (Football Quiz, 1-49)	1959	75p	£37.50
X49	Footballers (Football Quiz, 50-98)	1959	£1.00	£50.00
X42	Footballers (Black Back, 1-42)	1960	40p	£17.00
X42	Footballers (Black Back, 43-84)	1960	50p	£21.00
XF64	Footballers (Plain Back)	1961	75p	£48.00
XF44	Footballers (Plain Back, Scottish)	1961	£1.50	—
X82	Footballers (Bazooka)	1962	75p	—
X55	Footballers (Make-A-Photo, 1-55)	1963	75p	—
X55	Footballers (Make-A-Photo, 56-110)	1963	75p	—
X81	Footballers (Make-A-Photo, Scottish)	1963	—	—
X58	Footballers (Quiz, 1-58)	1964	75p	£45.00
X45	Footballers (Quiz, 59-103)	1964	£1.00	—
X46	Footballers (Quiz, 104-149)	1964	£1.00	—
X81	Footballers (Quiz, Scottish)	1964	£2.00	—
X110	Footballers (In Pairs, 1-110)	1966	60p	—
X110	Footballers (In Pairs, 111-220)	1966	60p	—
X33	Footballers (In Pairs, Scottish)	1966	£1.25	—
X55	Footballers (Star Players)	1967	10p	£5.50
X54	Footballers (Yellow, 1-54)	1968	50p	—
X47	Footballers (Yellow, 55-101)	1968	50p	£24.00
X65	Footballers (Football Facts, 1-64)	1969	40p	£26.00
X54	Footballers (Football Facts, 65-117)	1969	10p	£5.00
X55	Footballers (Football Facts, 117-170)	1969	10p	£5.00
MF36	Footballers	1969	50p	—
X42	Footballers (Football Facts, Scottish, 1-41) ...	1969	£1.00	—
X35	Footballers (Football Facts, Scottish, 42-75) ...	1969	£1.00	—
X84	Footballers (Orange Back, 1-84)	1970	6p	£5.00
X85	Footballers (Orange Back, 85-169)	1970	6p	£2.50
X86	Footballers (Orange Back, 170-255)	1970	25p	£20.00
X85	Footballers (Green Back, Scottish, 1-85) ...	1970	40p	—
X86	Footballers (Green Back, Scottish, 86-171) ...	1970	40p	—
X109	Footballers (Did You Know, 1-109)	1971	15p	£15.00
X110	Footballers (Did You Know, 110-219)	1971	15p	£16.50
X71	Footballers (Did You Know, 220-290)	1971	20p	£15.00
X73	Footballers (Did You Know, Scottish, 1-73) ...	1971	6p	£3.00
X71	Footballers (Did You Know, Scottish, 74-144)	1971	50p	—
23	Football Club Crests	1971	75p	—
X109	Footballers (Orange/Red, 1-109)	1972	6p	£6.00
X110	Footballers (Orange/Red, 110-219)	1972	6p	£6.00

A. & B. C. GUM—cont.

Qty		Date	Odds	Sets
B22	Football Card Game	1972	15p	£3.25
X89	Footballers (Rub Coin, Scottish, 1-89)	1972	50p	—
X89	Footballers (Orange/Red, Scottish, 90-179)	1972	50p	—
M32	Footballers (Autographed Photos)	1973	50p	£16.00
X131	Footballers (Blue Back, 1-131)	1973	6p	£8.00
X130	Footballers (Blue Back, 132-263)	1973	15p	—
X90	Footballers (Red Back, Scottish, 1-90)	1973	50p	—
X88	Footballers (Red Back, Scottish, 91-178)	1973	50p	—
X132	Footballers (Red Back, Rub Coin)	1974	6p	£10.00
X132	Footballers (Green Back, Scottish, Rub Coin)	1974	25p	—
X40	Fotostars	1961	40p	£16.00
X66	Funny Greetings	1961	40p	—
X66	Funny Valentines	1961	50p	—
X36	Golden Boys (Matt)	1958	30p	£11.00
XF40	Golden Boys (Glossy)	1958	40p	£16.00
L27	Grand Prix	1970	—	—
X55	Huck Finn	1968	15p	—
X60	Kung Fu	1974	20p	£12.00
X55	Land of the Giants	1969	50p	—
X36	Magic	1967	20p	—
X74	Man on the Moon	1969	25p	—
X55	Monkees (Black & White)	1967	12p	£6.50
X55	Monkees (Coloured)	1967	12p	£6.50
X30	Monkees Hit Songs	1967	16p	£5.00
X36	Olympics	1972	£1.00	—
X55	Partridge Family	1972	20p	—
X120	Planes	1960	30p	£36.00
X44	Planet of the Apes	1968	15p	—
X48	Railway Quiz	1958	30p	£15.00
X72	Railway Quiz	1959	30p	£20.00
M24	Royal Portraits	1953	£1.00	£24.00
X25	Sir Francis Drake	1961	80p	£20.00
X88	Space Cards	1958	40p	£35.00
X55	Star Trek	1969	£1.25	—
X66	Superman in the Jungle	1968	50p	£33.00
X16	Superman in the Jungle (Jig-saw)	1968	75p	£12.00
X25	The Girl from UNCLE	1965	30p	£7.50
X36	The High Chaparral	1969	20p	—
X54	The Legend of Custer	1968	50p	—
X55	The Man from UNCLE	1965	40p	—
X40	The Rolling Stones	1965	£2.00	—
X50	Top Stars	1964	75p	—
X40	Top Stars (different)	1964	75p	—
X56	TV Westerns	1959	50p	£28.00
P88	Wacky Plaks	1962	60p	—
X70	Who–Z–At Star?	1958	60p	£42.00
X55	Winston Churchill Cards	1965	10p	£5.00
X37	World Cup Footballers	1970	60p	£22.00
X66	You'll Die Laughing (Creature Feature)	1974	8p	£5.00
X48	You'll Die Laughing (Purple back)	1967	12p	—

P. A. ADOLPH ("Subbuteo")

24	Famous Footballers 1st	1954	—	£2.00
24	Famous Footballers 2nd	1954	—	£2.00

A. W. ALLEN LTD. (Confectionery, Australia)

Qty		Date	Odds	Sets
36	Cricketers (Brown front)	1932	£4.00	£150.00
36	Cricketers (Brown front, different)	1933	£5.00	—
36	Cricketers (Flesh tinted, frame back)	1934	£3.00	£100.00
36	Cricketers (Flesh tinted, no frame)	1936	£3.00	£100.00
36	Cricketers (coloured)	1938	£3.00	£100.00

ALMA CONFECTIONERY

25	James Bond 007 Moonraker	1980	25p	—

JAMES ALMOND (Confectionery)

25	Sports and Pastimes	1925	£3.00	£75.00

AMALGAMATED PRESS LTD.

24	Aeroplanes (Plain Back)	1930	75p	—
32	Aeroplanes & Carriers	1932	75p	£24.00
M32	Australian & English Cricket Stars	1932	£4.00	£125.00
M12	Catchy Tricks & Teasers	1933	£1.00	£12.00
M16	England's Test Match Cricketers	1928	£4.00	£64.00
M22	English League (Div. 1) Footer Captains	1926	£1.00	£22.00
M16	Exploits of the Great War	1929	60p	£10.00
16	Famous Aircraft	1927	£1.50	£24.00
M16	Famous Australian Cricketers	1929	£4.00	£64.00
16	Famous Film Stars	1927	£2.50	£40.00
M24	Famous Footer Internationals	1926	75p	£18.00
M32	Famous Test Match Cricketers	1926	£2.00	£65.00
24	Famous Trains & Engines	1932	75p	£18.00
16	Fighting Planes of the World	1934	75p	—
32	Football Fame Series	1936	75p	£24.00
M16	Great War Deeds	1927	75p	£12.00
M32	Great War Deeds (Different)	1928	75p	£24.00
M16	Heroic Deeds of the Great War	1927	60p	£10.00
32	Makes of Motor Cars & Index Marks	1923	60p	£20.00
32	Mechanical Wonders of 1935	1935	60p	—
32	Modern Motor Cars	1926	£2.50	—
24	Motors (Plain Back)	1932	£1.00	—
24	Ships of the World (Champion)	1924	60p	£15.00
33	Ships of the World (Different, Anonymous)	1935	75p	—
BF66	Sportsmen	1922	20p	£15.00
32	Sportsmen of the World	1934	50p	£16.00
M12	Sports Queeriosities	1933	£1.25	£15.00
M24	The Great War 1914-1918	1928	60p	£12.00
M16	The Great War 1914-1918 New Series	1929	60p	£10.00
M16	The R.A.F. at War (Plain Back)	1940	£1.50	—
M32	Thrilling Scenes from the Great War	1927	60p	£20.00
M16	Thrills of the Dirt Track	1929	£1.50	£24.00
M16	Tip Top Tricks and Teasers	1927	£1.25	£20.00
M14	V.C.'s & Their Deeds of Valour (Plain Back)	1928	£1.50	—
M24	Wonderful London	1926	£2.00	£48.00

AMARAN TEA

25	Coins of the World	1964	—	£1.50
25	Dogs' Heads	1965	—	60p
25	Do You Know?	1969	—	£1.25
25	Flags & Emblems	1964	—	£1.50

AMARAN TEA—cont.

Qty		Date	Odds	Sets
25	Naval Battles	1971	—	£2.50
25	Old England	1969	—	75p
25	Science in the 20th Century	1966	—	75p
25	The Circus	1966	—	£1.25
25	Veteran Racing Cars	1965	—	£2.00

AMPOL (Oil, Australia)

M32	Cars of To-day	1950	—	£5.00

THE ANGLERS MAIL (Periodical)

E3	Terminal Tackle Tips	1976	—	£1.00

ANGLO-AMERICAN CHEWING GUM LTD.

X66	The Horse	1966	—	£4.00
40	Underwater Adventure	1966	—	£1.50
50	Zoo Stamps of the World	1966	25p	£12.50

ANGLO CONFECTIONERY LTD.

X66	Captain Scarlet & The Mysterons	1968	£1.00	—
L12	Football Hints (Folders)	1970	25p	£3.00
X84	Football Quiz	1969	30p	£25.00
X66	Joe 90	1968	£1.00	—
X84	Railway Trains & Crests	1974	40p	£35.00
X66	Space	1967	15p	£10.00
X66	Tarzan	1967	12p	£8.00
X66	The Beatles—Yellow Submarine	1968	£1.50	—
X66	The Horse	1966	40p	—
X56	The New James Bond	1970	£1.00	—
X64	U.F.O.	1971	20p	—
M24	Vintage Cars Series	1970	£2.00	£48.00
X78	Walt Disney Characters	1971	75p	—
X66	Wild West	1970	30p	£20.00
X48	World Cup 1970	1970	50p	£25.00

ANONYMOUS

K24	Animal Jungle Game	1965	—	£2.00
50	Animals of the World	1954	—	75p
25	Bridges of the World	1958	—	50p
25	British Uniforms of the 19th Century	1957	—	50p
20	Budgerigars	1960	15p	£3.00
25	Cacti	1961	—	50p
25	Careless Moments	1922	—	£4.00
25	Castles of Britain	1962	—	£1.25
25	Children of All Nations	1958	—	50p
25	Dogs	1958	—	£1.00
25	Family Pets	1964	—	£1.50
25	Flags & Emblems	1961	—	£1.25
25	Flowers	1971	—	75p
25	Football Clubs & Badges	1962	—	50p
100	Miscellaneous Subjects (GUM)	1965	—	£5.00
25	Modern Aircraft	1958	—	50p
50	Motor Cars	1956	—	£2.00
25	Musical Instruments	1971	—	50p
25	Pigeons	1971	—	75p
25	Pond Life	1963	—	50p

ANONYMOUS—cont.

Qty		Date	Odds	Sets
1	Soldier—Bugler	1965	—	40p
1	Venice in London	1965	—	15p
BELGIAN ISSUES				
X100	Famous Men	1938	—	£6.00
U.S. ISSUES				
X30	Aeroplanes & Insignia	1945	—	£10.00
M48	America at War (101-148)	1942	—	£30.00
M48	America at War (501-548)	1943	—	£40.00
M48	America at War (601-648)	1943	—	£40.00
10	Boxers "A"	1926	—	£7.50
10	Boxers "B"	1926	—	£7.50
10	Boxers "C"	1926	—	£7.50
10	Boy Scouts	1926	—	£7.50
10	Film Stars "A"	1926	—	£6.00
10	Film Stars "B"	1926	—	£6.00
10	Film Stars "C"	1926	—	£6.00
M60	Pinocchio (Bread Issue)	1950	—	£6.00
10	Presidents "A"	1926	—	£6.00
10	Presidents "B"	1926	—	£6.00
10	Western Pioneers	1926	—	£7.50
SPANISH ISSUES				
X32	Footballers (P/C Backs)	1930	50p	£16.00

APLIN & BARRETT (Cheese)

X25	Whipsnade	1937	30p	£7.50

ARBUCKLE COFFEE CO. (U.S.A.)

P50	Animals	1890	£2.50	£125.00
P50	Cooking Subjects	1890	£2.50	—
P100	General Subjects (Unnumbered)	1890	£3.00	—
P50	General Subjects (51-100)	1890	£2.50	—
P50	History of Sports & Pastimes of the World	1890	£2.50	£125.00
P50	History of United States & Territories	1890	£2.00	£100.00
P50	Illustrated Atlas of U.S.	1890	£2.00	£100.00
P50	Illustrated Jokes	1890	£3.00	—
P50	Principal Nations of the World	1890	£2.00	£100.00
P50	Views from a Trip around the World	1890	£2.00	£100.00

ARDMONA (Tinned Fruit, Australia)

X50	International Cricket Series III	1980	—	£5.00

ARMITAGE BROS. LTD. (Pet Foods)

25	Animals of the Countryside	1964	—	50p
25	Country Life	1968	—	50p

ASKEY'S (Biscuits)

25	People & Places	1971	—	£2.00
25	Then & Now	1971	—	£2.00

AUSTIN MOTOR CO. LTD.

M13	Famous Austin Cars	1953	£1.00	—

AUTOBRITE (Car Polish)

25	Vintage Cars	1965	—	£2.00

AUSTRALIAN LICORICE PTY LTD. (Australia)

Qty		*Date*	*Odds*	*Sets*
?27	Australian Cricketers	1930	£4.00	—
24	Australian Cricketers	1931	£4.00	£100.00
24	English Cricketers (Blue Back)	1928	£4.00	£100.00
24	English Cricketers (Brown Back)	1930	£4.00	—
18	English Cricketers ("18 in set")	1932	£4.00	—
12	South African Cricketers	1931	£4.00	£50.00

AUTOMATIC MACHINE CO.

25	Modern Aircraft	1958	—	75p

AUTOMATIC MERCHANDISING CO.

X25	Adventure Twins & The Treasure Ship	1964	—	£10.00

AVON RUBBER CO. LTD.

30	Leading Riders of 1963	1963	30p	£9.00

B.B.B. PIPES

25	Pipe History	1926	£3.00	—

B.T. LTD. (Tea)

25	Aircraft	1961	—	£2.50
25	British Locomotives	1961	—	£3.00
25	Do You Know	1967	—	£3.00
25	Holiday Resorts	1963	—	75p
25	Modern Motor Cars	1962	—	£4.00
25	Occupations	1962	—	£3.00
25	Pirates & Buccaneers	1961	—	£3.00
25	The West	1964	—	£2.00

BADSHAH TEA CO.

25	British Cavalry Uniforms of the 19th Century	1963	—	£3.00
25	Butterflies & Moths	1971	—	50p
25	Fish & Bait	1971	—	60p
25	Fruits of Trees & Shrubs	1965	—	60p
25	Garden Flowers	1963	—	£2.50
25	Naval Battles	1971	—	£3.00
25	People & Places	1970	—	60p
25	Regimental Uniforms of the Past	1971	—	50p
25	Romance of the Heavens	1968	—	—
25	Wonders of the World (Series of 50)	1970	—	60p

BAKE-A-CAKE LTD.

56	Motor Cars	1952	£1.00	—

BARBERS TEA LTD.

1	Advertising Card	1956	—	25p
25	Aeroplanes	1956	—	£2.50
24	Cinema & Television Stars	1955	—	—
24	Dogs	1961	—	50p
25	Locomotives	1956	—	£4.00
24	Railway Equipment	1958	—	£2.50

JOHN O. BARKER (IRELAND) LTD. (Gum)

X24	Circus Scenes	1970	—	£5.00
X24	Famous People	1970	—	£5.00
25	The Wild West	1970	75p	—

BARRATT & CO. LTD. (Confectionery)

Qty		*Date*	*Odds*	*Sets*
M30	Aircraft (Varnished)	1941	£1.25	—
M30	Aircraft (Unvarnished)	1943	£1.50	—
25	Animals in the Service of Man	1964	—	60p
16	Australian Cricketers, Action Series	1926	£3.00	£50.00
15	Australian Test Players	1930	£6.00	—
25	Birds	1960	—	£2.50
50	Botany Quest	1966	75p	£37.50
25	British Butterflies	1965	£1.00	—
25	Butterflies & Moths	1969	—	75p
25	Cage & Aviary Birds	1960	—	£2.50
50	Captain Scarlet & The Mysterons	1967	—	—
50	Cars of the World	1965	75p	£37.50
B122	Characters from Film Cartoons	1940	£1.25	—
25	Coronation, 1911	1911	£6.00	—
20	Cricket Team Folders	1933	£5.00	—
?260	Cricketers, Footballers & Football Teams	1925	£2.50	—
L60	Disneyland "True Life"	1956	50p	£30.00
L50	F.A. Cup Winners	1935	£2.00	—
25	Fairy Stories	1926	£1.00	£25.00
B?240	Famous Cricketers (Various Series)	1936	£3.00	—
35	Famous Film Stars	1961	60p	£21.00
B248	Famous Footballers (Various Series)	1936	£1.25	—
B79	Famous Footballers (Non-Descriptive)	1947	£1.25	—
B50	Famous Footballers, New Series	1950	£1.00	—
B50	Famous Footballers, New Series (Different)	1952	£1.00	—
B50	Famous Footballers Series A1	1953	£1.00	—
B50	Famous Footballers Series A2	1954	£1.00	—
B50	Famous Footballers Series A3	1955	£1.00	—
60	Famous Footballers Series A4	1956	75p	—
60	Famous Footballers Series A5	1957	75p	—
60	Famous Footballers Series A6	1958	75p	—
60	Famous Footballers Series A7	1959	75p	—
50	Famous Footballers Series A8	1960	75p	—
50	Famous Footballers Series A9	1961	75p	£37.50
50	Famous Footballers Series A10	1962	40p	£20.00
50	Famous Footballers Series A11	1963	75p	£37.50
50	Famous Footballers Series A12	1964	75p	£37.50
50	Famous Footballers Series A13	1965	75p	£37.50
50	Famous Footballers Series A14	1966	60p	—
50	Famous Footballers Series A15	1967	—	£2.00
32/50	Famous Sportsmen	1971	—	£1.50
B45	Fastest on Earth	1953	60p	£27.00
32	Felix Pictures	1930	£6.00	—
25	Fish & Bait	1962	—	£2.50
100	Football Stars	1930	£3.50	—
?69	Football Team Folders	1933	£2.00	—
B66	Football Teams—1st Division	1928	£2.50	—
48	Giants in Sport	1959	£1.00	£48.00
25	Headdresses of the World	1962	—	£2.50
25	Historical Buildings	1960	—	£1.50
48	History of the Air	1959	50p	—
32	History of the Air	1959	—	—
25	History of the Air	1960	—	£4.00
25	Interpol	1964	£1.00	—

BARRATT & CO. LTD. (Confectionery)—cont.

Qty		*Date*	*Odds*	*Sets*
50	Leaders of Sport	1927	£2.50	—
35	Magic Roundabout	1968	—	£2.00
25	Merchant Ships of the World (Black Back) ...	1962	—	£5.00
25	Merchant Ships of the World (Blue Back) ...	1962	—	£1.50
L40	Modern Aircraft	1957	75p	£30.00
45	Modern British Aircraft	1959	£1.00	—
13	National Flags	1914	£7.50	—
64	Natural History (Plain Back)	1940	75p	—
B24	Naval Ships (Plain Back)	1939	£2.50	—
B6	Our King & Queen (Plain Back)	1940	£3.00	—
25	People & Places	1965	—	50p
25	Pirates & Buccaneers	1960	—	£1.50
12	Prominent London Buildings	1912	£6.00	—
30	Robin Hood	1961	75p	£22.50
36	Sailing into Space	1959	£1.00	—
50	Soccer Stars	1973	40p	—
50	Soldiers of the World	1966	—	£3.50
16	South African Cricketers	1929	£5.00	—
25	Space Mysteries	1965	—	£1.25
L20	Speed Series	1930	£3.00	—
50	Tarzan	1967	—	£4.00
35	Test Cricketers Series A	1956	£1.60	£56.00
48	Test Cricketers Series B	1957	£2.50	—
50	The Secret Service	1970	—	£6.00
24	The Wild West	1961	—	£2.00
25	The Wild West (Different)	1963	—	£1.50
50	The Wild Wild West	1969	—	£10.00
25	The Young Adventurer	1965	£1.25	—
50	Thunderbirds	1967	£1.00	—
50	Thunderbirds 2nd Series	1968	50p	—
50	Tom & Jerry	1970	—	£3.00
50	Trains	1970	—	£2.50
50	Trains of the World	1964	—	£5.00
35	TV's Huckleberry Hound & Friends	1961	75p	—
35	TV's Sea Hunt	1961	75p	—
35	TV's Yogi Bear	1969	£1.00	—
35	TV's Yogi Bear & Friends	1971	—	60p
70	U.F.O.	1971	—	£10.00
B35	Walt Disney Characters	1956	60p	£21.00
50	Walt Disney Characters, 2nd Series	1957	75p	£37.50
36	Walt Disney's Robin Hood	1957	75p	—
35	Walt Disney's True Life	1962	75p	—
25	Warriors Through the Ages	1962	—	£2.00
25	What Do You Know?	1964	—	60p
X72	Wild Animals	1972	30p	£22.00
M50	Wild Animals by George Cansdale	1954	80p	£40.00
36	Wild West Series No. 1	1959	80p	£30.00
25	Willum	1961	£1.25	—
50	Wisecracks	1970	—	£1.00
50	Wisecracks 2nd Series	1970	—	—
50	Wisecracks 3rd Series	1971	—	—
50	Wonders of the World	1962	—	£1.25
25	World Locomotives	1961	—	£3.50
50	Wunders Der Welt	1968	—	£2.00
50	Zoo Pets	1964	80p	£40.00

GEO. BASSETT & CO. LTD. (Confectionery)

Qty		Date	Odds	Sets
25	Motor Cars—Vintage & Modern	1968	—	£2.00
25	Nursery Rhymes	1966	—	75p
25	Popular Dogs	1967	—	£1.00
70	U.F.O.	1974	—	£1.50
25	Victoria Cross Heroes in Action	1970	—	£1.50

BARRATT DIVISION

50	Age of the Dinosaurs	1979	20p	—
40	Ali-Cat Magicards	1978	20p	—
50	Asterix in Europe	1977	10p	—
50	Athletes of the World	1980	6p	£3.00
50	Cricket	1978	60p	—
50	Cricket, 2nd Series	1979	75p	—
50	Disney—Health & Safety	1977	—	£1.00
50	Football Action	1977	20p	—
50	Football Action	1978	20p	—
50	Football 1978-79	1979	20p	—
50	Football 1979-80	1980	20p	—
50	Football 1980-81	1981	—	£4.00
50	Football 1981-82	1982	20p	—
50	Football Stars	1974	—	£2.50
50	Football Stars—1975-6	1975	20p	—
50	House of Horror	1982	10p	—
50	Living Creatures of Our World	1979	20p	—
50	Play Cricket	1980	10p	£5.00
25	Pop Stars	1974	—	75p
35	Secret Island 1st Series	1976	20p	—
40	Secret Island 2nd Series	1976	—	£1.00
50	Space 1999	1976	10p	—
50	Survival on Star Colony 9	1979	10p	—
40	Swim and Survive	1983	—	—
50	The Conquest of Space	1980	20p	—
50	Tom & Jerry	1974	30p	—
50	World Cup Stars	1974	—	£1.00
50	World of the Vorgans	1978	20p	—
49/50	Yogi's Gang	1976	—	£2.50

BATTLE PICTURE WEEKLY

80	Weapons of World War II	1975	—	£10.00

BEANO LTD. (Gum)

25	Fascinating Hobbies	1950	—	—
50	Modern Aircraft (Beano)	1951	—	—
50	Modern Aircraft (British Educational)	1951	—	£1.50
50	Ships of the Royal Navy	1955	—	£1.50
50	The Conquest of Space	1956	—	£1.50
50	This Age of Speed No. 1 (Aeroplanes)	1954	—	£5.00
50	This Age of Speed No. 2 (Buses & Trams)	1954	—	£10.00
50	Wonders of Modern Transport (Aircraft)	1955	—	—
25	Wonders of the Universe (Foto Gum)	1960	—	50p

S. N. BEATTIE & CO. (Commercial)

24	Safety Signs	1955	60p	—

J. J. BEAULAH (Canned Goods)

Qty		Date	Odds	Sets
1	Boston Stump	1953	—	25p
25	Coronation Series	1953	—	£15.00
24	Marvels of the World	1954	—	50p
24	Modern British Aircraft	1953	—	£1.00

THE BEEHIVE STORES

Qty		Date	Odds	Sets
25	British Uniforms of the 19th Century	1959		£6.00

BELLS SCOTCH WHISKY

Qty		Date	Odds	Sets
?36	Other Famous Bells (Shaped)	1975	25p	—

J. BELLAMY & SONS LTD. (Confectionery)

Qty		Date	Odds	Sets
25	Vintage & Modern Trains of the World	1975	—	£3.00

VAN DEN BERGHS LTD. (Margarine etc.)

Qty		Date	Odds	Sets
L24	Pirates	1965	80p	£20.00
M12	Recipes From Round the World	1958	75p	—
M12	Regional Recipes	1958	75p	—
L24	This Modern World	1965	80p	£20.00

DE BEUKELAER (Biscuits)

Qty		Date	Odds	Sets
KF100	All Sports	1932	12p	£7.50
KF1000	Film Stars (1-1000)	1932	20p	—
F100	Film Stars (1001-1100)	1937	20p	—
KF100	Film Stars (B1-100)	1935	25p	—
132	Film Stars (Gold Background)	1939	15p	£20.00

J. BIBBY & SONS LTD. (Cooking Fat)

Qty		Date	Odds	Sets
L25	Don't You Believe It	1955	60p	£15.00
L25	Good Dogs	1955	£1.00	£25.00
L25	How What and Why	1955	60p	£15.00
L25	Isn't it Strange	1955	60p	£15.00
L25	They Gave it a Name	1955	60p	£15.00
L25	This Wonderful World	1955	60p	£15.00

ALFRED BIRD & SONS (Custard)

Qty		Date	Odds	Sets
K48	Happy Families	1938	40p	—

BIRKUM (Cheese, Denmark)

Qty		Date	Odds	Sets
25	Motor Cars	1956	—	£6.00

BISHOPS STORTFORD DAIRY FARMERS (Tea)

Qty		Date	Odds	Sets
25	Dogs' Heads	1967	—	£1.00
25	Freshwater Fish	1964	—	—
25	Historical Buildings	1964	—	£3.00
25	History of Aviation	1964	—	—
25	Passenger Liners	1965	—	£1.50
25	Pond Life	1966	—	50p
25	Science in the 20th Century	1966	—	50p
25	The Story of Milk	1966	—	£1.00

BLAKEY BOOT PROTECTORS

Qty		Date	Odds	Sets
72	War Series	1916	£2.50	—

BLUE BAND SERIES (Stamps)

Qty		Date	Odds	Sets
24	History of London's Transport	1954	—	£4.00
24	History of London's Transport 2nd Series	1955	£1.00	—
16	See Britain by Coach	1954	—	£1.00

BLUE BIRD STOCKINGS

Qty		Date	Odds	Sets
P12	Exciting Film Stars	1963	—	£2.50
24	Star Cards	1963	£1.00	—

BLUE CAP LTD. (Cheese)

PACKAGE SERIES

12	Farm Series A	1953	30p	£4.00
12	Farm Series B	1953	30p	£4.00
12	Farm Series C	1953	30p	£4.00
12	Sports Series D	1953	50p	—
8	Sports Series E	1953	75p	—

E. H. BOOTH & CO. LTD. (Tea)

25	Badges & Uniforms of Famous British Regiments & Corps	1967	—	50p
25	Ships & Their Workings	1971	—	£1.50

BOW BELLS (Periodical)

BF6	Handsome Men on the British Screen	1922	£1.50	—

BOYS CINEMA (Periodical)

BF6	Famous Film Heroes	1922	£1.25	—
M24	Famous Heroes	1922	£1.00	£24.00
MF8	Film Stars (Brown Front)	1930	£1.50	£12.00
MF8	Film Stars (Black Front)	1931	£1.50	£12.00

BOYS FRIEND (Periodical)

3	Famous Boxers Series	1911	£3.00	—
3	Famous Flags Series	1911	£2.50	—
3	Famous Footballers Series	1911	£3.00	—
3	Famous Regiments Series	1911	£3.00	—
BF4	Footballers (½ Length)	1923	£1.00	£4.00
BF5	Footballers (2 Per Card)	1922	£1.00	£5.00
BF15	Rising Boxing Stars	1922	80p	£12.00

BOYS MAGAZINE (Periodical)

M8	Boxers	1922	£2.00	—
B8	Coloured Studies of Famous Internationals	1922	£1.50	£12.00
M10	Cricketers	1922	£3.50	—
F10	Famous Cricketers Series	1929	£3.00	£30.00
F12	Famous Footballers Series	1929	£1.25	£15.00
BF10	Football Series	1922	80p	£8.00
M30	Footballers (Picture 49 x 39 mm)	1922	£1.00	—
B64	Footballers & Sportsmen (Picture 56 x 35)	1922	£1.25	—
12	Zat Cards (Cricketers)	1930	£4.00	—
M11	Zat Cards (Cricketers)	1930	£4.00	—

BOYS REALM (Periodical)

BF15	Famous Cricketers	1922	£1.50	£22.50
BF9	Famous Footballers	1922	£1.00	£9.00

C. & T. BRIDGEWATER LTD. (Biscuits)

KF48	Coronation Series	1937	12p	£2.50
KF96	Film Stars 1st (CE over No.)	1932	15p	£15.00
KF96	Film Stars 2nd (E below No.)	1933	15p	—
KF96	Film Stars 3rd (Black & White)	1934	20p	£20.00
KF48	Film Stars 4th	1935	12p	—

C. & T. BRIDGEWATER LTD. (Biscuits)—cont.

Qty		Date	Odds	Sets
KF48	Film Stars 5th	1937	20p	—
KF48	Film Stars 6th (F before No.)	1938	25p	—
F48	Film Stars 7th	1939	20p	£10.00
KF48	Film Stars 8th	1940	12p	£2.50
KF48	Radio Stars 1st (Black & White)	1935	20p	£10.00
KF48	Radio Stars 2nd (Coloured)	1936	12p	£4.00

BRITISH AUTOMATIC CO. (Weight)

Qty		Date	Odds	Sets
24	British Aircraft	1950	30p	£7.50
24	British Birds	1950	40p	—
24	British Locomotives	1948	6p	£1.50
36	British Motor Cars	1954	75p	—
44	Coronation Information	1953	60p	—
32	Dogs 1st Series	1953	6p	£1.25
32	Dogs 2nd Series	1953	20p	£6.50
24	Famous Trains of the World 1st Series	1952	24p	£6.00
24	Famous Trains of the World 2nd Series	1952	20p	£5.00
32	Fortunes, 2nd Series	1953	15p	£5.00
24	Freshwater Fish	1950	40p	£10.00
24	History of Transport	1948	6p	75p
44	Jokes	1951	25p	£11.00
24	Olympic Games	1952	75p	—
24	Racing & Sports Cars	1957	60p	£15.00
24	Space Travel	1955	60p	£15.00
24	Speed	1949	6p	£1.00
24	Sportsmen	1955	60p	—
20	Twenty Questions	1952	75p	—
24	Warships of the World	1954	6p	£1.50

BROOKE BOND & CO. LTD. (Tea)

Qty		Date	Odds	Sets
50	Adventurers & Explorers	1973	6p	75p
50	African Wild Life	1962	6p	£1.00
50	Asian Wild Life	1962	6p	£1.00
50	Bird Portraits (no address)	1957	20p	£10.00
50	Bird Portraits (with address)	1957	20p	£10.00
20	British Birds	1954	40p	£8.00
50	British Butterflies	1963	6p	£1.25
50	British Costume	1967	6p	75p
50	British Wild Life (Brooke Bond Great Britain Ltd.)	1958	30p	£15.00
50	British Wild Life (Brooke Bond Tea Ltd.)	1958	6p	£3.00
50	British Wild Life (Brooke Bond & Co. Ltd.)	1958	30p	£15.00
50	Butterflies of the World	1964	6p	£1.00
50	Famous People	1969	6p	75p
50	Flags & Emblems of the World	1967	6p	75p
50	Freshwater Fish	1960	6p	£1.50
50	History of Aviation	1972	6p	75p
50	History of the Motor Car	1968	6p	75p
50	Inventors and Inventions	1975	6p	75p
40	Olympic Greats	1979	6p	75p
50	Out Into Space (Issued with . . .)	1956	50p	£25.00
50	Out Into Space (Issued in. . .)	1958	12p	£6.00
40	Play Better Soccer	1976	6p	75p
40	Police File	1977	6p	75p
X10	Poly Filla Modelling Cards	1974	20p	—
50	Prehistoric Animals	1972	6p	75p

BROOKE BOND & CO. LTD. (Tea)—cont.

Qty		Date	Odds	Sets
40	Queen Elizabeth I—Queen Elizabeth II	1982	6p	75p
40	Small Wonders	1981	6p	75p
50	The Race into Space	1971	6p	75p
50	The Saga of Ships	1970	6p	75p
50	The Sea—Our Other World	1974	6p	75p
50	Transport Through the Ages	1966	6p	75p
50	Trees In Britain	1966	6p	75p
50	Tropical Birds	1961	6p	£1.25
40	Vanishing Wildlife	1978	6p	75p
50	Wild Birds in Britain	1965	6p	75p
50	Wild Flowers 1st Series	1955	60p	£30.00
50	Wild Flowers 2nd Series (with issued by)	1959	6p	£1.25
50	Wild Flowers 2nd Series (no issued by)	1959	40p	£20.00
50	Wild Flowers 3rd Series	1964	6p	£1.00
50	Wild Life in Danger	1963	6p	75p
50	Wonders of Wildlife	1976	6p	75p
40	Woodland Wildlife	1980	6p	75p
BLACK BACK REPRINTS				
50	African Wild Life	1973	—	75p
50	British Butterflies	1973	—	75p
50	British Costume	1973	—	75p
50	Famous People	1973	—	75p
50	Flags & Emblems of the World	1973	—	—
50	Freshwater Fish	1973	—	75p
50	History of the Motor Car	1974	—	75p
50	The Race Into Space	1974	—	75p
50	The Saga of Ships	1973	—	75p
50	Transport Through the Ages	1973	—	—
50	Trees in Britain	1973	—	75p
50	Tropical Birds	1974	—	75p
50	Wild Birds in Britain	1973	—	75p
50	Wild Flowers Series 2	1973	—	75p
50	Wild Life in Danger	1973	—	75p
CARD GAMES BASED ON REGULAR SERIES				
L36	British Costume Card Game	1974	—	75p
L36	Flags & Emblems Snap Game	1974	—	75p
L36	Motor History Snap Game	1974	—	75p
CANADIAN ISSUES				
48	African Animals	1964	—	£7.50
48	Animals & Their Young	1972	—	£1.50
48	Animals of North America	1960	—	£20.00
48	Birds of North America	1962	—	—
48	Butterflies of North America	1965	—	—
48	Canadian/American Songbirds	1966	—	£12.50
48	Dinosaurs	1963	—	—
48	Exploring the Oceans	1971	—	£1.50
48	Indians of Canada	1974	—	£1.50
48	North American Wildlife in Danger	1970	—	£1.50
48	Songbirds of North America	1959	—	£35.00
48	The Arctic	1973	—	£1.50
48	The Space Age	1969	—	£1.50
48	Transportation Through the Ages	1967	—	—
48	Trees of North America	1968	—	—

BROOKE BOND & CO. LTD. (Tea)—cont.

Qty		*Date*	*Odds*	*Sets*
48	Tropical Birds	1964	—	£10.00
48	Wild Flowers of North America	1961	—	£15.00
RHODESIAN ISSUES				
50	African Birds	1965	60p	—
50	African Wild Life	1963	80p	£40.00
50	Asian Wild Life	1963	60p	£30.00
50	Butterflies of the World	1966	75p	£37.50
50	Tropical Birds	1962	60p	£30.00
50	Wildlife in Danger	1964	75p	—
SOUTH AFRICAN ISSUES				
50	Our Pets	1967	60p	£30.00
50	Out Into Space	1966	50p	£25.00
50	Wild Van Afrika (Bilingual)	1965	75p	£37.50
50	Wild Van Afrika (one language)	1965	—	—

BROOK MOTORS

G12	Motor Cycles (cut from calendars)	1975		£3.00
P12	Steam Engines	1973	—	£5.00
P12	Veteran Cars	1961	—	£7.50

DAVID BROWN (Tractors)

XF3	Is Your Slip Showing?	1954	—	£1.00

BROWN & POLSON (Custard)

X25	Recipe Cards	1925	£1.50	—

BROWNE BROS. LTD. (Tea)

25	Birds	1964	—	£3.00
25	British Cavalry Uniforms of the 19th Century ...	1964	—	£4.00
25	Garden Flowers	1965	—	—
25	History of the Railways 1st	1964	—	£2.50
25	History of the Railways 2nd	1964	—	£5.00
25	Passenger Liners	1966	—	—
25	People & Places	1965	—	50p
25	Tropical Birds	1966	—	50p
25	Wonders of the Deep	1965	—	50p
25	Wonders of the World	1970	—	£3.50

BUBBLES INC. (Gum)

X55	Mars Attacks	1965	£6.00	—
X50	Outer Limits	1966	75p	£37.50

BUCHANAN'S (Jam)

24	Birds and Their Eggs	1924	£3.00	—

BIRDALL & BURDALL (Gravy Salt)

30	Wild Animals	1924	£2.00	—

BURGER KING (Restaurants, U.S.A.)

X36	The Empire Strikes Back	1981	—	£4.00

BURTONS WAGON WHEELS (Biscuits)

25	Indian Chiefs	1972	—	50p
25	The West	1972	—	50p
25	Wild West Action	1972	—	50p

BUTTAPAT DAIRIES

?24	People of the World	1915	£7.50	—

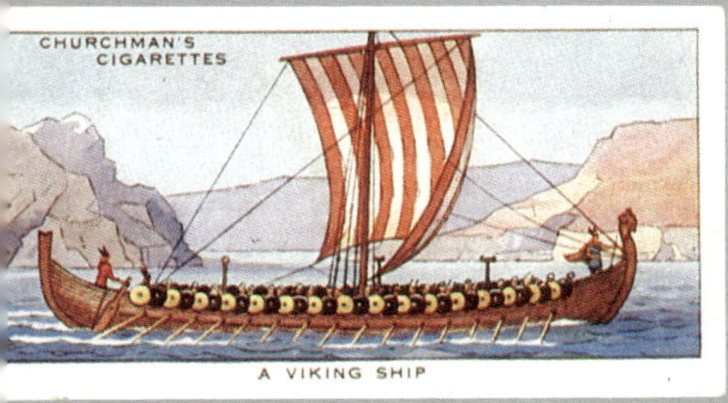

The Story of Navigation. Churchman

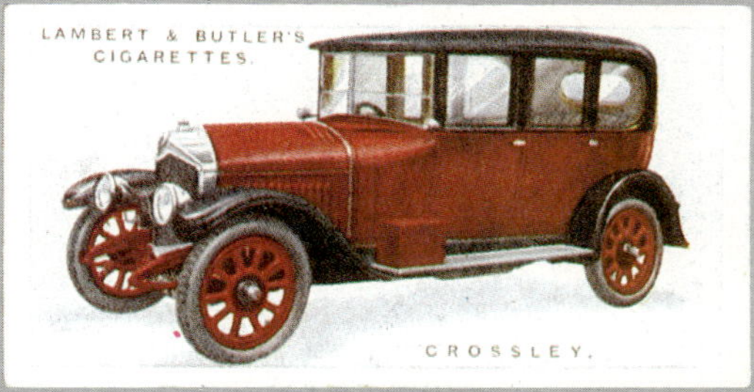

Motor Cars. Lambert & Butler

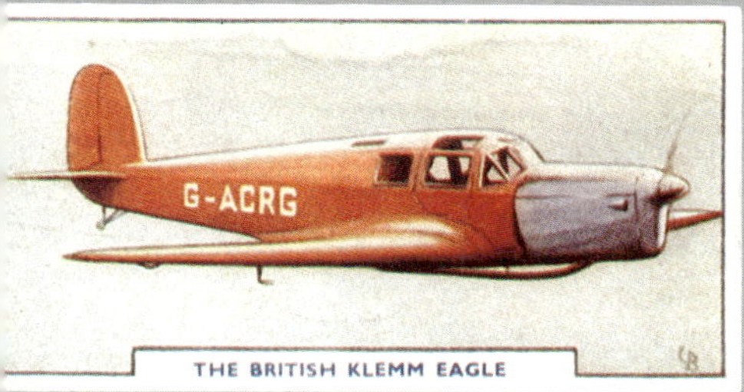

Aircraft (54). Phillips

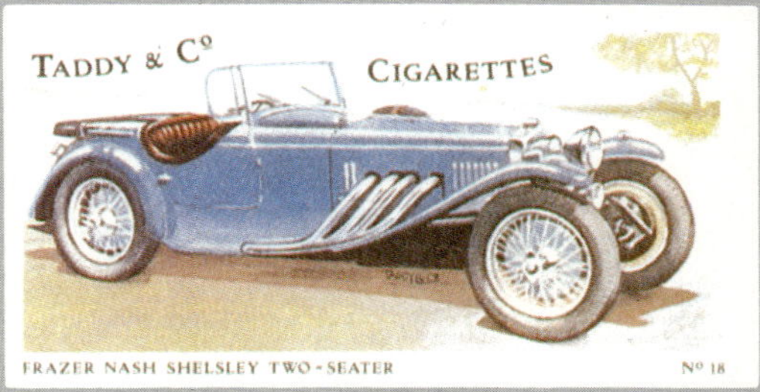

Motor Cars. Taddy

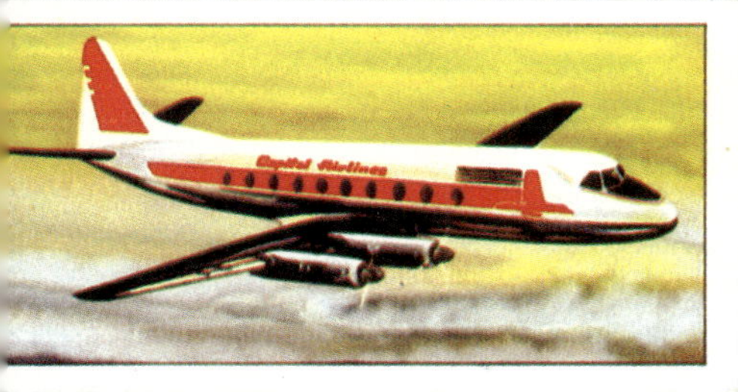

International Air Liners. Glengettie or Home Counties

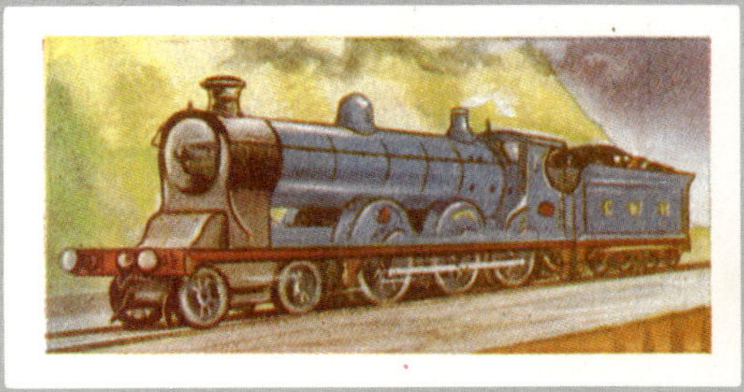

150 Years of Locomotives. Robert R. Miranda Ltd.

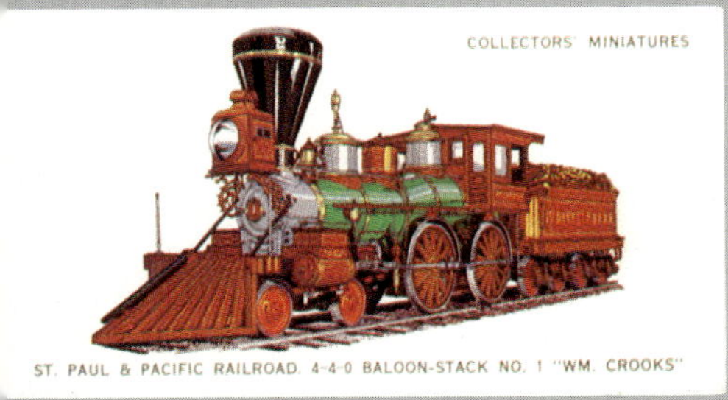

Railway Locomotives. Prescott-Pickup

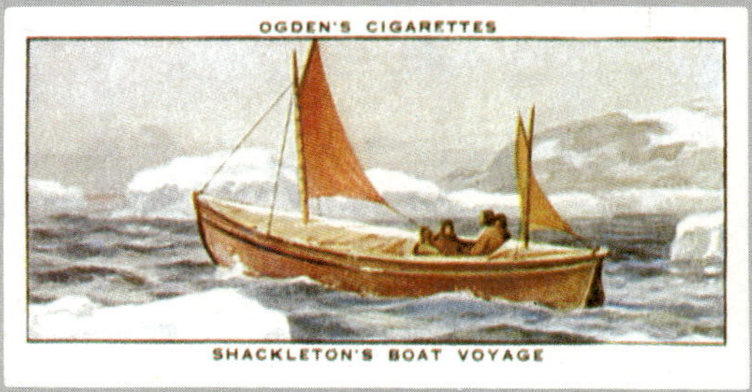

Sea Adventure. Ogden (also Hignett)

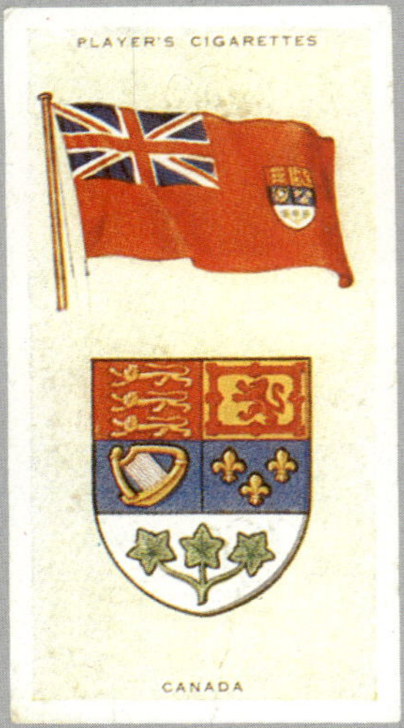

National Flags & Arms. Player

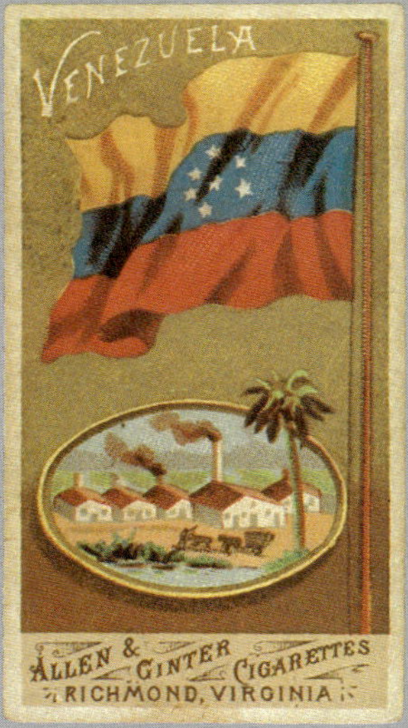

Flags of all Nations. Allen & Ginter

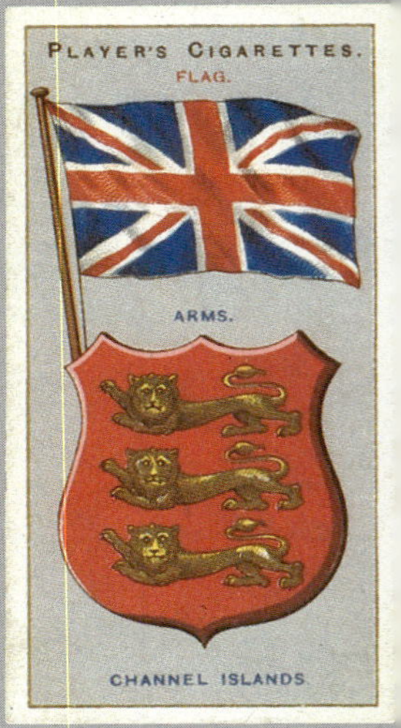

Countries Arms & Flags. Player

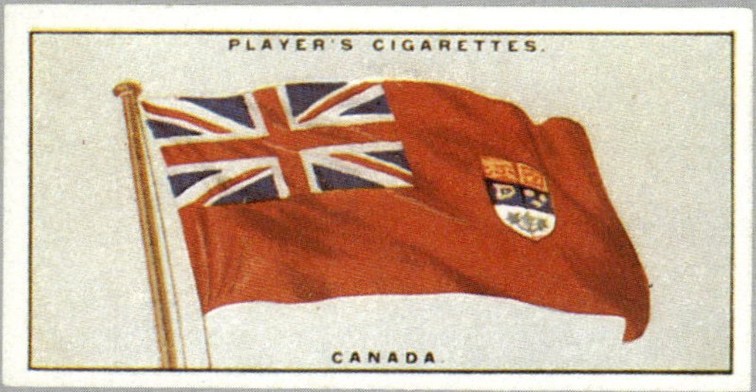

Flags of the League of Nations. Player

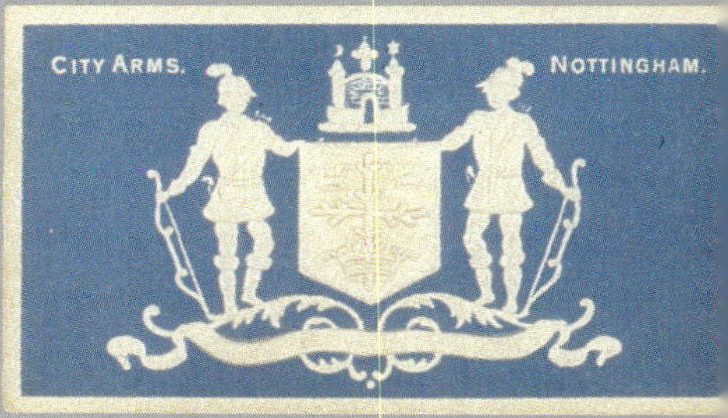

Borough Arms. Dexter

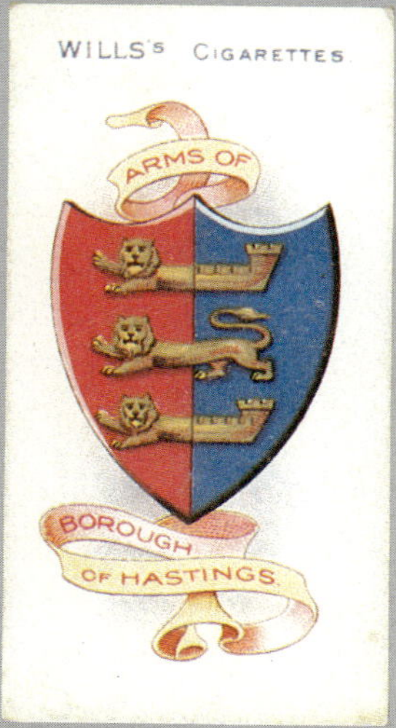

Borough Arms. Wills

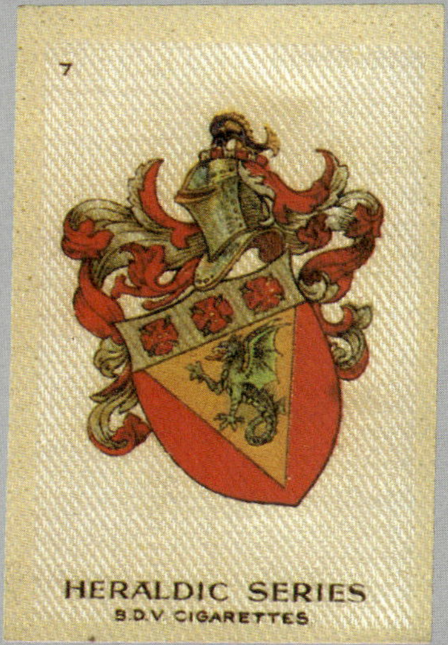

Heraldic Series (silk). Phillips

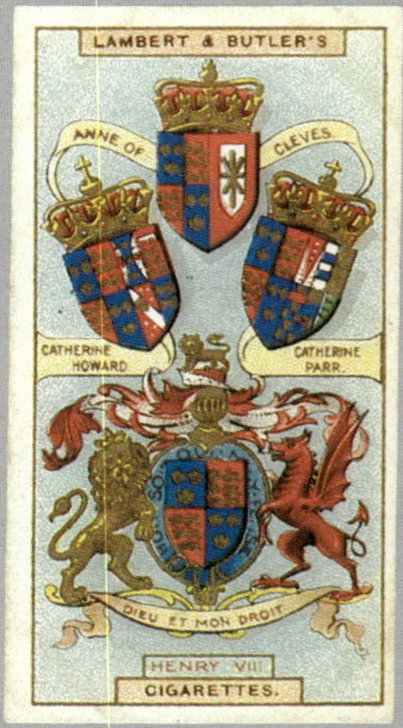

Arms of Kings & Queens of England. Lambert & Butler

C. & G. CONFECTIONERY LTD.

Qty		Date	Odds	Sets
25	Box of Tricks 1st Series	1965	60p	—
25	Box of Tricks 2nd Series	1965	60p	—

CADBURY BROS. LTD. (Chocolate)

C12	Antarctic Series	1913	£5.00	£60.00
X6	Bay City Rollers	1975	—	£1.00
L12	Birds in Springtime	1983	—	£2.50
6	Bournville Series B	1906	£7.50	—
P3	Bournville Views	1906	75p	£2.25
6	Bournville Village Series	1906	£5.00	—
P25	British Birds (Reward Cards)	1910	£3.50	—
12	British Birds & Eggs	1910	£3.50	—
P12	British Birds & Their Eggs (Reward Cards)	1910	£4.00	—
P32	British Butterflies & Moths (Reward Cards)	1910	£3.00	£100.00
6	British Colonies, Maps & Industries	1908	£5.00	£30.00
120	British Marvels	1936	25p	—
120	British Marvels Series 2	1936	25p	—
12	British Trees Series	1911	£1.50	£18.00
80	Cadbury's Picture Making	1936	75p	—
12	Cathedral Series	1913	£1.50	£18.00
6	Colonial Premiers Series	1908	£6.00	£36.00
12	Constellations Series	1912	£1.50	£18.00
24	Copyright (Inventors) Series	1914	£4.00	—
1	Coronation	1911	—	£7.50
48	Dangerous Animals	1970	—	£3.50
6	Dog Series	1908	£7.50	—
C12	English Industries	1908	£10.00	—
25	Fairy Tales	1924	80p	£20.00
27	Famous Steamships	1923	75p	£20.00
12	Fish	1910	£5.00	—
P6	Fish & Bait Series	1909	—	—
12	Flag Series	1912	60p	£7.50
C6	Flag Series (Joined Pairs)	1912	£1.25	£7.50
X12	Flight (Birds)	1982	40p	—
1	Largest Steamers in the World	1907	—	£7.50
6	Locomotive Series	1906	£8.00	£50.00
12	Match Puzzles	1906	£8.00	—
6	Old Ballad Series	1906	£7.50	—
X6	Panama Series	1910	£8.00	—
X5	Pop Stars	1975	20p	£1.00
X8	Prehistoric Monsters	1975	—	£1.25
P6	Rivers of the British Isles (Reward Cards)	1910	£7.50	—
24	Shadow Series	1914	£5.00	—
6	Shipping Series (4 Sizes)	1910	£4.00	—
X6	Sports Series	1906	—	—
24	Strange But True	1970	—	50p
12	The Age of the Dinosaur	1971	—	50p
25	Transport	1925	12p	£3.00

CADET SWEETS ("C.S.")

25	Arms & Armour	1961	—	50p
50	Buccaneers	1957	—	£2.00
50	Buccaneers (Different)	1959	—	£5.00
25	Daktari	1969	—	£2.00

CADET SWEETS ("C.S.")—cont.

Qty		Date	Odds	Sets
50	Doctor Who and the Daleks	1965	—	—
25	Dogs 1st Series	1958	—	£1.00
25	Dogs 2nd Series	1958	—	£1.00
25	Evolution of the Royal Navy	1959	—	50p
50	Fifty Years of Flying	1953	—	£12.50
50	Footballers	1956	—	£1.25
50	Footballers (Different)	1959	—	£1.25
50	Footballers & Club Colours	1963	—	£1.25
25	How?	1969	—	50p
50	Motor Cars	1954	—	£4.00
25	Prehistoric Animals	1961	—	£3.00
50	Railways of the World	1956	—	£1.50
50	Record Holders of the World	1956	—	£1.00
25	Record Holders of the World (Different) ...	1962	—	60p
25	Ships Through the Ages 1st Series	1963	—	75p
25	Ships Through the Ages 2nd Series	1963	—	75p
50	Stingray	1965	—	£2.50
48	The Adventures of Rin Tin Tin	1960	—	£2.00
50	The Conquest of Space	1957	—	£2.00
25	Treasure Hunt	1964	—	50p
50	UNCLE	1966	—	£1.00
25	What Do You Know?	1965	—	£7.50

A. J. CALEY & SON (Confectionery)

K24	Film Stars	1930	£2.00	—
48	Wisecracks (Mickey Mouse Weekly)	1932	£1.50	—

F. C. CALVERT & CO. LTD. (Toothpaste)

25	Dan Dare Series	1954	—	£7.50

CANDY GUM

M50	Autosprint	1975	—	£2.50
M30	Autosprint, 2nd Series	1975	—	£2.00
M30	Autosprint, 2nd Series (Plain Back)	1975	—	£2.50

CANDY NOVELTY CO.

B25/50	Dog Series—A1 Set	1953	—	50p

CANNINGS (Jam)

25	Types of British Soldiers	1914	£6.00	—

F. CAPERN (Bird Seed)

24	Picture Aviary	1964	—	—
1	Picture Aviary Introductory Card	1964	—	6p

CAPEZIO (Ballet Shoes, U.S.A)

XF12	Famous Dancers Gallery	1950	—	£10.00

CARR'S BISCUITS

E20	Cricketers	1967	75p	£15.00

CARSONS CHOCOLATE

72	Celebrities	1902	£7.50	—

CARTERS LITTLE LIVER PILLS

28	Dominoes	1911	50p	£14.00

F. C. CARTLEDGE (Razor Blades)

Qty		*Date*	*Odds*	*Sets*
X48	Epigrams "A"	1939	10p	£4.00
X64	Epigrams "B"	1939	10p	£5.00
X96	Epigrams "C"	1939	12p	—
50	Famous Prize Fighters	1938	20p	£10.00

CASH & CO. (Shoes)

20	War Series	1916	£3.50	—

CASSELLS (Periodical)

M6	British Engines	1923	£4.00	£24.00
B12	Butterflies & Moths Series	1923	£3.00	£36.00

CASTROL OIL

X18	Famous Riders	1958	75p	£15.00
X24	Racing Cars	1958	50p	£12.00

CAVE AUSTIN & CO. LTD. (Tea)

20	Inventors Series	1923	£5.00	—

CEDE LTD.

25	Coins of the World	1956	—	75p

CENTRAL ELECTRICITY AUTHORITY

B10	Interesting Careers	1961	—	60p

CEREBOS (Salt)

100	Sea Shells	1925	60p	£60.00

CEYLON TEA CENTRE

25	The Island of Ceylon	1955	—	50p

CHARTER TEA & COFFEE CO. LTD.

25	Prehistoric Animals 1st Series	1962	—	—
25	Prehistoric Animals 2nd Series	1962	—	—
25	Strange But True 1st Series	1961	—	£2.00
25	Strange But True 2nd Series	1961	—	£2.00
25	Transport Through the Ages 1st Series	1961	—	£4.00
25	Transport Through the Ages 2nd Series	1961	—	£4.00

CHIVERS & SONS LTD. (Preserves)

P6	Studies of English Fruits Series 1	1924	£3.00	£18.00
P6	Studies of English Fruits Series 2	1924	£3.00	£18.00
24	Wild Wisdom	1964	75p	—
48	Wild Wisdom in Africa	1964	75p	—
48	Wild Wisdom, River and Marsh	1964	75p	—
PACKAGE ISSUES				
L15	Children of Other Lands	1952	40p	£6.00
L15	Chivers British Birds	1951	40p	£6.00
L20	On Chivers Farms	1951	35p	£7.00

CHIX CONFECTIONERY CO. LTD.

X48	Famous Footballers No. 1 Series	1951	40p	—
X48	Famous Footballers No. 2 Series	1952	30p	£15.00
X48	Famous Footballers No. 3 Series	1953	40p	—
X50	Famous Last Words	1970	30p	—

CHIX CONFECTIONERY CO. LTD.—cont.

Qty		*Date*	*Odds*	*Sets*
X24	Footballers (Portrait & Action) 1-24	1952	—	£1.00
X24	Footballers (Portrait & Action) 25-48	1952	—	—
L50	Funny Old Folk	1970	—	£5.00
L50	Happy Howlers	1970	30p	—
L50	Krazy Kreatures from Outer Space	1970	—	£6.00
L50	Military Uniforms	1970	—	£7.50
L50	Moon Shot	1966	50p	—
X50	Ships of the Seven Seas	1968	50p	£25.00
X50	Soldiers of the World	1962	50p	£25.00
X50	Sports through the Ages	1968	75p	—
96	TV & Radio Stars	1954	40p	—

CHUMS (Periodical)

BF23	Cricketers	1923	£1.25	£30.00
BF20	Football Teams	1922	60p	£12.00
F8	Football Teams New Series	1923	£1.00	£8.00
X10	Real Colour Photos (Footballers)	1922	£2.00	—

CHURCH & DWIGHT (Baking Soda, U.S.A.)

M60	Beautiful Birds, New Series	1899	£1.25	£75.00
M60	Beautiful Birds of America	1898	£1.50	£90.00
M60	Beautiful Flowers	1899	£1.25	£75.00
X10	Birds of Prey	1976	—	£1.50
M30	Champion Dog Series	1902	£1.50	—
M30	Dairy Animals	1905	£2.00	—
M30	Fish Series	1900	£1.00	£30.00
M30	Game Bird Series	1904	£1.50	£45.00
M60	Interesting Animals	1903	£1.50	£90.00
M30	Mother Goose Series	1900	£2.50	
M30	New Series of Birds	1908	£1.00	£30.00
M30	New Series of Dogs	1910	£2.00	—
M30	Useful Birds of America	1915	£1.00	—
M30	Useful Birds of America, 2nd Series	1918	£1.25	—
M30	Useful Birds of America, 3rd Series	1922	£1.00	£30.00
M30	Useful Birds of America, Series 4	1924	£1.25	—
M15	Useful Birds of America, Series 5	1924	£1.00	£30.00
M15	Useful Birds of America, Series 6	1924	80p	£12.00
M15	Useful Birds of America, Series 7	1924	80p	£12.00
M15	Useful Birds of America, Series 8	1924	80p	£12.00
M15	Useful Birds of America, Series 9	1926	20p	£3.00
M15	Useful Birds of America, Series 10	1926	20p	£3.00

CLEVEDON CONFECTIONERY LTD.

50	British Aircraft	1958	75p	—
25	British Orders of Chivalry & Valour	1960	£1.00	—
50	British Ships	1959	75p	—
B50	British Trains & Engines	1958	£1.25	—
25	Dan Dare	1961	£1.00	—
40	Did You Know?	1963	£1.00	—
40	Famous Cricketers	1959	£2.50	—
25	Famous Cricketers	1962	£2.50	—
50	Famous Football Clubs	1964	40p	—
50	Famous Footballers	1961	40p	—
50	Famous International Aircraft	1963	40p	—
B50	Famous Screen Stars	1959	£1.00	—

CLEVEDON CONFECTIONERY LTD.—cont.

Qty		Date	Odds	Sets
40	Film Stars	1958	£1.00	—
50	Football Club Managers	1959	75p	—
50	Hints on Association Football	1961	75p	—
50	Hints on Road Safety	1962	75p	—
50	International Sporting Stars	1960	40p	—
B50	Regimental Badges	1959	£1.00	—
X25	Sporting Memories	1962	—	—
50	The Story of the Olympics	1961	40p	—
50	Trains of the World	1962	50p	—
B30	Wagon Train	1963	60p	—

CLOVER DAIRIES LTD.

25	Animals & Reptiles	1970	—	50p
25	British Rail	1973	—	50p
25	People & Places	1972	—	50p
25	Prehistoric Animals	1965	—	60p
25	Science in the 20th Century	1971	—	50p
25	Ships & Their Workings	1971	—	50p
25	The Story of Milk	1970	—	£1.00
25	Transport Through the Ages	1971	—	50p

COCA COLA (Drinks)

X20	America's Fighting Planes (U.S.A.)	1944	—	£12.50
M100	Our Flower Paradise (S. Africa)	1960	—	£4.00
X96	The World of Nature (U.S.A.)	1960	—	£5.00

CECIL COLEMAN LTD. (Confectionery)

24	Film Stars	1935	£2.00	—

COLGATE-PALMOLIVE (Toiletries)

M24	Famous Sporting Trophies	1979	—	£1.00

COLINVILLE LTD. (Gum)

L25	Prairie Pioneers	1959	£1.00	—
L28	Space Fantasy 1st Series (1-28)	1959	£1.00	—
L28	Space Fantasy 2nd Series (29-56)	1959	£1.00	—

COLLECTOR & HOBBYIST (Periodical)

25	Fascinating Hobbies	1950	—	50p

COLLECTORS SHOP

25	Bandsmen of the British Army	1960	—	£5.00
3	Bonus Cards	1961	—	—

COLT 45 (Drink)

X4	American Scenes (Beer Mats)	1975	—	75p

COMET SWEETS

25	A. & M. Denis on Safari 1st Series	1961	—	75p
25	A. & M. Denis on Safari 2nd Series	1961	—	75p
25	Modern Wonders	1961	—	50p
25	Olympic Achievements 1st Series	1960	—	60p
25	Olympic Achievements 2nd Series	1960	—	60p

COMIC LIFE (Periodical)

BF4	Sports Champions	1922	£1.25	—

COMMODEX (Gum)

Qty		Date	Odds	Sets
L88	Operation Moon	1969	50p	—
L120	Super Cars	1970	30p	£36.00

COMMONWEALTH SHOE & LEATHER CO. (U.S.A.)

M12	Makes of Planes	1930	£1.00	£12.00

COMO CONFECTIONERY PRODUCTS LTD.

L25	History of the Wild West 1st	1963	60p	—
L25	History of the Wild West 2nd	1963	—	£3.00
50	Lenny's Adventures	1961	40p	—
50	Noddy & His Playmates	1962	—	£4.00
L25	Noddy's Adventures 1st Series	1958	30p	—
L25	Noddy's Adventures 2nd Series	1958	30p	—
25	Noddy's Budgie & Feathered Friends 1st ...	1964	35p	—
25	Noddy's Budgie & Feathered Friends 2nd ...	1964	35p	—
L50	Noddy's Friends Abroad	1959	30p	—
L50	Noddy's Nursery Rhyme Friends	1959	30p	—
L50	Sooty's Adventures	1960	30p	—
L50	Sooty's New Adventures 2nd	1961	—	£3.00
L50	Sooty's Latest Adventures 3rd	1963	30p	—
25	Speed 1st Series	1962	—	—
25	Speed 2nd Series	1962	—	75p
25	Supercar 1st Series	1962	—	—
25	Supercar 2nd Series	1962	—	£6.00
25	Top Secret 1st Series	1965	60p	—
25	Top Secret 2nd Series	1965	60p	—
L26	XL5 1st Series	1965	—	—
L26	XL5 2nd Series	1966	—	—

COMPTON'S GRAVY SALT

22	Footballers Serie A (Black)	1924	£3.00	—
22	Footballers Serie A (Coloured)	1924	£4.00	—
22	Footballers Serie B (Black)	1924	£3.00	—
22	Footballers Serie B (Coloured)	1924	£4.00	—
22	Footballers Serie C	1924	£5.00	—
22	Footballers Serie D	1924	£5.00	—

COOPER & CO. LTD. (Tea)

50	Do You Know?	1962	—	75p
25	Inventions & Discoveries 1st Series	1962	—	—
25	Inventions & Discoveries 2nd Series	1962	—	—
25	Mysteries & Wonders of the World 1st Series	1961	—	75p
25	Mysteries & Wonders of the World 2nd Series	1961	—	75p
25	Prehistoric Animals 1st Series	1962	—	£7.50
25	Prehistoric Animals 2nd Series	1962	—	£7.50
25	Strange But True 1st Series	1961	—	50p
25	Strange But True 2nd Series	1961	—	50p
25	Transport Through the Ages 1st Series ...	1961	—	£2.50
25	Transport Through the Ages 2nd Series ...	1961	—	£2.50

CO-OPERATIVE SOCIETIES (Shops)

B48	World Cup Teams & Players. *Complete with Poster*	1982	—	£2.00
D306	Espana '82. *Complete with Album*	1982	—	£4.00
—	Special Poster for above (only if ordered at same time)	1982	—	50p

JOHN COURAGE (Brewers)

Qty		Date	Odds	Sets
X6	Sporting Heroes (Beer Mats)	1975	—	£2.00

COW & GATE (Baby Food)

X24	Advertisement Cards	1928	£1.00	£24.00
X48	Happy Families	1928	—	£15.00

CROMWELL STORES

25	Do You Know?	1963	—	£2.50
25	Racing Colours	1963	—	£3.00

CROSBIE (Preserves)

K54	Miniature Playing Cards	1938	40p	—

JOSEPH CROSFIELD & SONS LTD. (Soap)

36	Film Stars	1924	£1.50	—

CRYSELCO ELECTRIC LAMPS

X25	Beautiful Waterways	1939	24p	£6.00
X25	Buildings of Beauty	1938	50p	£12.50
X12	Interesting Events of 60 Years Ago	1955	—	£12.50

D. CUMMINGS & SON (Commercial)

64	Famous Fighters	1947	—	£10.00

DAILY EXPRESS (Newspaper)

X59	Car Cards	1971	—	£1.00

DAILY HERALD (Newspaper)

32	Cricketers	1954	£1.00	—
32	Footballers	1954	50p	—
32	Turf Personalities	1955	12p	—

DAILY ICE CREAM CO.

24	Modern British Locomotives	1954	—	£5.00

DAILY MAIL (Newspaper)

P176	War Photographs	1916	50p	—

DAILY MIRROR (Newspaper)

M100	Star Soccer Sides	1966	15p	£15.00

DAILY SKETCH (Newspaper)

40	World Cup Souvenir	1970	50p	£20.00

DAINTY NOVELS

10	World's Famous Liners	1912	£4.00	—

DANDY GUM

M160	Cars and Bikes	1977	15p	—
M200	Fables (F1-200)	1968	—	£25.00
M116	Flag Parade	1965	—	£15.00
M160	Flag Parade	1978	—	£20.00
B72	Motor Cars	1966	35p	—
B53	Our Modern Army (P/C Inset)	1958	—	£25.00
B43/53	Our Modern Army (P/C Inset)	1958	10p	£4.00
B53	Pin Ups (P/C Inset)	1956	75p	—

DANDY GUM—cont.

Qty		Date	Odds	Sets
B53	Pin Ups (P/C Inset, Different)	1978	—	£4.00
M100	Soldier Parade	1970	—	£20.00
M100	Wild Animals (H1-100)	1969	—	£15.00

LIAM DEVLIN & SONS LTD. (Confectionery)

Qty		Date	Odds	Sets
M36	Coaching Gaelic Football	1960	—	—
48	Corgi Toys	1971	—	£10.00
50	Do You Know?	1964	—	75p
B50	Famous Footballers (New Series)	1952	£1.50	—
B50	Famous Footballers (A1)	1953	£1.50	—
B50	Famous Footballers (A2)	1954	£1.50	—
50	Famous Footballers (A3)	1955	£1.50	—
B54	Famous Speedway Stars	1960	—	—
B45	Fastest on Earth	1953	£1.25	—
36	Flags of the Nations	1960	£1.00	—
48	Gaelic Sportstars	1960	—	—
48	Irish Fishing	1962	—	£4.00
50	Modern Transport	1966	—	£1.00
48	Our Dogs	1963	—	—
48	Right or Wrong?	1963	£1.25	—
B35	Walt Disney Characters	1956	£1.50	—
B50	Wild Animals by George Cansdale	1954	£1.50	—
48	Wild Wisdom	1970	£1.00	—
50	Wonders of the World	1972	—	£1.00
?100	World Flag Series	1970	—	—

DICKSON ORDE & CO. LTD. (Confectionery)

Qty		Date	Odds	Sets
50	Footballers	1960	—	75p
25	Ships Through the Ages	1961	—	—
25	Sports of the Countries	1962	—	50p

DINKIE PRODUCTS LTD. (Hair Grips)

Qty		Date	Odds	Sets
L20	Gone with the Wind (Series 5)	1948	—	—
X20	M.G.M. Films (Series 3)	1948	—	£5.00
L24	M.G.M. Films (Series 7)	1949	—	£5.00
L24	M.G.M. Films (Series 9)	1950	—	—
L24	Paramount Pictures (Series 8)	1950	—	£5.00
X24	Stars & Starlets (Series 1)	1947	—	£5.00
X20	Stars & Starlets (Series 2)	1947	—	£5.00
L24	Warner Bros. Artistes (Series 4)	1948	—	£5.00
L24	Warner Bros. Films (Series 6)	1949	—	£5.00

DIRECT TEA SUPPLY CO.

Qty		Date	Odds	Sets
25	British Uniforms of the 19th Century	1958	—	£7.50

F. M. DOBSON (Confectionery)

Qty		Date	Odds	Sets
100	Newcastle & Sunderland's 100 Greatest Footballers	1982	—	£3.00
2	Error Cards	1982	—	50p

A. & J. DONALDSON (Commercial)

Qty		Date	Odds	Sets
?500	Sports Favourites	1953	75p	—

DONRUSS (Gum, U.S.A.)

Qty		Date	Odds	Sets
X66	M.A.S.H.	1982	—	£5.00
X99	Rocky II	1981	—	£4.00

DONRUSS (Gum, U.S.A.)—cont.

Qty		Date	Odds	Sets
X22	Rocky II Stickers	1981	—	£3.50
X66	Sgt. Pepper's Lonely Hearts Club Band	1978	—	£3.50
X66	Space 1999	1976	—	£3.50

DOUBLE DIAMOND (Beer)

P5	Puzzle Pictures (beer mats)	1976	—	75p

DRYFOOD LTD. (Confectionery)

50	Animals of the World	1956	—	75p
K50	Zoo Animals	1955	—	75p

DUCHESS OF DEVONSHIRE DAIRY CO. LTD.

L25	Devon Beauty Spots	1936	£2.00	—

DUNHILLS (Confectionery)

25	Ships & Their Workings	1962	—	£2.00

DUNKIN (Confectionery, Spain)

X88	Martial Arts	1976	—	£10.00
M50	Motor Cycles of the World	1976	—	£10.00

DUNNS (Chocolate)

60	Animals	1924	£3.00	—

DUTTON'S BEER

12	Team of Sporting Heroes	1981	—	75p

THE EAGLE (Periodical)

M12	Marvels of this Modern Age	1965	—	£1.25
16	Wallet of Soccer Stars	1965	—	£1.50

J. EDMONDSON & CO. LTD (Confectionery)

4	Aeroplane Models	1939	£5.00	—
?40	Art Picture Series	1914	£5.00	—
15	Birds & Eggs	1924	£3.00	—
?20	Boy Scout Proficiency Badges	1924	£5.00	—
20	British Ships	1925	60p	£12.00
20	Dogs	1924	£1.50	—
20	Famous Castles	1925	£2.00	—
40	Flags of All Nations	1923	£3.00	—
24	Pictures from the Fairy Stories	1930	£2.00	—
24	Popular Sports	1930	£2.00	—
25	Sports & Pastimes Series	1916	£5.00	—
12	Throwing Shadows on the Wall	1937	£1.00	£12.00
25	War Series	1916	£5.00	—
12	Woodbine Village	1936	£1.00	£12.00
26	Zoo Alphabet	1935	£3.00	—

EDWARDS & SONS (Confectionery)

27	Popular Dogs	1954	75p	—
12	Products of the World	1957	—	50p
25	Transport Present & Future (Descriptive) ...	1956	—	50p
25	Transport Present & Future (Non-Descriptive)	1955	—	50p
25	Wonders of the Universe	1956	—	50p

ELKES BISCUITS LTD.

Qty		Date	Odds	Sets
25	Do You Know?	1964	—	50p

ELY BREWERY CO. LTD.

B24	Royal Portraits	1953	80p	£20.00

EMPIRE MARKETING BOARD

12	Empire Shopping	1926	75p	£9.00

H. E. EMPSON & SONS LTD. (Tea)

25	Birds	1962	—	£2.00
25	British Cavalry Uniforms of the 19th Century	1963	—	£4.00
25	Garden Flowers	1966	—	—
25	History of the Railways 1st Series	1966	—	—
25	History of the Railways 2nd Series	1966	—	—
25	Passenger Liners	1964	—	—
25	Tropical Birds	1966	—	—
25	Wonders of the Deep	1965	—	50p

ENGLISH & SCOTTISH C.W.S. (Shops)

25	Humorous Peeps into History (1-25)	1927	£1.00	£25.00
25	Humorous Peeps into History (26-50)	1928	£2.00	—
25	In Victoria's Days	1930	£1.00	£25.00
X12	The Rose of the Orient Film Series	1925	25p	£3.00
X12	The Rose of the Orient 2nd Film Series	1925	25p	£3.00
X12	The Story of Tea (Blue Back)	1925	30p	£3.50
X12	The Story of Tea (Brown Back)	1925	25p	£3.00

ESKIMO FOODS

P4	The Beatles	1965	—	£16.00

JOHN E. ESSLEMONT LTD. (Tea)

25	Before Our Time	1966	—	£1.00
25	Into Space	1966	—	£1.00

ESSO PETROLEUM CO.

M16	Squelchers (Football)	1970	60p	£10.00

ESTA MEDICAL LABORATORIES INC. (U.S.A.)

E6	Curiosa of Conception	1960	—	£3.00

EVERSHED & SON LTD. (Soap)

25	Sports and Pastimes	1914	£5.00	—

EVERY GIRL'S PAPER

BF17	Film Stars	1924	£1.00	—

EWBANKS LTD.

25	Animals of the Farmyard	1960	—	50p
25	British Uniforms	1956	—	60p
25	Miniature Cars & Scooters	1960	—	50p
50	Ports & Resorts of the World	1960	—	£1.25
25	Ships Around Britain	1961	—	50p
25	Sports & Games	1958	—	75p
25	Transport Through the Ages	1957	—	50p

EXPRESS WEEKLY (Periodical)

Qty		Date	Odds	Sets
25	The Wild West (No Overprint)	1958	—	£1.00
25	The Wild West (Red Overprint)	1958	—	60p

FACCHINO'S CHOCOLATE WAFERS

100	Cinema Stars	1936	10p	£10.00
50	How or Why	1937	16p	£8.00
50	People of All Lands	1937	75p	—
50	Pioneers	1937	60p	—

FAITH PRESS (Commercial)

10	Boy Scouts (LCC)	1928	£1.00	£10.00

FAMILY STAR (Periodical)

K52	Fortune Telling Cards	1952	—	£7.50

FARROWS (Sauces)

50	Animals in the Zoo	1925	£2.00	—

JOHN FILSHILL LTD. (Confectionery)

24	Birds & Their Eggs	1924	£2.00	—
25	Footballers	1924	£2.50	—

FINDUS (Frozen Foods)

20	All About Pirates	1967	—	£1.25

FINE FARE TEA

25	Inventions & Discoveries 1st Series	1965	—	£1.50
25	Inventions & Discoveries 2nd Series	1965	—	£1.50
12	Your Fortune in a Tea-cup	1966	—	£1.00

FISH MARKETING BOARD

18	Eat More Fish	1930	75p	—

FIZZY FRUIT (Confectionery)

25	Buses and Trams	1959	—	£7.50

FLEER GUM INC. (U.S.A.)

X66	Gomer Pyle, U.S.M.C.	1965	—	£7.50
X72	Here's Bo!	1980	—	£6.00
12	Posters	1980	—	£2.50
X66	McHale's Navy	1965	—	£7.50

FLEETWAY PUBLICATIONS LTD.

X72	Adventures of Sexton Blake	1968	20p	£15.00
P2	Pop Stars (Roxy)	1961	—	50p
50	Star Footballers of 1963	1963	25p	£12.50

FORD MOTOR CO. LTD.

M50	Major Farming	1955	£1.50	—

A. C. W. FRANCIS (Confectionery, Grenada)

25	Football Clubs & Badges	1967	—	£3.00
25	Pond Life	1967	—	£1.50
25	Sports of the Countries	1967	—	£2.50

LES FRERES (Shop)

25	Aircraft of World War II	1964	—	£2.00

J. S. FRY & SONS LTD. (Confectionery)

Qty		*Date*	*Odds*	*Sets*
50	Ancient Sundials	1924	£1.00	£50.00
50	Birds & Poultry	1912	80p	£40.00
24	Birds & Their Eggs	1912	£1.25	£30.00
15	China & Porcelain	1907	£2.50	—
P2	Coronation Postcards	1911	£5.00	—
25	Days of Nelson	1906	£2.50	£62.50
25	Days of Wellington	1906	£2.50	£62.50
25	Empire Industries	1924	£1.50	—
50	Exercises for Men & Women	1926	£2.00	—
48	Film Stars	1934	50p	—
50	Fowls, Pigeons & Dogs	1908	£1.00	£50.00
P12	Fun Cards	1972	—	50p
25	Match Tricks	1921	—	—
15	National Flags	1908	£1.50	£22.50
50	Nursery Rhymes	1917	80p	£40.00
50	Phil May Sketches	1905	£1.25	£62.50
25	Red Indians	1927	£1.50	—
25	Rule Britannia	1915	£2.50	£62.50
50	Scout Series	1912	£2.00	£100.00
48	Screen Stars	1928	£1.00	£50.00
120	This Wonderful World	1935	50p	—
50	Time & Money in Different Countries	1908	£1.00	£50.00
50	Tricks & Puzzles (Black Back)	1924	80p	£40.00
50	Tricks & Puzzles (Blue Back)	1918	80p	£40.00
25	With Captain Scott at the South Pole	1908	£2.50	£62.50

GAYCON PRODUCTS LTD. (Confectionery)

25	Adventures of Pinky & Perky 1st Series	1961	75p	—
25	Adventures of Pinky & Perky 2nd Series ...	1961	75p	—
50	British Birds & Their Eggs	1961	—	£1.25
25	British Butterflies	1962	—	£6.00
25	Do You Know? 1st Series	1964	75p	—
25	Do You Know? 2nd Series	1964	75p	—
50	Flags of All Nations	1963	60p	—
25	History of the Blue Lamp 1st Series	1962	—	£4.00
25	History of the Blue Lamp 2nd Series	1962	—	£4.00
30	Kings & Queens	1961	—	60p
25	Modern Motor Cars	1959	£1.00	—
25	Modern Motor Cars of the World 1st Series ...	1962	£1.00	—
25	Modern Motor Cars of the World 2nd Series ...	1962	£1.00	—
25	Red Indians 1st Series	1960	—	£1.50
25	Red Indians 2nd Series	1960	—	£1.50
25	Top Secret 1st Series	1963	£1.00	—
25	Top Secret 2nd Series	1963	£1.00	—

GEES FOOD PRODUCTS

30	Kings & Queens	1961	—	£4.00
16	See Britain by Coach	1959	—	50p

GEM LIBRARY (Periodical)

BF4	Footballers—Autographed Action Series ...	1923	75p	£3.00
BF6	Footballers—Autographed Real Action Photo Series	1922	75p	£4.50

GEM LIBRARY (Periodical)—cont.

Qty		Date	Odds	Sets
BF15	Footballers—Special Action Photo	1922	60p	—
L16	Marvels of the Future	1929	75p	£12.00

ALFRED GERBER (Cheese)

M143	Glorious Switzerland	1952	50p	—

GIRLS FRIEND (Periodical)

B6	Actresses (Silk)	1913	£4.00	—

GIRLS MIRROR (Periodical)

BF10	Actors & Actresses	1922	75p	—

GLENGETTIE TEA

25	Animals of the World	1964	—	50p
25	Birds & Their Eggs	1970	—	£2.00
25	British Locomotives	1959	—	75p
25	Do You Know?	1970	—	50p
25	Historical Scenes	1968	—	50p
25	History of the Railways 1st Series	1974	—	50p
25	History of the Railways 2nd Series	1974	—	50p
25	International Air Liners	1963	—	50p
25	Medals of the World (Black Back)	1959	—	50p
25	Medals of the World (Blue Back)	1959	—	£3.50
25	Modern Transport (Black Back)	1963	—	£3.50
25	Modern Transport (Blue Back)	1963	—	£7.50
25	Naval Battles	1971	—	50p
25	Rare British Birds	1967	—	75p
25	Sovereigns, Consorts & Rulers of G.B. 1st	1970	—	£5.00
25	Sovereigns, Consorts & Rulers of G.B. 2nd	1970	—	£5.00
25	The British Army (Black Back)	1976	—	60p
25	The British Army (Blue Back)	1976	—	60p
25	Trains of the World	1966	—	50p
25	Veteran & Vintage Cars	1966	—	£6.00
25	Wild Flowers	1961	—	60p

GLENTONS LTD. (Shop)

24	World's Most Beautiful Butterflies	1910	£2.00	—

J. GODDARD & SONS LTD. (Metal Polish)

L4	Cleaning a Silver Teapot	1928	£1.25	—
L3	Four Generations	1923	50p	£1.50
L12	London Views	1925	25p	£3.00
L12	Old Silver	1924	30p	£3.50
L9	Old Silver at the Victorian & Albert Museum	1933	£1.00	£9.00
L12	Ports of the World	1928	75p	£9.00
L12	Present Day Silverware	1937	60p	£7.50
L4	Silverware with Flowers I	1928	60p	£2.50
L8	Silverware with Flowers II	1933	£1.00	£8.00
L2	Use & Cleaning of Silverware I	1926	25p	50p
L6	Use & Cleaning of Silverware II	1937	£2.00	—
L8	Views of Leicester	1934	£1.00	£8.00
L12	Views of Old Leicester	1928	£1.00	£12.00

GOLDEN GRAIN TEA

25	Birds	1970	—	£2.50
25	British Cavalry Uniforms of the 19th Century	1964	—	£1.50

GOLDEN GRAIN TEA—cont.

Qty		Date	Odds	Sets
25	Garden Flowers	1971	—	50p
25	Passenger Liners	1970	—	50p

GOLDEN WONDER (Potato Crisps)

14	Space Cards (round corners)	1979	—	50p
14	Space Cards (square corners)	1979	—	50p
24	Sporting All Stars	1979	—	85p
24	TV All Stars	1979	—	60p

GOODIES LTD. (Confectionery)

25	Flags & Emblems	1961	—	75p
25	Indian Tribes	1975	50p	£12.50
25	Mini Monsters	1975	50p	£12.50
25	Olympics	1972	60p	£15.00
25	Pirates	1976	60p	—
25	Prehistoric Animals	1969	50p	—
25	Robbers & Thieves	1976	50p	—
25	The Monkees 1st Series	1967	—	£1.00
25	The Monkees 2nd Series	1968	60p	—
25	Vanishing Animals	1977	50p	£12.50
25	Weapons Through the Ages	1974	50p	—
25	Wicked Monarchs	1973	50p	£12.50
25	Wide World/People of Other Lands	1968	50p	£12.50
25	Wild Life	1977	50p	£12.50
25	World Cup '74	1974	50p	£12.50

D. W. GOODWIN & CO. (Flour)

36	Careers for Boys & Girls	1930	£5.00	—
24	Extra Rhymes, 2nd Series	1930	—	—
36	Flags of All Nations	1930	£4.00	—
?30	Jokes Series	1930	£5.00	—
?30	Optical Illusions	1930	£4.00	—
?30	Ships Series	1930	£5.00	—
?36	World Interest Series	1930	£4.00	—

WILLIAM GOSSAGE & SONS LTD. (Soap)

48	British Birds & Their Eggs	1924	80p	£40.00
48	Butterflies & Moths	1924	60p	£30.00

GOWERS & BURGONS (Tea)

25	British Birds & Their Nests	1970	—	£2.50
25	Family Pets	1964	—	60p
25	People & Places	1970	—	50p
25	Prehistoric Animals	1969	—	£6.00
25	Sailing Ships Through the Ages	1971	—	£7.50
25	The Circus	1964	—	—
25	Veteran and Vintage Cars	1965	—	£5.00
25	Veteran Racing Cars	1964	—	—

GRANGERS NO. "1"

12	Dr Mabuse Series	1926	£5.00	—

GRANOSE FOODS LTD.

M48	Adventures of Billy the Buck	1956	—	75p
M16	Air Transport	1957	—	75p

GRANOSE FOODS LTD.—cont.

Qty		Date	Odds	Sets
M16	Animal Life	1957	—	75p
M16	Aquatic & Reptile Life	1957	—	75p
M48	King of the Air	1956	15p	—
M48	Life Story of Blower the Whale	1956	15p	—
M48	Lone Leo the Cougar	1955	15p	—
M16	Out Winged Friends	1957	20p	—
M16	Plant Life	1957	—	—
M48	Silver Mane, the Timber Wolf	1955	—	£2.50
M16	Space Travel	1957	—	£2.50
M48	Tippytail the Grizzly Bear	1956	—	75p
M16	Water Transport	1957	—	75p
M16	World Wide Visits	1957	—	75p

GREGG (Jelly, New Zealand)

B48	Aquatic Birds	1974	—	£3.00

HALPINS (Tea)

25	Aircraft of the World	1958	—	50p
L20	Aircraft of the World (Double, as Above)	1958	—	£3.00
25	Nature Studies	1958	—	£1.50

HAPPY HOME (Periodical)

B8	Child Studies (Silk)	1912	£4.00	—
M9	Flags (Silk)	1914	£2.50	£20.00
B9	Our Lucky Flowers (Silk)	1912	—	—
K14	The Happy Home Silk Button (Silk)	1914	£3.00	£40.00
M12	Women on War Work	1915	£3.00	£36.00

HARDEN BROS. & LINDSAY LTD. (Tea)

50	Animals of the World	1960	—	—
50	British Birds & Their Eggs	1960	—	—
50	National Pets	1961	—	75p

JOHN HAWKINS & SONS LTD. (Cotton)

LF30	The Story of Cotton	1925	£2.00	—

HEINEKEN (Beer)

P12	The Heineken Story (beer mats)	1976	—	£1.00

HEINZ (Foods)

E1	Australian Cricket Team	1964		75p

HITCHMAN'S DAIRIES LTD.

25	Aircraft of World War II	1966	—	£4.00
25	Animals of the World	1964	—	£3.00
25	British Birds & Their Nests	1970	—	—
25	British Railways	1971	—	60p
25	Buses & Trams	1966	—	£1.50
25	Merchant Ships of the World	1970	—	£3.00
25	Modern Wonders	1962	—	£4.00
25	Naval Battles	1971	—	50p
25	People & Places	1971	—	£1.50
25	Regimental Uniforms of the Past	1973	—	50p
25	Science in the 20th Century	1966	—	60p
25	The Story of Milk	1965	—	£7.50
25	Trains of the World	1970	—	—

HOADLEY'S CHOCOLATES LTD.—(Australia)

Qty		*Date*	*Odds*	*Sets*
?33	Cricketers (black fronts)	1928	£5.00	—
36	Cricketers (brown fronts)	1933	£4.00	—
50	Empire Games and Test Teams	1932	£3.00	—
40	Test Cricketers	1936	£3.00	—
B36	Test Cricketers (different)	1938	£5.00	—

THOMAS HOLLOWAY LTD. (Pharmaceutics)

X39	Natural History Series (Animals Heads)	1900	£3.50	£140.00
X39	Natural History Series (Birds)	1900	£3.50	£140.00
X60	Natural History Series (Full Length)	1900	£3.00	£180.00
X50	Pictorial History of the Sports and Pastimes of all Nations	1900	£4.00	—

HOME & COLONIAL STORES LTD.

26	Advertising Alphabet	1914	£3.00	—
M100	Flag Pictures	1916	£1.25	—
M40	War Heroes	1916	£1.50	—
M40	War Pictures	1916	£1.50	—
100	War Pictures (Different)	1916	£1.25	£125.00

HOME COUNTIES DAIRIES TEA

25	Country Life	1964	—	50p
25	International Air Liners	1965	—	50p
25	The Story of Milk	1965	—	£1.00

HOME MIRROR (Periodical)

M4	Cinema Star Pictures (Silk)	1919	£4.00	—

HOME WEEKLY (Periodical)

12	Little Charlie Cards	1920	£6.00	—

HORNIMAN (Tea)

48	Dogs	1961	—	75p
48	Pets	1960	—	75p
48	Wild Animals	1958	—	75p

HORSLEY'S STORES

25	British Uniforms of the 19th Century	1968	—	£2.50
25	Castles of Britain	1968	—	£3.50
25	Family Pets	1968	—	£2.50

VAN HOUTEN (Chocolate)

M4	Dutch Costumes (Wrappers)	1953	—	£2.00

HUNT CROP & SONS (Vedast)

12	Characters from Dickens	1912	£4.00	—

HUNTLEY & PALMER (Biscuits)

P12	Animals	1900	£3.00	£36.00
P12	Aviation	1900	—	—
P12	Biscuits in Various Countries	1900	£2.50	£30.00
P6	Biscuits with Travellers	1900	£2.50	£15.00
P12	Children of Nations I (Gold Border)	1900	£3.00	£36.00
P12	Children of Nations II (White Border)	1900	£3.00	£36.00
P12	Children at Leisure & Play	1900	£3.00	—

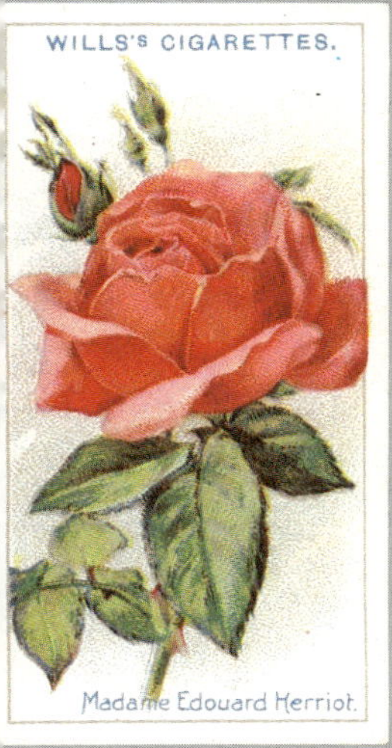

Roses. Wills

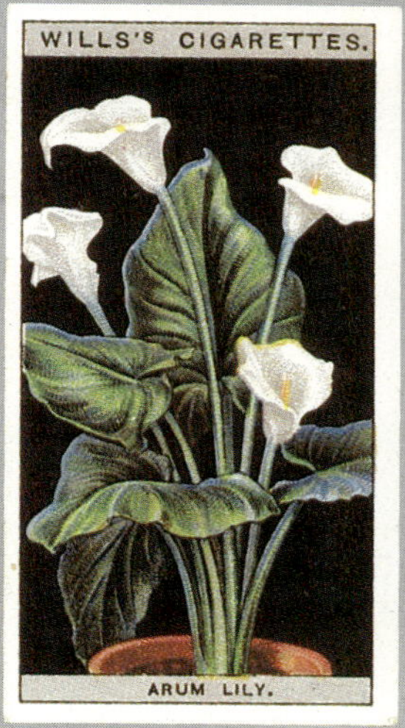

Flower Culture in Pots.
Wills (also I.T.C. Canada)

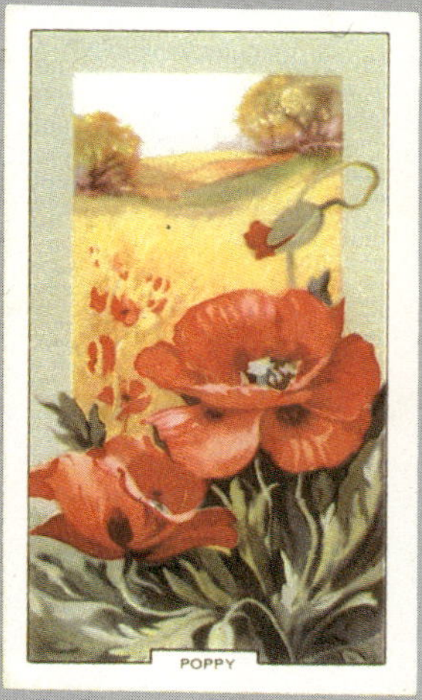

Wild Flowers. Gallaher

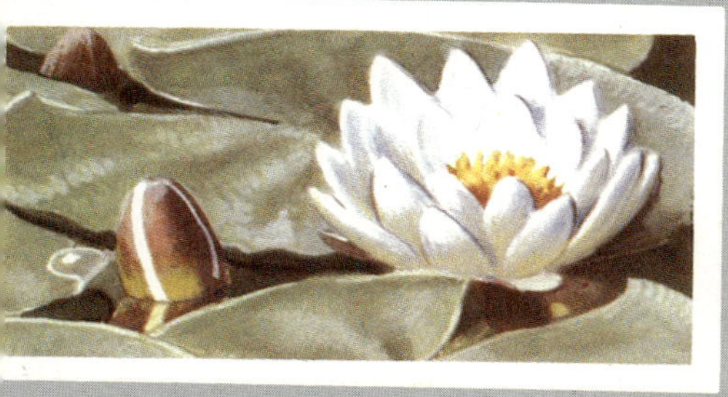

Wild Flowers. Brooke Bond

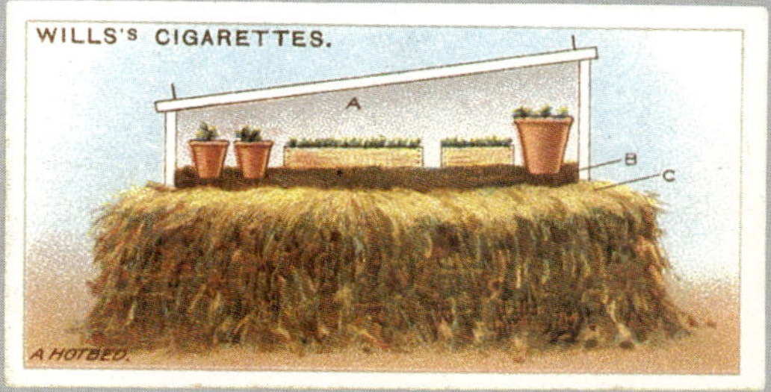

Gardening Hints. Wills (also I.T.C. Canada)

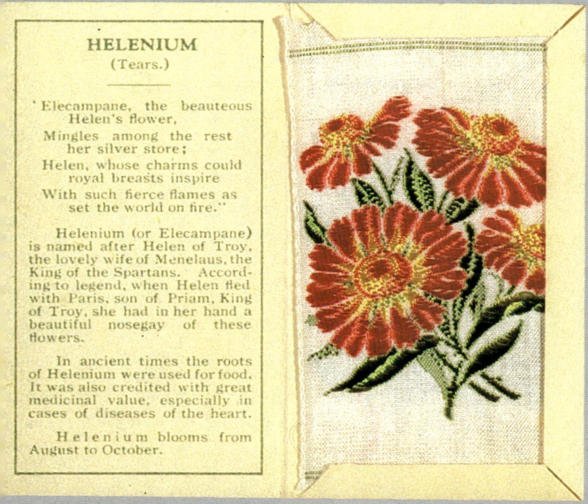

Kensitas Flowers. Wix

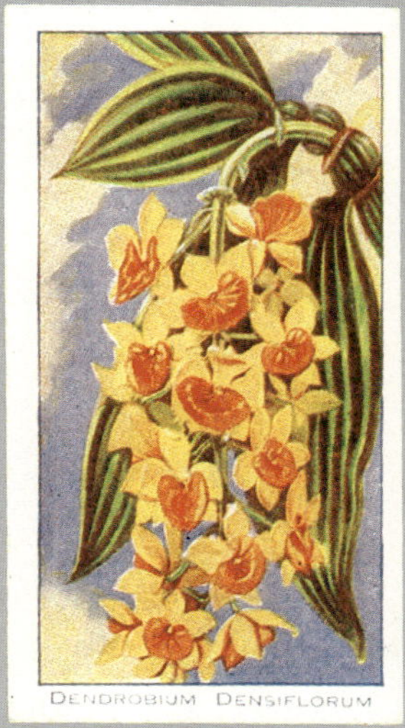

Orchids. Carreras

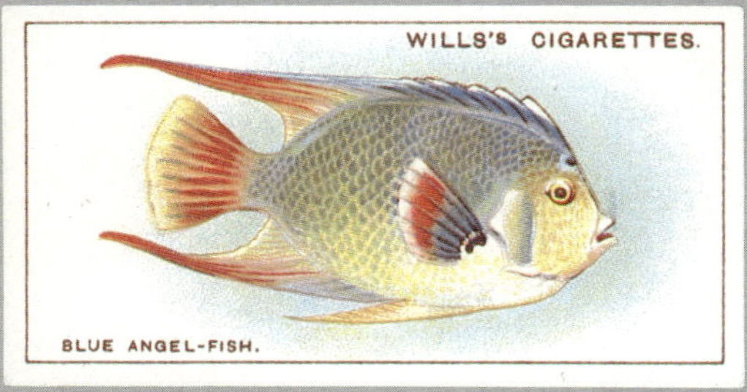

Wonders of the Sea. Wills (also B.A.T.)

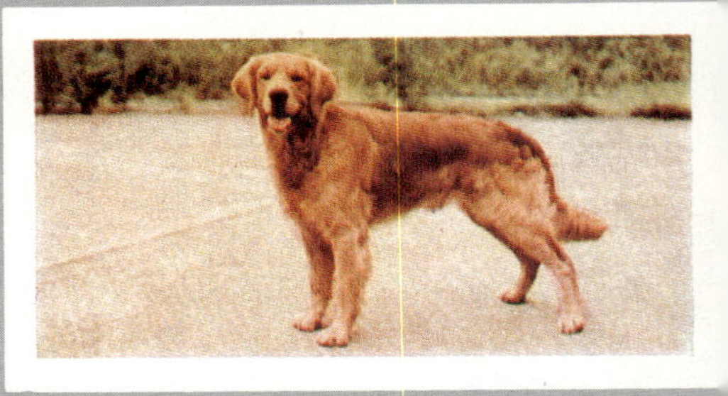

Dogs. Horniman

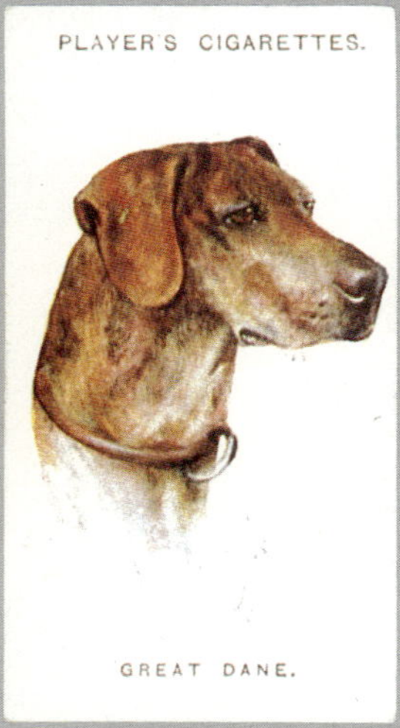

Dogs Heads by Wardle. Player

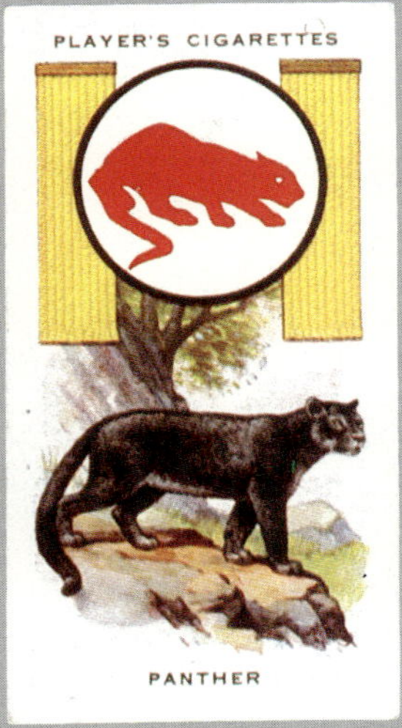

Boy Scout and Girl Guide. Player

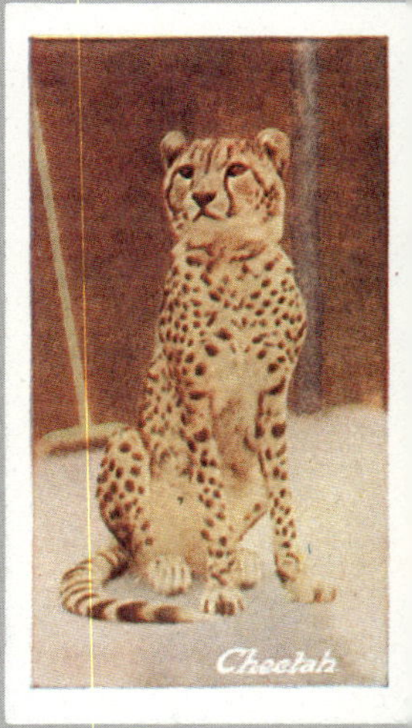

Zoo Series. Typhoo or Sword

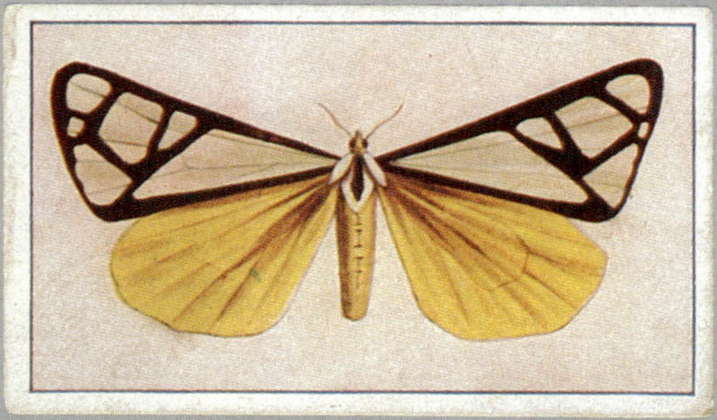

Butterflies & Moths. Sniders & Abrahams

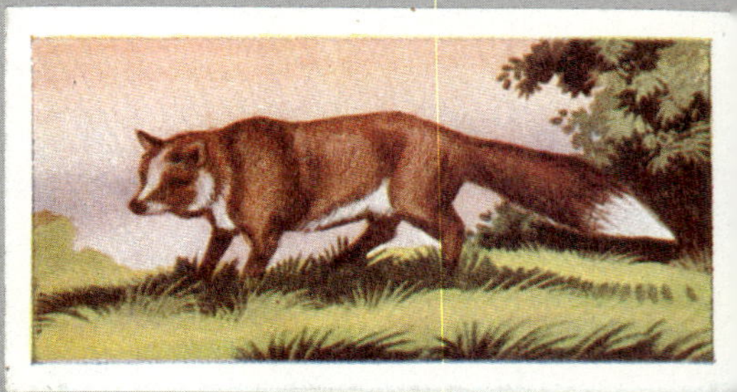

Interesting Animals. Neilson

HUNTLEY & PALMER (Biscuits)—cont.

Qty		Date	Odds	Sets
P12	Harvests of the World	1900	£10.00	—
P12	Hunting	1900	—	—
P8	Inventors	1900	£10.00	—
X12	Rhondes Enfantines	1900	£7.50	—
P12	Scenes with Biscuits	1900	£3.00	£36.00
X8	Shakespearian Series	1900	£3.00	£24.00
P12	Soldiers of Various Countries	1900	£6.00	—
P12	Sports (Semi-Circular Background)	1900	£3.50	£42.00
P12	Sports (Plain Background)	1900	£3.50	£42.00
P12	The Seasons	1900	£4.00	—
P12	Travelling During the 19th Century	1900	—	—
P12	Views of Italy & the French Riviera	1900	£3.50	—
P12	Warships of Nations	1900	£5.00	—
P8	Watteau	1900	£3.00	£25.00
P8	Wonders of the World	1900	—	—

HUSTLER SOAP

20	Animals 1st Series	1925	35p	£7.00
20	Animals 2nd Series	1925	50p	£10.00
20	Animals 3rd Series	1925	40p	£8.00
30	Regimental Nicknames	1924	80p	£24.00

R. HYDE & CO. LTD. (Bird Seed)

80	British Birds	1928	60p	£48.00
80	Cage Birds	1930	50p	£40.00
80	Canary Culture	1930	40p	£35.00
M10	Cartoons	1908	£5.00	—

I.P.C. MAGAZINES LTD.

M25	Lindy's Cards of Fortune	1975	—	£2.00

JACOB & CO. (Biscuits)

D24	Banknotes That Made History (With Album)	1975	—	75p
D32	Famous Picture Cards From History (With Album)	1978	—	£1.00
25	Vehicles of All Ages	1924	£1.00	£25.00
25	Zoo Series (Brown Back)	1924	50p	£12.50
25	Zoo Series (Green Back)	1924	24p	£6.00

JESK (Confectionery)

25	Buses & Trams	1959	—	£4.00

JIBCO (Tea)

K53	Miniature Playing Cards	1956	£1.00	—
K50	Puzzle Cards	1955	£1.00	—
K25	Screen Stars	1955	60p	—
K25	Screen Stars, 2nd Series	1956	—	50p

R. L. JONES & CO. LTD. (Drink)

24	Jet Aircraft of the World	1956	—	50p

JUBBLY (Drink)

50	Adventurous Lives	1967	—	75p

JUNIOR PASTIMES (Commercial)

52	Popular Players (Footballers)	1951	50p	—
52	Popular Railway Engines	1951	60p	—
L80	Star Pix	1951	35p	—

K.P. NUTS

Qty		Date	Odds	Sets
12	Sports Adventure Series	1978	—	£3.00

KANE PRODUCTS LTD. (Confectionery)

36	ATV Stars (Packets)	1957	50p	—
50	British Birds & Their Eggs	1960	—	£7.50
25	Cricket Clubs & Badges	1957	—	60p
L50	Disc Stars	1960	25p	—
X50	Disc Stars	1960	10p	£5.00
50	Dogs	1955	40p	—
X72	Film Stars (Plain Back)	1955	40p	£30.00
50	Flags of All Nations	1959	—	£3.00
25	Football Clubs & Colours	1956	—	50p
50	Historical Characters	1957	—	£1.50
25	International Football Stars	1957	—	£3.00
30	Kings & Queens	1959	—	£2.50
X30	Kings & Queens	1959	—	£3.50
25	Modern Motor Cars	1959	—	£3.00
50	Modern Racing Cars	1954	—	£1.25
25	National Pets Club 1st Series	1958	—	£1.50
25	National Pets Club 2nd Series	1958	—	—
25	1956 Cricketers 1st Series	1956	—	£1.50
25	1956 Cricketers 2nd Series	1956	—	£3.00
25	Red Indians 1st Series	1957	—	£1.50
25	Red Indians 2nd Series	1957	—	75p
25	Roy Rogers Colour Series	1958	20p	£5.00
25	Roy Rogers Series	1957	40p	£10.00
50	Space Adventure	1955	—	£10.00
50	20th Century Events	1955	40p	£20.00
K50	Wild Animals	1954	—	75p

KARDOMAH (Tea)

K?500	General Interest (various series)	1900	£1.00	—

KEILLER (Confectionery)

LF18	Film Favourites	1926	£2.50	—
25	Scottish Heritage	1976	—	£4.00

KELLOGG LTD. (Cereals)

16	A History of British Military Aircraft	1963	10p	£1.50
16	Animals (3D)	1968	£1.25	£20.00
12	Famous Firsts	1963	6p	50p
12	International Soccer Stars	1963	6p	50p
40	Motor Cars	1950	50p	£20.00
40	Motor Cars (Coloured, as above)	1951	60p	£24.00
16	Ships of the British Navy	1962	30p	£5.00
12	The Story of the Bicycle	1964	£1.25	£15.00
16	The Story of the Locomotive 1st Series	1963	30p	£5.00
16	The Story of the Locomotive 2nd Series	1963	30p	£5.00
16	Veteran Motor Cars	1962	20p	£3.00

KIDDYS FAVOURITES LTD. (Commercial)

52	New Popular Film Stars	1950	50p	—
52	Popular Boxers	1950	60p	—
52	Popular Cricketers	1950	£1.00	—
65	Popular Film Stars	1950	50p	—

KIDDYS FAVOURITES LTD. (Commercial)—cont.

Qty		Date	Odds	Sets
52	Popular Footballers	1950	50p	—
52	Popular Olympics	1950	75p	—
75	Popular Players (Hearts on Front)	1950	50p	—
52	Popular Players (Shamrocks on Front)	1950	60p	—
52	Popular Speedway Riders	1950	75p	—

KINGS LAUNDRIES LTD. (Walthamstow, E. London)

25	Famous Railway Engines	1953	£1.00	—
25	Modern British Warplanes	1953	£1.00	—
25	Modern Motor Cycles	1953	£1.00	—
25	Radio & Television Stars	1953	£1.00	—

KINGS OF YORK (Laundry)

25	Flags of All Nations (Silk)	1954	80p	£20.00
30	Kings & Queens of England	1954	—	60p

KINGS SPECIALITIES (Food Products)

26	Alphabet Rhymes	1915	£5.00	—
?25	"Dont's" or Lessons in Etiquette	1915	£4.00	—
25	Great War Celebrities	1915	£5.00	—
25	Heroes of Famous Books	1915	£4.00	—
25	King's "Discoveries"	1915	£4.00	—
25	King's "Servants"	1915	£4.00	—
?25	Proverbs	1915	£4.00	—
37	Unrecorded History	1915	£4.00	—
?25	War Pictures	1915	£5.00	—
?25	Where King's Supplies Grow	1915	£4.00	—

KNOCKOUT (Periodical)

20	Super Planes of Today	1956	—	50p

KRAFT CHEESE

12	Historic Military Uniforms	1971	—	50p

LACEY'S CHEWING GUM

50	Footballers	1923	£4.00	—
?24	Uniforms	1923	£7.50	—

F. LAMBERT & SONS LTD. (Tea)

25	Before Our Time	1961	—	50p
25	Birds & Their Eggs	1962	—	—
25	Butterflies & Moths	1960	—	75p
25	Cacti	1962	—	50p
25	Car Registration Numbers 1st Series	1959	—	£1.50
25	Car Registration Numbers 2nd Series	1960	—	£5.00
25	Football Clubs & Badges	1958	—	50p
25	Game Birds & Wild Fowl	1964	—	£1.50
25	Historic East Anglia	1961	—	50p
25	Interesting Hobbies	1965	—	£5.00
25	Passenger Liners	1965	—	£4.00
25	Past & Present	1964	—	50p
25	People & Places	1966	—	—
25	Pond Life	1964	—	£3.50
25	Sports & Games	1964	—	50p

LAMPORT & HOLT (Shipping)

Qty		Date	Odds	Sets
L1	TSS Vandyck & TSS Voltaire	1925	—	£4.00

LEAF BRANDS INC. (Confectionery)

X50	Cliff Richard	1960	40p	£20.00
X50	Do You Know?	1961	6p	£2.50
X50	Famous Discoveries & Adventures	1962	60p	—
X50	Footballers	1961	12p	£6.00
X40	The Flag Game	1960	20p	£8.00
X50	Totem Pole Talking Signs	1962	30p	—

LETRASET

12	Star Wars	1978	—	50p

LEVER BROS. (Soap)

20	British Birds & Their Nests	1961	—	60p
F150	Celebrities	1900	£1.50	—
L39	Celebrities	1901	£2.00	—

LIEBIG EXTRACT OF MEAT CO. (see also Oxo)

This firm issued nearly 2,000 different sets throughout Europe between 1872 and 1974. Because inclusion of all these in this volume would be impracticable it is intended to produce a separate catalogue of Liebig Cards. See separate announcement for details. Some recent Italian issues are included below as a sample of the scope of these series.

Qty		*Date*	*Odds*	*Sets*
X6	1839 Ancient Cavalry	1970	—	75p
X6	1840 Ancient Helmets	1970	—	£1.00
X6	1799 Antique Pistols	1964	—	75p
X6	1837 Astronomy 1st Series	1970	—	60p
X6	1838 Astronomy 2nd Series	1970	—	60p
X6	1856 Beethoven	1973	—	60p
X6	1848 Bullfighting 1st Series	1970	—	60p
X6	1849 Bullfighting 2nd Series	1970	—	60p
X6	1825 Carabinieri (Military Police)	1968	—	£1.50
X6	1833 Chess Pieces	1969	—	60p
X6	1844 Conquest of the Moon 1st Series	1971	—	75p
X6	1851 Conquest of the Moon 2nd Series ...	1972	—	75p
X6	1818 Cradles	1967	—	60p
X6	1842 Dangerous Occupations 1st Series ...	1970	—	60p
X6	1843 Dangerous Occupations 2nd Series ...	1970	—	60p
X6	1824 Early Aviation	1968	—	75p
X6	1812 Ecumenical Councils	1966	—	60p
X6	1852 Famous Duels	1972	—	60p
X6	1819 Famous Places from "The Promised Bride"	1967	—	60p
X6	1841 Giovanni Pascoli	1970	—	60p
X6	1817 History of Photography	1965	—	£1.00
X6	1854 History of Typewriters	1972	—	60p
X6	1855 How Animals See 1st Series	1973	—	60p
X6	1858 How Animals See 2nd Series	1973	—	60p
X6	1832 Italian Aviation	1969	—	75p
X6	1836 Life & Works of Rossini	1969	—	60p
X6	1820 Life of Massimo D'Azeglio	1967	—	60p
X6	1795 Lithographic Art	1964	—	60p
X6	1834 Locomotives	1969	—	£1.00
X6	1831 Modern Aviation	1969	—	75p
X6	1828 Old Uniforms 1st Series	1968	—	75p
X6	1829 Old Uniforms 2nd Series	1968	—	75p
X6	1830 Old Uniforms 3rd Series	1968	—	75p
X6	1826 Philosophy & Science	1968	—	60p
X6	1764 Pinocchio	1962	—	75p
X6	1835 Principal Middle East States	1969	—	60p
X6	1801 Protected Birds	1964	—	75p
X6	1853 Resurrection (Paintings)	1972	—	60p
X6	1857 Search for Microbes 1st Series	1973	—	60p
X6	1860 Search for Microbes 2nd Series	1973	—	60p
X6	1850 Self Portraits	1972	—	60p
X6	1783 Story of Guns 1st Series	1962	—	£2.00
X6	1790 Story of Guns 2nd Series	1963	—	£1.00
X6	1859 Story of the Circus 1st Series	1973	—	75p
X6	1861 Story of the Circus 2nd Series	1974	—	75p
X6	1846 Symbols of Power 1st Series	1971	—	60p
X6	1847 Symbols of Power 2nd Series	1972	—	60p
X6	1863 The Animal Kingdom	1974	—	60p
X6	1862 Warships	1974	—	£1.00
X6	1771 World's Motorways	1962	—	60p

LIFEGUARD PRODUCTS (Soap)

Qty		Date	Odds	Sets
25	British Butterflies	1955	—	50p

JOSEPH LINGFORD & SON LTD. (Baking Powder)

Qty		Date	Odds	Sets
36	British War Leaders	1949	—	£12.50

LIPTON LTD. (Tea)

Qty		Date	Odds	Sets
60	Flags of the World	1967	—	£3.00
50	The Conquest of Space	1962	—	£2.00

LONGLEAT HOUSE

Qty		Date	Odds	Sets
25	Longleat House	1967	—	50p

LOT-O-FUN (Periodical)

Qty		Date	Odds	Sets
BF4	Champions	1922	£1.25	—

G. F. LOVELL & CO. LTD. (Confectionery)

Qty		Date	Odds	Sets
36	British Royalty Series	1910	£10.00	—
36	Football Series	1910	—	—
25	Photos of Football Stars	1926	£2.50	—

J. LYONS & CO. LTD. (Ice Cream & Tea)

Qty		Date	Odds	Sets
40	All Systems Go	1968	50p	£20.00
48	Australia	1959	6p	£1.00
25	Birds & Their Eggs	1962	—	75p
40	British Wildlife	1970	30p	£12.00
L16	Catweazle Magic Cards	1971	—	50p
40	European Adventure	1969	35p	—
40	Famous Aircraft	1965	6p	£1.50
40	Famous Cars	1966	50p	£20.00
40	Famous Locomotives	1964	75p	£30.00
48	Famous People	1966	25p	£12.50
32	HMS 1902-1962	1962	6p	75p
L35	Illustrated Map of the British Isles	1959	20p	£7.00
40	International Footballers	1972	40p	—
40	Into the Unknown	1969	40p	£16.00
15	Jubilee	1977	40p	£6.00
50	100 Years of Motoring	1964	30p	—
40	On Safari	1970	35p	£14.00
40	Pop Scene	1971	40p	—
40	Pop Stars	1970	40p	—
40	Soccer Stars	1971	40p	£16.00
40	Space Age Britain	1968	40p	£16.00
40	Space Exploration	1963	50p	£20.00
25	Space 1999	1976	40p	—
50	Train Spotters	1962	15p	£7.50
K100	Tricks & Puzzles	1926	75p	—
40	Views of London	1967	50p	£20.00
48	What Do You Know?	1957	6p	£1.50
24	Wings Across the World	1962	6p	50p
24	Wings of Speed (Advertisement Back)	1961	6p	£1.00
24	Wings of Speed (Descriptive Back)	1961	6p	50p

MACFISHERIES (Shops)

Qty		Date	Odds	Sets
L12	Gallery Picture	1924	35p	£4.25
L14	Japanese Colour Prints	1924	50p	£7.00

MACFISHERIES (Shops)—cont.

Qty		Date	Odds	Sets
L12	Poster Pointers	1925	30p	£3.50
L12	Sporting Prints	1923	50p	£6.00

MADDISON CONFECTIONERY PRODUCTIONS LTD.

X31	Christmas Greeting Cards	1957	£1.00	—
X48	Disc Jockey 1st Series	1957	30p	£15.00
X48	Disc Jockey 2nd Series	1958	50p	—
X50	Recording Stars	1958	40p	£20.00

MAGNET LIBRARY (Periodical)

BF15	Footballers	1922	75p	£12.50
BF6	Football Teams	1922	75p	£4.50
BF4	Football Teams	1923	75p	£3.00

MANCHESTER EVENING NEWS

L30	Footballers	1976	—	£4.00

MAPLE LEAF GUM

K90	Motor Car & Motor Cycle Badges (Metal)	1960	30p	—
K75	National Flags (Metal)	1960	25p	—

R. MARCANTONIO LTD. (Ice Lollies)

50	Interesting Animals	1953	—	75p

MARS CONFECTIONS LTD.

25	Ceremonies of the Coronation	1937	25p	£6.25
50	Famous Aeroplanes, Pilots & Airports	1938	30p	£15.00
50	Famous Escapes	1937	30p	£15.00
50	Famous Film Stars	1939	30p	£15.00
25	Wonders of the Queen Mary	1936	30p	£7.50

JAMES MARSHALL (GLASGOW) LTD. (Food)

1	Marshall's Products Illustrated	1926	—	£2.00
40	Recipes	1926	£2.00	—

MASTER VENDING CO. LTD. (Gum)

X25	A Bombshell for the Sheriff	1959	40p	£10.00
X50	Cardmaster Football Tips	1958	30p	£15.00
X16	Cricketer Series—New Zealand 1958	1958	40p	£6.50
X50	Did You Know? (Football)	1959	10p	£5.00
X100	Jet Aircraft of the World	1958	20p	£30.00
X25	Taxing the Sheriff	1959	16p	£4.00
X36	Tommy Steele	1958	40p	£15.00

MAXILIN MARKETING CO.

25	Motor Cars	1951	—	50p

MAYNARDS LTD. (Confectionery)

12	Billy Bunter Series	1926	£5.00	—
?20	Football Clubs	1926	£4.00	—
18	Girl Guide Series	1921	£3.00	—
50	Girls of All Nations	1921	£1.50	£75.00
12	Strange Insects	1935	£2.00	£24.00
8	The European War Series	1916	£6.00	—
12	Wonders of the Deep	1935	£2.00	£24.00
12	World's Wonder Series (Numbered)	1930	£2.00	—
10	World's Wonder Series (Unnumbered)	1930	£3.00	£30.00

MAYPOLE (Grocers)

Qty		Date	Odds	Sets
25	War Series	1915	£2.50	£62.50

MAZAWATTEE (Tea)

X39	Kings and Queens	1902	£2.00	£80.00

MEADOW DAIRY CO.

50	War Series	1915	£2.50	—

MELOX (Dog Food)

L50	Famous Breeds of Dogs	1937	£1.25	—

MERRYSWEETS LTD.

X48	Telegum TV Stars	1958	10p	£5.00
X48	World Racing Cars	1959	40p	—

GEOFFREY MICHAEL PUBLISHERS LTD.

40	Modern Motor Cars	1953	—	£3.00

MILK MARKETING BOARD

25	Prehistoric Animals	1963	—	60p

MILLERS (Tea)

25	Animals & Reptiles	1962	—	50p

MILLER

MF20	Tough Men of the Screen	1958	—	£1.50

ROBERT R. MIRANDA LTD. (Confectionery)

50	150 Years of Locomotives	1956	—	75p
50	100 Years of Motoring	1955	—	75p
25	Ships Through the Ages	1957	—	£2.50
50	Strange Creatures	1961	—	£1.00

MISTER SOFTEE LTD. (Ice Cream)

B20	County Badge Collection	1976	—	£2.00
M12	Did You Know?	1976	—	—
15	Moon Mission	1962	—	£5.00
L10	Steam Power	1978	—	£1.50
P12	Top Ten (Black Back)	1965	—	£1.00
P12	Top Ten (Blue Back, Different)	1964	—	60p
20	Top Twenty	1963	—	£1.25
25	TV Personalities	1962	—	—
P12	Your World	1963	—	75p

MITCHAM FOODS LTD.

25	Aircraft of Today	1955	—	£1.50
25	Aquarium Fish 1st Series	1957	—	£7.50
25	Aquarium Fish 2nd Series	1957	—	50p
50	Butterflies & Moths	1959	60p	£30.00
25	Footballers	1956	—	£1.00
50	Mars Adventure	1958	£1.00	—
25	Motor Racing	1960	—	£2.50

MOBIL OIL CO. LTD.

X36	The Story of Grand Prix Motor Racing	1971	—	£1.00
25	Veteran & Vintage Cars	1962	—	£6.00
24	Vintage Cars	1966	—	£1.50

THE MOLASSINE CO. (Dog Food)

Qty		Date	Odds	Sets
50	Dogs (Full Length)	1963	—	£7.50
50	Dogs (Heads)	1964	40p	—
25	Dogs at Work	1970	—	£1.00
12	Dogs of All Countries	1925	£2.00	£24.00
50	Puppies	1967	40p	—

MONTAGUE MOTOR MUSEUM

M24	Veteran & Vintage Cars	1965	—	£24.00

MONTY GUM

L72	Flag Parade	1972	—	£5.00
L72	International Football Teams	1970	—	£15.00
M54	Kojak (P/C Inset)	1976	—	£7.50
L56	Motor Cars (P/C Inset)	1956	—	£25.00
M124	The High Chaparral	1970	—	£7.50

MORNING FOODS LTD.

1	Advertisement Card	1953	—	40p
F25	British Planes	1953	—	£3.00
F50	British Trains	1952	£1.25	—
25	British Uniforms	1954	—	50p
50	Modern Cars	1954	—	£2.00
50	Our England	1955	—	£1.25
25	Test Cricketers	1953	—	£3.00
12	The Cunard Line (Black Back)	1957	—	50p
12	The Cunard Line (Blue Back)	1957	—	75p
25	World Locomotives (Black Back)	1954	—	50p
25	World Locomotives (Blue Back)	1954	—	£2.50

E. D. L. MOSELEY (Confectionery)

B25	Historical Buildings	1954	—	75p

V. MUHLENEN & CO. (Cheese)

B6	Swiss Views, Series III	1955	—	£3.00

MURCO PETROLEUM

B50	World's Airlines	1978	—	£1.50

MUSGRAVE BROS. LTD. (Tea)

25	Birds	1961	—	£1.00
25	Into Space	1961	—	60p
25	Modern Motor Cars	1962	—	£2.00
25	Pond Life	1963	—	£3.00
25	Products of the World	1961	—	50p
25	Tropical Birds	1964	—	50p
25	Wild Flowers	1961	—	50p

MYERS & METREVELI (Gum)

KF48	Film Stars	1953	50p	—
X48	Film Stars & Biographies	1953	£1.00	—
X60	Holywood Peep Show	1953	£1.00	—
L50	Spot the Planes	1953	£1.50	—

MY WEEKLY (Periodical)

M9	Battle Series (Silk)	1916	£3.00	£27.00
M12	Floral Beauties (Silk)	1914	£2.50	£30.00

MY WEEKLY (Periodical)—cont.

Qty		Date	Odds	Sets
M15	Language of Flowers (Silk)	1914	£2.50	—
M54	Lucky Emblems (Silk)	1912	£3.50	—
M6	Lucky Flowers (Silk)	1913	—	—
M12	Our Soldier Boys (Silk)	1915	£3.00	£36.00
M14	Soldiers of the King (Silk)	1915	£3.00	£42.00
M6	Sweet Kiss Series (Silk)	1913	£2.50	£15.00
M6	War Heroes (Silk)	1916	£3.00	£18.00

NABISCO FOODS LTD.

12	British Soldiers	1971	—	50p
12	E.T.	1983	—	£2.50
L24	Footballers	1970	30p	£7.50
L10	History of Aviation	1970	75p	£7.50
AUSTRALIAN ISSUES				
32	Leading Cricketers (Crispies etc.)	1948	£1.50	£48.00
M66	Popular Pets	1962	—	£4.00
L24	United Nations in Action	1968	—	£4.00

EDWARD NASSAR & CO. LTD. (Coffee, Gold Coast)

25	Transport, Present & Future	1955	—	£1.25

NATIONAL SPASTICS SOCIETY

24	Famous County Cricketers (Booklet)	1958	—	£10.00
24	Famous Footballers	1959	—	60p

NEILSONS (Confectionery)

50	Interesting Animals	1954	—	75p

NELSON LEE LIBRARY (Periodical)

BF15	Footballers	1922	65p	£10.00
BF6	Modern British Locomotives	1922	£3.00	£18.00

NESTLE LTD. (Chocolate)

L12	Animal Bars (Wrappers)	1970	—	50p
24	Animals of the World	1962	—	£3.50
49	Happy Families	1935	30p	£15.00
100	Stars of the Silver Screen Vol. I	1936	40p	—
50	Stars of the Silver Screen Vol. II	1937	40p	—
136	This England	1936	25p	—
X24	Wild Animals Series II	1910	£2.50	—
156	Wonders of the World Vol. I	1932	20p	—
144	Wonders of the World Vol. II	1933	20p	—

NEW ENGLAND CONFECTIONERY CO. (U.S.A.)

M12	Real Airplane Pictures	1929	50p	£6.00

NEW HOLLAND MACHINE CO.

P12	Traction Engines	1960	£1.25	£15.00

NEWS CHRONICLE (Newspaper)

L13	Barrow RFC	1955	—	£1.25
L11/13	Birmingham	1955	—	£1.50
L14	Blackburn Rovers FC	1955	—	£1.25
L12	Bradford City FC	1955	—	£1.25

NEWS CHRONICLE (Newspaper)—cont.

Qty		Date	Odds	Sets
L12/13	Bury FC	1955	—	£1.25
L11	Chesterfield FC	1955	—	£1.25
L12	Everton FC	1955	—	£1.25
L15	Manchester City FC	1955	—	£2.00
L12	Newcastle United FC	1955	—	£2.00
L14	Rochdale Hornets RFC	1955	—	£1.25
L13	Salford RFC	1955	—	£1.00
L13	Swinton RFC	1955	—	£1.00
L11	Workington AFC	1955	—	£1.25
L11	York City FC	1955	—	£1.25

NEWTON, CHAMBERS & CO. (Toilet Rolls)

P18	More Rhyme Time (19-36)	1934	£1.00	£18.00
P18	Nursery Rhymes (1-18)	1934	£1.00	£18.00

NEW ZEALAND BUTTER

X50	Super Cricket Card Series, 1982-3	1983	—	£6.00

NEW ZEALAND MEAT PRODUCERS BOARD

X25	Scenes of New Zealand Lamb	1930	£1.25	—

NORTHERN CO-OPERATIVE SOCIETY LTD. (Tea)

25	Birds	1963	—	—
25	History of the Railways 1st Series	1964	—	£2.00
25	History of the Railways 2nd Series	1964	—	£5.00
25	Passenger Liners	1963	—	50p
25	Then & Now	1963	—	£2.00
25	Tropical Birds	1962	—	60p
25	Weapons of World War II	1962	—	£3.00
25	Wonders of the Deep	1965	—	50p

NORTON'S (Shop)

25	Evolution of the Royal Navy	1965	—	£10.00

NUGGET POLISH CO.

X30	Allied Series	1910	£6.00	—
50	Flags of all Nations	1925	£2.50	—
X40	Mail Carriers and Stamps	1910	£6.00	—

NUNBETTA (Grocer)

25	Motor Cars	1955	£1.25	—

O.V.S. TEA

K25	Modern Engineering	1955	—	£2.00

TONY L. OLIVER (Commercial)

25	Aircraft of World War II	1964	—	—
50	German Orders & Decorations	1963	—	£5.00
50	German Uniforms	1971	—	£3.00
M25	Vehicles of the German Wehrmacht	1965	—	£12.50

OVALTINE (Beverage)

25	Do You Know?	1965	—	£2.00

OXO LTD. (Meat Extract)

K20	British Cattle	1934	£1.00	£20.00
15	Bull Series	1937	40p	£6.00

OXO LTD. (Meat Extract)—cont.

Qty		Date	Odds	Sets
K24	Feats of Endurance	1934	75p	£18.00
K20	Furs & Their Story	1932	£1.00	£20.00
K36	Lifeboats & Their History	1935	£1.00	£36.00
K30	Mystery Painting Pictures	1928	£1.00	£30.00
P6	Oxo Cattle Studies	1930	£6.00	—
25	Oxo Recipes	1936	80p	£20.00

P.M.R. ASSOCIATES LTD. (Commercial)

25	England, The World Cup, Spain '82	1982	—	75p

H. J. PACKER LTD. (Confectionery)

50	Humorous Drawings	1936	£1.00	£50.00

PAGE WOODCOCK WIND PILLS

20	Humorous Sketches by Tom Browne	1902	£10.00	—

PALS (Periodical)

B8	Famous Footballers	1922	£1.50	£12.00
BF12	Football Series	1922	80p	£10.00

PANINI (Commercial)

M268	World of Cricket '83 (with Album)	1983	—	£9.00

JAMES PASCALL LTD. (Confectionery)

48	Boy Scout Series	1912	£2.50	—
24	British Birds	1925	60p	£15.00
30	Devon Ferns	1927	75p	£22.50
30	Devon Flowers	1927	75p	£22.50
24	Devon Worthies	1927	£1.00	£24.00
18	Dogs	1924	£1.00	£18.00
10	Felix the Film Cat	1928	—	—
30	Flags & Flags with Soldiers	1905	£4.00	—
30	Glorious Devon	1929	75p	£22.50
36	Glorious Devon 2nd Series (Black Back) ...	1929	60p	£20.00
36	Glorious Devon 2nd Series (Green Back) ...	1929	60p	£20.00
2	King George V & Queen Mary	1910	—	—
44	Military Series	1912	—	—
20	Pascall's Specialities	1926	£4.00	—
12	Royal Naval Cadet Series	1912	£5.00	—
28	Town and other Arms	1914	—	—
50	Tricks & Puzzles	1926	£2.00	—
?13	War Portraits	1915	—	—

J. PATERSON & SON LTD. (Biscuits)

M48	Balloons	1960	—	£3.50

GEORGE PAYNE (Tea)

26	American Indian Tribes	1962	—	50p
25	British Railways	1962	—	50p
12	Characters from Dickens Works (numbered) ...	1912	£6.00	—
6	Characters from Dickens Works (unnumbered) ...	1912	£7.50	—
25	Dogs' Heads	1963	—	50p
25	Science in the 20th Century	1963	—	50p

PEEK FREAN & CO. (Biscuits)

Qty		Date	Odds	Sets
X12	English Scenes	1884	£4.00	—
X4	Shakespeare Scenes	1884	£4.00	—

PENNY MAGAZINE

BF12	Film Stars	1931	£1.25	—

PETERKIN (Foods)

B8	English Sporting Dogs	1930	£3.50	—

PETPRO LTD.

35	Grand Prix Racing Cars	1966	—	75p

PHILADELPHIA CHEWING GUM CORP.

X88	War Bulletin	1965	40p	£35.00

PHILATELIC POSTCARD PUBLISHING CO. (Commercial)

P10	Philatelic Anniversary Postcards Set 1	1983	—	£1.00
P12	Philatelic Anniversary Postcards Set 2	1983	—	£1.20
P10	Philatelic Anniversary Postcards Set 3	1983	—	£1.00

PHILLIPS (Tea)

25	Army Badges Past & Present	1964	—	50p
25	British Birds & Their Nests	1966	—	—
25	British Rail	1965	—	60p

PLANET LTD. (Gum)

X50	Racing Cars of the World	1965	60p	£30.00

PLANTERS NUT & CHOCOLATE CO. (U.S.A.)

M25	Hunted Animals	1933	30p	£7.50

PLUCK (Periodical)

BF27	Famous Football Teams	1922	60p	£15.00

POLAR PRODUCTS LTD. (Ice Cream, Barbados)

25	International Air Liners	1970	—	£4.00
25	Modern Motor Cars	1970	—	£4.00
25	Tropical Birds	1970	—	£4.00
25	Wonders of the Deep	1970	—	£4.00

H. POPPLETON & SONS (Confectionery)

50	Cricketers Series	1926	£6.00	—
16	Film Stars Series	1928	£1.50	—

POPULAR MOTORING (Periodical)

L4	P.M. Car Starter	1972	—	50p

POSTER STAMP ASSOCIATION

25	Modern Transport	1957	—	60p

PRESCOTT (Confectionery)

L36	Speed Kings	1966	—	£2.00

PRESCOTT-PICKUP & CO. (Commercial)

P15	Charles & Diana in Canada	1983	—	£1.50

PRESCOTT-PICKUP & CO. (Commercial)—cont.

Qty		*Date*	*Odds*	*Sets*
P30	Charles & Diana in the Antipodes	1983	—	£3.00
P6	Prince William (from above set)	1983	—	60p
P63	Falklands Task Force	1982	—	£6.00
	Special Album			£3.50
P60	Interregnum (Napoleonic Wars)	1978	—	£6.00
P60	Papal Visit	1982	—	£6.00
P60	Railway Locomotives	1977	—	£6.00
50	Railway Locomotives	1977	—	£1.25
P70	Royal Family—Birth of a Prince	1982	—	£7.00
	Special Album			£3.50
P60	The Royal Wedding	1981	—	£6.00
	Special Album			£3.50
P60	Thirty Years Elizabeth Regina	1982	—	£6.00
	Special Album			£3.50
P60	Tramcars & Tramways	1977	—	£6.00
P63	War in the South Atlantic	1983	—	£6.00

PRESTON DAIRIES (Tea)

25	Country Life	1966	—	50p

PRICES PATENT CANDLE CO. LTD.

P12	Famous Battles	1910	£4.00	£50.00

PRIMROSE CONFECTIONERY CO. LTD.

24	Action Man	1976	40p	—
50	Amos Burke—Secret Agent	1970	—	£10.00
50	Andy Pandy	1960	—	£1.00
50	Bugs Bunny	1964	—	£2.50
50	Burke's Law	1967	—	—
50	Chitty Chitty Bang Bang	1971	—	£1.00
50	Cowboy	1960	—	£1.50
25	Cup Tie Quiz	1973	—	50p
25	Dad's Army	1973	—	75p
50	Famous Footballers F.B.S.I.	1961	—	£2.50
25	Football Funnies	1974	—	75p
25	Happy Howlers	1975	—	60p
50	Joe 90	1969	—	—
50	Krazy Kreatures from Outer Space	1970	—	£1.25
50	Laramie	1964	—	£3.00
50	Laurel & Hardy	1968	—	—
50	Popeye	1960	—	—
50	Popeye 2nd Series	1961	—	£5.00
50	Popeye 3nd Series	1962	—	£1.25
50	Popeye 4th Series	1963	—	£1.25
50	Queen Elizabeth II	1969	—	£2.00
50	Quick Draw McGraw	1964	—	—
50	Space Patrol	1970	—	£1.25
50	Space Race	1969	—	£1.25
12	Star Trek	1971	—	75p
50	Superman	1968	—	£5.00
50	The Flintstones	1963	—	£1.00
50	Yellow Submarine	1968	—	£25.00
50	Z Cars	1968	—	£1.50

S. PRIOR (Bookshop)

25	Do You Know?	1964	—	—

PRIORY TEA CO. LTD.

Qty		Date	Odds	Sets
50	Aircraft	1961	—	£2.00
50	Birds	1962	—	£5.00
24	Bridges	1960	—	£1.25
24	Cars	1958	£1.00	£24.00
50	Cars (Different)	1964	—	£3.50
50	Cycles & Motorcycles	1963	40p	£20.00
24	Dogs	1957	—	50p
24	Flowering Trees	1959	—	50p
24	Men at Work	1959	—	£1.00
24	Out & About	1957	—	£1.00
24	People in Uniform	1956	60p	£15.00
24	Pets	1957	—	£1.00
50	Wild Flowers	1963	30p	£15.00

PROPERT SHOE POLISH

25	British Uniforms	1955	—	£1.00

PUKKA TEA CO. LTD.

50	Aquarium Fish	1961	—	£15.00

PYREX LTD. (Glassware)

P16	Guide to Simple Cooking	1976	—	£1.50

QUAKER OATS

X12	Armour Through the Ages	1968	25p	£3.00
M54	Historic Arms of Merrie England	1938	35p	—
X8	Historic Ships	1967	£1.25	—
X12	Prehistoric Animals	1967	£1.25	—
X12	Space Cards	1968	—	—
X12	Vintage Engines	1967	£1.50	£18.00

PACKAGE ISSUES

12	British Customs	1961	16p	£2.00
L36	British Landmarks	1961	20p	—
12	Famous Explorers	1961	16p	£2.00
12	Famous Inventors	1961	16p	£2.00
12	Famous Ships	1961	16p	£2.00
12	Famous Women	1961	16p	£2.00
12	Fascinating Costumes	1961	16p	£2.00
12	Great Feats of Building	1961	16p	£2.00
L36	Great Moments of Sport	1961	25p	—
12	History of Flight	1961	20p	£2.50
12	Homes & Houses	1961	16p	£2.00
L36	Household Hints	1961	20p	—
12	On the Seashore	1961	16p	£2.00
L36	Phiz Quiz	1961	20p	—
L36	Railways of the World	1961	25p	—
L36	The Story of Fashion	1961	20p	—
12	The Wild West	1961	16p	£2.00
12	Weapons & Armour	1961	16p	£2.00

QUEEN ELIZABETH LAUNDRY

45	Beauties	1912	£10.00	—

QUEENS (Laundry)

30	Kings & Queens of England	1955	—	£10.00

QUORN SPECIALITIES LTD. (Foods)

Qty		*Date*	*Odds*	*Sets*
25	Fish and Game	1963	£1.00	—

RADIO FUN (Periodical)

20	British Sports Stars	1956	—	50p

RADIO REVIEW (Periodical)

L36	Broadcasting Stars	1936	75p	£27.00
E20	Broadcasting Stars	1936	£1.00	—

RALEIGH BICYCLES

L48	Raleigh the All Steel Bicycle	1957	—	£20.00

REDDINGS TEA CO.

25	Castles of Great Britain	1965	60p	£15.00
25	Cathedrals of Great Britain	1964	60p	£15.00
25	Heraldry of Famous Places	1966	60p	£15.00
48	Ships of the World	1964	—	£1.00
25	Strange Customs of the World	1970	—	50p
48	Warriors of the World	1962	40p	£20.00

REDDISH MAID CONFECTIONERY

50	Famous International Aircraft	1955	£1.00	—
25	Famous International Athletes	1955	£1.00	—
25	International Footballers of Today	1955	£1.00	—

RED HEART (Pet Food)

P6	Cats	1954	—	£5.00
P6	Dogs	1953	—	£4.00
P6	Dogs 2nd Series	1953	—	£5.00
P6	Dogs 3rd Series	1954	—	£5.00

RED LETTER (Periodical)

P29	Charlie Chaplin Cards	1920	£3.00	—
X98	Midget Message Cards	1920	£1.25	—

REEVES LTD. (Confectionery)

25	Cricketers	1912	£7.50	—

REGENT OIL

X25	Do You Know?	1965	—	50p

RIDGWAY'S TEA

X20	Journey to the Moon	1958	£1.50	—

RINGTONS LTD. (Tea)

25	Aircraft of World War II	1962	—	£7.50
25	British Cavalry Uniforms of the 19th Century ...	1971	—	£2.00
25	Do You Know?	1964	—	50p
25	Fruits of Trees & Shrubs	1964	—	50p
25	Headdresses of the World	1973	—	50p
25	Historical Scenes	1964	—	50p
25	Old England	1964	—	50p
25	People & Places	1964	—	60p
25	Regimental Uniforms of the Past	1966	—	£1.25
25	Sailing Ships Through the Ages	1967	—	£1.25

RINGTONS LTD. (Tea)—cont.

Qty		Date	Odds	Sets
25	Ships of the Royal Navy	1961	—	75p
25	Sovereigns Consorts & Rulers 1st	1961	—	£2.00
25	Sovereigns Consorts & Rulers 2nd	1961	—	£2.00
25	The West	1968	—	£1.50
25	Then & Now	1970	—	—
25	Trains of the World	1970	—	50p

RISCA TRAVEL AGENCY

25	Holiday Resorts	1957	—	£7.50

D. ROBBINS & CO. (Commercial, U.S.A.)

P24	Frontiers of Freedom	1942	—	£10.00
P24	Good Neighbors of the Americas	1942	—	£10.00
P24	Indians of the U.S.A.	1942	—	£20.00
P24	Modern Wonders of the World	1942	—	£10.00
P24	Our Friend—The Dog	1942	—	£10.00
P24	Story of Transportation	1942	—	£10.00

ROBERTSON LTD. (Preserves)

10	Musical Gollywogs (Shaped)	1962	40p	—
10	Sporting Gollywogs (Shaped)	1962	40p	—

ROBERTSON & WOODCOCK LTD. (Confectionery)

50	British Aircraft Series	1930	75p	£37.50

ROBINSON BROS. & MASTERS (Tea)

25	Tea from the Garden to the Home	1930	£1.50	—

ROCHE & CO. LTD. (Matches)

K49/50	Famous Footballers	1927	75p	—

THE ROCKET (Periodical)

BF11	Famous Knockouts	1923	£1.00	£11.00

ROSSI'S (Ice Cream)

M48	Flags of the Nations	1975	10p	£4.00
	Album		—	50p
25	The History of Flight 1st Series	1963		£2.00
25	The History of Flight 2nd Series	1963		£2.00
25	World's Fastest Aircraft	1964		£1.50

ROWNTREE & CO. (Confectionery)

M20	Merrie Monarchs	1978	—	£1.50
M18	Prehistoric Monsters	1978	—	£1.25
L6	Punch & Judy Show	1976	—	£1.50
X42	Railway Engines (Caramac)	1976	—	£5.00
M10	Texan Tall Tales of the West	1977	30p	£3.00
48	The Old & The New	1934	£1.50	—

ROYAL NATIONAL LIFEBOAT INSTITUTION

M16	Lifeboats	1979	—	60p

ROYAL SOCIETY FOR PREVENTION OF ACCIDENTS

24	Modern British Cars	1954	20p	£5.00
22	Modern British Motor Cycles	1953	—	£7.50

ROYAL SOCIETY FOR PREVENTION OF ACCIDENTS—cont.

Qty		Date	Odds	Sets
25	New Traffic Signs	1958	—	£1.25
24	Veteran Cars 1st Series	1955	—	£3.50
24	Veteran Cars 2nd Series	1957	—	£7.50

ROYAL LEAMINGTON SPA

25	Royal Leamington Spa	1975	—	50p

RUBY (Periodical)

X10	Famous Beauties of the Day	1923	£1.25	£12.50
X6	Famous Film Stars	1923	£1.50	£9.00

SAGION STUFFING

28	Dominoes Without the Dot	1939	10p	£2.50

J. SAINSBURY LTD. (Groceries)

M12	British Birds	1924	£2.50	£30.00
M12	Foreign Birds	1924	£2.50	£30.00

SANDERS BROS. (Custard)

25	Birds, Fowls, Pigeons & Rabbits	1925	£1.00	£25.00
20	Dogs	1926	30p	£6.00
25	Recipes	1924	£1.00	£25.00

SANITARIUM HEALTH FOOD CO. (New Zealand)

X12	Animals of New Zealand	1974	—	£3.50
L30	Another Look at New Zealand	1971	—	£2.50
L30	Antarctic Adventure	1972	—	£3.50
L20	Cars of the Seventies	1976	—	£2.50
L20	Conservation—Caring for Our Land	1974	—	£2.00
L20	Discover Indonesia	1977	—	£2.00
L24	Famous New Zealanders	1971	—	£2.50
M30	Fascinating Orient	1974	—	£1.50
X12	Jet Aircraft	1974	—	£3.50
L20	Looking at Canada	1978	—	£2.00
L25	National Costumes of the Old World	1968	—	£3.50
L30	New Zealand National Parks	1973	—	£4.00
L20	New Zealand's Booming Industries	1975	—	£1.50
M30	New Zealand To-Day	1974	—	£3.00
L20	N.Z. Energy Resources	1976	—	£2.50
X12	N.Z.R. Steam Engines	1976	—	£4.00
L20	Spectacular Sports	1974	—	£2.50
L20	Super Cars	1972	—	£3.00
L20	The Story of New Zealand Aviation	1977	—	£3.00
L20	The Story of New Zealand in Stamps	1977	—	£3.50
L20	Timeless Japan	1975	—	£2.50
L20	Vintage Cars	1973	—	£3.50

SAVOY PRODUCTS LTD. (Foods)

M56	Aerial Navigation	1926	40p	—
M56	Aerial Navigation Series B	1927	40p	£22.50
M56	Aerial Navigation Series C	1928	40p	—
M56	Famous British Boats	1928	40p	£22.50

SCANLEN'S (Gum, Australia)

X90	World Series Cricket	1982	—	£10.00

THE SCHOOL FRIEND (Periodical)

Qty		Date	Odds	Sets
L6	Famous Film Stars	1927	£1.50	—
X10	Popular Girls of Cliff House School	1922	£4.00	—
XF6	Popular Pictures	1923	£1.50	—

THE SCHOOLGIRL (Periodical)

BF12	Zoological Studies	1923	£1.00	—

THE SCHOOLGIRLS WEEKLY (Periodical)

XF1	HRH The Duke of York	1922	—	£2.00
XF4	Popular Pictures	1922	£1.25	—

THE SCOUT (Periodical)

L9	Birds' Eggs	1925	£1.50	£13.50
M12	Railway Engines	1924	£2.00	£24.00

SCRAPBOOK MINICARDS

27	Pendon Museum (model railway etc.)	1978	—	60p

SECRETS (Periodical)

K52	Film Stars (Miniature Playing Cards)	1935	50p	£25.00

SELLOTAPE PRODUCTS LTD. (Adhesive Tape)

35	Great Homes & Castles	1974	—	£4.00

SEYMOUR MEAD & CO. LTD. (Tea)

24	The Island of Ceylon	1964	—	50p

SHARMAN (Newspapers)

T24	Golden Age of Flying	1979	—	£1.25
T24	Golden Age of Motoring	1979	—	£1.25
T24	Golden Age of Steam	1979	—	£1.25

EDWARD SHARP & SONS (Confectionery)

25	Hey Presto !	1970	—	50p
K53	Miniature Playing Cards	1924	£1.50	—
100	Prize Dogs	1924	£1.25	—

SHELL (Oil)

M16	Animals (3-D)	1975	40p	£1.60
14	Bateman Series	1930	£3.00	—
P20	Great Britons	1972	12p	£2.50
NEW ZEALAND ISSUES				
B48	Aircraft of the World	1970	—	£2.00
B60	Cars of the World	1970	—	£3.00
B48	Racing Cars of the World	1970	—	£2.50
40	Vintage Cars (Transfers)	1970	—	£2.00

SHEPHERD'S DAIRIES

100	War Series	1915	£3.00	—

SHERMANS POOLS LTD.

P8	Famous Film Stars	1940	7p	60p
P37	Famous Teams	1938	75p	—
P2/37	Famous Teams (Aston Villa/Blackpool)	1938	—	20p
P38	Searchlight on Famous Players	1937	£1.00	—

SHIPTON

Qty		Date	Odds	Sets
75	Trojan Gen Cards	1959	40p	£30.00

SHUREYS PUBLICATIONS LTD.

P?750	Views (Various Printings)	1906	30p	—

SINGER SEWING MACHINE CO. (U.S.A.)

P36	Costumes of All Nations	1892	£3.00	£100.00
P18	Costumes of All Nations (Different)	1894	£5.00	£90.00

SKETCHLEY CLEANERS

25	A Nature Series	1960	—	£2.00
25	Communications	1960	—	£2.50
25	Tropical Birds	1960	—	£4.00

SLADE & BULLOCK LTD. (Confectionery)

25	Cricket Series	1924	—	—
25	Football Terms	1924	—	—
25	Modern Inventions	1925	£2.50	—
20	Now & Then Series	1925	£3.00	—
25	Nursery Rhymes	1925	—	—
25	Science & Skill Series	1925	£2.50	—
25	Simple Toys & How to Make Them	1925	—	—

P. SLUIS (Bird Food)

X30	Tropical Birds	1962	—	£2.50

SMART NOVELS (Periodical)

BF12	Stage Artistes & Entertainers	1924	£1.00	—

JOHN SMITH (Brewers)

P5	Limericks (Beer Mats)	1976	—	£1.00

SNAP CARDS (Gum)

L50	ATV Stars 1st Series	1960	40p	£20.00
L48	ATV Stars 2nd Series	1959	20p	£10.00
L50	Associated Rediffusion Stars	1960	40p	£20.00
L50	Dotto	1959	25p	£12.50

H. A. SNOW (Films)

12	Hunting Big Game in Africa	1923	£2.00	£24.00

SOCCER BUBBLE GUM

M48	Soccer Teams No. 1 Series	1960	—	£3.50
M48	Soccer Teams No. 2 Series	1961	30p	£15.00

SODASTREAM (Confectionery)

25	Historical Buildings	1957	—	50p

SOMPORTEX LTD. (Gum Vending)

L60	Famous TV Wrestlers	1966	80p	—
X60	Film Scene Series James Bond 007	1966	80p	—
L72	John Drake Danger Man	1966	75p	—
L50	The Exciting World of James Bond 007	1965	£1.00	—
L72	The Saint	1967	£1.00	—
L72	Thunderball	1967	30p	—

SOMPORTEX LTD. (Gum Vending)—cont.

Qty		Date	Odds	Sets
X73	Thunderbirds (Coloured)	1967	£1.00	—
X72	Thunderbirds (Black/White)	1967	75p	£55.00
X36	Weirdies	1968	40p	£15.00
26	You Only Live Twice (Film Strips)	1969	—	—

SOUTH WALES CONSTABULARY

X36	British Stamps	1983	—	£6.00
X35	The '82 Squad (Rugby)	1982	50p	—

SPAR GROCERS

X30	Disney on Parade	1972	—	£6.00

SPILLERS NEPHEWS (Biscuits)

25	Conundrum Series	1910	£7.50	—
40	Views of South Wales & District	1910	£7.50	—

SPORT AND ADVENTURE (Periodical)

M46	Famous Footballers	1922	60p	£30.00

SPRATTS PATENT LTD. (Pet Food)

K100	British Bird Series (Numbered)	1935	£1.00	—
K50	British Bird Series (Unnumbered)	1935	75p	—
42	British Birds	1926	£1.00	—
36	Champion Dogs	1926	£1.25	—
K20	Fish	1935		—
K100	Poultry Series	1935	£1.50	—
25	The Bonzo Series	1924	£1.50	£37.50

STAMP CORNER

25	American Indian Tribes	1963		£7.50

STAR JUNIOR CLUB

10	Animals	1960	50p	—
10	Sports & Games (Numbered)	1960	50p	—
5	Sports & Games (Unnumbered)	1960	50p	—

STOLL (Films)

25	Stars of To-day	1930	£3.00	—
25	The Mystery of Dr. Fu-Manchu	1930	£4.00	—

STOLLWERCK (Chocolate)

T144	Animal World	1902	50p	—

THE SUN (Newspaper)

M134	Football Swap Cards	1970	12p	£16.00
1000	Soccercards	1980		£25.00
P50	3D Gallery of Football Stars	1975	20p	—

SUNBLEST TEA

25	Inventions & Discoveries 1st Series	1960	—	—
25	Inventions & Discoveries 2nd Series	1960	—	—
25	Prehistoric Animals 1st Series	1960	—	£1.25
25	Prehistoric Animals 2nd Series	1960	—	£1.25

SUNBLEST (Australia)

M25	Sunblest Explorer Cards	1975	—	£2.50

SUNDAY STORIES (Periodical)

Qty		Date	Odds	Sets
M5	Flags (Silk)	1916	£5.00	—
M6	The King & His Soldiers (Silk)	1916	£5.00	—

SWEETACRE (Confectionery, Australia)

36	Cricketers (Minties)	1926	£4.00	£150.00
24	Cricketers (Caricatures)	1938	£5.00	—
32	Prominent Cricketers (33-64)	1932	£2.00	£65.00
48	Sports Champions	1930	£1.00	—
32	Test Records (1-32)	1932	£2.00	£65.00

SWEETULE PRODUCTS LTD. (Confectionery)

18	Aircraft (Packet)	1954	£1.00	£18.00
25	A Nature Series	1960	—	£1.25
25	Animals of the Countryside	1959	—	60p
25	Archy Andrews Jokes	1957	£1.25	—
25	Birds & Their Eggs	1954	—	60p
25	Birds & Their Eggs (Black Back)	1959	—	£1.00
25	Birds & Their Eggs (Blue Back)	1959	—	£1.00
25	Birds & Their Haunts	1958	£1.50	—
52	Birds, Fish & Flowers (P/C Inset)	1961	—	£4.00
25	Birds of the British Commonwealth (Black Back)	1954	—	75p
25	Birds of the British Commonwealth (Blue Back)	1954	—	75p
M12	Coronation Series (Packet)	1953	£2.00	—
25	Do You Know?	1963	—	75p
25	Family Crests	1961	—	75p
25	Famous Sports Records	1957	—	75p
25	Football Club Nicknames	1959	—	75p
K18	Historical Cars & Cycles	1957	—	£1.00
18	Home Pets (Packet)	1954	£1.50	—
25	International Footballers (Packet)	1962	£1.00	£25.00
25	Junior Service Quiz	1959	—	60p
18	Landmarks of Flying (Packet)	1961	£1.00	£18.00
50	Modern Aircraft	1954	—	75p
25	Modern Transport	1955	—	50p
18	Motor Cars (Packet)	1952	—	—
50	Motor Cycles Old & New	1963	—	£12.50
30	National Flags & Costumes	1962	—	£4.50
25	Naval Battles	1959	—	75p
25	Products of the World	1958	—	60p
18	Railway Engines—Past & Present (Packet)	1953	£1.50	—
25	Sports Quiz	1958	—	£1.00
1	Stamp Card (Real Stamp Attached)	1962	—	15p
25	Stamp Series	1961	—	£1.00
25	The Wild West (Black Back)	1960	—	£1.00
25	The Wild West (Blue Back)	1960	—	75p
X30	Trains of the World	1960	—	—
25	Treasure Island	1957	—	£1.25
25	Tropical Birds	1954	—	60p
25	Vintage Cars	1964	—	75p
25	Weapons of Defence	1959	—	60p
25	Wild Animals	1958	—	50p
25	Wild Flowers	1961	—	50p
25	Wonders of the World	1956	—	50p

SWETTENHAM (Tea)

Qty		Date	Odds	Sets
25	Aircraft of the World	1959	—	£2.50
25	Animals of the Countryside	1959	—	75p
25	Birds & Their Eggs	1958	—	60p
25	British Coins & Costumes	1958	—	75p
25	Butterflies & Moths	1958	—	50p
25	Evolution of the Royal Navy	1957	—	60p
25	Into Space	1959	—	75p
25	The Island of Ceylon (Conqueror Tea)	1964	£1.00	—
25	Wild Animals	1958	—	£2.50

W. SWORD & CO. (Biscuits)

25	British Empire at Work	1925	£4.00	—
20	Dogs	1926	£4.00	—
20	Inventors & their Inventions	1926	£4.00	—
25	Safety First	1927	£4.00	—
25	Sports & Pastimes Series	1926	£5.00	—
25	Vehicles of all Ages	1924	£4.00	—
25	Zoo Series (brown)	1928	£3.00	—
25	Zoo Series (coloured)	1928	£4.00	—

TEACHER'S WHISKY

L12	Scottish Clans & Castles (circular)	1955	40p	£5.00

TEASDALE & CO. (Confectionery)

25	Great War Series	1916	£5.00	—

TETLEY TEA

48	British Birds	1970	—	£7.50

D. C. THOMSON & CO. LTD. (Periodical)

L30	Adventure Pictures	1929	75p	£22.50
B16	Badges of the Fighting Fliers	1939	60p	£10.00
P26	Battles for the Flag	1939	£1.25	—
K80	Boys of All Nations	1935	30p	—
20	British Birds & Their Eggs	1930	75p	£15.00
F11	British Team of Footballers	1923	60p	£6.50
L20	Canvas Masterpieces (Silk)	1925	£2.50	—
16	Catch-My-Pal Cards	1939	60p	£10.00
X12	Coloured Photos of Star Footballers	1927	£1.25	—
64	County Cricketers	1955	75p	£50.00
16	Cricket Crests	1934	£2.50	£40.00
KF8	Cricketers	1923	60p	£5.00
X24	Cricketers	1933	£3.00	—
12	Dandy Dogs	1928	£1.00	—
K28	Dominoes—School Caricatures	1936	75p	—
20	Easy Scientific Experiments	1930	75p	£15.00
BF18	Famous British Footballers (English)	1923	40p	£7.00
K80	Famous Feats	1935	30p	—
25	Famous Footballers	1955	40p	£10.00
24	Famous Footballers (Different)	1956	40p	£10.00
20	Famous Liners	1930	£1.50	£30.00
L32	Famous Ships	1932	£1.25	—
16	Flags of All Nations	1934	75p	£12.00
K80	Flags of the Sea	1935	30p	—

D. C. THOMSON & CO. LTD. (Periodical)—cont.

Qty		Date	Odds	Sets
KF137	Footballers	1923	25p	—
X8	Footballers	1933	£1.25	—
F18	Footballers	1923	40p	£7.50
K52	Footballers—Hunt the Cup Cards	1937	50p	£25.00
24	Footballers—Motor Cars (Double-Sided)	1928	£1.50	£36.00
BF22	Footballers—Signed Real Photos (English)	1923	40p	£9.00
F40	Football Photos	1925	£1.50	—
48	Football Stars	1957	30p	£15.00
44	Football Stars of 1959	1959	30p	£13.00
K61/64	Football Team Cards	1934	25p	£15.00
64	Football Tips & Tricks	1955	30p	£20.00
L32	Football Towns & Their Crests	1932	£1.50	—
12	Guns in Action	1938	60p	£7.50
M8	Hidden Treasure Clue Cards	1930	£5.00	—
6	Ju Jitsu Cards	1925	£1.50	£9.00
24	Motor Bike Cards	1926	£2.00	—
20	Motor Cycles	1930	£2.00	£40.00
K100	Motor Cars	1934	30p	—
36	1930 Speedway Stars	1930	£1.50	—
K80	Punishment Cards	1935	30p	—
12	Queer Animals	1928	75p	—
16	Queer Birds	1934	75p	£12.00
K80	Secrets of Cricket	1935	75p	—
36	Spadgers Monster Collection of Spoofs	1936	50p	—
48	Speed	1937	40p	£20.00
12	Speedsters of the Wilds	1928	75p	—
48	Stars of Sport & Entertainment	1960	40p	£20.00
P22	Star Teams of 1961	1961	50p	£11.00
20	The Wireless Telephone	1930	75p	£15.00
32	The World's Best Cricketers (Green Back)	1932	60p	£18.00
36	The World's Best Cricketers (Mauve Back)	1930	£2.50	£90.00
72	The World's Best Cricketers	1958	75p	£54.00
X12	The World's Biggest	1937	£4.00	—
24	This Year's Top Form Footballers	1924	50p	£12.00
10	Vanguard Photo Gallery	1923	£4.00	—
96	VP Flips	1925	60p	—
24	Warrior Cards (Sectional Back)	1936	60p	£15.00
K28	Warrior Cards (Domino Back)	1936	60p	£17.00
K80	Warrior Cards	1935	30p	—
20	Why?	1930	75p	£15.00
K28	Wild West Dominoes	1936	75p	—
20	Wonders of the Rail	1930	£2.00	£40.00
20	Wonders of the World	1930	75p	£15.00
64	World Cup Footballers	1958	40p	£25.00

THURMER & SYMES (Biscuits)

B96	Ocean Giants	1954	75p	—

TIMARU MILLING CO. (Cereals, New Zealand)

36	Focus on Fame	1948	—	£6.00
37	Peace & Progress	1947	—	£6.00
36	Victory Album Cards	1946	—	£7.50

TIMES CONFECTIONERY CO. LTD.

Qty		Date	Odds	Sets
BF24	Roy Rogers—In Old Amarillo (Plain Back) ...	1955	—	50p
B24	Roy Rogers—In Old Amarillo (Printed Back) ...	1955	—	£2.00
BF24	Roy Rogers—South of Caliente (Plain Back) ...	1955	—	50p
B24	Roy Rogers—South of Caliente (Printed Back)	1955	—	£2.00

TIP TOP (Ice Cream, New Zealand)

M10	Galactic Bar	1977	—	£3.00
M15	R2D2 Space Ice	1977	—	£5.00

TIT-BITS (Periodical)

K54	Pin-Ups (P/C Inset)	1976	—	75p
TF17	Star Cover Girls	1953	£1.00	—

CHOCOLAT TOBLER LTD.

50	Famous Footballers	1939	£1.00	—
T192	General Interest Series	1900	50p	—

TOMMY GUN (Toys)

50	Medals (Plain Back)	1971	—	75p

TOM THUMB (New Zealand)

M24	Supercars	1980	—	£2.00

TONIBELL (Ice Cream)

12	Action Soldiers	1976	—	75p
M20	Banknotes	1974	12p	£2.50
L12	Beautiful Butterflies	1974	12p	£1.50
M20	County Badges	1974	8p	£1.50
25	Did You Know?	1963	—	50p
L12	Did You Know?	1975	25p	—
X12	England's Soccer Stars	1970	—	£7.00
D19	Famous Sports Trophies	1976	—	£3.00
D12	Farmyard Stencils	1977	—	£3.00
M24	1st Division Football League Club Badges ...	1978	40p	£10.00
25	Inventions that Changed the World	1963	—	50p
X10	Junior Champs	1983	25p	£2.50
K36	Team of all Time	1971	50p	—
25	The World's Passenger Liners	1963	—	50p
25	This Changing World (With "LTD")	1963	—	75p
25	This Changing World (Without "LTD") ...	1963	—	£1.25
25	Wonders of the Heavens	1963	—	£1.50

TOP FLIGHT (Confectionery)

25	Top Flight Stars	1959	—	£1.50

TOPICAL TIMES (Periodical)

BF8	Football Teams	1924	£1.00	£8.00
L24	Great Players	1938	60p	£15.00
C24	Miniature Panel Portraits	1937	60p	£15.00
E?120	Panel Portraits	1932	75p	—
E16	Panel Portraits (coloured)	1939	£1.25	£20.00
C24	Stars of To-day	1938	60p	£15.00

TOPPS CHEWING GUM INC.

X99	Autos of 1977	1977	20p	—
X132	Battlestar Galactica	1979	10p	—

TOPPS CHEWING GUM INC.—cont.

Qty		*Date*	*Odds*	*Sets*
X66	Bay City Rollers	1978	10p	—
X49	Comic Book Heroes	1977	20p	£10.00
X220	Footballers (Red Back)	1975	10p	—
X88	Footballers (Scottish, Blue Back)	1975	20p	—
X330	Footballers (Blue Back)	1976	10p	—
X132	Footballers (Scottish, Red Back)	1976	20p	—
X330	Footballers (Red Back)	1977	10p	—
X132	Footballers (Scottish, Yellow Back)	1977	20p	—
X396	Footballers (Orange Back)	1978	6p	£12.00
X132	Footballers (Scottish Green Back)	1978	10p	—
X396	Footballers (Pale Blue Back)	1979	10p	—
X132	Footballers (Scottish, Red Back)	1979	10p	—
X66	Footballers (Pink Back)	1980	10p	—
X65	Footballers (Blue Back)	1981	10p	—
E18	Football Posters	1980	10p	—
X21	Funny Puzzles	1978	20p	—
X49	Marvel Super Heroes	1980	—	£5.00
X66	Planet of the Apes	1974	10p	£5.00
X50	Shocking Laffs	1977	15p	—
X88	Star Trek, The Motion Picture	1980	—	—
X66	Star Wars (1-66)	1978	10p	—
X66	Star Wars (1A-66A)	1978	10p	—
X66	Superman the Movie 1st Series (1-66)	1979	—	£4.00
X66	Superman the Movie 2nd Series (67-132)	1979	—	£4.00
X88	The Black Hole	1980	10p	£5.00
X42	Wanted Posters	1978	15p	—
U.S. ISSUES				
X88	Buck Rogers in the 25th Century	1979	—	£4.00
X55	Mysteries of India	1967	—	£10.00
X88	Raiders of the Lost Ark	1981	—	£6.00

JOHN TORDOFF & SON LTD. (Tea)

25	Safety First	1926	£2.00	—
25	The Growth and Manufacture of Tea	1926	£3.00	—

TOWER TEA

24	Illustrated Sayings	1910	£7.50	—

TREBOR/SHARP (Confectionery)

25	Famous Pets	1972	—	50p

TRUCARDS (Commercial)

M30	Animals	1972	—	50p
M30	Battle of Britain	1972	—	50p
M30	Flowers	1972	—	50p
M30	History of Aircraft	1972	—	50p
M30	Sport	1972	—	50p
M30	Veteran and Vintage Cars	1972	—	£1.00
M30	World War I	1972	—	50p
M30	World War II	1972	—	50p

TUCKETT'S (Confectionery)

25	Photos of Cricketers	1925	£7.50	—
50	Photos of Film Stars	1935	£2.00	—

W. & E. TURNER (Shoes)

Qty		Date	Odds	Sets
20	War Pictures	1915	£3.00	—

TWININGS TEA

Qty		Date	Odds	Sets
30	Rare Stamps	1960	25p	£7.50
30	Rare Stamps 2nd Series	1960	6p	£1.25
30	Rare Stamps 2nd Series (Red Overprint)	1961	—	50p

TYDOL GASOLINE (U.S.A.)

Qty		Date	Odds	Sets
X40	Aeroplanes	1937	—	£25.00

TYPHOO TEA LTD.

Qty		Date	Odds	Sets
25	Aesop's Fables	1924	80p	£20.00
25	Ancient & Annual Customs	1922	60p	£15.00
T25	Animal Friends of Man	1927	£1.50	£37.50
T25	Animal Offence & Defence	1926	30p	£7.50
T25	A Tale of Two Cities	1931	80p	£20.00
24	British Birds & Their Eggs	1914	£2.50	£60.00
T25	British Birds & Their Eggs	1936	16p	£4.00
29/30	British Empire at Work	1925	60p	£17.50
25	Calendar 1934	1933	—	—
25	Calendar 1936	1935	£4.00	—
T1	Calendar 1937	1936	—	£2.00
T25	Characters from Shakespeare	1937	12p	£2.50
25	Common Objects Highly Magnified	1925	50p	£12.50
25	Conundrums	1915	£5.00	—
T30	David Copperfield	1929	£1.00	£30.00
24	Do You Know?	1962	—	50p
T25	Famous Voyages	1934	30p	£7.50
M20	Flags & Arms of Countries	1916	£4.00	—
24	Great Achievements	1962	—	£6.00
T25	Historic Buildings	1936	24p	£6.00
T25	Homes of Famous Men	1934	20p	£5.00
T25	Horses	1935	24p	£6.00
T25	Important Industries of the British Empire	1939	12p	£2.00
T25	Interesting Events in British History	1938	12p	£2.00
T25	John Halifax—Gentleman	1932	80p	£20.00
T25	Lorna Doone	1930	£1.50	£37.50
10	Nursery Rhymes	1914	£7.50	£75.00
24	Our Empire's Defenders	1916	£7.50	—
48	Puzzle Series	1913	£7.50	—
T30	Robin Hood & His Merry Men	1928	£1.25	£37.50
M12	The Amazing World of Dr Who	1976	—	£4.00
T25	The Swiss Family Robinson	1935	12p	£2.50
24	Travel Through the Ages	1962	—	50p
T25	Trees of the Countryside	1938	12p	£3.00
T25	Whilst We Sleep	1928	80p	£20.00
24	Wild Flowers	1961	—	75p
T25	Wild Flowers in their Families	1936	16p	£4.00
T25	Wild Flowers in their Families 2nd Series	1937	12p	£2.00
T26	Wonder Cities of the World	1933	60p	£15.00
M24	Wonderful World of Disney	1975	—	£12.50
T25	Work on the Farm	1933	60p	£15.00
25	Zoo Series	1932	20p	£5.00

TYPHOO TEA LTD.—cont.

Qty		Date	Odds	Sets
PACKAGE ISSUES				
20	By Pond & Stream	1955	12p	£2.50
20	Common British Birds	1955	12p	£2.50
20	Costumes of the World	1955	12p	£2.50
24	Do You Know?	1962	20p	—
20	Famous Bridges	1955	12p	£2.50
20	Famous Buildings	1955	12p	£2.50
24	Famous Football Clubs	1962	15p	£3.50
24	Famous Football Clubs, 2nd Series	1963	25p	£6.00
35	Football Club Plaques	1973	35p	—
24	Football Stars, New Series	1973	35p	—
24	Great Voyages of Discovery	1962	25p	—
24	International Football Stars	1964	30p	—
24	International Football Stars, 2nd Series	1969	30p	—
24	100 Years of Great British Achievements ...	1972	30p	—
20	Pets	1955	12p	£2.50
20	Some Countryside Animals	1955	12p	£2.50
20	Some Popular Breeds of Dogs	1955	12p	£2.50
20	Some World Wonders	1955	12p	£2.50
24	Travel Through the Ages	1962	20p	—
20	Types of Ships	1955	12p	£2.50
20	Wild Animals	1955	12p	£2.50
24	Wild Flowers	1961	20p	—
PREMIUM ISSUES				
E24	Famous Football Clubs	1964	£1.50	£36.00
E24	Famous Football Clubs, 2nd Series	1965	£1.50	£36.00
E24	Football Stars	1973	£1.50	£36.00
G24	Great Voyages of Discovery	1967	£1.50	—
E24	International Football Stars	1969	£1.50	£36.00
G24	100 Years of British Achievements	1972	—	£7.50

TYSON & CO. (Soap)

28	Semaphore Signals	1912	£5.00	—

UNION JACK (Periodical)

BF6	Monarchs of the Ring	1923	£1.00	£6.00
B8	Police of All Nations	1922	£1.50	£12.00

UNITED AUTOMOBILE SERVICES

25	Castles (Series No. 1)	1925	£2.00	—
25	Churches (Series No. 2)	1925	£2.00	—
25	Places of Interest (Series No. 4)	1925	£2.00	—
25	"United" (Series No. 3)	1925	£2.00	—

UNITED DAIRIES

25	Aquarium Fish	1962	—	60p
25	Birds & Their Eggs	1961	—	50p
25	British Uniforms of the 19th Century ...	1962	—	£1.25
25	The Story of Milk	1966	—	£2.50
25	The West	1963	—	£1.00

UNIVERSAL AUTOMATICS LTD.

X30	Trains of the World	1958	—	£7.50

VAL GUM

Qty		Date	Odds	Sets
L144	Animals of the World	1954	50p	—
L144	Birds of the World	1954	50p	—
L292	Film Stars	1954	40p	—
L50	Footballers	1935	60p	—
L48	Natural History Sketches	1954	—	—
L72	Popeye	1954	—	—
L?	Shirley Temple Cards	1935	—	—

VERKADE'S FABRIEKEN N.V. (Biscuits, Holland)

X140	De Bloemen En Haar Vrienden	1933	—	£7.00
X140	De Boerderij	1935	—	£8.00
X138	Hans De Torenkraai	1936	—	£8.00
X132	Kamerplanten	1928	—	£15.00
X126	Mijn Aquarium	1925	—	£12.50

CHOCOLAT DE VILLARS

24	British Birds & their Eggs	1926	£1.00	£24.00

VOMO AUTOMATICS

X50	Flags of the World	1965	30p	£15.00

JONATHAN WALES LTD.

25	The History of Flight 1st Series	1963	£1.00	—
25	The History of Flight 2nd Series	1963	£1.00	—

WALKER, HARRISON & GARTHWAITE LTD. (Dog Food)

M15	Dogs	1902	£2.50	—

T. WALL & SONS (Ice Cream)

24	Do You Know?	1965	—	£1.00
36	Dr Who Adventure	1966	—	£20.00
48	Moon Fleet	1967	—	£2.00
M6	Prehistoric Animals (Magicards)	1971	—	50p
P6	Sea Creatures	1971	—	50p
20	Skateboard Surfer	1978	—	60p

WALTERS PALM TOFFEE

50	Some Cap Badges of Territorial Regiments	1938	10p	£5.00

WAND CONFECTIONERY LTD.

X10	Chubby Checker—How to do the Twist	1964	—	—
25	Commemoration Stamp Series	1963	£1.20	£30.00
X35	Pop D.J.'s	1964	£1.00	£35.00
25	They Gave Their Name	1963	—	£5.00
23/25	They Gave Their Name	1963	—	£1.00

WARWICK DISTRICT COUNCIL

30	England's Historic Heartland	1980	—	£1.25

WEBCOSA & CO.

X20	Trail Town	1963	50p	£10.00

WEEKLY WELCOME (Periodical)

12	Lest We Forget Cards	1916	£3.00	—

WEETABIX LTD. (Cereals)

TS25	Animal Cards	1962	—	60p
B28	Asterix—His Friends & Foes	1976	10p	—

WEETABIX LTD. (Cereals)—cont.

Qty		Date	Odds	Sets
TS25	British Bird Cards	1962	50p	—
TS25	British Cars	1963	60p	—
L25	Conquest of Space, Series A	1959	—	£3.00
L25	Conquest of Space, Series B	1959	—	£3.00
B25	Dr Who (Coloured Background)	1977	—	—
B24	Dr Who (White Background)	1975	—	—
TS25	Our Pet Cards	1961	—	60p
L25	The Western Story	1959	—	£1.00
TS25	Thrill Cards	1960	50p	—
TS25	Working Dog Cards	1961	—	£2.00

JAMES O. WELSH (Confectionery, U.S.A.)

50	Comics	1950	—	£40.00

WELSH RUGBY UNION

50	Great Welsh Rugby Players	1981	—	£1.00

WESTCO (Confectionery)

F60	Westco Autocards	1954	£1.00	—

J. WEST FOODS LTD.

M8	Famous Sea Adventures	1972	—	50p

WEST LONDON SYNAGOGUE

50	Jewish Life in Many Lands	1961	—	£5.00
50	Jewish Symbols & Ceremonies	1961	—	£2.00
25/50	Jewish Symbols & Ceremonies	1961	—	50p

WESTON BISCUIT CO. LTD. (Australia)

L24	Veteran & Vintage Cars 2nd Series	1962	—	£1.50

WEST RIDING COUNTY COUNCIL

20	Health Cards	1924	£1.50	—

WHITBREAD & CO. LTD. (Brewers)

M1	Duke Without a Head	1958	—	£1.00
M50	Inn Signs, 1st Series (Metal)	1951	80p	£40.00
M50	Inn Signs, 2nd Series (Metal)	1951	80p	£40.00
M50	Inn Signs, 3rd Series (Metal)	1952	£1.00	£50.00
M50	Inn Signs, 3rd Series (Card)	1952	£1.25	—
M50	Inn Signs, 4th Series	1952	80p	£40.00
M50	Inn Signs, 5th Series	1953	80p	£40.00
M25	Inn Signs, Bournemouth	1973	75p	—
M25	Inn Signs, Devon & Somerset	1973	60p	£15.00
M25	Inn Signs, Isle of Wight	1974	75p	—
M25	Inn Signs, Kent	1973	75p	—
M15	Inn Signs, London	1973	50p	—
M10	Inn Signs, London (Different)	1974	60p	—
M25	Inn Signs, Marlow	1973	75p	—
M25	Inn Signs, Portsmouth	1973	75p	—
M4	Inn Signs, Special Issue	1955	75p	£3.00
M25	Inn Signs, Stratford-Upon Avon	1974	75p	—
M25	Inn Signs, West Pennines	1973	75p	—
M25	Maritime Inn Signs	1974	20p	£5.00
M1	The Britannia Inn	1958	—	£15.00
M1	The Railway	1958	—	£1.00
M1	The Startled Saint	1958	—	£12.50

WHITE FISH AUTHORITY

Qty		Date	Odds	Sets
25	The Fish We Eat	1954	—	50p

WHITEHAVEN LIBRARY

M6	The Port of Whitehaven	1978	—	50p

WHITEHEAD (Lollies)

X25	Kings & Queens	1980	—	£1.00

WIKO (Confectionery, Germany)

50	Soldaten Der Welt	1969	—	£1.00

WILCOCKS & WILCOCKS LTD. (Tea)

25	Birds	1965	—	—
25	British Cavalry Uniforms of the 19th Century ...	1963	—	£2.50
25	Garden Flowers	1964	—	75p
25	Passenger Liners	1967	—	£5.00
25	People & Places	1966	—	75p
25	Tropical Birds	1965	—	£1.25
25	Wonders of the Deep	1965	—	£1.25
25	Wonders of the World	1971	—	£2.50

A. S. WILKIN LTD. (Confectionery)

25	Into Space	1960	—	£1.25

WILKINSON LTD. (Tools)

K4	Wilkinson Tools	1962	25p	£1.00

W. R. WILKINSON & CO. (Confectionery)

B25	Footballers	1956	£1.50	—

WIMPY (Restaurants)

M20	Super Heroes Super Villains	1979	30p	£6.00

WOMAN'S FRIEND (Periodical)

K52	Fortune Telling Cards	1925	50p	—

WOMAN'S OWN (Periodical)

F8	Film Stars	1955	£1.00	£8.00

WRIGHTS BISCUITS LTD.

24	Marvels of the World	1954	—	50p
24	Mischief Goes to Mars (Mischief Club)	1954	—	60p
24	Mischief Goes to Mars (Wright Ltd.)	1954	—	50p

YORKSHIRE WATER AUTHORITY

X10	Know Your Reservoirs	1983	—	£2.00

YOUNG BRITAIN (Periodical)

BF15	Favourite Cricketers Series	1922	£2.00	£30.00

SPECIAL OFFERS

8 different pre 1940 sets, our selection (no pages)	**£7.50**
40 different post 1945 sets, our selection	**£10.00**
8 different sets of Trucards	**£3.00**
Liebig starter selection. 19 modern sets + 1 pre 1914	**£7.00**
20 different cigarette packets, mainly unusual	**£5.00**
Book selection. Cigarette Cards & Novelties + 2 Jacob's albums complete (Famous Picture Cards, Banknotes)	**£5.50**

JACOB'S BISCUITS
FAMOUS PICTURE CARDS FROM HISTORY (1978)

A series of 32 colour reproductions from 32 different sets dealing with Transport & Natural History.

Together with a superb album including details of each card, a general introduction on card collecting, **and** a superb full colour reproduction of a set of Taddy "Clowns & Circus Artistes".

A collector's item in their own right, the cards and album together form an interesting introduction to card collecting.

Available NOW for only £1.00!

Wards (Colour Printers) Dunston Tyne & Wear Tel. 0632 605915